THE REALITY OF APOCALYPSE

Society of Biblical Literature

Symposium Series

Christopher R. Matthews, Editor

Number 39

THE REALITY OF APOCALYPSE
Rhetoric and Politics
in the Book of Revelation

edited by
David L. Barr

THE REALITY OF APOCALYPSE
Rhetoric and Politics in the Book of Revelation

edited by
David L. Barr

Society of Biblical Literature
Atlanta

THE REALITY OF APOCALYPSE
Rhetoric and Politics
in the Book of Revelation

Copyright © 2006 by the Society of Biblical Literature

All rights reserved. No part of this work may be reproduced or transmitted in any form or by any means, electronic or mechanical, including photocopying and recording, or by means of any information storage or retrieval system, except as may be expressly permitted by the 1976 Copyright Act or in writing from the publisher. Requests for permission should be addressed in writing to the Rights and Permissions Office, Society of Biblical Literature, 825 Houston Mill Road, Atlanta, GA 30333-0399, USA.

Cover photo of the leaf of Papyrus 46 containing 2 Cor 11:33–12:9 courtesy of the Papyrology Collection, Graduate Library, University of Michigan.

Library of Congress Cataloging-in-Publication Data

The reality of Apocalypse : rhetoric and politics in the book of Revelation / edited by David L. Barr.
    p. cm. — (Society of Biblical Literature symposium series ; no. 39)
Includes index.
ISBN-13: 978-1-58983-218-3 (paper : alk. paper)
ISBN-10: 1-58983-218-3 (paper : alk. paper)
  1. Bible. N.T. Revelation—Socio-rhetorical criticism—Congresses. I. Barr, David L., 1942–. II. Series: Symposium series (Society of Biblical Literature) ; no. 39.

BS2825.52.R44 2006
228'.06—dc22   2005036839

13 12 11 10 09 08 07 06   5 4 3 2 1

Printed in the United States of America on acid-free, recycled paper
conforming to ANSI/NISO Z39.48-1992 (R1997) and ISO 9706:1994
standards for paper permanence.

Table of Contents

Abbreviations vii

Introduction 1

Part One: Rhetoric and Reality

1. Reading the Apocalypse as Apocalypse: The Limits of Genre
   Gregory L. Linton 9

2. Apocalypse Renewed: An Intertextual Reading of the
   Apocalypse of John
   David E. Aune 43

3. Beyond Genre: The Expectations of Apocalypse
   David L. Barr 71

4. Hearing and Seeing but Not Saying: A Rhetoric of Authority
   in Revelation 10:4 and 2 Corinthians 12:4
   Jean-Pierre Ruiz 91

5. To Rejoice or Not to Rejoice? Rhetoric and the Fall of Satan
   in Luke 10:17–24 and Rev 12:1–17
   Edith M. Humphrey 113

6. Sarcasm in Revelation 2–3: Churches, Christians, True Jews,
   and Satanic Synagogues
   Steven J. Friesen 127

Part Two: Politics and Reality

7. The "Synagogue of Satan": Crisis Mongering and the
   Apocalypse of John
   Paul Duff 147

8. Symptoms of Resistance in the Book of Revelation
   Greg Carey 169

9. Dragon Myth and Imperial Ideology in Revelation 12–13
   Jan Willem van Henten 181

10. The Lamb Who Looks Like a Dragon? Characterizing Jesus
    in John's Apocalypse
    David L. Barr 205

11. Betwixt and Between on the Lord's Day: Liturgy and the Apocalypse
    Jean-Pierre Ruiz 221

12. Babylon the Great: A Rhetorical-Political Reading
    of Revelation 17–18
    Elisabeth Schüssler Fiorenza 243

Select Bibliography 271

Contributors 277

Index of Ancient Writings 279

Index of Modern Authors 291

Subject Index 299

Abbreviations

AB	Anchor Bible
ANRW	*Aufstieg und Niedergang der römischen Welt: Geschichte und Kultur Roms im Spiegel der neueren Forschung.* Edited by H. Temporini and W. Haase. Berlin, 1972–
ATR	*Australasian Theological Review*
BAGD	Bauer, W., W. F. Arndt, F. W. Gingrich, and F. W. Danker. *Greek-English Lexicon of the New Testament and Other Early Christian Literature.* 2d ed. Chicago, 1979
BBB	Bonner biblische Beiträge
BETL	Bibliotheca ephemeridum theologicarum lovaniensium
BHT	Beiträge zur historischen Theologie
Bib	*Biblica*
BibInt	*Biblical Interpretation*
BR	*Biblical Research*
BZNW	Beihefte zur Zeitschrift für die neutestamentliche Wissenschaft
CahT	Cahiers Théologiques
CAT	Commentaire de l'Ancien Testament
CBQ	*Catholic Biblical Quarterly*
CC	Continental Commentary
CdE	*Chronique d'Egypte*
CH	Church History
CNT	Commentaire du Nouveau Testament
ConBNT	Coniectanea neotestamentica
CSEL	Corpus scriptorum ecclesiasticorum latinorum
EPRO	Etudes préliminaires aux religions orientales dans l'empire romain
ESCJ	Études sur le christianisme et le judaïsme
EvQ	*Evangelical Quarterly*
ExAud	*Ex auditu*
FOTL	Forms of the Old Testament Literature

FRLANT	Forschungen zur Religion und Literatur des Alten und Neuen Testaments
GNS	Good News Studies
GTJ	*Grace Theological Journal*
HDR	Harvard Dissertations in Religion
HNT	Handbuch zum Neuen Testament
HNTC	Harper's New Testament Commentaries
HR	*History of Religions*
HSM	Harvard Semitic Monographs
HTR	*Harvard Theological Review*
ICC	International Critical Commentary
IDBSup	*Interpreter's Dictionary of the Bible: Supplementary Volume.* Edited by K. Crim. Nashville, 1976
Int	*Interpretation*
JAAR	*Journal of the American Academy of Religion*
JBL	*Journal of Biblical Literature*
JEA	*Journal of Egyptian Archaeology*
JHS	*Journal of Hellenic Studies*
JJS	*Journal of Jewish Studies*
JR	*Journal of Religion*
JSNT	*Journal for the Study of the New Testament*
JSNTSup	Journal for the Study of the New Testament: Supplement Series
JSOTSup	Journal for the Study of the Old Testament: Supplement Series
JSP	*Journal for the Study of the Pseudepigrapha*
JSPSup	Journal for the Study of the Pseudepigrapha: Supplement Series
JSS	*Journal of Semitic Studies*
JSSR	*Journal for the Scientific Study of Religion*
KEK	Kritisch-exegetischer Kommentar über das Neue Testament (Meyer-Kommentar)
LCL	Loeb Classical Library
LEC	Library of Early Christianity
LSJ	Liddell, H. G., R. Scott, H. S. Jones, *A Greek-English Lexicon.* 9th ed. with revised supplement. Oxford, 1996
LumVie	*Lumière et vie*
NCB	New Century Bible
Neot	*Neotestamentica*
NHC	Nag Hammadi Codices
NICNT	New International Commentary on the New Testament
NIGTC	New International Greek Testament Commentary
NovT	*Novum Testamentum*
NTOA	Novum Testamentum et Orbis Antiquus
NTS	*New Testament Studies*

QJS	*Quarterly Journal of Speech*
RAC	*Reallexikon für Antike und Christentum.* Edited by T. Kluser et al. Stuttgart, 1950–
RB	*Revue biblique*
RelSRev	*Religious Studies Review*
RevExp	*Review and Expositor*
RHPR	*Revue d'histoire et de philosophie religieuses*
RivBSup	Rivista biblica italiana Supplement Series
RSR	*Recherches de science religieuse*
SBLDS	Society of Biblical Literature Dissertation Series
SBLRBS	Society of Biblical Literature Resources for Biblical Study
SBLSP	Society of Biblical Literature Seminar Papers
SBM	Stuttgarter biblische Monographien
SBT	Studies in Biblical Theology
SCHNT	Studia ad corpus hellenisticum Novi Testamenti
SNT	Studien zum Neuen Testament
StABH	Studies in American Biblical Hermeneutics
TANZ	Texte und Arbeiten zum neutestamentlichen Zeitalter
TDNT	*Theological Dictionary of the New Testament.* Edited by G. Kittel and G. Friedrich. Translated by G. W. Bromiley. 10 vols. Grand Rapids, 1964–1976
TF	Theologische Forschung
THKNT	Theologischer Handkommentar zum Neuen Testament
TJ	*Trinity Journal*
TPQ	*Theologisch-praktische Quartalschrift*
TZ	*Theologische Zeitschrift*
VD	*Verbum domini*
WBC	Word Biblical Commentary
WMANT	Wissenschaftliche Monographien zum Alten und Neuen Testament
WTJ	*Westminster Theological Journal*
WUNT	Wissenschaftliche Untersuchungen zum Neuen Testament
ZNW	*Zeitschrift für die neutestamentliche Wissenschaft und die Kunde der älteren Kirche*
ZTK	*Zeitschrift für Theologie und Kirche*

INTRODUCTION

It was my great privilege to chair the "Seminar on the Apocalypse: The Intersection of Literary and Social Methods" in the context of the Annual Meeting of the SBL for seven years—and related consultations for another six years. Of the many essays read, responded to, and discussed over that time, I have selected these to represent the work of the seminar.[1] Each of them tries to negotiate the intersection; each is in dialogue with the others; each explores the lively interplay between imagination and history, between rhetoric and politics, between words and worlds. Taken together, they explore the reality of the Apocalypse. For far from being a fantasy of what will never be, the Apocalypse represents a reality that already existed, creating a social world that provided both community and individual identity to its audience.

The scholars contributing to this volume have worked together for more than a decade focusing their research first on methods for understanding the historical and social context of the Apocalypse and later on the contexts, both ancient and modern, that shape our interpretations. This volume represents some of the fruit of that shared agenda. As we worked together, responded critically to each others work, and developed our own insights, new issues—indeed new paradigms for scholarship—began to emerge.

These new paradigms affected both the way we worked (cooperatively not competitively, letting go of the notion that there is one best way to interpret the Apocalypse) and the issues we addressed. These issues are not always novel but our approach soon deviated from what had been done before. We started with the firm conviction that the Apocalypse is a work of literary invention that has to be read (and interpreted) rhetorically. Our access to John's historical and social situation would always be through an analysis of the performance of the text.

We have chosen to focus the volume around two themes: rhetoric and politics, both broadly conceived, interrelated, and overlapping. Essays in the section "Rhetoric and Reality" focus both on the general rhetorical strategies of the work, including its genre and intertextual relationships, and on its specific rhetorical tactics. These essays also show how the rhetoric fits the situation in Roman Asia Minor and the struggle within the community of the Apocalypse. Essays in the section "Politics and

---

1. Another collection of the work of the seminar addressed to the needs of students has been published in the SBL series Resources for Biblical Studies: David L. Barr, ed., *Reading the Book of Revelation: A Resource for Students* (Atlanta: Society of Biblical Literature, 2003).

Reality" pursue further the conflicts within the community and conflicts with the broader culture. These essays also show how myth, symbol, and liturgy all function as means of resistance in an imperial setting.

The first three essays reflect new ways of thinking about the genre of the Apocalypse, ways that incorporate and seek to extend the formative work of the SBL Genres project.[2] Greg Linton ("Reading the Apocalypse as Apocalypse: The Limits of Genre") notes how the Apocalypse refuses to stay within the generic boundaries readers try to construct for it. The Apocalypse exhibits a high degree of intertextuality and is best understood as a hybrid genre that contains a combination of literary features. The first part of the essay examines how readers construct genres to guide their reading of texts. Some texts are easy to classify, but hybrid texts require the reader to make decisions and thus invite the participation of the reader in the production of its meaning. The second part of the essay describes the Apocalypse of John as a hybrid genre. Its high degree of intertextuality requires readers to focus on certain literary conventions to the exclusion of others, since more than one choice is available. The hybrid nature of the text contributes to the multiple interpretations offered by various readers.

David Aune ("Apocalypse Renewed: An Intertextual Reading of the Apocalypse of John") pursues the idea of intertextuality in greater detail. He investigates the major textual units of the Apocalypse, imagining how the implied audience might have perceived the variety of intertextual connections as they read or heard the work unfold before them. This investigation shows that the Apocalypse is a work containing a variety of literary forms in a sequence that conforms to no known ancient literary conventions. Many of these forms are associated with either apocalyptic or prophetic writings, but not both. The synthesis of these two traditions, coupled with the lack of pseudonymity, suggests that John is doing something essentially different from what is being done in other Apocalypses. By placing apocalyptic traditions within a prophetic framework (Rev 1–3 and 22:6–20), and by juxtaposing apocalyptic with prophetic elements throughout the entire composition, the author appears to have attempted to give a new lease on life to apocalyptic traditions that could not and did not long retain their vitality in early Christianity because of their indissoluble association with nationalistic myths connected with the royal ideology of ancient Israel.

David Barr ("Beyond Genre: The Expectations of Apocalypse") expands the discussion of genre by seeking the social context of the performance of an apocalypse. After reviewing the development of scholarly attempts to define the genre, first through listing the common traits, later through a conceptual model, he addresses the issue of what a verbal apocalypse shares with other forms of "revelation"—from entrails to oracles. He focuses on the effect of such revelations on the audience, arguing that by understanding the social setting of the various media the ancients understood as revelatory we have a better understanding of the social function of John's Apocalypse.

---

2. See *Semeia* 14 (1979), edited by John J. Collins with the theme "Apocalypse: The Morphology of a Genre.".

John-Pierre Ruiz ("Hearing and Seeing but Not Saying: A Rhetoric of Authority in Revelation 10:4 and 2 Corinthians 12:4") shifts our focus from the audience to the author, or rather, to how the audience is expected to construct the author. He compares the prohibition found in Rev 10:4, "Seal up what the seven thunders have said and do not write it down," with 2 Cor 12:4, where Paul tells of someone "who heard things that are not to be told, that no mortal is permitted to repeat," suggesting that the juxtaposition of these two texts sheds interesting light on the rhetorical strategies of John and Paul. Each uses the tension between what is said and what remains unsaid to establish his authority with the addressees of the document. Paul's defense of his apostolic mission relies on the proclamation of the power of weakness, which takes written form in the text of his correspondence with the Corinthian church; John's defense of his prophetic mission rests on the testimony of the document in which that mission finds expression among the churches of Asia.

Edith M. Humphrey ("To Rejoice or Not to Rejoice? Rhetoric and the Fall of Satan in Luke 10:17–24 and Revelation 12:1–17") also attempts to illuminate John's text by setting it alongside another first-century text, comparing John's version of Satan's fall to earth (12:1–17) with that attributed to Jesus (Luke 10:17–24). After addressing the question of if and how to apply the conventions of classical rhetoric to narrative texts, she argues that both of these passages mount an implicit argument through visionary narrative, though they differ in the degree to which they have been informed by classical rhetoric. A comparison of these two allusive passages explores the value and limits of rhetorical criticism, demonstrates how a tailor-made literary-rhetorical method is helpful in analyzing such texts, and attempts to highlight (at least in a preliminary way) the interaction between Greco-Roman and Hebrew rhetoric. Despite their differences, both pieces share an interest in authority, in ambiguity, and in dualism, so that they speak with a more-or-less distinct "Christian accent."

Steve Friesen ("Sarcasm in Revelation 2–3: Churches, Christians, True Jews, and Satanic Synagogues") finishes off the first section with an exploration of how the rhetoric of slander functions to define the communities that John included and excluded. After reviewing scholarly appraisals of John's rhetoric as "vilification" or "polemic" and considering especially who and what John means by the expression "synagogue of Satan," he suggests ways to cast the discussion in new terms. First, we need to recognize the ironic strategies employed by the author of Revelation. The sarcasm directed against opponents must be read as sarcasm; it is not a claim to be the true Israel. Second, we need to reject the term "Christian" as an appropriate description of John, his text, or his congregations. The term is an anachronistic retrojection that diverts the discussion. John's imagery and language depict the churches as an eschatological movement that cannot be described with the terms "Jew," "Israel," or "Christian." John was guilty of sarcastic name-calling, but not of supercessionist ideology. We begin to see how rhetoric also implies a politics and an ethics of interpretation, the major themes of the next section.

Paul Duff ("The 'Synagogue of Satan': Crisis Mongering and the Apocalypse of John") inaugurates this second section by focusing particularly on the "synagogue of

Satan" accusation that occurs in two of the so-called letters, those addressed to the churches in Smyrna and Philadelphia. Traditionally this accusation has been understood to refer to the Jewish communities in these cities, and the hostility has been linked to the supposed cooperation of the Jews in the persecution of Christians. After reviewing recent studies that question this identification, Duff argues that the traditional view is (partly) right: John does intend the Jewish synagogue. He also argues that the Apocalypse itself contains little evidence (indeed, none outside what some infer from these expressions) of any Jewish hostility toward John's community. Based upon this and that John's overall attitude toward Judaism is positive throughout the Apocalypse, Duff argues that John demonized the local Jewish communities in order to drive a wedge between his most conservative churches and the synagogues in their respective cities. Faced with the ascendancy of the liberal "Jezebel" faction in some of John's churches, John was trying to discourage his most loyal (and most conservative) allies from deserting their churches for the synagogue, a place where it might be easier for his followers to maintain the high walls between themselves and the larger society.

Greg Carey ("Symptoms of Resistance in the Book of Revelation") shifts our attention from the community and its relation to other minority communities to the broader context of the Roman Empire. He addresses one of the most problematic aspects of the Apocalypse, its portrayal of violence, vengefulness, and misogyny. He argues that these aspects of the Apocalypse are best understood by analyzing it as an example of resistance literature. Revelation emerges in an imperial context and manifests traces of the imperial other. Its resort to violence and parody rely upon imperial discourses for their force. And its polemics against "the inhabitants of the earth," other Jewish communities, and alternative voices in the churches reflect the compulsion to articulate group identity over against Rome's hegemonic claims. Revelation is not simply good, bad, or in between, but its symptoms of resistance include rigid communal boundaries, competition with other group leaders, tension with neighbors, hybrid forms of discourse, and the reinscription of imperial values.

Jan Willem van Henten ("Dragon Myth and Imperial Ideology in Revelation 12–13") explores these imperial values further, examining especially the propaganda portraying the emperor as world savior. Despite recent attempts to read the visions in Rev 12 and 13 largely or entirely against a Hebrew Bible/Old Testament background, most scholars still think that John the prophet incorporated non-Jewish mythological traditions in both visions. Whether one chooses the older paradigm of searching for tradition-historical interdependencies or the newer paradigm of literary analysis, a reading that links John's visions to sources that express imperial ideology directly (e.g. in documents about the emperor cult) or indirectly (e.g., in applications of mythological traditions to the emperor) seems to be highly relevant, because such a reading highlights the political message of the visions.

The visions in Rev 12–13 show close correspondences with Greco-Roman combat myths (e.g., the Apollo-Python-Leto and Horus-Seth/Typhon-Isis myths), which, as a matter of fact, play an important role in the imperial ideology. The emperors, for example, were often associated with Apollo or Zeus, gods who were famous for their role as slayer of a dragon. If one would contextualize the book of Revelation by linking it to such political applications of those myths, the combat as presented in Revelation seems to imply an inversion of roles to the readers: not only is the obvious claim of the ruler cult to a divine status for the emperor refuted, but the radical message is that the emperors should be associated with the dragon or the chaos monsters in their own myths, the opposite of Zeus or Apollo who triumphs over the agent of chaos.

Thus, the emperor's ideology would be deconstructed on two grounds: (1) John's insiders' ground of the Jewish prohibition to venerate any other god than the God of Israel, and (2) the emperor's own propaganda, which should be turned upside down.

David L. Barr ("The Lamb Who Looks Like a Dragon? Characterizing Jesus in John's Apocalypse") looks at the other side of this imperial coin: if the emperor begins to look like the dragon, does Jesus begin to look like the emperor? A narrative reading of the Apocalypse reveals a story that stands squarely against coercion and domination, yet, ironically, the usual reading of that story endorses just such tyranny—with Jesus now acting with all the oppressive power of the emperor. This chapter explores this contradiction from the triple perspectives of symbolism, morality, and narrative analysis, concluding with a deconstructive reading of Revelation as a call to persistent resistance to Roman imperial domination through keeping the word of God and the testimony of Jesus, that is, through suffering. Barr argues that those who read the Apocalypse as predicting a second coming of Jesus wherein he will obliterate the forces of evil in some final battle and force the earth to accept God's rule are profoundly wrong. Rather, in John's story, evil is ever and only defeated through resistance and faithful suffering.

Jean-Pierre Ruiz ("Betwixt and Between on the Lord's Day: Liturgy and the Apocalypse") employs literary-critical and social-scientific perspectives to examine the rhetoric and the politics of ritual in the Apocalypse of John. He does a thorough review of how ritual studies have been employed to understand John's text and then argues that John's authority over the text's addressees was established as a matter of control over the production of a text for recitation and reception in a ritual setting: John's voice was heard across a distance that the text simultaneously created and mediated. Because John's voice was but one among the many that competed for attention of Christians in western Anatolia, rite made might by claiming the superiority of this text's authority over against the manifest sociopolitical, economic and ideological expressions of Roman imperial authority.

In the final chapter, Elisabeth Schüssler Fiorenza ("Babylon the Great: A Rhetorical-Political Reading of Revelation 17–18") draws together many of the strands of method and results of earlier chapters. She reviews the work of the seminar and, more broadly, the development of the academic study of the Apocalypse over the past two decades, arguing that a paradigm shift has taken place. In this new paradigm all language and all knowledge of the world is understood to be rhetorical. Not only the Apocalypse, but also our interpretations of the Apocalypse are articulated in specific social situations and serve political ends. This necessitates a hermeneutics of suspicion and a practice of ethical inquiry that asks whether proposed interpretations of Revelation do justice to its own rhetoric of resistance.

More specifically, the chapter analyzes the feminist debate over the gendered language of the Apocalypse, which is an elite male-centered language that has often produced misogynist readings. Still, she argues it is a mistake to read this language as if it were natural language, for that poses the danger of reinforcing the Western sex/gender system. Rather, a rhetorical, political reading must assess both the reality envisioned in the text and also the reality created by our interpretations of the text—both understood as rhetorical constructs. Revelation must be read not only in terms of gender but also in terms of the multiple and interacting systems of oppression, both in John's world and our own.

This symposium aims to demonstrate how a diverse group of scholars, employing several methods and disagreeing on many points, has attempted to make sense of the Apocalypse not simply as a fantasy about the end of the world, but more particularly as a record of a struggle against and within the Roman imperial system. Careful attention to the rhetoric and politics (both of the work and of its interpreters) reveals the reality of apocalypse.

PART ONE

Rhetoric and Reality

Reading the Apocalypse as Apocalypse: The Limits of Genre

Gregory L. Linton

Identifying a text's genre is crucial for determining its meaning, yet the Apocalypse resists classification in one pure genre. Interpreters have categorized it as prophecy, apocalypse, letter, drama, liturgy, and myth. Most offer various combinations of these genres. Some will identify one as primary and view the others as secondary elements. The multiple connections of the Apocalypse with various types of literature complicate the attempt to pin down its generic identity. One way to express this is to say the Apocalypse has a high degree of intertextuality, since genre is an aspect of intertextuality.[1]

Maria Corti's definition of genre emphasizes this connection: "Genre serves as the place where the individual work enters into a complex network of relations with other works."[2] Similarly, Tzvetan Todorov says that "genres are precisely those relay-points by which the work assumes a relation with the universe of literature."[3] To specify the genre of a text is to clarify and delineate the text's intertextual relations with other texts. The interpreter compares the text with other texts, notes the similarities and differences, and then determines which of those other texts are most

---

An earlier version of this essay was published in the *Society of Biblical Literature Seminar Papers* (Atlanta: Scholars Press, 1991), 161–86.

1. Fredric Jameson notes that "a systematic construction of that imaginary entity designated as intertextuality is at work in all genre criticism." He defines intertextuality as that phenomenon "in which a number of texts are superposed, and the notion of some larger one, which encompasses them all and includes them within itself, proposed" ("Magical Narratives: Romance as Genre," *New Literary History* 7 [1975]: 155). For other explanations of the connection between intertextuality and genre, see Gérard Genette, *Palimpsestes: La littérature au second degré* (Paris: Seuil, 1982), 11; Laurent Jenny, "The Strategy of Form," trans. R. Carter, in *French Literary Theory Today: A Reader* (ed. Tzvetan Todorov; Cambridge: Cambridge University Press, 1982), 42–43; Steven Mailloux, *Interpretive Conventions: The Reader in the Study of American Fiction* (Ithaca, N.Y.: Cornell University Press, 1982), 151–52.

2. Maria Corti, *An Introduction to Literary Semiotics* (trans. Margherita Bogat and Allen Mandelbaum; Bloomington: Indiana University Press, 1978), 115.

3. Tzvetan Todorov, *The Fantastic: A Structural Approach to a Literary Genre* (trans. Richard Howard; Ithaca, N.Y.: Cornell University Press, 1975), 8.

similar to it. Through this process of comparison and differentiation, interpreters separate and categorize literary works into groups, which are called genres. By drawing boundaries around certain groups of works, interpreters partition and organize the vast field of textuality.

However, the intertextuality of texts also undermines the effort to identify genres because all texts have connections with others outside their particular genre. All texts refuse to stay in their generic boundaries to a greater or lesser extent. The Apocalypse of John is a text that overruns its boundaries to a high degree. It is a hybrid genre that refuses to stay within any particular set of generic boundaries. It is similar to many different kinds of texts but not identical to any of them. When compared with any other literary genre, the Apocalypse lacks some of its features while possessing others that do not belong to that genre. Because it combines the conventions of other genres in a unique way, it offers readers the opportunity to select which conventions they will foreground as their dominant reading strategy. To narrow its intertextual connections to a primary genre, interpreters opt for one of two strategies. Either they redefine the genre so that the Apocalypse fits into it more neatly, or they gloss over the book's differences from other works of that genre.

This essay will describe ways that interpreters deal with the hybrid genre of the Apocalypse. The first section shows how readers create literary genres for pragmatic and rhetorical purposes. The second section describes how the Apocalypse's intertextuality causes confusion about its genre and therefore produces multiple interpretations.

THE CREATION OF GENRES

A genre is a group of literary works that have been connected by readers who have judged their similarities to be of greater number and significance than their differences. The following discussion of genre theory will explain why readers construct genres, how genres affect interpretation, and how highly intertextual works mix literary conventions. This overview of genre theory will provide the foundation for discussing the search for the genre of the Apocalypse.

THE NECESSITY OF GENRE

Literary scholars of various persuasions agree that every text belongs to at least one genre.[4] Writers cannot write without having in mind other writings they have

---

4. John Barton, *Reading the Old Testament: Method in Biblical Study* (Philadelphia: Westminster, 1984), 16; Ralph Cohen, "Do Postmodern Genres Exist?" *Genre* 20 (1987): 244; Jacques Derrida, "The Law of Genre," trans. Avital Ronell, *Critical Inquiry* 7 (1980): 65; Alastair Fowler, *Kinds of Literature: An Introduction to the Theory of Genres and Modes* (Cambridge: Harvard University Press, 1982), 20; Hans Robert Jauss, "Theory of Genres and Medieval Literature," in *Toward an Aesthetics of Reception* (trans. Timothy Bahti; Minneapolis: University of Minnesota Press, 1982), 79; José Ortega y Gasset, "Notes on the Novel," in *The Dehumanization of Art and Other Essays on Art, Culture, and Lit-*

read, which become for them models to be imitated, transformed, or opposed.[5] No writing is created ex nihilo. According to E. D. Hirsch Jr., generic conceptions are necessary not only for communication between author and reader but to stimulate the imagination of the writer.[6]

The second reason why every text belongs to at least one genre is that genres have not only a generative function but also a hermeneutic function. They are necessary both for writers to be able to write and for readers to be able to read. As Sheldon Sacks states, "[T]raditional generic distinctions employed by some critics in discussions of literature are forms of intuitive knowledge actually used by readers to comprehend and writers to create literary works."[7] Readers cannot read and understand a work unless they are able to relate it to other works that they have read. They must be able to set the work in "some context of familiar types."[8] Ralph Cohen says that "if each piece of writing were different from all others there would be no basis for theorizing or even for communication."[9]

It is impossible for a writing to be completely different from all others or to be completely unintelligible to the reader (provided it is written in a language known to the reader). Readers have amazing powers of recuperation and naturalization that allow them to relate any work—no matter how avant-garde it may be—to other works so that it may take on meaning. According to Jonathan Culler, readers naturalize the texts they read by bringing the strange and deviant text "into relation with a type of discourse or model which is already, in some sense, natural and legible." This process is one of the basic activities of the human mind. Culler argues that we can make anything signify, whether it is random sentences spit out by a computer, or a play by Beckett, or a story by Robbe-Grillet.[10]

Readers naturalize texts by placing them in a literary *con-text*, which means "a weaving together." They trace the threads of textuality in the text back to other similar texts that they have read.[11] When they notice that certain works seem to have

---

erature (Princeton: Princeton University Press, 1968), 58, cited in Robert Scholes, *Protocols of Reading* (New Haven: Yale University Press, 1989), 135.

5. Robert Scholes, *Structuralism in Literature: An Introduction* (New Haven: Yale University Press, 1974), 130.

6. E. D. Hirsch Jr., *Validity in Interpretation* (New Haven: Yale University Press, 1967), 104.

7. Sheldon Sacks, "The Psychological Implications of Generic Distinctions," *Genre* 1 (1968): 106.

8 Fowler, *Kinds of Literature*, 36, 259.

9. Cohen, "Do Postmodern Genres Exist?" 244. See also Adena Rosmarin, *The Power of Genre* (Minneapolis: University of Minnesota Press, 1985), 45.

10. Jonathan Culler, *Structuralist Poetics: Structuralism, Linguistics, and the Study of Literature* (Ithaca, N.Y.: Cornell University Press, 1975), 137–38.

11. The Latin word *texere* means "to weave," and *intertexere* means "to weave into," or "to intermix by weaving." Thus Roland Barthes can say that "the metaphor of the text is that of the *network*." A text is a web, fabric, or network. See Roland Barthes, "From Work to Text," in *Image-Music-Text* (trans. Stephen Heath; Glasgow: Fontana, 1977), 161; Hans-George Ruprecht, "Intertextualité," *Texte: Revue de critique et de théorie littéraire* 2 (1983): 13 (volume published as *L'Intertextualité: Intertexte, autotexte, intratexte* [ed. Brian T. Fitch and Andrew Oliver; Toronto: Editions Trintexte, 1983]); E. R. Harty, "Text, Context, Intertext," *Journal of Literary Studies* 1 (1985): 1–6.

close intertextual connections, they group them into a genre. Thus reading is by nature an intertextual, and therefore generic, activity; otherwise, readers could not make sense of texts. Culler says: "A work can only be read in connection with or against other texts, which provide a grid through which it is read and structured by establishing expectations which enable one to pick out salient features and give them a structure."[12] Every text belongs to at least one genre so that writers can write and readers can read.[13]

GENRE'S ROLE IN INTERPRETATION

How readers identify a text's genre affects how they interpret that text. The purpose of identifying a work's genre is to orient and guide the reader's encounter with the text.[14] Tremper Longman III points out that readers must make at least an unconscious genre identification, which triggers a certain reading strategy in their mind.[15] E. D. Hirsch has emphasized that different types of texts require different types of interpretation. Consequently, the question of a text's genre is the most important question an interpreter can ask, "since its answer implies the way it should be understood with respect to its shape and emphasis as well as the scope and direction of its meanings." He says that the interpreter's "preliminary generic conception of a text is constitutive of everything that he subsequently understands."[16]

The identification of a text's genre shapes not only the reader's overall view of the text but also interpretation of specific details of the text. Hirsch notes that "an interpreter's notion of the type of meaning he confronts will powerfully influence his understanding of details."[17] Heather Dubrow illustrated this point by offering a hypothetical opening paragraph of a novel. She then proceeded to show that one's understanding of the novel as a murder mystery causes one to attach different meanings to various details than if it is viewed as a *Bildungsroman*. The various elements take on different meaning according to the generic presuppositions of the reader.[18]

---

12. Culler, *Structuralist Poetics*, 139.
13. Hans Robert Jauss ("Theory of Genres," 79) argues the same point: "Even where a verbal creation negates or surpasses all expectations, it still presupposes preliminary information and a trajectory of expectations against which to register the originality and novelty. This horizon of the expectable is constituted for the reader from out of a tradition or series of previously known works, and from a specific attitude, mediated by one (or more) genre and dissolved through new works. Just as there is no act of verbal communication that is not related to a general, socially or situationally conditioned norm or convention, it is also unimaginable that a literary work set itself into an informational vacuum, without indicating a specific situation of understanding. To this extent, every work belongs to a genre—whereby I mean neither more nor less than that for each work a preconstituted horizon of expectations must be ready at hand (this can also be understood as a relationship of 'rules of the game') to orient the reader's (public's) understanding and to enable a qualifying reception."
14. Culler, *Structuralist Poetics*, 136; Fowler, *Kinds of Literature*, 37–38.
15. Tremper Longman III, "Form Criticism, Recent Developments in Genre Theory, and the Evangelical," *WTJ* 47 (1985): 51, 67.
16. Hirsch, *Validity in Interpretation*, 113, 263, 74.
17. Ibid., 75.
18. Heather Dubrow, *Genre* (Critical Idiom 42; London: Methuen, 1982), 1–2.

Thomas L. Kent also offers an example of the way in which genre identification contributes to the reader's perception of the meaning of a text. He describes a letter to the editor of the *Des Moines Register* in which the writer complained about an editorial cartoon that he or she thought was typical of the paper's desire to cater to the wealthy and affluent. Although the cartoon belonged to the sub-genre "satiric cartoon," the reader viewed it as belonging to the genre of "household hints." Consequently, the writer interpreted the cartoon opposite of the way he or she should have.[19]

Longman offers a biblical example of the interrelation of genre and interpretation. He shows that biblical scholars translate *yhwh malak* in certain psalms differently based on their identification of the psalm's genre. If they identify the psalm as an enthronement ceremony, they translate the phrase as "Yahweh is becoming king." If they do not view the psalm as an enthronement ceremony, they translate the phrase as "Yahweh reigns."[20]

Different generic identities provide the reader with different expectations and therefore different interpretations. According to Terence Hawkes, our understanding of the genre of a work "'programmes' our reading of it, reduces its complexity, or rather gives it a knowable shape, enabling us literally to 'read' it, by giving it a context and a framework which allows order and complexity to appear."[21] Disagreements about the interpretation of a text are often disagreements about its genre.[22] Kent forcefully argues this point:

> Through history, interpretations of a text change. One way to view these different readings is to see interpretations growing out of different generic perceptions of texts. . . . Literary texts are interpreted differently when their generic categories are perceived differently. For example, to read *Moby-Dick* as predominantly an allegorical romance means that the text will be interpreted differently than if it were read as predominantly realistic novel. This observation is another way of saying that when a text shifts generic categories or when it is perceived as changing categories—which amounts to the same thing—it also changes meaning.[23]

The reason interpreters expend so much energy determining the generic identity of the Apocalypse is that their decision will affect how they interpret and understand it. The genre provides an interpretive strategy, an encompassing framework in which to fit the smaller details of the text.[24]

---

19. Thomas L. Kent, "Interpretation and Genre Perception," *Semiotica* 56 (1985): 134–36; idem, *Interpretation and Genre: The Role of Generic Perception in the Study of Narrative Texts* (Lewisburg, Pa.: Bucknell University Press, 1986), 16–19.
20. Longman, "Form Criticism," 62–63.
21. Terence Hawkes, *Structuralism and Semiotics* (New Accents Series; Berkeley: University of California Press, 1977), 103. See also Culler, *Structuralist Poetics*, 136–37.
22. Hirsch, *Validity in Interpretation*, 98; Kent, *Interpretation and Genre*, 22; Jonathan Culler, *The Pursuit of Signs: Semiotics, Literature, Deconstruction* (Ithaca, N.Y.: Cornell University Press, 1981), 59.
23. Kent, *Interpretation and Genre*, 151.
24. Fowler, *Kinds of Literature*, 38; Hirsch, *Validity in Interpretation*, 222.

The connection between genre and interpretation must be qualified somewhat by noting that readers can understand some aspects of a text apart from their understanding of its genre. As Marie-Laure Ryan points out, a reader may appreciate a sonnet even if one has never encountered that form before or is unaware of its conventions.[25] Some aspects of the meaning of a text are available even to naive readers with little literary competence because readers can always connect the text with something with which they are familiar.

Also, the identification of a work's genre does not always determine or control the interpretation of every element. Often, the genre provides a general, overall orientation or viewpoint that sometimes affects interpretation of particular points and sometimes does not. For example, those who emphasize the epistolary character of the Apocalypse usually conclude that one must keep in mind that the book was written for a particular group of people in a particular situation.[26] Obviously, this perspective will affect interpretation of some verses directly, some indirectly, and some perhaps not at all. Some interpretation can occur without reference to the genre of the text, but, for the most part, genre and interpretation are closely connected.

THE LITERARY CONVENTIONS OF GENRE

A genre consists of a cluster of implicit or explicit conventions that guide writers as they write and readers as they read. Literary or generic conventions act as norms, rules, prescriptions, restrictions, or prohibitions that determine or condition how writers write a certain kind of work and how readers read it. According to Hirsch, the term *convention* embraces "the entire system of usage traits, rules, customs, formal necessities, and proprieties which constitute a type of verbal meaning."[27] Literary conventions include numerous aspects of literary works, such as form, content, function, modes of publication and delivery, interpretive strategies, and so forth.[28]

Literary conventions result from a shared understanding that has arisen among a community of readers either in implicit or explicit fashion. At times they are codified and made explicit by influential theorists such as Aristotle or Boileau. If they are never codified in this way, they remain unconscious and implicit, forming what Renato Poggioli refers to as the "unwritten poetics" of an age.[29] Kent refers to these two

---

25. Marie-Laure Ryan, "Toward a Competence Theory of Genre," *Poetics* 8 (1979): 329.
26. G. R. Beasley-Murray, *The Book of Revelation* (NCB; Grand Rapids: Eerdmans, 1974), 12–14.
27. Hirsch, *Validity in Interpretation*, 92.
28. Jeremy Hawthorn, *Unlocking the Text: Fundamental Issues in Literary Theory* (London: Edward Arnold, 1987), 49.
29. Renato Poggioli, "Poetics and Metrics," in *Comparative Literature: Proceedings of the Second Congress of the International Comparative Literature Association*, vol. 1, ed. Werner Friederich (Chapel Hill: University of North Carolina Press, 1959), 194–95. Poggioli argues that unwritten poetics exist in every age, either alone or alongside written ones. He writes: "In primitive ages, we have only unwritten poetics; in eclectic, composite, and decadent epochs, they predominate over the written ones; in classical or neo-classical periods they are less influential than the written ones, affecting preferably those special or minor currents which flow apart from the main stream" (195).

types of literary conventions as formulated and unformulated. Formulated literary conventions are the static, synchronic, formal elements of a text, whereas unformulated literary conventions are fluid, changeable, diachronic, and nonprescriptive.[30] Whether explicit or implicit, formulated or unformulated, the conventional nature of genres causes them to take on the character of institutions that "function as 'horizons of expectation' for readers, and as 'models of writing' for authors."[31]

When a person becomes aware of literary conventions by means of education and experience, that person possesses "literary competence."[32] John Barton defines literary competence as the ability to recognize genre.[33] Literary competence is generic competence. According to Kent, readers may have varying degrees of literary competence. He proposes a spectrum that stretches between the naive reader, "who has yet to internalize the generic conventions of a large number of genres," and the sophisticated reader, "who recognizes the conventions of a large number of genres." Most readers fall somewhere in between these two extremes.[34]

Writers draw upon on their literary competence, or in this case "authorial competence."[35] Their knowledge of literary conventions shapes the context in which or against which they write.[36] When they write in an explicit genre and signal its use through paratextual indications such as titles, subtitles, prefaces, or other less obvious means, then they are in effect offering a contract to the reader.[37] As Dubrow says: "[The author] in effect agrees that he will follow at least some of the patterns and conventions we associate with the genre or genres in which he is writing, and we in turn agree that we will pay close attention to certain aspects of his work while realizing that others, because of the nature of the genres, are likely to be far less important."[38]

Viewing genre as a contract emphasizes the communicative and hermeneutical functions of genre. As Paul Ricoeur says, "[T]he function of literary genres is to mediate between speaker and hearer by establishing a common *dynamics* capable of ruling both the production of discourse as a work of a certain kind and its interpreta-

---

30. Kent, *Interpretation and Genre*, 36–40.
31. Tzvetan Todorov, "The Origin of Genres," trans. Richard M. Berrong, *New Literary History* 8 (1976): 163.
32. Culler, *Structuralist Poetics*, 113–30; Barton, *Reading the Old Testament*, 8–19; Ryan, "Toward a Competence Theory," 329–30.
33. Barton, *Reading the Old Testament*, 16; see also Kent, *Interpretation and Genre*, 38.
34. Kent, "Interpretation and Genre Perception," 134–38; idem, *Interpretation and Genre*, 19.
35. Corti, *Introduction to Literary Semiotics*, 117.
36. Culler, *Structuralist Poetics*, 116; Longman, "Form Criticism," 51; Kent, *Interpretation and Genre*, 146.
37. Northrop Frye, *Anatomy of Criticism: Four Essays* (Princeton: Princeton University Press, 1957), 76; Genette, *Palimpsestes*, 9; Culler, *Structuralist Poetics*, 147; Hirsch, *Validity in Interpretation*, 93–94; Jameson, "Magical Narratives," 135.
38. Dubrow, *Genre*, 31.

tion according to the rules provided by the 'genre.' "[39] Longman also emphasizes the communicative function of genres. After examining the metaphors used for genre such as contract, institution, game, code, deep structure, and patterns of expression, he draws these three conclusions: "(1) Genre explains the possibility of communication in a literary transaction; (2) Genres rest upon expectations which arise in readers when they confront a text; (3) Authors can be coerced in composition to conform to genre expectations."[40]

If a text does not clearly signal its generic category, or if its generic conventions are part of "the unwritten poetics" of an era, then readers construct some constraints or guidelines for interpretation. They compare the work with similar works in order to hypothesize the conventions the text is following. Readers cannot read in a vacuum. They must naturalize the text by identifying intertextual relation with other texts they have read. As they continue reading, they may continually modify their hypotheses, but, as Hirsch admits, "the interpreter can never be completely certain what that genre is and can never completely codify its proprieties in all their complexity."[41]

Genre's Role in Setting Boundaries

By constructing a generic category, interpreters place boundaries around a group of works to set them off from others. By including an individual work within one of these categories, they place boundaries around it to set it off from some works and alongside others. Placing boundaries or frames around a text is an attempt to restrict the text so that one can interpret it. Identifying the genre of a work sets limits on its dissemination of meaning. Genre plays a paradoxical role in setting these boundaries because, as Jacques Derrida claims, the mark of belonging or inclusion that is the distinctive trait of a genre does not itself belong to any genre or class: "The re-mark of belonging does not belong." Genre labels are supplements to the text that place "within and without the work, along its boundary, an inclusion and exclusion with regard to genre in general, as to an identifiable class in general." He concludes that "every text participates in one or several genres, there is no genreless text; there is always a genre and genres, yet such participation never amounts to belonging." While genre groupings are necessary, no sooner are they posited than they are violated by texts.[42]

Derrida compares the status and role of genre with the parergon in artistic works.[43] The *parergon,* a term borrowed from Kant, is something that lies against, beside, and in addition to the work, such as clothes on a statue, columns on a building,

---

39. Paul Ricoeur, "The Hermeneutical Function of Distanciation," trans. David Pellauer, *Philosophy Today* 17 (1973): 136.
40. Longman, "Form Criticism," 53.
41. Hirsch, *Validity in Interpretation,* 94.
42. Derrida, "The Law of Genre," 63–66; idem, "Living On: Border Lines," trans. James Hulbert, in Harold Bloom et al., *Deconstruction and Criticism* (New York: Continuum, 1979), 86.
43. Jacques Derrida, "II. The Parergon," in *The Truth in Painting* (trans. Geoff Bennington and Ian McLeod; Chicago: University of Chicago Press, 1987), 53–64. For a helpful discussion of this

or picture frames. It is neither simply outside nor simply inside the work; it stands out both from the work and from its milieu. It stands out against two grounds, but with respect to each of those two grounds, it merges into the other. From one perspective, a picture frame blends in with the picture, but from another perspective, it blends in with the wall. It never really belongs to either one. Genre works in the same way: It serves to distinguish the individual work from other literature, but it does not belong to the work or to the field of literature that serves as its background. It resides in a liminal area between an individual text and the broader field of textuality, obtaining and maintaining its existence only by its difference from other things.

Genres are not metaphysical entities that live independently of texts or readers, so interpreters should not reify or hypostatize genres. Rather, genres are heuristic devices constructed by readers to help them explain and interpret texts.[44] Gustavo Pérez Firmat points out that genre is itself a text compiled from other texts so that it is always less than and different from any of those particular texts. Genre is a "text of texts" that exists only in critical discourse.[45] Similarly, John G. Cawelti uses the term "supertext" for genre: "The supertext (genre) claims to be an abstract of the most significant characteristics or family resemblances among many particular texts, which can accordingly be analyzed, evaluated, and otherwise related to each other by virtue of their connection with the supertext."[46]

Constructing these supertexts is a circular and deductive process. Adena Rosmarin shows that constructing genres entails reading one thing as another, which is an "edifying mistake of classification" that allows criticism to begin. She demonstrates that all generic descriptions and definitions result from deductive reasoning, despite claims of inductiveness by those who construct them. The process of genre definition proceeds from purpose to premise to particular texts rather than from the opposite direction.[47] Pérez Firmat also shows that descriptions of genre are circular and deductive in nature. One cannot argue empirically from works to theories because one must always rely on a prior principle of selection to isolate the texts that are compared.[48] Similarly, Eliseo Vivas concludes that "because classes must be defined inductively, they must be considered open concepts." However, in order to read and interpret, critics and readers must close the concept arbitrarily so that works can be classified in

---

article, see Jonathan Culler, *On Deconstruction: Theory and Criticism after Structuralism* (Ithaca, N.Y.: Cornell University Press, 1982), 193–200.

44. John J. Collins, *The Apocalyptic Imagination: An Introduction to Jewish Apocalyptic Literature* (2d ed.; Biblical Resource Series; Grand Rapids: Eerdmans; Livonia, Mich.: Dove, 1998), 8; idem, "Preface," *Semeia* 14 (1979): iv; Edgar V. McKnight, *Postmodern Use of the Bible: The Emergence of Reader-Oriented Criticism* (Nashville: Abingdon, 1988), 243–44.

45. Gustavo Pérez Firmat, "The Novel as Genres," *Genre* 12 (1979): 278.

46. John G. Cawelti, "The Question of Popular Genres," *Journal of Popular Film and Television* 13 (1985): 55.

47. Rosmarin, *Power of Genre*, 22–25.

48. Pérez Firmat, "Novel as Genres," 271, 274–77. He appeals to Karl Popper's argument in *The Logic of Scientific Discovery* that "all inductive reasoning presupposes an antecedent, non-inductive step" (276 n. 11).

some way.⁴⁹ Rosmarin concludes from these facts that genre critics should adopt an explicitly deductive approach that would be pragmatic and rhetorical in nature. In her view, genres are pragmatic rather than natural, defined rather than found, used rather than described.⁵⁰

The Mixed Conventions of Hybrid Genres

The process of identifying a text's generic conventions becomes even more complicated when the text seems to have mixed conventions, thus offering multiple possibilities to the reader. Some works slavishly follow the conventions of a genre, and others violate the rules. The former is typical of popular literature, such as detective fiction, which tends to be formulaic in its characterization and plot development. Kent labels these as "automatized texts," because they are formulaic, predictable, high in redundancy, and low in information.⁵¹ The term "easy reading" applies to these works because they do not offer any difficulty or challenge to the reader.

As Kent points out, every text must follow conventions to some extent so that communication may take place. A text that shifted ceaselessly from one set of generic conventions to another would prevent the competent reader from fixing it as a specific kind. Its generic inconsistency would cause so much uncertainty and provide so little redundancy that it would be uninterpretable. It would impart no information to the competent reader. On the other hand, the completely formulaic text would not impart any information either since the competent reader "would know precisely the generic conventions that constitute the text and what the formulaic text intends to communicate." Most texts fall somewhere in between the two extremes.⁵²

Literary works valued most highly by sophisticated readers depart from generic conventions in some way in order to distinguish themselves by their creativity and originality. Kent identifies literariness with hybridization or deformation of generic conventions:

> Certain formally organized sign systems appear strange; they seem to either incorporate or deform the conventions we commonly associate with other kinds of texts. These texts that break generic conventions—texts that we usually consider literary—appear to form new generic categories. They appear to be like no other text we have ever read before.⁵³

Elsewhere he notes that "most highly regarded literary texts go beyond formulas by

---

49. Eliseo Vivas, "Literary Classes: Some Problems," *Genre* 1 (1968): 104.
50. Rosmarin, *Power of Genre*, 23–50.
51. Kent, *Interpretation and Genre*, 48, 53, 57–58, 62, 65, 68, 70, 78, 81–101, 142–43, 146.
52. Kent, "Interpretation and Genre Perception," 138–39; idem, *Interpretation and Genre*, 20–21, 103.
53. Kent, *Interpretation and Genre*, 16.

either deforming genres, like Hopkins deforms the sonnet, or combining genres, like Sterne succeeds in doing in *Tristram Shandy*."⁵⁴

Kent illustrates these assertions by showing that one work by Herman Melville, *Pierre*, is a formulaic example of tragedy, while another work, *Moby-Dick*, combines a number of generic elements. He shows that three different scholars all agree on the generic identification of the former and their low evaluation of it. They sharply disagree, however, on the generic identification of the latter, viewing it as a tragedy, a phenomenological text, and a dialectical novel. The hybrid character of *Moby-Dick* produces two results: (1) Scholars offer different interpretations of the book based on their generic identifications; and (2) They agree on the high degree of the book's aesthetic value.⁵⁵ Hybrid texts result in multiple interpretations, which readers generally find more pleasing than the formulaic text that is easier to interpret.

Todorov also argues that "the major work creates, in a sense, a new genre and at the same time transgresses the previously valid rules of the genre." Therefore, "one might say that every great book establishes the existence of two genres, the reality of two norms: that of the genre it transgresses, which dominated the preceding literature, and that of the genre it creates." He concludes that "as a rule, the literary masterpiece does not enter any genre save perhaps its own; but the masterpiece of popular literature is precisely the book which best fits its genre."⁵⁶ Similarly, Rosalie Colie has shown that "the greatness of such works as *Paradise Lost* and *King Lear* derives in large part from their being encyclopedic works of 'mixed genre' which incorporate and juxtapose virtually the entire range of generic conventions, displaying through these different 'fixes' on experience the full range of human possibilities."⁵⁷

Other theorists maintain that *every* true work of art violates the rules in some

---

54. Ibid., 40. Kent's identification of the quality of literariness with deformation of generic conventions is consistent with formalist attempts to define the "literary" as those works that defamiliarize the known. In the current theoretical climate, the identification of literariness with certain formal properties of the text is very problematic. Marxist theorists above all have exposed the historical, social, and political influences that affect judgments concerning a text's literariness (see Tony Bennett, *Formalism and Marxism* [New Accents; New York: Methuen, 1979], 59–60). In contrast to current literary tastes, in certain cultures and periods of literary history the most conventional work was valued most highly and considered a classic. Such opinions reflect cultural values; therefore, literariness is not simply a matter of certain properties of a text. Nevertheless, it is true that those texts, like the Apocalypse of John, that have remained popular over the centuries are those that are not formulaic and univocal. Both the literary and social aspects of these decisions should be kept in mind.

55. Ibid., 140–44.

56. Tzvetan Todorov, "The Typology of Detective Fiction," in *The Poetics of Prose* (trans. Richard Howard; Ithaca, N.Y.: Cornell University Press, 1977), 43. For similar views, see Corti, *Introduction to Literary Semiotics*, 132; Dubrow, *Genre*, 32; Fowler, *Kinds of Literature*, 23–24; Jauss, "Theory of Genres," 89; Thomas L. Kent, "The Classification of Genres," *Genre* 16 (1983): 10–12; idem, *Interpretation and Genre*, 16, 20, 40, 58, 78, 103; Oswald Ducrot and Tzvetan Todorov, *Encyclopedic Dictionary of the Sciences of Language* (trans. Catherine Porter; Baltimore: Johns Hopkins University Press, 1979), 150–51.

57. Barbara K. Lewalski, foreword to *Resources of Kind: Genre-Theory in the Renaissance*, by Rosalie Colie (ed. Barbara K. Lewalski; Berkeley: University of California Press, 1973), viii.

way. Benedetto Croce provided the classic statement for this view when he asserted that each work of art is a genre unto itself because the artist must always do something different with his materials.[58] Adrian Marino articulates this Romantic rejection of generic criticism:

> Literary works, unique and irrepeatable in essence and definition, therefore "original," defy rigorous subcategorization and all leveling pigeonholes. They form distinctive structures, irreducible to the category of a genre, which is always denied by the particular coefficient of invention, specific to every genuine creation. In fact, people know only about tragedies, not about *tragedy*; about novels, not about *the novel*, both being theoretical abstractions, while each and every work is an absolute, incomparable individuality. . . . In this way, each literary work can be written *only* "in its own genre," belongs to its own genre, and starts a *new genre*. . . . There are as many true genres and species as there are true poets.[59]

To a certain extent, Croce and his followers are right to say that "each and every work is an absolute, incomparable individuality" since every work will contain more than any generic description can comprehend. As Rosmarin says: "Genres can never be perfectly coincident with texts unless we posit as many genres as texts." The genres that readers construct will do violence in some way to the particularity, originality, and individuality of literary works. Nevertheless, readers must group and classify works in order to interpret them, which is always possible because writers must follow some conventions if their work is to be understandable at all.[60] Adherents of the Crocean view unconsciously recognize this necessity because, when they speak of works of art transgressing norms, they admit that norms must always be present.[61] Similarly, Kent points out that "it is important to remember that even if a text appears strange, even if it transgresses generic boundaries, we understand the transgression only because we recognize the generic boundaries that have been violated."[62]

---

58. Croce also criticized genre criticism for diverting the reader from a proper intuitive response to the work of art to an improper logical response. For discussions of Croce's theory, see William K. Wimsatt Jr. and Cleanth Brooks, *Romantic and Modern Criticism*, vol. 2: *Literary History: A Short History* (Chicago: University of Chicago Press, Midway Reprints, 1983), 499–519; Dubrow, *Genre*, 83–84; Jauss, "Theory of Genres," 77–79.

59. Adrian Marino, "Toward a Definition of Literary Genres," in *Theories of Literary Genre* (ed. Joseph P. Strelka; Yearbook of Comparative Literature 8; University Park: Pennsylvania State University Press, 1978), 51.

60. Rosmarin, *Power of Genre*, 45. Murray Krieger also discusses the tension between a text and its "shadow text" or genre. He notes that in texts we see "both the attempt by the shadow text, seen as a universalized shadow genre, to claim, indeed to subsume, the single text at hand, thus keeping it generically open, and the attempt by the text itself to make its claim as a unique play of forces that would seal it off in its own breakaway freedom." The text is never equivalent with its shadow because within the text "the genre is carnivalized, converted into *genera mixta*, its language exploded into a heteroglossia" (*A Reopening of Closure: Organicism against Itself* [Wellek Library Lectures; New York: Columbia University Press, 1989], 75–77).

61. Todorov, *The Fantastic*, 8.

62. Kent, "Interpretation and Genre Perception," 134.

Although each literary work is a unique, individual artistic expression, readers must relate texts to similar texts so that they can use similar interpretative strategies on them. Writers must also follow conventions established by previous writings—even if they are transformed or mixed in some unique way—in order to communicate a message to readers. If texts were pure individual expressions without any connection to what preceded them, no one could read them or understand them. Vivas states that "no artist, however talented, can make objects each of which is in a class by itself. If he could, his work would be totally idiotic, utterly private, each job would be a monad without windows or pre-established harmony. His work would say nothing to anyone but himself, the maker—if it did that much."[63] Although many works of art do not fit completely into any one genre, this does not make such works genres unto themselves, without any connections to other works.[64]

THE HYBRID GENRE'S EFFECT ON INTERPRETATION

Genres are artificial constructs of readers, interpreters, critics, and theorists that supplement, bind, and limit texts in order to aid in their interpretation. Some texts are easy to limit in this way, but others are more difficult to classify in one category. The latter often are more highly intertextual than the former, and therefore they resist grouping on the basis of similarities more than texts whose intertextuality is not quite so extensive.[65] While some texts attempt to limit the options of classification for the interpreter, others have multiple and extensive intertextual relations that complicate the attempt to classify them in one particular genre. As Patrick O'Donnell and Robert Con Davis note:

> Dynamic in nature, intertextuality "at work" inevitably takes the form of boundary-crossing; it creates crises, aporiae, ideology wherever it goes—for, as is inherent in the nature of signs, the intertextual relation generates the deferral and rewriting of "parent" texts, themselves bastardized deformations of the texts that came before them. Intertextuality challenges those systems of signification which allow

---

63. Vivas, "Literary Classes," 103.
64. Jauss refutes Croce's view in this same way ("Theory of Genres," 79).
65. Gustavo Pérez Firmat, in "Apuntes para un modelo de la intertextualidad en literatura," *Romanic Review* 69 (1978): 2, notes that "intertextuality is not an absolute value but a quantitative phenomenon. Not all texts show the same degree of intertextuality: in some, intertextuality constitutes the generating principle of the text (the work of Lautréamont); in others, it appears only in an accidental manner (the realistic novel)" [my translation]. This view contrasts with deconstructionist views of intertextuality, which see it as infinite and unlimited in every text. For an example of this latter view, see Joseph N. Riddell, "From Heidegger to Derrida to Chance: Doubling and (Poetic) Language," in *Martin Heidegger and the Question of Literature: Toward a Postmodern Literary Hermeneutics* (ed. William V. Spanos; Bloomington: Indiana University Press, 1979), 231–52, and Vincent B. Leitch's discussion of Riddell's article in *Deconstructive Criticism: An Advanced Introduction* (New York: Columbia University Press, 1983), 87–102. If one views intertextuality strictly in terms of literary relations between texts, then the amount of intertextuality in a work would depend on the extent of a writer's literary competence and the writer's use of it in that work. It would also depend on the extent of the reader's literary competence, which would enable the latter to recognize the degree of intertextuality.

us to mark off the formal terrains of "literary period," "genre," "author," "subject," "nation," "text."[66]

These highly intertextual texts are often called "mixed" or "hybrid" genres.[67]

Kent explains that hybrid genres deform or incorporate conventions commonly associated with other kinds of texts. They do this through a process he calls "syntagmatic foregrounding," which is "the disappointment of a specific generic expectation that is created by the repetition of a narrative element in an unexpected context, or by the omission of an important narrative element from the text." The result of combining different generic categories in unexpected ways is that "uncertainty is manufactured about the hybrid genre's true generic category."[68] "Paradigmatic foregrounding" establishes generic expectations at the beginning of a text, and when these are satisfied, the text is automatized.[69] Syntagmatic foregrounding deautomatizes a text by introducing "designed uncertainty," which overcomes the tendency towards "systemic closure" in the text. According to information theory, the higher the uncertainty, the greater the information content.[70] Consequently, the hybrid genre is open to multiple interpretations, as Kent says of his example *Moby-Dick*: "Because of its mixture of generic categories, *Moby-Dick* becomes a tapestry of possible interpretations."[71]

The hybrid genre provides so many possibilities to readers that they must choose one on which to focus their attention. An analogy from everyday life can illustrate this process. People are continuously bombarded with more sensory stimuli than they can possibly be aware of at one time. Consequently, they choose to respond selectively to certain ones and ignore the others, an ability termed "selective attention."

An example of selective attention is the "cocktail party effect," which occurs when a person stands in a crowded room where multiple conversations are occurring.

---

66. Patrick O'Donnell and Robert Con Davis, "Introduction: Intertext and Contemporary American Fiction," in *Intertextuality and Contemporary American Fiction* (ed. Patrick O'Donnell and Robert Con Davis; Baltimore: Johns Hopkins University Press, 1989), xiv. See also p. xv.

67. Fowler refers to the hybrid as a work in which two or more complete generic repertoires are present in such proportions that neither one dominates. These are usually neighboring or contrasting kinds that have some external form in common. He thinks this is a rather rare phenomenon. More common is what he calls "modulation," which occurs when a modal abstraction with a token repertoire is combined with a genre (*Kinds of Literature*, 107, 183, 191). Kent similarly contends that "a particular text in a hybrid genre will employ one dominant pure genre as a kind of base on which other formulated conventions are constructed" ("Classification of Genres," 11; *Interpretation and Genre*, 69). Both of these theorists tend to reify genres rather than viewing them as readerly creations. This is clear in Kent when he argues that "a finite number of genres exist, and all other more complex literary structures are a combination of these genres" ("Classification of Genres," 10; *Interpretation and Genre*, 67–68). If a finite number of genres do indeed exist, it is because those are the only ones that readers have so far agreed upon.

68. Kent, *Interpretation and Genre*, 50.
69. Ibid., 50–51, 57.
70. Ibid., 53, 56, 61–62, 65, 69, 104.
71. Ibid., 25.

A person can shift attention from one to the other, simultaneously blocking out the others that might interfere with reception. The mechanism by which humans can do this has not been identified definitively, but one of the most popular theories is the "Broadbent filter theory." According to Donald Broadbent, the brain possesses only one information processing channel—and a limited one at that. Incoming sensory stimuli are stored in a short-term sensory register, and from this register the filter selects the message to be received. Studies have shown that this selection mechanism can shift between different sensory input channels twice a second. In addition, the filter's selection of a message may be influenced by biases toward those stimuli that are novel, more intense, more probable, considered more valuable, or that best match the contextual information derived from recent inputs and memories.[72]

Selective attention becomes obvious with ambiguous cognitive illusions or the figure-ground phenomenon. The paintings of Salvador Dali provide well-known examples. Other common examples are the duck-rabbit, vase-faces, and the Necker cube. These phenomena offer competing sensory stimuli simultaneously to the observer. When the observer focuses on one input, it becomes the "figure," which appears to have a hard surface with a recognizable shape and definable boundaries. Simultaneously, the observer must divert attention from the other stimuli, which become the "ground," perceived as less surface-like and without definite boundaries. In these illusions, one notices the figure and ground alternating as perception shifts from one competing picture or object to the other. In this alternation of perception, the observer is entertaining alternative perceptual hypotheses concerning what the object is or where its parts lie in space.[73]

Like these perceptual phenomena, a hybrid genre containing a mixture of conventions offers multiple possibilities to readers, who must foreground one set of conventions and background the others.[74] Readers read with great difficulty a text as if it belonged simultaneously to more than one genre. Trying to do this would provide no foundation on which to interpret the text consistently. Since human beings desire order, coherence, and consistency, in these cases they reduce the complexity of the text by focusing attention on one cluster of conventions—even if it is incomplete.[75] They foreground one intertextual relation or generic connection and background the

---

72. Neville Moray, "Attention," in *The Oxford Companion to the Mind* (ed. Richard L. Gregory; Oxford: Oxford University Press, 1987), 59–61; Donald H. McBurney and Virginia B. Collings, *Introduction to Sensation/Perception* (2d ed.; Englewood Cliffs, N.J.: Prentice-Hall, 1984), 251–54.

73. Richard L. Gregory, "Figure-Ground," "Illusions," "Perception as Hypotheses," in Gregory, *Oxford Companion to the Mind*, 263–64, 337–43, 608–10; Julian Hochberg, "Gestalt Theory," in Gregory, *Oxford Companion to the Mind*, 288–91. One can find illustrations of these illusions in Gregory, "Illusions," 340.

74. Steve Moyise uses a different analogy to illustrate the "competing voices" that result from intertextual allusions: When a radio dial is incorrectly tuned, the listener must choose which broadcast will receive attention ("Intertextuality and the Book of Revelation," *ExpTim* 104 [July 1993]: 296).

75. Ducrot and Todorov note the role of the Russian formalists' principle of dominance in determining the genre of a text, but they admit that we do not know how to measure the dominance of generic elements in a text (*Encyclopedic Dictionary*, 150).

others; one becomes figure and the others become ground. As Temma F. Berg notes, "[T]o read is to forget much that one has read."[76] Berg cites I. A. Richards, whose comments are relevant to the current topic: "But in all reading whatsoever much must be left out. Otherwise we could arrive at no meaning. The omission is essential in the twofold sense: without omission no meaning would form for us; and through the omission what we are trying to grasp becomes what it is."[77]

When reading a work with mixed conventions, the reader must choose which conventions to follow and which ones to ignore, which ones to foreground and which to background. Other readers of the same text may choose a different perspective and foreground a different cluster. Also, the same reader may regard the same text differently upon a second or third reading. The different decisions result from the biases, predispositions, or experiences of the reader at the time of reading. Such hybrid texts may provide evidence of various kinds that would support each of these possibilities without fully committing themselves to any one of them.

A text that is highly intertextual and intergeneric has as a result a high degree of polyvalence. Julia Kristeva notes this fact:

> If one grants that every signifying practice is a field of transpositions of various signifying systems (an inter-textuality), one then understands that its 'place' of enunciation and its denoted 'object' are never single, complete, and identical to themselves, but always plural, shattered, capable of being tabulated. In this way polysemy can also be seen as the result of a semiotic polyvalence—an adherence to different sign systems.[78]

Similarly, Kent concludes that "a hybrid genre is higher in uncertainty and information content than a pure genre" and that "the greater the degree of foregrounding activity within a text, the higher is the uncertainty and the information content within that text."[79] Thus, a greater degree of intertextuality and intergenericity opens a text to multiple interpretations. Its meaning and relevance appear inexhaustible. This kind of text is often considered a "classic."[80]

Roland Barthes's concept of "writerly" texts and Umberto Eco's similar concept

---

76. Temma F. Berg, "Reading in/to Mark," *Semeia* 48 (1989): 189.

77. I. A. Richards, *How to Read a Page: A Course in Effective Reading, with an Introduction to a Hundred Great Works* (New York: Norton, 1942), 93, cited in Berg, "Reading in/to Mark," 189.

78. Julia Kristeva, *Revolution in Poetic Language* (trans. Margaret Waller; New York: Columbia University Press, 1984), 60.

79. Kent, "Classification of Genres," 11–12. His terminology is borrowed from Abraham A. Moles, *Information Theory and Esthetic Perception* (trans. Joel E. Cohen; Urbana: University of Illinois Press, 1966). Although his confidence that pure genre conventions can always be identified and separated within a hybrid text is unwarranted, his explanation that texts high in levels of information and uncertainty are those that combine a great many genre convictions is helpful.

80. Frank Kermode in *The Classic: Literary Images of Permanence and Change* (Cambridge: Harvard University Press, 1983) argues that classics are characterized by indeterminacy of meaning and the possibility of multiple interpretations. Complexity and richness of meaning give these works staying power. What makes a work a classic is highly debated today because of increasing awareness that value judgments are influenced by the social, political, and economic situations of those passing judgment.

of "open" texts can be applied to hybrid genres. According to Barthes, the "readerly" text puts readers in the position of a passive consumer. It does not allow for much creativity or participation on the part of readers. The "writerly" text, on the other hand, allows readers to participate in the text as producer of its meaning; readers are allowed to enter the play of signifiers and write the text themselves.[81] Readers can actively construct meaning from the various possibilities offered by the text.

In Eco's view, writers compose closed works of art with the intention to guide the addressee along a straight and narrow path towards a single, determinate meaning. The author presents the work as "a finished product with the intention that his particular composition should be appreciated and received in the same form as he devised it." Open works, however, are composed with an indeterminate structure that allows the performer or reader to complete it so that the performer is simultaneously the composer and the reader simultaneously the writer. Eco recognizes that even closed works will be susceptible to different interpretations because the reader's "comprehension of the original artifact is always modified by his particular and individual perspective." Nevertheless, he believes that works can be distinguished by how much their composers try to ignore or repress this fact or try to exploit the inevitable openness of works and turn that openness into "a positive aspect of [their] production, recasting the work so as to expose it to the maximum possible 'opening.' "[82]

The highly intertextual text that mixes generic conventions is a "writerly text" or an "open work." It allows readers greater space in which to create their own meaning from the text. Robert T. Eberwein correctly concludes that "generically fragmented" works are writerly texts because they allow readers to provide the ordering principle themselves rather than derive it from the stabilizing conventions of the genre.[83] As Barthes says: "The more plural the text, the less it is written before I read it."[84] Since the role of producer is an inherently more interesting, though less secure, one for readers, this kind of text gives greater pleasure to the reader.[85] The Apocalypse of John is this kind of text. It is highly intertextual, it has mixed conventions of different kinds, and therefore it is open to multiple interpretations. The following section will show that the Apocalypse is a mixed genre that invites readers to participate in constructing its identity and producing its meaning.

---

81. Roland Barthes, *S/Z* (trans. Richard Miller; New York: Hill and Wang, 1974), 4–5.

82. Umberto Eco, "The Poetics of the Open Work," in *The Role of the Reader: Explorations in the Semiotics of Texts* (Bloomington: Indiana University Press, 1979), 49–50. Barthes makes the same distinctions between the *écrivant* and the *écrivain*.

83. Robert T. Eberwein, "Genre and the Writerly Text," *Journal of Popular Film and Television* 13 (1985): 64.

84. Barthes, *S/Z*, 10.

85. This point is emphasized by Roland Barthes in *The Pleasure of the Text* (trans. Richard Miller; New York: Hill and Wang, 1975). Barthes distinguishes the text of pleasure (*plaisir*) and the text of bliss (*jouissance*). The former is linked to a comfortable practice of reading, while the latter discomforts and unsettles the reader (14). But the latter text is the one that leads to the greatest pleasure, which he describes in erotic terms throughout his book.

The Mixed Genre of the Apocalypse of John

Interpreters have offered various generic identities for the Apocalypse of John through the centuries, but, as in the case of the Gospels, they have reached no consensus. Like the Gospels, the Apocalypse offers many generic possibilities to the reader without fully supporting any one of the categories. It mixes conventions from various genres so that the reader must decide which ones to foreground and which ones to background. This kind of mongrel text with its "matrix of generic features"[86] is frustrating to the reader who looks for a simple, consistent interpretative strategy to make sense of the text. But it can also supply much pleasure since it allows the reader a greater role in the production of its meaning.

Mixture of Literary Conventions in 1:1–20

A close examination of the first chapter of the Apocalypse reveals its intertextual and intergeneric character. Texts often begin with the phenomenon that Kent calls "paradigmatic foregrounding." Writers will indicate the use of a genre at the beginning of a work by means of a title or subtitle, preface, foreword, or some other paratextual reference. If the genre is not specified in such paratextual ways, then readers must begin reading with a hypothesis concerning the work's genre in mind. As they read, they alter and adjust their hypothesis as the evidence supporting it or contradicting it accumulates.[87]

The opening of the Apocalypse is so highly intertextual that it frustrates the reader who tries to categorize the book in a single genre. By verse 20, the reader must continue reading with the hypothesis of a blend of conventions. Since readers cannot focus on different sets of literary conventions simultaneously, they will view one set as primary and background the others. Different readers select different conventions to foreground and background.

The first three words of the Apocalypse offer hope for a quick solution to the question of its genre. The nominative absolute Ἀποκάλυψις followed by the genitives Ἰησοῦ Χριστοῦ appear to entitle the book. Similarly, Mark began his Gospel with a self-description: Ἀρχὴ τοῦ εὐαγγελίου Ἰησοῦ Χριστοῦ. Just as Mark's self-description εὐαγγέλιον became the technical generic title for works similar to it, John's self-description ἀποκάλυψις became the generic name for similar works. This word was probably adopted as a generic label for two reasons: (1) The Apocalypse was the most influential and popular of the Christian examples of these writings; and (2) "apocalypse" provides a helpful description of these works since they claimed to be unveilings of the spiritual dimension, God's will, the future, and so on.

---

86. Eberwein, "Genre and the Writerly Text," 65.

87. Hirsch uses the term "heuristic genre" to refer to the vague, broad, preliminary guess that the interpreter narrows in the course of interpretation until he arrives at the "intrinsic genre," the correct guess that can account for all the meanings of the utterance (*Validity in Interpretation*, 88). Although his concept of intrinsic genre is problematic, his general description of the way readers modify their generic hypotheses during the temporal process of reading is helpful.

The application of the term to a group of works similar to the Apocalypse apparently did not occur until the patristic writers of the second century and later began using it this way.[88] No writing before the Apocalypse ever used the term as a generic title. Morton Smith concludes after an investigation of the ancient uses of the terms ἀποκαλύπτω and ἀποκάλυψις: "Remarkable is the rarity of the words in works now commonly called 'apocalypses.' I do not know any such text prior to the New Testament Apocalypse which either describes itself or the proceedings in it as *apokalypseis* or even uses the verb *apokalypto* for the whole of the revelation."[89] Leon Morris draws the proper conclusion from these facts:

> We should make it clear that "apocalyptic" is our term. It is not one which the ancients used, at least in this way. It is not even certain that they regarded the books we speak of as apocalyptic as constituting a definite class. Doubtless they saw some similarities, but whether they were as impressed by them as are modern scholars, we do not know. If they were, they have not left it on record. There is quite a range of apocalyptic opinion, and the men who wrote this kind of literature seem to have come from all parties and from none. It may well not have occurred to the men of antiquity, accordingly, to group their writings together. They may have been more impressed by the differences than the resemblances. In antiquity then there is neither the name (i.e. as applied to a class of books; the term occurs but is used otherwise), nor the classification.[90]

Likewise, Elisabeth Schüssler Fiorenza notes the lack of evidence that ἀποκάλυψις was a technical term for revelatory literature and concludes that "it is doubtful that the author chose this title in order to qualify his prophecy as an apocalyptic document."[91] Since John juxtaposes the description of his book as "the words of the prophecy" (1:3) with the description of it as ἀποκάλυψις (1:1), it seems reasonable to conclude that the latter term "is a synonym for *propheteia* for John." This identification is supported by the fact that the noun and verb forms are used elsewhere for Christian prophecy, as in Shepherd of Hermas, Gal 1:12, and 1 Cor 14.[92] As Adela

---

88. Morton Smith, "On the History of ΑΠΟΚΑΛΥΠΤΩ and ΑΠΟΚΑΛΥΨΙΣ," in *Apocalypticism in the Mediterranean World and the Near East* (ed. David Hellholm; Tübingen: Mohr Siebeck, 1983), 13, 18–19; Philipp Vielhauer, "Introduction: Apocalypses and Related Subjects," trans. David Hill, in *New Testament Apocrypha* (ed. Edgar Hennecke and Wilhelm Schneemelcher; Philadelphia: Westminster, 1965), 2:582.
89. Smith, "On the History of ΑΠΟΚΑΛΥΠΤΩ," 14.
90. Leon Morris, *Apocalyptic* (London: InterVarsity Press, 1973), 20–21.
91. Elisabeth Schüssler Fiorenza, *The Book of Revelation: Justice and Judgment* (Philadelphia: Fortress, 1985), 150. See also R. H. Charles, *The Revelation of St. John* (Edinburgh: T&T Clark, 1920), 1:4; Robert H. Mounce, *The Book of Revelation* (rev. ed.; NICNT; Grand Rapids: Eerdmans, 1998), 40.
92. M. Eugene Boring, "The Apocalypse as Christian Prophecy: A Discussion of the Issues Raised by the Book of Revelation for the Study of Early Christian Prophecy," in *Society of Biblical Literature Seminar Papers 1974* (ed. G. W. MacRae; Missoula, Mont.: Society of Biblical Literature, 1974), 47; Elizabeth Schüssler Fiorenza, *Invitation to the Book of Revelation* (Doubleday New Testament Commentary; Garden City, N.Y.: Image Books, 1982), 32; Mazzaferri, *Genre of the Book of Revelation*, 276.

Yarbro Collins notes, "[T]he author does not seem to have distinguished between an apocalyptic and a prophetic book."[93] When one compares the term with its use in the Pauline and deutero-Pauline traditions, one can see that for John and his readers it most likely denoted "a visionary, ecstatic experience similar to prophecy."[94]

Despite these facts, some commentators view the first three words of the Apocalypse as a self-designation of its genre. For example, G. B. Caird says that this phrase "not only describes its content, but classifies it as a recognized type of literature."[95] David Hellholm also argues that ἀποκάλυψις serves as a genre designation because it refers to a written form and because it has an emphatic position at the beginning of the title.[96] The term functions as a genre designation for modern readers because the genre apocalypse now exists in critical discourse, but to claim that it served as a genre designation for the original readers is not accurate since this was the first time the word was used to refer to a complete written work.

The first word of the Apocalypse appears to offer the reader various alternatives for its generic identity. It may be simply a synonym for prophecy, or it may refer to a genre that may be distinguished from prophecy to some degree, a genre that the reader must construct by determining the quality and quantity of that difference. The reader must continue looking for evidence in the book to confirm or refute either hypothesis.

As readers proceed, they notice that the revelation is mediated to John by an angel, a phenomenon that they can connect with other literature such as Daniel, *1 Enoch*, and Shepherd of Hermas. They will then continue to examine the book to see how prominent is the role of the angel-interpreter. Another word in verse 1, ἐσήμανεν, will encourage readers to compare the writing with other symbolic works.

Verse 2 contains the phrase "word of God," which reminds readers of the way Old Testament prophets referred to their revelations. Verse 3 contains a beatitude, which was a linguistic form used by the prophets of Israel (Isa 19:25; 30:18; 56:2; Jer 17:7). This verse also indicates that the work was written as an oral performance, which suggests a liturgical character.[97] In the midst of this beatitude, John refers to his work as "the words of the prophecy," which will cause the reader to scrutinize the book for similarities to other prophetic works. The phrase "the time is near" indicates

---

93. Adela Yarbro Collins, *The Apocalypse* (New Testament Message 22; Wilmington, Del.: Glazier, 1979), 5.

94. Schüssler Fiorenza, *Book of Revelation*, 150–51.

95. G. B. Caird, *A Commentary on the Revelation of St. John the Divine* (HNTC; New York: Harper & Row, 1966; repr., Peabody, Mass.: Hendrickson, 1987), 9.

96. David Hellholm, "The Visions He Saw or: To Encode the Future in Writing," in *Text and Logos: The Humanistic Interpretation of the New Testament* (ed. Theodore W. Jennings Jr.; Atlanta: Scholars Press, 1991), 112–14, 121–23.

97. David L. Barr, "The Apocalypse of John as Oral Enactment," *Int* 40 (1986): 243–56; Jean-Pierre Ruiz, "Betwixt and Between on the Lord's Day: Liturgy and the Apocalypse," in *Society of Biblical Literature Seminar Papers, 1992* (Atlanta: Scholars Press, 1992), 663; see chapter 11 of this volume.

a view of eschatology that must be compared with eschatological writings to determine with which ones it is most similar.

Up to this point, the Apocalypse begins similar to many Old Testament prophetic books, but beginning with verse 4 the reader encounters a new generic alternative. Suddenly, the book begins to follow the conventions of a letter as it was developed in the Hellenistic world and modified by Paul. Normally, the epistolary prescript occurs at the beginning of letters. The verse contains the typical references to the sender and recipients and Paul's peculiar form of greeting, which includes the blessings of grace and peace. Verses 5 and 6 contain a doxology similar to the one found in the epistolary prescript of Gal 1:1–5. This element might raise expectations of a liturgical identity for the book.

Verses 7 and 8, however, contain two prophetic utterances unrelated to the epistolary opening. The language is based on Dan 7 and Zech 12. The title "the Alpha and the Omega" may reflect a divine name used in magical papyri.[98] As readers continue examining the book for epistolary conventions, they will not find any more until the very end. In those closing verses, they must decide which verses to include in the epistolary postscript.[99]

Verses 1–8 are an example of syntagmatic foregrounding. The work begins by paradigmatically foregrounding conventions many readers will associate with Old Testament prophecy, but then epistolary conventions enter the syntagmatic progression of the narrative, thereby frustrating the generic expectations that have been raised in the reader. Just as suddenly, these epistolary conventions disappear until the end of the book. This example of syntagmatic foregrounding—and no doubt there are many more in the Apocalypse—introduces designed uncertainty into the narrative, which deautomatizes it and allows the reader the option of choosing which conventions to continue to follow.[100]

The whole work seems to be set in an epistolary frame so that the reader must decide whether the letter form is the dominant genre or a secondary element. Since the epistolary conventions function as a frame and do not extend throughout the book, how important is the epistolary character for understanding the work? The interpreter must choose whether to foreground or background the epistolary elements. By the end of verse 8, the reader can choose among several options: Is the book an

---

98. David E. Aune, "The Apocalypse of John and Greco-Roman Revelatory Magic," *NTS* 33 (1987): 481–501; idem, *Revelation 1–5*, 57.

99. Common suggestions are verse 21, verses 10–21, or verses 6–21.

100. Michael Anthony Harris, "The Literary Function of Hymns in the Apocalypse of John" (Ph.D. diss., Southern Baptist Theological Seminary, 1989), 252–58, illustrates how the alternation between apocalyptic and epistolary conventions in the first chapter makes the Apocalypse a "deformulated apocalypse." Although he states that "because of the nature of the narrative, it is a mistake to valorize one generic element over the other," a few sentences later he concludes that "the narrative should still be broadly regarded as apocalyptic, since the apocalyptic visions dominate the narrative" (253). He makes few references to the prophetic conventions followed in the first chapter. Like most interpreters, he neglects to see how extensive is the Apocalypse's intertextuality and that the line between prophetic and apocalyptic conventions is ultimately the creation of the interpreter.

epistolary prophecy, or a prophetic letter, or an apocalypse in the form of an apostolic letter, or some other combination?[101]

Verse 9 begins to describe a vision experienced by the author. This vision calls to mind certain prophetic call narratives, such as Isa 6, Jer 1, and Ezek 1–3. In verse 10, the reader discovers that the vision occurred when John was "in the Spirit." Here, the reader must decide whether the phrase refers to the gift of prophecy or a trance-like state experienced by apocalyptic visionaries. Verse 11 contains the command to write to the seven churches, again emphasizing the character of the book as a circular letter. Some readers also connect this feature with apocalypse because, in contrast to the oral phenomenon of prophecy, apocalyptic writings take a self-consciously written form. The description of the Son of Man in verses 12–20 contains numerous images adopted from the Old Testament, although some of them occur in other Jewish writings. Verse 18 may contain an image drawn from the mythology of the goddess Hekate, a connection that encourages the reader to search for other mythological elements in the book.[102] Verse 19 contains a phrase that some readers connect with a common formula of that era for describing prophecy.[103]

Readers also note another detail in the first chapter that may provide a key to its genre. Eleven times the word "seven" appears, and it continues to play a key role throughout the book. Four sections of the book are clearly divided into seven parts, a pattern that tempts some readers to divide the rest of the book according to this pattern. James L. Blevins has connected this pattern of sevens with the theater of

---

101. For example, the following commentators minimize the epistolary conventions: Adela Yarbro Collins, "The Early Christian Apocalypses," *Semeia* 14 (1979): 70–71; David E. Aune, *The New Testament in Its Literary Environment* (LEC 8; Philadelphia: Westminster, 1987), 240–41; idem, *Revelation 1–5* (WBC 52; Dallas: Word, 1997), lxxxiii; idem, "Intertextuality and the Genre of the Apocalypse," in *Society of Biblical Literature 1991 Seminar Papers* (ed. Eugene H. Lovering Jr.; Atlanta: Scholars Press, 1991), 146; and W. S. Vorster, "'Genre' and the Revelation of John: A Study in Text, Context, and Intertext," *Neot* 22 (1988): 114–15. Frederick David Mazzaferri also views the epistolary framework as incidental due to John's circumstances of exile (*The Genre of the Book of Revelation from a Source-Critical Perspective* [BZNW 54; Berlin: de Gruyter, 1989], 231–33).

Other commentators emphasize its epistolary character: Richard Bauckham, *The Theology of the Book of Revelation* (New Testament Theology; Cambridge: Cambridge University Press, 1993), 12–17; Schüssler Fiorenza, *Book of Revelation*, 169; D. A. Carson, Douglas J. Moo, and Leon Morris, *An Introduction to the New Testament* (Grand Rapids: Zondervan, 1992), 479; Martin Karrer, *Die Johannesoffenbarung als Brief: Studien zu ihrem literarischen, historischen und theologischen Ort* (Göttingen: Vandenhoeck & Ruprecht, 1986); J. Ramsey Michaels, "Jewish and Christian Apocalyptic Letters: 1 Peter, Revelation, and 2 Baruch 78–87," in *Society of Biblical Literature 1987 Seminar Papers* (ed. Kent Harold Richards; Atlanta: Scholars Press, 1987), 268–75; idem, *Interpreting the Book of Revelation* (Guides to New Testament Exegesis; Grand Rapids: Baker, 1992), 30–33; M. Eugene Boring, *Revelation* (Interpretation: A Bible Commentary for Teaching and Preaching; Louisville: Knox, 1989), 5–8; and Jürgen Roloff, *The Revelation of John: A Continental Commentary* (trans. John E. Alsup; Minneapolis: Fortress, 1993), 8.

102. Aune, *Revelation 1–5*, 104–5.

103. W. C. van Unnik, "A Formula Describing Prophecy," *NTS* 9 (1962–63): 86–94. A thorough discussion of alternative interpretations for this verse is provided by G. K. Beale, *The Book of Revelation: A Commentary on the Greek Text* (NIGTC; Grand Rapids: Eerdmans, 1999), 152–70.

Ephesus, which is the only one in the ancient world that has seven thuromata, or openings for scenery.[104] Consequently, he views the Apocalypse as a drama in seven acts. However, those who argue for its identity as drama usually combine that genre with some other genre such as liturgy or prophecy.[105]

By the end of the first chapter, the reader can discern no single, clear generic identity. Aune rightly observes: "From the perspective of the original reader, it has become obvious that the sequence of literary forms in the Apocalypse conforms to no known ancient literary conventions."[106] In chapters 2 and 3, another unusual element occurs: Seven letters to different churches are included. But these letters are not like the ones Paul wrote. Instead, they seem to be more like prophetic proclamations[107] or royal edicts.[108] Incorporating seven letters into a book's structure is unusual for both prophecy and apocalypse. These seven letters complicate further the search for the genre of the Apocalypse.

As one continues through the book, other elements complicate any generic hypothesis. For example, the numerous hymns and the fact that the book was to be read in a worship setting lead some to view the dominant genre as liturgy.[109] Others foreground the mythological elements of the book and refer to it as myth.[110] Other readers deemphasize these elements as merely constituent parts of a more inclusive genre. By the end of the book, the great amount of syntagmatic foregrounding will enable the reader to link the book with many different kinds of works. Thus, the Apocalypse is a deformed text or a hybrid genre, which allows readers to choose which conventions they will foreground and which ones they will background and which ones they will ignore altogether.[111]

Aune suggests that "the conception of 'mixed genres' is theoretically infelici-

---

104. James L. Blevins, "The Genre of Revelation," *RevExp* 77 (1980): 393–408.
105. John Wick Bowman, "The Revelation to John: Its Dramatic Structure and Message," *Int* 9 (1955): 436–53.
106. Aune, "Intertextuality and the Genre of the Apocalypse," 159.
107. Klaus Berger, "Apostelbrief und apostolische Rede/Zum Formular frühchristlicher Briefe," *ZNW* 65 (1974): 190–231.
108. Aune, *Revelation 1–5*, 124–29.
109. Barr, "The Apocalypse of John as Oral Enactment," 243–56; Edouard Cothenet, "Earthly and Heavenly Liturgy according to the Book of Revelation," in *Roles in the Liturgical Assembly* (trans. Matthew J. O'Connell; New York: Pueblo, 1981), 115–35; W. Hulitt Gloer, "Worship God! Liturgical Elements in the Apocalypse," *RevExp* 98 (winter 2001): 35–58; Otto Piper, "The Apocalypse of John and the Liturgy of the Ancient Church," *CH* (1951): 10–22; M. H. Shepard, *The Paschal Liturgy and the Apocalypse* (Richmond: Knox, 1960).
110. John G. Gager, *Kingdom and Community: The Social World of Early Christianity* (Prentice-Hall Studies in Religion Series; Englewood Cliffs, N.J.: Prentice-Hall, 1975), 49–57.
111. For a discussion of some of these options and their shortcomings along with an attempt to identify the "complex literary type" of the Apocalypse by doing justice to the various generic connections of the book, see Schüssler Fiorenza, *Book of Revelation*, 165–70. For an analysis of the intertextual connections that occur throughout the Apocalypse, see Aune, "Intertextuality and the Genre of the Apocalypse," 145–59, and the second chapter of my dissertation: Gregory L. Linton, "Intertextuality in the Revelation of John," (Ph.D. diss., Duke University, 1993), 61–110.

tous and should be used only as a court of last resort, for if the notion of *mixtum compositum* is too quickly applied to a problematic text, the possibility of achieving a generic understanding of the structure of the entire text is given up without a struggle."[112] In this comment, Aune concedes that his concern is narrowing the generic choices to provide a reading strategy. His attempt to identify the genre of the Apocalypse is pragmatic and rhetorical. In fact, every text is a *mixtum compositum* to a greater or lesser extent, but in order to make sense of a text, the reader has to place restrictions on it by focusing on one set of generic conventions. In the case of highly intertextual works like the Apocalypse of John, this attempt often requires a greater "struggle." Despite Aune's reluctance to accept the obvious conclusion, a reader of the Apocalypse would not "too quickly" characterize it as a hybrid genre, considering the designed uncertainty of its first chapter and the numerous identifications of its genre that result.

READING THE APOCALYPSE AS AN APOCALYPSE

Perhaps the most popular identification of the genre of the Apocalypse among current scholars is apocalypse. The genre apocalypse, however, did not exist when John wrote since its conventions had not yet been formulated. Apocalypse is an example of a genre whose conventions remained unformulated and implicit for many years—in this case, centuries—until a critic formulated them.[113] Some genre theorists, such as Jauss and Pérez Firmat, suggest that ancient genres should be constructed on the basis of "poetological documents." In this process, "one would piece together the scattered critical observations of the day in order to recover the conception of the genre that oriented the composition and reception of such works." In fact, Pérez Firmat argues that genres do not exist until they are constructed in critical discourse.[114]

Unfortunately, this process of genre construction is more complicated with works that contemporary readers did not recognize as belonging to a new and different genre. Because readers assumed that such works belonged to already recognized genres, they offered no critical comments on them.[115] Some genres are *a posteriori* constructions, proposed by later interpreters who have come to recognize that certain works shared enough similarities to each other and differences from other works to justify categorizing them in their own genre. "Apocalypse" is an example of a genre that did not exist until it was constructed and defined in critical discourse. Since the genre of apocalypse was not yet formulated, the writers of apocalypses themselves did not realize that they were writing apocalypses. Apparently, many, if not all, of them

---

112. David E. Aune, "The Apocalypse of John and the Problem of Genre," *Semeia* 36 (1986): 67. See chapter 2 of this volume.

113. See the section above on literary conventions, pp. 14–16.

114. Gustavo Pérez Firmat, "Genre as Text," *Comparative Literature Studies* 17 (1980): 16–25; idem, "Novel as Genres," 284–91.

115. Longman, "Form Criticism," 58–59.

thought that they were writing prophecies.[116] Certainly, John himself thought he was writing prophecy, since he says so six times (1:3; 19:10; 22:7, 10, 18, 19).

Readers did not recognize apocalypse as a discrete genre until the second century at the earliest. Even then, the use of the term may simply indicate the influence of the Apocalypse of John on the work rather than the category of literature to which the work belonged. In 1822, the German scholar K. I. Nitzsch coined the term "apocalypse" for the genre. The first critic to attempt to identify its conventions was Friedrich Lücke, who published a study of apocalyptic literature in 1832. The attempt to identify the conventions of apocalypse continues until this day. These attempts result from the fact that later readers have recognized that a certain group of works—including at the very least Daniel, *1 Enoch*, *4 Ezra*, *2 Baruch*, and the Apocalypse of John—shared similarities that distinguished them from other genres such as prophecy.[117] Critics have recognized that the writers of these works were unconsciously following tacit conventions that formed an unwritten poetics. They have attempted to specify and codify those conventions, thereby drawing boundaries around a certain group of works to set it off from others. They disagree, however, on the nature and placement of those boundaries. This procedure of marking boundaries is difficult to perform with a highly intertextual phenomenon like apocalypse, especially in early Christianity where apocalypse and prophecy were tightly interwoven.[118]

Those who read the Apocalypse as an apocalypse select certain characteristics of the book that it shares with other books in order to read it *as if* it were one of those books. They place boundaries around those works on the basis of certain similarities and give them the name "apocalypse" because the Apocalypse of John is often used as the starting point for comparison. For example, Paul Hanson advised using the Apocalypse as the paradigm or starting point for defining the genre apocalypse and then to "consider which other compositions of the same era show sufficient similarity to justify extension of the term to them as well."[119] Leonard L. Thompson advises the same approach when he says that "a work may be called an apocalypse if it resembles the Revelation of John."[120] He refers to the Apocalypse as "the source for delineating apocalyptic literature."

This approach begs the question of the Apocalypse's generic identity by setting it up as the prototype for all other apocalypses. The attempt to identify the genre "apocalypse" begins by assuming, rather than proving, that the Apocalypse is a prime example. The power of this assumption is revealed in Thompson's statement in re-

---

116. Schüssler Fiorenza cites *4 Esdras* 12:42; 14:22, 26, in this connection (*Book of Revelation*, 140, 153 n. 21).

117. Klaus Koch, *The Rediscovery of Apocalyptic* (trans. Margaret Kohl; London: SCM, 1972), 23. Also see the discussion of these issues in chapter 3 of this volume, p. 74.

118. Schüssler Fiorenza, *Book of Revelation*, 168–69; Carson, Moo, and Morris, *Introduction to the New Testament*, 479.

119. P. D. Hanson, "Apocalypse, Genre," *IDBSup*, 27.

120. Leonard L. Thompson, *The Book of Revelation: Apocalypse and Empire* (New York: Oxford University Press, 1990), 18.

sponse to Walter Schmithals's view that the Apocalypse does not embody apocalyptic thinking: "The Apocalypse is not apocalyptic!"[121] He describes Schmithals's view as an example of an "odd twist" in generic classification. With an exclamation mark and an appeal to the reigning consensus, he dismisses the whole debate as unworthy of further discussion. Similarly, many scholars simply assume the majority view that the Apocalypse is an apocalypse and feel no need to defend it. Those who resist the current consensus, on the other hand, must always defend their views.

Because the Apocalypse is highly intertextual, it includes elements not found in other apocalypses and omits other elements found in apocalypses. To use the Apocalypse as the prototype for the genre apocalypse requires foregrounding and emphasizing certain aspects of the book and backgrounding others. Elements of other apocalypses that are missing from the Apocalypse must be considered as not essential for the genre.

The Apocalypse Group of the SBL Genres Project followed the procedure of constructing the genre apocalypse by analogy with the Apocalypse of John. The group attempted to bring precision and rigor to the definition of apocalypse by advancing the discussion beyond the lists of characteristics provided by H. H. Rowley, Klaus Koch, and D. S. Russell. They began by gathering those works that were considered apocalypses by modern scholars. Then they tabulated their features of form and content. The features that occurred in every one of the works were included in the definition of "apocalypse," which was published in *Semeia* 14:

> "Apocalypse" is a genre of revelatory literature with a narrative framework, in which a revelation is mediated by an otherworldly being to a human recipient, disclosing a transcendent reality which is both temporal, insofar as it envisages eschatological salvation, and spatial insofar as it involves another, supernatural world.[122]

The process they followed involved circular reasoning, a typical feature of genre definitions.[123] This project illustrates a question that vexes all genre theorists: How can one define apocalypse before one knows on which works to base the definition; yet how can one know on which works to base the definition before one has defined apocalypse?[124] The Apocalypse Group decided from the outset which works were apocalypses so that the results were predetermined. By relying on scholarly consensus as their starting point, they included the Apocalypse in their list of books to be compared. The entire project hinged on their selection of works to be examined. Their selection process adopted a synchronic approach that grouped together works from a wide span of time (250 B.C.E.–250 C.E.).

Such an approach neglects the diachronic development of the unformulated

---

121. Ibid., 213.
122. John J. Collins, "Introduction: Towards the Morphology of a Genre," *Semeia* 14 (1979): 9.
123. See Dubrow, *Genre*, 46; Claudio Guillén, *Literature as System* (Princeton: Princeton University Press, 1971), 129; Paul Hernadi, *Beyond Genre: New Directions in Literary Classification* (Ithaca, N.Y.: Cornell University Press, 1972), 2–6; Pérez Firmat, "Novel as Genres," 271–77.
124. Hernadi, *Beyond Genre*, 2.

conventions followed by the authors of these books. Aune remarks: "In some respects, the dichotomy between prophecy and apocalyptic is a false one, since neither 'prophecy' nor 'apocalypse' designates a static type of literature; rather, each represents a spectrum of texts composed over centuries."[125] The authors of these texts imitated and modified previous writings. When viewed diachronically, some of these works departed from the unwritten poetics of apocalypse by excluding or transforming some of the conventions.

When the Apocalypse is examined from the perspective of the diachronic development of the conventions of apocalypses, several anomalies become evident. All of the works considered apocalypses that were written prior to the Apocalypse were pseudonymous. The consensus among commentators is that the Apocalypse is not pseudonymous. From John's own standpoint in the first century, his writing was something new and different from previous similar writings. His text departed significantly from the unformulated conventions followed by similar visionary works up to his day.[126] He also transformed these conventions by avoiding historical reviews. He complicated the connection with these other works by setting his work in an epistolary framework. When one considers these features of the Apocalypse, one must conclude that it did not follow exactly the conventions of any prior group of texts.[127]

Those who have predetermined that the Apocalypse is an apocalypse minimize its lack of pseudonymity. Although all fifteen of the Jewish apocalypses and nineteen out of twenty-four of the early Christian apocalypses included in the investigation are pseudonymous, the Apocalypse Group excluded pseudonymity from its definition.[128] Adela Yarbro Collins minimizes the importance of pseudonymity for apocalypse by noting that pseudonymity was a characteristic of many other kinds of works.[129] As Mazzaferri notes, the same might also be said for most, if not all, of the other elements of apocalypse.[130]

---

125. Aune, *Revelation 1–5*, lxxv.

126. Richard Bauckham argues that the author of the Apocalypse probably had not read any apocalypses but was familiar with apocalyptic traditions that circulated in his circle of Christian prophets (*The Climax of Prophecy: Studies on the Book of Revelation* [Edinburgh: T&T Clark, 1993], 38–91). Helmut Koester also notes that "apocalyptic concepts and traditions are widely used in the writing," but he argues that "its intention is rather to present a critical discussion of already existing apocalyptic views and speculations" (*History and Literature of Early Christianity* [vol. 2 of *Introduction to the New Testament*; 2d ed.; New York: de Gruyter, 2000], 253).

127. Harris, "Literary Function of Hymns," 258 n. 55, also recognizes that the lack of pseudonymity and the addition of epistolary conventions deformulates apocalyptic conventions, yet he continues to refer to the Apocalypse as an apocalypse.

128. Elisabeth Schüssler Fiorenza believes that only six of the works surveyed in Yarbro Collins's article on early Christian apocalypses are both Christian and early ("The Phenomenon of Early Christian Apocalyptic: Some Reflections on Method," in *Apocalypticism in the Mediterranean World and the Near East* [ed. David Hellholm; Tübingen: Mohr Siebeck, 1983], 299).

129. Yarbro Collins, "Early Christian Apocalypses," 71.

130. Mazzaferri, *Genre of the Book of Revelation*, 226–27.

John J. Collins explains that the lack of pseudonymity, *ex eventu* prophecy, and esotericism in the Apocalypse is due to the reemergence of prophecy in early Christianity and the resultant "heightened eschatological fervor," which rendered these elements superfluous.[131] Others question whether the creative impact of prophecy on John's use of the apocalyptic genre has skewed the features of the latter to the point that his work can no longer be considered a pure apocalypse.[132]

Whether a work includes a particular element of a genre is a matter of subjective judgment. The presence of such elements may be a matter of degree. For example, another feature of apocalypses, the angel who mediates revelation, appears infrequently in the Apocalypse (1:1; 17:1–18; 18:1–3, 21–24; 19:9; 21:9–14; 22:6ff.). When he does appear, he rarely offers an interpretation. Also, whether the same angel always speaks to John is not clear. More frequently, the revelation is given directly by a voice from heaven and by Christ himself.[133] Although the Apocalypse largely lacks this identifying element of apocalypse, the Apocalypse Group considers its minimal presence enough to include the Apocalypse within the category of apocalypse.

The Apocalypse also has elements that other apocalypses do not. Most interpreters recognize that it is the only apocalypse set in an epistolary framework. The inclusion of epistolary conventions causes some to doubt that the Apocalypse is an apocalypse, but others minimize the importance of the epistolary elements.[134]

The attempt to categorize the Apocalypse as an apocalypse reveals two aspects of the role of the reader. First, readers construct and define the genre of apocalypse by deciding which conventions will be considered essential. Second, the reader foregrounds the aspects of the Apocalypse that conform to those conventions. If that categorization is challenged, ingenuity and effort are required to make it more secure. Other generic connections of the book may have been overlooked in order to make it fit the category of apocalypse.

The Role of Genre in Interpretation of the Apocalypse

The interpreter's understanding of the genre of the Apocalypse will affect what significance one attaches to the various details of the text. Commentators often point out that a proper understanding of this work's genre is essential for its interpretation. For example, Dave Mathewson declared that "a consideration of genre will help to

---

131. John J. Collins, "Pseudonymity, Historical Reviews, and the Genre of the Revelation of John," *CBQ* 39 (1977): 329–43.

132. Schüssler Fiorenza, "Phenomenon," 310; Vielhauer, "Introduction," 623; Mazzaferri, *Genre of the Book of Revelation*, 227–28.

133. Vielhauer, "Introduction," 623; Mazzaferri, *Genre of the Book of Revelation*, 228, 276–78, 293–94.

134. Although Mazzaferri argues against identifying the Apocalypse as an apocalypse, he also minimizes the importance of the epistolary elements by viewing them as an incidental consequence of John's banishment. He employs this strategy to maintain his identification of the Apocalypse as classical prophecy (*Genre of the Book of Revelation*, 231–33).

prevent interpretations from running awry."[135] Robert Mounce states: "It is difficult to say what anything means until one has decided in a sense what everything means." He admonishes that "an informed sensitivity to the thought forms and vocabulary of apocalyptic is the *sine qua non* of satisfactory exegesis."[136] G. R. Beasley-Murray also contends that one must understand the traditional symbolism of apocalypse, which he compares to the modern political cartoon, if one is to understand John's message.[137]

Yarbro Collins also warns that "misunderstanding will result if a reader brings inappropriate expectations to a work." She argues that the Apocalypse's apocalyptic nature makes it an allegorical narrative in which the "old story" of the myth of cosmic combat is used to tell the new story about the confrontation of Jesus' followers with the Roman Empire. In her view, one correctly interprets the book when one follows its recapitulated apocalyptic pattern of persecution, punishment, and salvation.[138] Similarly, Schüssler Fiorenza says that a correct understanding of the Apocalypse's apocalyptic imagery will make the reader realize that "its images and visions should not be understood in terms of historical description nor in terms of future prediction." Instead, an appreciation of its "mythological symbolization" will keep one from robbing its images of their power of persuasion by phrasing them in "propositional, logical, factual language."[139]

Commentators such as these suggest that a correct interpretation depends on a correct understanding of the book's genre, but one's prior understanding of the nature of the genre under consideration affects how one then interprets the book. One must not only have a "correct" understanding of the generic identity of the work but also a "correct" understanding of the genre itself. Different scholars may consider the Apocalypse to be an apocalypse, but if they have different views of the conventions that constitute apocalypse, they will interpret apocalypses in different ways. Consequently, they would interpret the Apocalypse, or at least parts of it, differently from each other.

For example, if interpreters assume that the Apocalypse is an apocalypse and that apocalypse is literature of the oppressed that combines revelation with the promise of restoration and reversal,[140] then they will highlight those aspects of the book. If one

---

135. Dave Mathewson, "Revelation in Recent Genre Criticism: Some Implications for Interpretation," *TJ*, n.s., 13 (1992): 208.

136. Mounce, *Book of Revelation*, xiii.

137. Beasley-Murray, *Book of Revelation*, 16–19. He tries to keep this perspective as he interprets specific passages. For example, in his exegesis of 14:19–20, he says that "John's prophecy should be recognized as a typical apocalyptic cartoon of the messianic judgment at the parousia, and be interpreted in the light of the nature of apocalypse" (230).

138. Yarbro Collins, *Apocalypse*, x–xiv.

139. Schüssler Fiorenza, *Invitation to the Book of Revelation*, 16–22.

140. E. P. Sanders, "The Genre of Palestinian Jewish Apocalypses," in *Apocalypticism in the Mediterranean World and the Near East* (ed. David Hellholm; Tübingen: Mohr Siebeck, 1983), 447–59.

assumes it is an apocalypse but that apocalypse is a revelation of heavenly mysteries,[141] then the mystical and revelatory aspects will carry greater significance than the eschatological. If one thinks that apocalypse is a flight from history into a cosmic vision of divine deliverance due to a pessimistic view of reality,[142] then elements supporting this view will become more significant than those that relate the cosmic vision to everyday reality. If one views apocalyptic symbols as "steno-symbols" or simple allegorical codes for historical persons and events contemporary with the writer,[143] then one will interpret the symbols of the Apocalypse as referring to particular persons and events in John's day. Interpreters who understand apocalyptic to be a reflection of the hope for transcendence of death on the part of oppressed people will focus on the visions of the afterlife in the book and will interpret the rest of the book as reflecting those concerns.[144] Those who adopt a sociology-of-knowledge approach to apocalyptic and see it as offering an alternative symbolic universe to readers will downplay the historical, "real-world" connections of the book and highlight its construction of a story in which suffering of the righteous makes sense.[145] These examples suggest that one's view of the pragmatic aspects of a genre—that is, its function, purpose, or referentiality—especially determines how one interprets it.

Of course, the book will take on a somewhat different character for the reader who assumes it is a prophecy or a drama or a liturgy, depending on the reader's understanding of those genres. The various methods or schools of interpretation that have been applied to the Apocalypse most likely resulted from disagreements over its genre and the significance of each of those genres.[146] Other elements that affect interpretation factor into the process of reading, but the identification of the genre determines to a great extent the interpreter's general orientation.

---

141. Christopher Rowland, *The Open Heaven: A Study of Apocalyptic in Judaism and Early Christianity* (New York: Crossroad, 1982).

142. Paul D. Hanson, *The Dawn of Apocalyptic: The Historical and Sociological Roots of Jewish Apocalyptic Eschatology* (rev. ed.; Philadelphia: Fortress, 1979).

143. Norman Perrin, *Jesus and the Language of the Kingdom: Symbol and Metaphor in New Testament Interpretation* (Philadelphia: Fortress, 1976), 30–32, 44–45, 59–60, 76–78.

144. John J. Collins, "The Symbolism of Transcendence in Jewish Apocalyptic," *BR* 19 (1974): 5–22.

145. David L. Barr, "The Apocalypse as a Symbolic Transformation of the World: A Literary Analysis," *Int* 38 (1984): 39–50; Paul D. Hanson, "Apocalypticism," *IDBSup*, 31.

146. These methods have been labeled in many ways, some of which are synonymous or overlapping: *kirchengeschichtlich, zeitgeschichtlich, weltgeschichtlich, endgeschichtlich, geschichtlichtstheologisch, heilsgeschichtlich, geschichtlichtsphilosophisch, religionsgeschichtlich, traditionsgeschichtlich,* recapitulation theory, chiliastic, allegorical, spiritual, idealist, historicist, futurist, preterist, dispensational premillennial, historic premillennial, amillennial, and postmillennial. For analyses of these approaches, see R. H. Charles, "History of the Interpretation of the Apocalypse," in *Studies in the Apocalypse* (2d ed.; Edinburgh: T&T Clark, 1915); John M. Court, *Myth and History in the Book of Revelation* (Atlanta: Knox, 1979), 1–19; Mounce, *Book of Revelation*, 24–30; Schüssler Fiorenza, *Book of Revelation*, 35–45.

Conclusion

A survey of the various hypotheses of the Apocalypse's genre reveals two patterns. First, most scholars recognize that the book does not belong to just one genre. They often consider one generic aspect as the form into which some other generic content has been poured. Schüssler Fiorenza views it as Christian prophetic-apocalyptic in the form of a circular, authoritative apostolic letter, but she views prophecy as the primary aspect.[147] Willem S. Vorster describes it in one place as a first-person narrative in the form of a circular letter containing apocalyptic eschatology[148] and elsewhere as a narrative of fantasy.[149] According to John Wick Bowman, it consists of prophetic content constructed as a drama in seven acts with the form of a letter superimposed on it.[150] Blevins describes it as a syncretistic combination of a prophetic message and the form of Greek tragic drama.[151] Aune says that it is an extended vision report, or apocalypse, framed by an epistolary prescript and postscript and introduced by a title.[152] Elsewhere, he describes it as a "prophetic apocalypse."[153] Beasley-Murray views it as a unique combination of epistle, apocalypse, and prophecy.[154] David Hill regards it as prophetic in intention and character but concedes that it employs much of the traditional apparatus of apocalyptic while lacking many of apocalyptic's characteristic features.[155] D. A. Carson, Douglas J. Moo, and Leon Morris view it as "a prophecy cast in an apocalyptic mold and written down in a letter form."[156] Jürgen Roloff calls it "a prophetic writing that contains numerous apocalyptic motifs and elements of style, but whose form is chiefly characterized by the purpose of epistolary communication."[157]

The options can be multiplied, but all seem to recognize that this book has mixed generic conventions so that it cannot be categorized in one pure genre. In fact, the adjective that frequently appears with reference to the form of the book is "unique."[158] Even those few who attempt valiantly but unsuccessfully to categorize the book in one genre often recognize the many other generic features contained in it and therefore must concede that its inclusion of these various elements in one book

---

147. Schüssler Fiorenza, *Book of Revelation*, 133–56; idem, *The Apocalypse* (Herald Biblical Booklets; Chicago: Franciscan Herald Press, 1976), 14–26.
148. Willem S. Vorster, "1 Enoch and the Jewish Literary Setting of the New Testament: A Study in Text Types," *Neot* 17 (1983): 11–12.
149. Vorster, "'Genre' and the Revelation of John," 111–20.
150. Bowman, "Revelation to John," 436–53.
151. Blevins, "Genre of Revelation," 393.
152. Aune, *New Testament in Its Literary Environment*, 240.
153. Aune, *Revelation 1–5*, xc.
154. Beasley-Murray, *Book of Revelation*, 12–29.
155. David Hill, *New Testament Prophecy* (New Foundations Theological Library; Atlanta: Knox, 1979), 75.
156. Carson, Moo, and Morris, *Introduction to the New Testament*, 479.
157. Roloff, *Revelation of John*, 8.
158. Beasley-Murray, *Book of Revelation*, 12; Aune, *New Testament in Its Literary Environment*, 240; Hill, *New Testament Prophecy*, 75.

makes it unique. For example, Aune describes the Apocalypse as an apocalypse but emphasizes that no other apocalypse is framed by epistolary conventions.[159]

The second pattern of hypotheses of the Apocalypse's genre is that, no matter what genre is considered primary, someone can always point out ways in which the book does not quite fit into that genre. If one says it is an apocalypse, others will point out that it lacks pseudonymity, *ex eventu* prophecies, esotericism, heavenly journeys, an angel-interpreter, pessimism concerning the present age, determinism, and lists of revealed things.[160] If one says it is a drama, someone else will point out that it does not contain the dialogue one normally finds in drama nor do the hymns really function as choruses.[161] These disagreements result from different views of what characteristics constitute the genre under consideration. Disagreements over the Apocalypse's generic identity may have origins in a prior disagreement about the genre with which it is compared.

Disagreements over the Apocalypse's generic identity result from the process of comparing a particular text to its generic paradigm. In the case of the Apocalypse, some of the genres with which it is compared, such as prophecy and apocalypse, were not clearly defined and recognized in antiquity. Therefore, the interpreter's identification of the Apocalypse is dependent on one's prior reconstruction of the ancient genre. In the case of other genres, such as drama, that were formulated to some extent, the Apocalypse just does not seem to fit comfortably into any of them. It seems that no matter what genre or blend of genres one chooses for its identity, the Apocalypse will always be more and less than that identity. Some surplus will always be unaccounted for by the generic choice, and the text will refuse to fit completely and neatly into any generic identification. This text constantly overruns any boundaries placed around it. It refuses to stay in bounds.

The Apocalypse is a highly intertextual work, a mixed genre. It offers multiple possibilities to the reader without fully supporting any one option. Readers cannot read a text from multiple perspectives simultaneously, so in the case of highly intertextual works, they will focus on one alternative or try to create some blend of two or three. The Apocalypse gives the reader the opportunity to focus on one or a combination of several alternatives, but whatever boundaries the reader places around it cannot bind the text. It will not stay in bounds. It is constantly breaking out of its frame. Consequently, it can be described as a writerly text or an open work, one that

---

159. Aune, *New Testament in Its Literary Environment*, 240. Examples of those who attempt to minimize other missing generic elements in order to classify the Apocalypse in one genre include Collins, "Pseudonymity," *CBQ* 39 (1977): 329–43; Yarbro Collins, "Early Christian Apocalypses"; and Mazzaferri, *Genre of the Book of Revelation*.

160. Bauckham, *Theology of the Book of Revelation*, 9–12; Hill, *New Testament Prophecy*, 71–76; Bruce W. Jones, "More about the Apocalypse as Apocalyptic," *JBL* 87 (1968): 325–27; George Eldon Ladd, "The Revelation and Jewish Apocalyptic," *EvQ* 29 (1957): 94–100; James Kallas, "The Apocalypse—An Apocalyptic Book?" *JBL* 86 (1967): 69–80; Mazzaferri, *Genre of the Book of Revelation*, 223–51; Mounce, *Book of Revelation*, 6–8; Schüssler Fiorenza, *Book of Revelation*, 168–69; and Vielhauer, "Introduction," 623.

161. Schüssler Fiorenza, *Book of Revelation*, 167; Vorster, "'Genre' and the Book of Revelation," 116.

allows the reader to participate in producing its meaning. Because of its intertextuality, it is also polyvalent, allowing readers to produce multiple interpretations. Thus, this book is both a bane and blessing to interpreters. It provides simultaneous frustration and pleasure to the reader.

Apocalypse Renewed: An Intertextual Reading of the Apocalypse of John

David E. Aune

Intertextuality plays a central role in both the production and reception of texts, so that critics can focus on either the author who constructed the text or the reader who reconstructs the text, or both. Intertextuality is a way of reading a text that sees it as a network of references to other texts, a phenomenon that may be approached at the levels of the word, the phrase, and the sentence, but that becomes particularly evident in larger textual units within a composition that have parallels or analogues in the constituent literary units of other texts. In the initial sequential reading of a text, connections with other textual units known to the reader are forged, which may upon the completion of the reading task lead the reader to an association with analogous self-contained literary texts, that is, to a conception of the genre to which a given text belongs.

1. Intertextuality as a Critical Method

From the standpoint of intertextuality, a particular text only exists as part of a larger literary tradition, or "canon" (culture itself can be considered an intertext). A given text is part of a web of relationships with earlier texts that must be known in order fully to understand the focal text, at least from the perspective of the author who constructed it and the readers who reconstructed it. Texts are necessarily written and read in light of the familiarity that both authors and readers have of earlier texts. The writers of texts use a variety of strategies as they write in the light of a circle of texts that they consider significant. Intertextuality is not as concerned with identifying the sources of a document as it is with understanding the impact and function of both earlier and contemporary texts in a given text. In fact, texts take on distinctive features when they intentionally deviate from their precursors, and this may suggest the particular function of a textual unit.

An earlier version of this chapter appeared as "Intertextuality and the Genre of the Apocalypse," in *Society of Biblical Literature 1991 Seminar Papers* (SBLSP 30; Atlanta: Scholars Press, 1991), 142–60.

Normally intertextuality centers on the modern reader (i.e., the literary critic as reader), and the intertext out of which the text is read and understood is the one known to that reader. An intertextual reading is not usually limited to the intertext of the author or to that of the original readers. In this essay, however, I focus on the intertextual reconstruction of the Apocalypse of John by a hypothetical original circle of readers. While the intertext of the modern critical reader is (at least theoretically) completely accessible to that reader, any attempt to reconstruct the intertext of the original readers can only be partially and imperfectly realized. While no two early Christian readers would have understood the Apocalypse in precisely the same way (since their knowledge of precursor texts would necessarily have been different), it is also likely that particular congregations of readers would have a relatively homologous understanding of the Apocalypse because of their shared knowledge of antecedent texts. The modern critic, on the other hand, can never become fully aware of the range of ancient responses to the Apocalypse for the simple reason that many (perhaps even most) of the precursor texts that the ancient reader would have assumed have been lost and are consequently unknown to us. Though some might regard our focus on the reader of the late first and early second century C.E. as inappropriate, in my view it is a completely legitimate enterprise that does not, however, invalidate other approaches to the response of readers to this particular text. Indeed, there can be no privileged approach to the reading and understanding of written texts. In the present context it is not possible to provide a detailed analysis of all of the intertexts that might have shaped the responses of an ancient reader to the Apocalypse of John. In what follows, however, I provide a sequential survey of the various textual units that comprise the Apocalypse and make suggestions regarding the particular precursor texts that might very well have guided readers during the late first and early second centuries C.E.

2. Aspects of the Literary Character of the Apocalypse

A. The Participant Transmitter

The textual history of most early Jewish and early Christian apocalypses suggests that the popular conception of the task of the ancient "copyist" as a faithful transcriber and transmitter of a stable sacred text is largely an imaginary construction. For many early Jewish and early Christian scribes, the task of recopying a text provided the opportunity (perhaps even the obligation) to rewrite that text.[1] In many instances it is even likely that the primary motivation for recopying a text was based on the desire to *rewrite* that text, since scribes often appear to have had agendas of

---

1. For a discussion of the same phenomenon in the history of Gospel manuscripts, see David C. Parker, *The Living Text of the Gospels* (Cambridge: Cambridge University Press, 1997). For a more recent discussion of the creative role of scribes, see Kim Haines-Eitzen, *Guardians of Letters: Literacy, Power, and the Transmitters of Early Christian Literature* (Oxford: Oxford University Press, 2000).

their own.² In such instances the reader's response was transmuted (or transmogrified) into the literal re-creation of the text, suggesting that the modern distinction between author and reader may not apply in a straightforward way to certain types of ancient compositions including apocalypses. Unlike many other early Christian apocalypses, all the manuscripts of the Apocalypse of John appear to derive from one exemplar. The eventual canonical status of the Apocalypse may be the major reason why earlier versions have not survived. Source criticism (see below) can provide a way of reconstructing how the author and his predecessors responded to the texts and partial texts that he (and they) revised.

B. Source-Critical Issues

During the last two centuries, many source-critical theories of the origin of the Apocalypse have been generated by scholars struck by the many aporias, doublets, pleonastic phrases, glosses, and grammatical peculiarities that permeate the text. While a holistic literary approach to the Apocalypse may choose to bracket out these problematic features (or even attempt to explain such textual phenomena in a way that makes an appeal to the hypothetical sources and redactional techniques of the author unnecessary), sooner or later these features of the Apocalypse must be dealt with. The Apocalypse is far from a finished, unified composition, and it is my view that only a careful source-critical analysis can explain the many peculiarities of the text.³

C. Types of Intertexts, Real or Imagined

The following three types of intertexts certainly do not exhaust the literary precursors within which the Apocalypse of John could be read, but they are among the more significant.

1. *Old Testament allusions.* From the perspective of the ancient reader, the Apocalypse signaled its relationship to various precursor texts in a variety of ways. One way was certainly the allusions to the OT that permeate the composition. The most recent edition of the Nestle-Aland Greek text uses its margins to suggest that there are 734 quotations or allusions to the OT in the Apocalypse, though this number is somewhat excessive. Another, more complex way in which the OT functions as the intertext of the Apocalypse is in the replication of structures found in various OT compositions.

2. *The anaphoric definite article.* One very particular way in which the author reflects an intertext (whether written or oral) is reflected in his use of the anaphoric

---

2. For examples of theological motivations exhibited by scribes, see Bart D. Ehrman, *The Orthodox Corruption of Scripture: The Effect of Early Christological Controversies on the Text of the New Testament* (Oxford: Oxford University Press, 1993).

3. I have proposed such an analysis in David E. Aune, *Revelation 1–5* (WBC 52; Dallas: Word Books, 1997), cv–cxxxiv.

definite article. Part of the style of apocalyptic literature is the use of already familiar persons and things drawn from stock apocalyptic imagery that are introduced the first time with the definite article.[4] Each of the following seventeen nouns occurs with the definite article upon its first occurrence, apparently because the author assumes that the readers are already familiar with the reality that the substantive represents: (1) οἱ ἑπτὰ ἄγγελοι οἳ ἐνώπιον τοῦ θεοῦ ἑστήκασιν, "the seven angels who stand before God" (8:2, 6, 8, 10, 12, 13; 9:1, 13, 14). (2) οἱ τέσσαρες ἄγγελοι οἳ δεδεμένοι ἐπὶ τῷ ποταμῷ τῷ μεγάλῳ Εὐφράτῃ, "the four angels who are bound at the great river Euphrates" (9:14). (3) ὁ ἀετός, "the eagle" (12:14). (4) αἱ ἑπτὰ βρονταί, "the seven thunders" (10:3). (5) ἡ γυνή, "the wife [of the Lamb]" (19:7; 21:9). (6) ἡ εἰρήνη τῆς γῆς, "the peace of the earth" (6:4). (7) τὸ θηρίον, "the Animal" (11:7). (8) ἡ ἶρις, "the rainbow" (10:1). (9) ἡ κιβωτὸς τῆς διαθήκης, "the ark of the covenant" (11:19). (10) οἱ δύο μάρτυρές μου, "my two witnesses" (11:3). (11) ἡ πλατεῖα τῆς πόλεως τῆς μεγάλης, "the street of the great city" (11:8). (12) τὰ ἑπτὰ πνεύματα, "the seven spirits" (1:4; 3:1; 4:5; 5:6). (13) ὁ πόλεμος, "the war" (16:14). (14) ἡ πόρνη, "the whore" (17:1, 15, 16; 19:2). (15) τὸ τέκνον, "the child" (12:4). (16) ὁ υἱὸς τοῦ θεοῦ, "the son of God" (2:18). (17) τὸ φρέαρ τῆς ἀβύσσου, "the shaft of the abyss" (9:1).

3. Constituent literary forms. A third type of intertext consists of the constituent literary units within a composition that the reader has encountered in other texts. This analysis focuses on the sequential identification of what initially appear to be coherent units of text containing codes that trigger in the reader a particular set of intertextual associations. When a different set of associations is triggered, it is apparent that a new unit of text with a different set of codes is before the reader. Discrete units of text are usually introduced with recognizable formulas that prepare the reader to look for new associations. The intertext within which each unit of text is read suggests both similarities and differences to the reader. However, while these units might initially appear to be relatively independent, the process of reading and association quickly makes connections between contiguous textual units (by virtue of their sequential proximity, the repetition of formulaic phrases encountered earlier, and by virtue of verbal and thematic associations that the reader discovers during the process of reading and rereading, or hearing and rehearing). It is precisely the retrospective association of what initially appeared to be discrete textual units that brings readers to associate this text, more or less in its entirety, with other discrete texts in their experience. Further, it is important to consider a dimension of reading often neglected, that is, interactive reading or reading aloud as a social experience in which the verbal and behavioral responses of the audience constitute signals productive of a more homoge-

---

4. Josef Schmid, *Studien zur Geschichte des griechischen Apokalypse-Textes* (Munich: Zink, 1955), 2:194–95; G. Mussies, *The Morphology of Koine Greek as Used in the Apocalypse of St. John: A Study in Bilingualism* (NovTSup 27; Leiden: Brill, 1971), 187–88.

neous experience than one might otherwise expect in readers who belong to a social network, but who read the text in isolation from others.[5]

3. Intertextual Analysis of the Apocalypse

This section will discuss twenty-one major textual units within Rev 1–22 for the purpose of suggesting the various associations that the original circle of readers might have had with each discrete literary form.[6] This level of generic intertext is particularly important for analyzing a composition such as the Apocalypse of John precisely because of the conventional, episodic, highly stylized, and formulaic character of Jewish and Christian apocalypses generally.

1. *Revelation 1:1–3.* Ancient expectations regarding the function of the opening sentence of Revelation are revealed in Epiphanius *Pan.* 1.1.1:[7]

The authors of old used to give hints of the subject they were to treat in the prefaces or remarks that they composed as a sort of title.

> Hence we too shall use this style in writing our preface for you, beloved brothers, and we shall briefly summarize the essential matter of [our work composed?] against the sects.

This suggests the obvious, namely, that Rev 1:1–3 functions as a title and conforms to the ancient tendency to describe the essential contents of a literary work. In content, however, this text clearly suggests that the composition it introduces is a particular type of literary text, namely one that mediates divine revelation. Revelatory literature is a broad category of texts clearly identifiable by both form and content.[8] Similar titles or introductory sentences occur in both prophetic and apocalyptic works (Jer 1:1–2; Ezek 1:1–3; Amos 1:1; *1 Enoch* 1:1; 93:1–3; *3 Apoc. Bar. praef* 1–2). When the author claims that the revelation of Jesus Christ was made known to him by an *angel*, that would have suggested immediately the stock apocalyptic figure of the *angelus interpres*, although no such figure actually appears until 17:1–18 and 21:9–22:11 (the conclusion of this section is difficult to specify). The content of the revelation, "what must soon take place" (v. 1), underlines the imminence of the revealed events, and the fact that "the time is near" (v. 3) indicates that eschatological events are in view. Describing his composition as "prophetic words" (cf. 22:7, 10, 18, where the

---

5. Cf. Linda Dégh and Andrew Vázsony, "Legend and Belief," in *Folklore Genres* (ed. Dan Ben-Amos; Austin: University of Texas Press, 1976), 100–103, who consider the interaction of those who narrate legends and their audience an essential feature of the legend genre.

6. The seven proclamations of Rev 2–3 are considered subunits within a single major unit of text. This analysis has been limited to Rev 1–18 primarily because of the limitations of space.

7. Philip R. Amidon, trans. and ed., *The Panarion of St. Epiphanius, Bishop of Salamis: Selected Passages* (New York: Oxford University Press, 1990), 5.

8. David E. Aune, *The New Testament in Its Literary Environment* (Philadelphia: Westminster, 1987), 231–38.

parallel phrase "prophetic book" occurs), the author was undoubtedly encouraging the reader to associate this work with earlier prophetic books in the Israelite and early Jewish tradition. The concluding emphasis on obeying the message of the book (v. 3) emphasizes the paraenetic function of the work which is certainly more characteristic of prophecy than of apocalyptic. Since the present version of the Apocalypse is characterized as "prophetic words" or "prophetic oracles" that must be obeyed (1:3), and yet that were revealed by an *angelus interpres* (1:1), the original readers would readily have associated the title as a combination of prophetic and apocalyptic features.

2. *Revelation 1:4–5a* is an epistolary prescript that is abruptly introduced since such prescripts *never* follow titles. That this one does would very probably have triggered *literary* associations; that is, this particular letter is meant to be "published" in the sense of copied many times for distribution and circulation. Since this composition contains an epistolary prescript near the beginning, the ancient reader would have expected an epistolary closing formula at the end and would not have been disappointed (22:21). While it is certain that these epistolary formulas reflect a distinctive early Christian adaptation of liturgical formulas, it is not clear that this adaptation was (as many maintain) a Pauline innovation. Regardless of their origin, these epistolary formulas would connect the Apocalypse with the role and function of other early Christian letters, particularly the Pauline letters. In the salutation in v. 4, the author does not simply identify the source of grace and peace as God, but rather as "the one who is and who was and who is coming," a formula that modifies the widespread *Dreizeitenformel* used of God in the Hellenistic world by changing the timeless "who will be" to the eschatological "who is coming," that is, "who will come." The jarring solecism ἀπὸ ὁ ὤν, "from the one who is," provides a foretaste of coming grammatical incongruities. Despite the fact that the Apocalypse is framed with epistolary conventions, the entire text does not appear to have been affected by epistolary features.[9]

> [Ugo Vanni connects the units of text in Rev 1:4–8 in a very different way. He has suggested that Rev 1:4–8 reflects a "liturgical dialogue," and that recognition of this fact solves the problem of the apparent lack of unity in this section.[10] He points to

---

9. Contrary to the view of Martin Karrer, *Die Johannesoffenbarunq als Brief* (Göttingen: Vandenhoeck & Ruprecht, 1986).

10. U. Vanni, "Un esempio di dialogo liturgico in Ap 1:4–8," *Bib* 57 (1976): 453–67; idem, *L'Apocalisse: Ermeneutica, exegesi, teologia* (Bologna, Italy: Edizioni dehoniane, 1988), 101–13. The schema that Vanni finds is the following ("Dialogo Liturgico," 460f.; *L'Apocalisse*, 107f.):

> Lector (ὁ ἀναγινώσκων):
> [4b] Grace to you and peace
> from him who is and who was and who is to come,
> and from the seven spirits who are before his throne,
> [5] and from Jesus Christ the faithful witness,
> the firstborn from the dead, and the ruler of kings on earth.
> Assembly (οἱ ἀκούοντες):

several features which suggest the presence of such a dialogue: (1) Revelation 1:3 has revealed the existence of a reader or lector and a group of listeners, the assembly. (2) The two amens (vv. 6, 7) lend a liturgical flavor to the passage. (3) An abrupt change of person occurs in the passage between 1:4–5a (χάρις ὑμῖν, "grace to you," a second-person plural pronoun) and 1:5b–6 (τῷ ἀγαπῶντι ἡμᾶς καὶ λύσαντι ἡμᾶς . . . καὶ ἐποίησεν ἡμᾶς, "to the one who loved *us*, and washed *us* . . . and made *us*," three first-person plural pronouns). Attractive though this proposal is, it is highly speculative since there are no analogous liturgical dialogues in existence in early Christianity that might prove the actual existence of such a liturgical genre.]

3. *Revelation 1:5b–6* is a doxology that is liturgically sonorous yet appropriate following an epistolary prescript since Gal 1:1–5 exhibits a close parallel. Doxologies are frequently used to conclude early Jewish and early Christian religious compositions (3 Macc 7:23; 4 Macc 18:24; Tob 14:15; *1 Clem* 64:2; *2 Clem* 20:5) or to conclude a constituent unit of text, particularly in letters (Rom 11:36; 1 Tim 1:17; 1 Pet 4:11; *1 Clem* 20:12; 32:4; 38:4). The inclusion of this doxology would probably have increased the liturgical expectations of the reader, a fact that gives some weight to Vanni's suggestions.

4. *Revelation 1:7–8* contains what appear to be two prophetic oracles (the first ends with a climactic ναί, ἀμήν). The first (v. 7) is a third-person prediction of the coming of Jesus Christ using the words of Dan 7:13 and Zech 12:10b. The second (v. 8) is a brief first-person speech of the Lord God in which he uses the "I am" formula to claim that he is the Alpha and the Omega, and to reiterate the revised *Dreizeitenformel* (v. 4), perhaps to authenticate the ultimate source of the revelation that John is transmitting. Both of these oracles reinforce the propriety of the phrase "words of prophecy" that the author used to characterize his work, although the first appears to be predominantly apocalyptic (focusing as it does on the parousia), while the second has predominantly prophetic associations (i.e., in divine self-predications in Isaiah).

To him who loves us
and has freed us by his blood
⁶ and made us a kingdom, priests to his God and Father,
to him be glory and dominion for ever and ever. Amen.
Lector:
⁷ Behold, he is coming with the clouds
and every eye will see him,
every one who pierced him;
and all tribes of the earth will wail on account of him.
Assembly:
Even so. Amen.
Lector:
⁸ I am the Alpha and the Omega
—says the Lord God—
who is and who was and who is to come,
the Almighty.

5. *Revelation 1:9–20* is a relatively short first-person singular narrative of a vision of the exalted Christ in which John receives a command to write what he sees in a book and to send it to the seven Christian congregations. This narrative style is maintained throughout the rest of the work and is generally characteristic of apocalyptic or prophetic vision or dream reports, an important factor contributing to their authenticity. Yet it has often been noted that while Jewish and Christian apocalypses are pseudonymous, the Apocalypse of John is apparently not. While there is no reason to suspect that John was aware of the pseudonymous character of all earlier apocalypses, he would have been cognizant of the fact that among the putative authors of apocalypses, none wrote later than Ezra. John's self-consciously autobiographical style, therefore, may be linked to prophetic books. The command to "write what you see" is given twice (and expressed in two different ways: v. 11: ὃ βλέπεις γράψον; v. 19: γράψον οὖν ἃ εἶδες) and then reiterated through the repetition of the aorist imperative γράψον in the introduction to each of the seven proclamations. Similar commands to write also occur in 14:13; 19:9 and 21:5. Two major aspects of this epiphany may well have impressed the readers: (1) It identifies the exalted Jesus with the Ancient of Days through allusions to Dan 7:9–14 and 10:5–9,[11] and (2) it provides divine legitimation for the composition of the Apocalypse through the reiterated command to write down the visions that John is about to see. Commands issued by God or angels to write down a revelatory message occasionally occur in the OT and early Jewish texts (Isa 30:8; Exod 34:27–28; Deut 31:19, 21; *Jub.* 1:5–7; cf. Tob 12:20; 4 Ezra 14), although they are much more frequent in Greco-Roman texts (Plato *Phaedo* 4.60e–61b; Callimachus *Aetia* 1.1.21–22; Propertius 3.3; Cicero *Academica priora* 2.16.51; Pausanias 1.21.2; Pliny *Ep.* 3.5.4; Aelius Aristides *Or.* 48.2; Dio Cassius 73.23.2). The author's autobiographical style (1:9) is characteristic of prophetic self-consciousness, while the command to write is a more general phenomenon characteristic of ancient revelatory literature. Revelation 1:9–20 is not an inaugural call (comparable to the call narratives in Isa 6, Jer 1, or Ezek 1–3), for John is not called to a new vocation but rather commissioned for a particular task.

6. *Revelation 2:1–3:22.* By the time the reader has finished the vision of commission narrated in 1:9–20, there is no reason to expect that the exalted Christ will dictate seven individual messages to each of the seven congregations. This section consists of seven units of text, often incorrectly styled "letters" that share an extraordinarily large number of stereotypical formulas. This literary device has no parallels in other apocalypses and must therefore be regarded as one of the author's more innovative moves. In all probability, early Christian readers would have associated these

---

11. This identification of the human figure with the Ancient of Days in Dan 7:13 was already assumed in Mss. 88 and 687, the only two extant LXX manuscripts of Daniel. Cf. the reading of Dan 7:13 in Ms. 967 (A. Giessen, *Der Septuaginta-Text des Buches Daniel*, 108): ηρχετο ως υιος ανθρωπου και ως παλαιος ημερω(ν) παρην και οι παρεστηκοτες προσηγαγον αυτω ("he came like a son of man and like the Ancient of Days was present, and those who were near approached him").

seven closely related textual units with royal or imperial decrees that were preserved on stone in important urban centers throughout the Roman province of Asia, and that the author has freely adapted for use in the present context.[12] Since each of the seven "proclamations" (a more appropriate designation than "letters") is dictated by the exalted Jesus, who knows the intimate details of each of the seven Christian communities, these texts clearly fit the general rubric of revelatory literature, although there are no close parallels in other Jewish or Christian apocalypses. Since the language used by the exalted Jesus in these proclamations is in a subtly higher register than that of the rest of the Apocalypse, Jesus is presented as more eloquent than the author.[13] The reading and rereading of the entire text suggests that using the form of royal or imperial proclamations is in fact part of the author's strategy of contrasting God and Christ with the Roman emperor, who is but a diabolical imitation of the former. Further, these proclamations are permeated with paraenesis (2:4–6, 14–16, 20–22; 3:14, 15–19) and in that respect they have a strikingly prophetic character, for paraenesis is almost entirely lacking in apocalypses.[14]

7. *Revelation 4:1–6:17 (and 8:1)* constitutes an extended throne-vision narrative that begins with the heavenly ascent "in spirit" of the author, followed by a vision of the throne of God and the liturgy of angelic beings in the heavenly court. It is introduced somewhat abruptly, although the abruptness is mitigated by the continuity in trumpet-like voices (1:10; 4:1). Although the reader has been given no hint that such a visionary ascent is in the works, such ascents, coupled with visions of the heavenly throne room, are stock features of many apocalypses. According to a cosmology widespread in the Hellenistic world, the earth was the lowest part of the cosmos surrounded by seven planetary spheres; in the early Jewish version of this cosmology, God's throne was located in the seventh heaven. Surprisingly, this cosmology is absent from John's conception, which is apparently that of the older cosmology of

---

12. David E. Aune, "The Form and Function of the Proclamations to the Seven Churches (Revelation 2–3)," *NTS* 36 (1990): 182–204.

13. The adversative particle ἀλλά occurs frequently in Hellenistic Greek literature, but just thirteen times in Revelation, of which eight of those instances occur in Rev 2–3 (2:4, 6, 9 [2x], 14, 20; 3:4, 9). The common connective particle δέ also occurs three times Rev 2–3 (2:5, 16, 24), and just four times in the rest of Revelation. These two stylistic features suggest that the author is providing the words of the exalted Christ with what he regarded as a dignified style; cf. J. A. L. Lee, "Some Features of the Speech of Jesus in Mark's Gospel," *NovT* 27 (1985): 1–26. Also relevant is that while 73.8 percent of the 337 sentences in Rev begin with καί, Rev 2–3 contains forty-four sentences, just nine of which begin with καί, that is, 20.5 percent. Not a single sentence begins with καί in the Proclamation to the Ephesians, and the other occurrences of καί occur only at the beginning of each proclamation (2:8, 12, 18; 3:1, 7, 14), with the exception of the Proclamation to Thyatira, where καί is used at the beginning of three of the eight sentences in the Proclamation (2:21, 23, 26).

14. For a qualification of this generalization, see J. C. H. Lebram, "The Piety of Jewish Apocalyptists," in *Apocalypticism in the Mediterranean World and the Near East* (ed. David Hellholm; Tübingen: Mohr Siebeck, 1983), 171–210.

a three-tiered universe consisting of heaven above, earth beneath, and the underworld below the earth (Rev 5:3, 13).

Throne visions function in one of at least six different ways, that is, (1) as *enthronement* scenes (Dan 7:13–14; 4 Ezra 2:42–48; Ezekiel the Tragedian *Exagoge* 68–82; *Odes Sol.* 36; cf. Rev 3:21), (2) as *judgment* scenes (Dan 7:9–12; *1 Enoch* 25:3; 45:3; 47:3–4; 62:1–6; *Apoc. Moses* 22:1–29:6; Matt 19:28–30 [and par. Luke 22:28–30]; 25:31–46; Rev 20:4–6; 20:11–15), (3) as *commission* scenes (1 Kgs 22:19–22; Job 1:6–12; 2:1–6; Isa 6:1–13; Ezek 1:4–3:11; *1 Enoch* 14:8–16:4; *Asc. Isa.* 10:1–16; cf. Rev 3:21), (4) as *eschatological heavenly festal gathering* scenes (Rev 7:9–12; Heb 12:22–24; *Odes Sol.* 36), (5) as *the goal of Merkavah mysticism* (*3 Enoch* 1:6–12; 7:1; cf. *Sepher ha-Razim* 7 [ed. M. Morgan, 81–86]), and (6) as a *literary device* used for commenting on earthly events in the narrative, much like the chorus in Greek tragedy (2 Kgs 22:19–20; Job 1:6–12; 2:1–6; Rev 4:1–6:17; 11:15–18; 14:1–5; 19:1–8).

Since throne visions typically functioned in one of the six ways mentioned above, the readers might well wonder about the purpose of this particular throne vision. Revelation 4:1–6:17 is a textual unit that presents the readers with three distinct subunits. (1) In 4:1–11 the author relates his vision of God enthroned and the angelic liturgy in the heavenly court room. One group of heavenly beings, the twenty-four elders, is found only in the Apocalypse; the quest for their identity has been the cause for much fruitless speculation. The four cherubim, or "living creatures," however, are familiar from many parts of the OT, where they often function as the divine throne, although John's description of the cherubim differs significantly from how they are depicted in the OT. In Ezekiel's initial vision (Ezek 1:4–28), the four cherubim figure significantly, and the competent reader would have been aware of this text. While in Ezekiel each of the four cherubim has four faces, the cherubim of the Apocalypse are each unique: one looks like a lion, one like an ox, one with a human face, and one like a flying eagle (4:7). While the cherubim of Ezekiel and the Apocalypse are "covered with eyes" (symbolizing divine omniscience), the cherubim in Ezekiel are each associated with a wheel, together constituting the four-wheeled divine throne-chariot (Ezek 1:15–21). The narrative pace is leisurely and serves to slow down and even delay the narrative. There is a degree of suspense in this narrative, for the function of the throne vision has not yet become clear. (2) In 5:1–14, a short drama is enacted in which the slain Lamb, first paradoxically identified as the lion of the tribe of Judah (v. 5), is found worthy to open the scroll. The figure of the Lamb is not found in any other Jewish or Christian apocalypse and constitutes an innovation on the part of the author. The first of twenty-nine occurrences of ἀρνίον in 5:6 is anarthrous, suggesting that the author assumed that this figure was unfamiliar to the readers. In 5:6–14, the author gradually focuses on the Lamb and carefully builds up the suspense to the point where the scroll actually begins to be unsealed. The reader remains in suspense, for the function of the throne scene has not yet become clear. (3) In 6:1–17, when the seals are opened, it becomes obvious that this throne vision constitutes an unusual form of judgment scene. The four horsemen bring waves of slaughter upon the people of the earth, although no basis for these punishments has yet been given (motivations for behavior are often missing from apocalypses; here the apocalyptic framework permits the reader to assume that those who dwell on the earth are irredeemably wicked). Finally, in vv. 9–11, an implied motive for the preceding judgments appears to have been divine revenge for the slaughter of Christians. After the opening of the sixth seal (6:12–17), the reader is left hanging, since only six of the seven seals have been opened, while an entirely different scene begins in 7:1 (the readers' expectation that the seventh seal will be opened is of course eventually fulfilled in a rather strange, anticlimactic way in 8:1).

8. *Revelation 7:1–17* is introduced abruptly because the reader expects the opening of the seventh seal, which is postponed until 8:1. Revelation 7:1–17 consists of two distinct, but related,[15] textual units, 7:1–8 and 7:9–17. The first unit, Rev 7:1–8, consists of three subunits of text. (1) The first is an *angelic epiphany*, a form that occurs three more times in Revelation (8:2; 15:1; 20:1–3) and each time exhibits a similar structure: (*a*) Introductory phrase: καί εἶδον. (*b*) Object of vision: ἄγγελον or ἀγγέλους. (*c*) Brief description of the action of the angel(s). (*d*) Followed by an abrupt change of subject. The author presents these brief angelic epiphanies as an outside observer; the angel(s) he sees and whose action he describes neither interacts with him nor he with it. This is a peculiar form with few if any parallels in Jewish or Christian apocalyptic literature, although they seem appropriate in the context of a vision report. (2) Revelation 7:2–3 contains an *angelic speech*. This form occurs eight more times in Revelation (10:1–7; 14:6–7; 14:8; 14:9–11; 14:14–16; 14:18–20; 18:1–3; 19:17–18), and again has few parallels in Jewish and Christian apocalyptic literature. The *angelic speech* in Revelation exhibits the following structural features: (*a*) Introductory phrase: καί εἶδον. (*b*) Object of vision: ἄλλον ἄγγελον. (*c*) The angel moves (ascends, descends, flies, emerges) to the center of the action. (*d*) The angel "cries with a loud voice." (*e*) The angel utters a brief statement on divine authority that must be understood as divine commentary on events in the eschatological drama. (3) Finally, the roster of the 144,000 who are sealed is given in 7:4–8 (although the sealing scene itself is omitted between vv. 3 and 4), which somewhat surprisingly consists of a list of twelve Israelite tribes, from each of which 12,000 are selected for this magical ritual of divine protection. Whether the readers understand the 144,000 to be Christians of pagan and/or Jewish origin, the list of tribes underscores the continuity between Judaism and Christianity.

Revelation 7:9–17 is yet another throne vision, in this instance one that functions as an eschatological heavenly festal gathering scene (Rev 14:1–5; Heb 12:22–24;[16] 4 Ezra 2:42–45; 13:5–50; *Odes Sol.* 36). This type of throne vision dramatizes the

---

15. A similar two-part structure occurs in *1 Enoch* 39:6–40:10.
16. In Heb 12:22–24, this type-scene is used metaphorically (cf. Heb 12:18: "you have not come to what may be touched"), a fact that suggests that it was widely familiar in early Jewish and early Christian circles.

final gathering before the heavenly throne of God of all the righteous in the company of the angelic beings engaged in the celebration of the victory and majesty of God. The constituent motifs in Heb 12:22–24 indicate the typical elements found in this scene: (1) Mount Zion, the heavenly Jerusalem (the setting), (2) an innumerable angelic host in festal gathering, (3) the assembly of the first-born, (4) God the judge of all, (5) the assembly of righteous people, apparently distinct from "the assembly of first-born," (6) Jesus, and (7) the sprinkled blood (implying the figurative presence of the ark).

9. *Revelation 8:2–9:21* centers on a series of seven plagues that are inflicted on the earth and its inhabitants, unleashed by the blowing of seven trumpets. The strikingly anticlimactic opening of the seventh seal in 8:1 is followed by two short angelic epiphanies, the first consisting of the brief introduction of the seven trumpet angels (v. 2) and the second consisting of a brief scene involving an angel at the heavenly altar who casts fire down upon the earth (vv. 3–5). This emphasizes the point (like the throne vision in 4:1–6:17) that divine retribution originates in heaven, that is, with God. As in the case of the seven seals, there is an interruption (10:1–11:14) before the blowing of the seventh trumpet (11:15–18). There is a widespread tendency, which is essentially correct, to understand the seven trumpet plagues (and the seven bowl plagues in 16:1–21) as an eschatological counterpart to the ten plagues inflicted by Moses upon the Egyptians. Although the particular schema found in Rev 8:2–9:21 (with 11:15–18) has no counterpart in other Jewish or Christian apocalypses (and so must be considered an innovation by the author), the constituent features are all thoroughly at home in Jewish apocalypticism. First, there is the tendency to conceive of the end of the world as a time when God will punish the unrighteous inhabitants of the world with plagues (ten are enumerated in *Apoc. Abr.* 30:3–8; *T. Dan* 5.8).[17] Second, there is (the admittedly rare) use of trumpet blasts as a structuring device for eschatological events (*Apoc. Zeph.* 9–12), though the trumpet did become a minor though staple feature of early Jewish and early Christian apocalyptic imagery (Isa 27:3; Zech 9:14; Matt 24:31; 1 Thess 4:16; 1 Cor 15:52; Did 16:6), often associated with eschatological judgment (Isa 58:1; Joel 2:2–3; Zeph 1:15–16; 4 Ezra 6:23; *Sib. Or.* 4.174f.; *Apoc. Mos.* 22:3; *Par. Jer.* 3:2; 4:1; *Apoc. Zeph.* 12:1; *Grk. Apoc. Ezra* 4:36). Third, there is the observable tendency to reduce the ten plagues of Exodus to seven (Ps 78:43–51; Ps 105:27–36; Amos 4:6–11; Artapanus [Eusebius *Praep. evang.* 9.27.1–37]; Wis 11:1–19:9; cf. *T. Benj.* 7:1–4; *m. Abot* 5.8). Nevertheless, although some of the trumpet plagues resemble some of the plagues of Exodus, the correlation is far from striking. This thoroughly apocalyptic section concludes on a prophetic note in 9:20–21, which seems to imply that the people punished could have repented, but chose not to do so.

---

17. Although the Egyptian plagues were a recurring theme in early Jewish literature, they are rarely interpreted eschatologically.

10. *Revelation 10:1–11:2* is a unit of text consisting of three separate sections; the first two are linked only by virtue of the fact that a single angel and a voice from heaven figure prominently in both episodes. Since the author had already interrupted the opening of the seventh seal, it comes as no great surprise that he interrupts the blowing of the seventh trumpet with two major units of text, 10:1–11 and 11:1–14. It does come as a surprise, however, that in a passage that delays the blowing of the seventh trumpet, the angelic revealer expressly swears that there will be no more delay (10:6). The first episode (10:1–7) looks like a cross between an *angelic epiphany* and an *angelic speech* (see above under Rev 7:1–8), although with one major difference: in both episodes John interacts with the heavenly voice, and in the second episode he interacts with the angelic revealer as well. The peculiarity of the content of this episode[18] suggests that it was composed entirely by the author for its present context and that he followed no obvious exemplars. At the end of the first episode the readers would very likely anticipate the blowing of the seventh trumpet, particularly since "there will be no more delay" (10:6b). The second episode (10:8–11) appears to have been consciously modeled after that part of the prophetic call of Ezekiel found in Ezek 2:8–3:3 and would be naturally understood as a prophetic commission by those familiar with that text. That it functions as a prophetic commission is made clear in 10:11: "you must again prophecy about many peoples and nations and tongues and kings." This section therefore contributes to the perception of the author as a prophet in the tradition of the OT prophets.[19] The third episode occurs in 11:1–2 (although it is difficult to decide whether v. 2 or v. 3 concludes the section).[20] Revelation 11:1–2 should be construed as a continuation of 10:8–11 (no typical Johannine formulas suggest a new unit of text), for John is given a measuring rod and told what to measure and what not to measure; this is the language of commission and is therefore appropriately placed after 10:8–11.

11. The abrupt appearance of *Rev 11:3–13* is mitigated by the fact that in vv. 1b–3 the brief speech of God or Christ slides from one subject to another, from a command to measure the temple to a prediction that the two witnesses will prophecy for 1,260 days (from a source-critical perspective this is an obvious seam). The reader expects the delayed blowing of the seventh trumpet to occur momentarily, but this event is delayed. Revelation 11:3–13 exhibits a literary character quite different from anything that the reader has yet confronted in the Apocalypse. It is not presented as a

---

18. This section has all the features of an *angelic speech*, were it not for the fact that what the angel says is not recorded, and when John begins to write down the response of the seven thunders, he is explicitly commanded not to write down what they said.

19. The author's prophetic role is also emphasized in Rev 22:16; cf. David E. Aune, "The Prophetic Circle of John of Patmos and the Exegesis of Revelation 22:16," *JSNT* 37 (1989): 103–16.

20. The problem is that there is a brief speech, apparently by God or Christ (cf. *"my* two witnesses" in v. 3a), in vv. 1b–3. What the voice says in v. 3, however, has no logical connection with what was said in vv. 1b–2, but seems to belong to vv. 4–13. It may well be that the author has intentionally created this dovetail joint to link vv. 1–2 to vv. 4–13.

vision (the author's characteristic "I saw" is conspicuous by its absence), but rather as a prophetic narrative, which appears to begin as a commentary on Zech 4:1–14, although that passage soon disappears from view. The quasi-visionary form of 11:3–13 is suggested by the clusters of verb tenses. There are thirty-six verbs in Rev 11:3–13. The author begins with three future tenses in v. 3, then shifts largely to the present tense in vv. 4–6 (eight verbs). He shifts back to the future in v. 7 (three verbs), then back largely to the present in vv. 8–10 (five verbs). The future tense (usually characteristic of predictions in apocalyptic literature) appears just once in v. 10, then twelve aorists are used in vv. 11–13. This phenomenon of a shifting from one group of tenses to another is characteristic of Johannine vision reports,[21] and while it may provide criteria for source-critical analysis, an intertextual approach to this peculiar style suggests that the original readers would probably understand 11:3–13 as at least the functional equivalent of a vision. It appears to be the first of several scenarios borrowed from Jewish apocalyptic folklore (similar material occurs in close proximity in Rev 12 and 13). While several parallel texts suggest that John's readers were familiar with the story of the martyrdom of the two witnesses (note the occurrence of the anaphoric article used with the first occurrence of the phrase "my two witnesses" in 11:3),[22] a particularly close parallel is found in a text preserved in Lactantius *Div. Inst.* 7.17. The parallels can be seen more clearly in a synoptic presentation in which the only change in order is the placement of Rev 11:6 before 11:5.[23]

There are several reasons for supposing that Lactantius is dependent here on the

---

21. Mussies, *Morphology*, 330–36, 340.

22. Two such texts are found in *Apoc. Elijah* 4:7–17 and 14:9–15:7. The *Apoc. Elijah* is probably late (150 to 275 c.e.), and 4:7–19 may be dependent, at least in part, on Rev 11:3–13. However, *Apoc. Elijah* 14:9–15:7 is a doublet featuring the woman Tabitha that appears to be independent of Rev 11:3–13 (P. Chester Beatty 2018; trans. Pietersma): "The young woman whose name is Tabitha will hear that the shameless one has made his appearance in the holy places. She will dress in her linen clothes and hurry to Judea and reprove him as far as Jerusalem, and say to him, 'O you shameless one, O you lawless one, O you enemy of all the saints!' Then the shameless one will become angry with the young woman. He will pursue her to the region of the setting of the sun. He will suck her blood in the evening and toss her onto the temple, and she will become salvation for the people. At dawn she will rise up alive and rebuke him saying, 'You shameless one, You have no power over my soul, nor over my body, because I live in the Lord always, and even my blood which you spilled on the temple became salvation for the people.'"

23. Here is the entire passage in Lactantius *Div. Inst.* 7.17 (M. F. McDonald, trans., *Lactantius The Minor Works* [Washington, D.C.: Catholic University of America Press, 1965], 517–18): "Now, when the end of these times is imminent, a great prophet [*magnus propheta*] will be sent from God to convert men to recognition of God, and he will have the power of working miracles. Whenever men will not hear him, he will close heaven and will hold back the rains; he will change water into blood, and will torture them with thirst and hunger; and fire will proceed from his mouth and burn whoever will attempt to hurt him. By these prodigies and powers, he will convert many to the worship of God. When these works of his have been carried out, another king will rise from Syria, born of the evil spirit, the overthrower and destroyer of the human race, who will destroy the remains of that previous evil one together with itself. This one will fight against the prophet of God; he will conquer and kill him and suffer him to lie unburied. But after the third day, he will rise again and will be taken into heaven while all look on and marvel."

Oracles of Hystaspes[24] or some otherwise unknown Jewish source and *not* on Rev 11:3–13, based on a comparison of these two texts. (1) A single prophet is found in Lactantius, compared with two prophets in Revelation. (2) The result of closing the heavens and turning the waters into blood in Lactantius is to torment people with hunger and thirst, while this effect is absent from Revelation. (3) The narrative in Revelation is consistently told with verbs in past tenses, while that in Lactantius is told using future tenses. (4) The text in Revelation contains a number of explanatory glosses, none of which appears in the account of Lactantius. (5) The narrative in Lactantius continues to describe events similar to those in Rev 13:1–10 but lacks allusions to Rev 11:14–12:17. (6) Since Lactantius lived from ca. 250–325 it is not impossible that he may have been influenced by the text of Revelation, yet he does not elsewhere reflect a very profound knowledge of that work.[25]

Assuming, then, that Rev 11:3–13 was a particular eschatological scenario with which the readers were familiar, what might they have made of it? First, the prophetic role of the two witnesses is clear, and that prophetic role appropriately follows the prophetic commissions in 10:8–11 and 11:1–2. Second, like other eschatological scenarios from Jewish apocalyptic folklore, the participants in the melodramatic conflict are not named, so that the readers can only speculate on their identity. Indeed, the author appears to encourage such speculation.

12. In *Rev 11:15–18*, the seventh trumpet is finally blown. Presumably, it was in order to avoid the problem of relating Rev 11:19–12:17 to 11:3–13 (i.e., the chronological order in the eschatological scheme is thereby obscured) that the author has inserted the blowing of the seventh trumpet with its consequences. However, rather than introduce an expected seventh set of plagues, it rather signals the introduction of a brief (and relatively awkward) throne vision that begins as something John *hears* in heaven (vv. 15b–16), but soon turns into a throne vision that John ap-

---

24. The view of David Flusser, "Hystaspes and John of Patmos," in *Irano-Judaica: Studies Relating to Jewish Contacts with Persian Culture throughout the Ages* (ed. S. Shaked; Jerusalem: Ben-Zvi Institute for the Study of Jewish Communities in the East, 1982), 12–75.

25. Outside of *Div. Inst.* 7.17, Lactantius appears to reflect an awareness of Revelation when he speaks of the second resurrection after a thousand years (*Div. Inst.* 7.26.5–7; cf. Rev 20:11–13, although the term "second resurrection" does not occur in Revelation). A comparison with Lactantius *Epitome* 66.9 (a later work in which the *Divine Institutes* are presented in abbreviated form) reflects an alteration of what he had originally written in *Div. Inst.* 7.17.7, apparently made in light of Rev 13:16. Lactantius was thoroughly familiar with classical sources and also with the Sibylline Oracles and Hermetic writings (R. M. Ogilvie, *The Library of Lactantius* [Oxford: Clarendon Press, 1978], 28–36), and even with early Christian extracanonical literature (Ogilvie, *Library of Lactantius*, 105–8), but less familiar with the Bible (Ogilvie, *Library of Lactantius*, 96–110), where he concludes that the seventy-three biblical quotations in *Div. Inst.* 4 are closely related to Cyprian's *Ad Quirinum*, although Lactantius cannot have drawn these quotations from the *Ad Quir.* in its present state). Outside of *Div. Inst.* 7 (with its seventy-three quotations of the Bible), the rest of *Div. Inst.* contains just seven quotations (Ogilvie, *Library of Lactantius*, 107f.), and the other works of Lactantius contain no biblical quotations at all (with the exception of the later *Epitome*).

parently *sees*, complete with a thanksgiving hymn sung by the twenty-four elders (the other denizens of the heavenly court are, for the nonce, absent).

13. In *Rev 11:19–12:17*, the author inserts another eschatological scenario that centers on the conflict between the Woman and the Dragon. Because this section is immediately preceded by the episode involving the blowing of the seventh trumpet (11:14–18), the reader is somewhat insulated from the problem of the relationship between the story of the two witnesses (11:3–13) and the story of the Woman and the Dragon (11:19–12:17), both with regard to chronology and characters. There is no continuity in *dramatis personae*, who are for the most part not named (challenging the ingenuity of the readers). In 12:7–9, however, the combatants are specifically named Michael and the Devil or Satan. In the rest of the story, the identities of the Messiah, that is, Christ (v. 3) and faithful Christians (v. 17b) are obvious. The author has apparently sandwiched two stories together by placing the narrative of Satan's defeat and expulsion from heaven, complete with commentary by the heavenly "chorus" (vv. 7–12), into the frame of the narrative of the Woman and the Dragon (vv. 1–6, 13–17). Adela Yarbro Collins (and others before her) has demonstrated the pre-Christian existence of the component elements of these combats in Greco-Roman and Jewish folklore. Important as this recognition is for the source criticism of the Apocalypse, it is also important for reconstructing the intertext within which the Apocalypse was read. Variants of two stories familiar to the readers, the Leto-Apollo-Python myth and the protological combat myth in which angels who remained faithful to God expelled rebel angels from heaven, have been linked in such a way as to demonstrate that pre-Christian myth contains basic truths about the Christian dispensation. Again, this complex scenario is not introduced or punctuated by the phrases typically used to introduce vision reports, such as "I saw," or "I saw, and behold" (the unusual introduction in v. 1, "A great sign appeared [ὤφθη] in heaven," is not simply a parallel expression, since in 15:1 the author begins a new segment with the phrase "And I saw another great and marvelous sign in heaven"). Further, the narrative style departs considerably from that of other vision reports in the Apocalypse. There are forty-five verbs in Rev 12, thirty-four are aorists (the basic narrative tense), two are perfects (note the fusion of aorist and perfect indicatives in Hellenistic Greek), nine are presents; the future tense does not occur. Revelation 12:1–17, therefore, would certainly not have been understood as a vision report by the original readers.

14. *Revelation 13:1–18*, in contrast to 11:3–13 and 11:19–12:17, is explicitly cast in the form of a vision report divided into two major segments, one concerning the Beast from the Sea (vv. 1–10), and the other concerning the Beast from the Land (vv. 11–18). Since the Beast from the Sea has seven heads and ten horns (v. 1), the readers would have identified it immediately with the great red Dragon of 12:3. But this first impression is not correct, since the Dragon is very quickly distinguished as both different from and superior to the Beast from the Sea (v. 2b). The seven heads

and ten horns of the latter must rather be attributed to family resemblance. Despite the awkwardness of vv. 1–2 read as a continuation of 11:19–12:17, it is obvious that the original readers would have understood 13:1–18 precisely as a continuation of that story. Among the known protological and eschatological myths of Jewish apocalyptic there is no close parallel to Rev 13. The reader would probably be aware, however, that the author has selected some elements from the early Jewish Leviathan and Behemoth myths (*1 Enoch* 60:7–11, 24; 4 Ezra 6:49–52; *2 Apoc. Bar.* 29:4; *b. B. Bat.* 74b–75a) and combined them with motifs from the eschatological antagonist myth. The eschatological Antagonist myth appears to have had two primary variants, one of which was based on the tradition of the godless tyrannical ruler (largely dependent on the depiction of Antiochus IV in Daniel) and the other of which was based on the figure of the false and seductive prophet. These traditions are presented separately in Rev 13:1–10 and 13:11–18, respectively, but blended (for example) in 2 Thess 2:3–12. In Christian apocalyptic, a presentation of the antics of the eschatological Antagonist was perhaps *de rigueur* (this figure is noteworthy by his absence in Rev 11:3–13, although he is present in parallel eschatological scenarios such as Lactantius *Div. Inst.* 7.17). The author's retention of *two* eschatological Antagonists very probably corresponds to his desire to encourage the reader to speculate about the particular identities of the *dramatis personae* in these traditional myths (this reaches a high point with the gematria puzzle in v. 18).

15. *Revelation 14:1–20.* There are four units of text in Rev 14: (1) 14:1–5, (2) 14:6–12, (3) 14:13, (4) 14:14–20, each of which presents a unique set of problems (14:13 will not be discussed here). Revelation 14:1–5 provides an effective contrast to the terrifying developments narrated in Rev 13. The reader would naturally link the 144,000 with the earlier mention of the same number of those sealed in Rev 7:4–8. The entire pericope is introduced with the formula "I saw, and behold" (v. 1) and is followed by three structural segments: (1) the earthly vision of the 144,000 in v. 1; (2) the audition of the New Song sung in heaven in vv. 2–3, which constitutes a brief throne vision; and (3) the interpretive explanation in vv. 4–5, which elaborates on the identity of the 144,000 using three οὗτοι clauses.

Revelation 14:6–12 is a group of three angelic visions (vv. 6–7, 8, 9–11), all introduced with the phrase "then I saw" (v. 6) and concluded when the author inserts an explanatory statement in v. 12. Each of the angelic visions is introduced by the mention of a new angelic revealer, the second and third of which are specifically enumerated: "another angel" (v. 6), "another angel, a second one" (v. 8), and "another angel, a third one" (v. 9).

Revelation 14:14–20 is introduced with one of the author's customary formulas for beginning a new subject, "I saw and behold" (v. 14), and concludes in v. 20, which is followed by an introductory phrase indicating the beginning of a major new section of the composition, "I saw another sign" (15:1). Revelation 14:14–20 consists of two units, the first in vv. 14–16 and the second in vv. 17–20, which are essentially doublets:

Revelation 14:14–17	*Revelation 14:17–20*
v. 14 figure with sickle seated on cloud	v. 17 figure with sickle comes out of temple
v. 15a another angel comes out of the temple	v. 18a another angel comes out from the altar
v. 15b calls with loud voice to first figure	v. 18b calls with loud voice to first figure
v. 15c "Put in your sickle" [πέμψον τὸ δρέπανόν σου]	v. 18c "Put in your sickle" [πέμψον σου τὸ δρέπανον]
v. 15d to harvest	v. 18d to gather clusters
v. 15e for harvest is ripe	v. 18e for grapes are ripe
v. 16a first figure used his sickle on the earth	v. 19a first angel used his sickle on the earth
v. 16b the earth was reaped	v. 19b vintage of earth gathered

The parallelism ceases with vv. 19c–20, where the imagery of the grape harvest is continued by mentioning the "great wine press of the wrath of God," into which the grapes are placed. The juxtaposition of the imagery of the grain harvest and the grape harvest as metaphors for divine judgment in vv. 14–20 is also found in Joel 3:13: "Put in the sickle, for the harvest is ripe. Go in, tread, for the wine press is full. The vats overflow, for their wickedness is great."[26]

16. *Revelation 15:1–16:21* is a unit of text in the form of a vision report that narrates the plagues unleashed by the seven bowl angels. It is important to observe that the first readers would hardly have anticipated another round of plagues, particularly after the result of the seventh trumpet (11:14–18), which signals heavenly rejoicing over the commencement of God's reign. This section begins with a title (15:1), and thereafter there are two subunits of text: (1) 15:2–8, a scene in the heavenly temple that narrates the commission of the seven bowl angels, and (2) 16:1–20, the plagues in the bowls are poured out upon the earth. These seven bowl plagues have rough parallels with the seven trumpet plagues, to the extent that the earliest readers would very probably have understood them together.

17. *Revelation 17:1–18* is a very distinctive textual unit in the Apocalypse, though it is part of a larger section consisting of 17:1–19:10 (this becomes evident only when the careful reader has read 19:9–10 and has become aware that the men-

---

26. Elsewhere the cutting of the grape clusters and/or the treading of the vintage is used alone as a metaphor for divine judgment (Isa 63:1–6; Jer 25:30–31), as is the metaphor of the grain harvest and/or the image of the threshing floor (Isa 17:4–5; Jer 51:33; Micah 4:13; Matt 3:12 [= Luke 3:17]; Matt 9:37–38 [= Luke 10:2; *Gos. Thom.* 73]; Mark 4:29; cf. Gal 6:7–9).

tion of the angel in 17:1–18 is part of an *inclusio* framing 17:1–19:10 [see below]). This realization will be reinforced in an even more forceful way when the competent reader comes to recognize the parallel structure that exists between 21:9–22:9 and 17:1–19:10. However, since the first reader would not be aware of this when reading 17:1–18, it is appropriate to discuss 17:1–19:10 in terms of its two constituent parts (17:1–18 and 18:1–19:10). As we begin reading 17:1–18, it is clear that it is an angelic revelation consisting of a vision (17:1–6) paired with an interpretation by the angelic guide (17:7–18). Even though the role of the *angelus interpres* has been accentuated in the title in 1:1 (and reappears at the end in 22:8, one of several clues linking the larger units of text), only in Rev 17 does this stock figure of apocalyptic literature appear in his stereotypical role (note that in 21:9–22:5, though John has an angelic guide, the guide offers no interpretation of what the author sees and hears). This particular vision report involves the transport of the visionary "in the spirit" to a remote location, a motif apparently based on the Elijah cycle that in turn influenced Ezekiel (cf. 1 Kgs 18:12; 2 Kgs 2:16; Ezek 3:14; 40:2; Rev 21:10; Hermas *Vis.* 1.1.3; 2.1.1). Another distinctive feature of this vision lies in the fact that it is a *tableau;* that is, there is no movement in what John sees. It is very likely that the vision itself in vv. 3–6 is an *ekphrasis,* that is, a description of a work of art. The work of art in question, probably a marble bas relief or series of bas reliefs, survives only on a series of bronze sestertii of Vespasian minted in 71 C.E.[27] The reverse depicts the goddess Roma in military dress seated on the Seven Hills of Rome, with a parazonium in her left hand, and her right foot touches the anthropomorphic figure of the river god Tiber. The readers, familiar with this marble bas relief and its numismatic counterpart as instruments of imperial propaganda, would have shared this inside allegorical joke with the author. While *ekphraseis* in the restricted sense of "description [of a work of art]" are not typical of apocalypses, a description of a painting does occur in *Apoc. Abr.* 21:7–29:21, while Hermas *Vis.* 3 and *Sim.* 6 and 9 appear to reflect *ekphraseis* in dependence on the *Tabula* of Cebes. By the Second Sophistic (second century C.E.), there were two major ways in which *ekphraseis* were used in literature. One approach centers on the necessity of understanding and interpreting the work of art itself, while the other (with examples in Cebes and Lucian) stresses the hidden meanings conveyed by the work of art that can usually be made clear through allegorical interpretation.[28] While the allegorical meaning of some *ekphraseis* is obvious, in others the meaning must be carefully explained. In Lucian's *Hercules* and Cebes' *Tabula,* the narrator is puzzled over the meaning of the work of art, not unlike the surprise and wonder expressed by John in v. 6b over what he has just seen in vv. 1–6a. Although Rev 17 is probably the result of a complex redactional process, in its present form

---

27. F. Castagnoli, "Note Numistiche," *Archeologia Classica* 5 (1953): 104–11; R. Beauvery, "L'Apocalypse au risque de la numismatique: Babylone, la grande Prostituée et le sixième roi Vespasien et la déese Rome," *RB* 90 (1983): 243–60.

28. Shadia Bartsch, *Decoding the Ancient Novel: The Reader and the Role of Description in Heliodorus and Achilles Tatius* (Princeton: Princeton University Press, 1989), 22–31.

it represents a particular type of apocalyptic vision report, while in content it uses a contemporary piece of propagandistic Roman art as an allegorical vehicle for a forceful condemnation of Rome; the conventionality of the vision report is combined with the unconventionality of the *ekphrasis* at its core.

18. In the poetic parallelism of *Rev 18:1–19:10*, the prose style in the Apocalypse reaches its highest and most lyrical level. This textual unit consists of two parts, 18:1–24, centering on a proleptic vision of the fall of Babylon, followed by a scene shift to a heavenly court in which the inhabitants rejoice over the destruction. The mention of the fall of Babylon evokes memories of the destruction of Jerusalem by the Babylonians on the Ninth of Ab in 586 B.C.E., a memory that survives in modern Jewish synagogue liturgy linked, as it is in the Apocalypse of John, with the fall of Jerusalem in 70 C.E. For the author, however, "Babylon" is a symbol for the present world power, Rome, responsible for the fall of Jerusalem in 70 C.E. In 18:1–24, the strophes are arranged to produce a particular effect on the readers. After announcing the fall of Babylon (vv. 1–3), events *preceding* that fall are narrated (vv. 4–7), after which events *subsequent* to the fall are described (vv. 8–21), first in future tenses in vv. 8–11 (seven future verbs) and then, following v. 18, exclusively in past tenses. Finally, the prophecy that Babylon will be destroyed is reiterated in v. 21. Three different types of poetic composition are connected in celebration of the fall of Babylon: (1) a ritual lament (vv. 1–3, 9–20; strikingly reminiscent of ritual laments over Tyre in Ezek 26:15–18 and 27:1–8, 26–36), interrupted by (2) a command to flee (vv. 4–8; cf. Jer 4:4–5; 6:1; 48:6–8; 50:8–10; 51:6–10; 51:45–48), and (3) a symbolic action and its interpretation: an angel casts a millstone into the sea, comparing it with the violence attending the overthrow of Babylon (vv. 21–24; cf. prophetic symbolic actions in 1 Kgs 22:11; 2 Kgs 13:14–19; Isa 7:10–12). The literary forms in this chapter are strikingly dependent on the writing prophets of the OT (the pervasive influence of Jeremiah is particularly prominent) rather than on early Jewish apocalyptic traditions. The author uses these biblical allusions to create a shared destiny of Israel and the followers of Jesus.

Revelation 19:1–10 consists of three subunits (19:1–4, 5–8, 9–11), all of which are introduced with the auditory formula "After this, I heard." The first unit consists of an initial hymn or praise, which introduces another scene from the heavenly throne room consisting of an initial hymn rejoicing over the destruction of Babylon-Rome (19:1b–3), followed by an affirmative response from the twenty-four elders and the four cherubim (19:4). The readers' emotional response to the exquisitely detailed description of the destruction of Babylon-Rome would naturally have been one of joy over the deserved misfortune of others, and this response is validated by the similar reaction of the denizens of the heavenly court. The second subunit of this section (19:5–8) is a call to praise (19:5), paired with a hymnic response (vv. 6–8), a hymnic continuation of the auditory throne scene that began in 1:1b–4. In this hymnic response, a puzzling bit of information is provided for the reader: "Let us rejoice and exult and give him the glory, for the marriage of the Lamb has come, and his bride has made herself ready" (19:7). This reference to "the marriage of the Lamb" has the anaphoric definite article before a phrase that has not occurred earlier in the book, an indication that the author is assuming that the expression is already known to the readers (whether it actually is or not). This phrase occurs just twice in the Apocalypse, here and in v. 9, and is not mentioned later. The phrase is amplified somewhat by the mention of the "bride" in v. 7, which is later picked up when the New Jerusalem is referred to under the metaphor of the bride in 21:2, 9, which is striking because it clearly suggests to the reader the metaphorical nature of the New Jerusalem itself.[29] The metaphors of Christ as the bridegroom and the people of God as the bride were relatively widespread in early Christianity. For example, the metaphor of the (Corinthian) church as a chaste virgin to Christ as husband occurs in 2 Cor 11:2. This metaphor is picked up again in Eph 5:25–32, where the archetype for the appropriate relationship between husbands and wives is the self-sacrificial love of Christ for the church. He cleanses her by his death and is thereby able to present her to himself at his return as a pure bride. The Synoptic tradition also seems to equate the figure of the bridegroom with Christ in a parabolic context (Mark 2:20; Matt 9:15b; Luke 5:35; cf. *Gos. Thom.* 104).

The third subunit consists of vv. 9–11, in which the author is commanded by an angel to write down a beatitude—"Blessed are those who are invited to the wedding banquet of the Lamb" (v. 9)—thereby emphasizing the reference in the immediately preceding hymn to the marriage of the Lamb and the preparation of the bride for that event in v. 7. The new element here is the specific mention of the "banquet" (δεῖπνον) of the wedding of the Lamb, an emphasis found only here in the Apocalypse. This metaphor was readily comprehensible, however, as a variant of the widespread tradition of the messianic banquet,[30] that is, the metaphor of an eschatological meal (a time of gladness and rejoicing) to which those blessed with final salvation are invited by God or his accredited agent. The beatitude in v. 9 is reminiscent of Luke 14:15—"Blessed is he who shall eat bread in the kingdom of God"—and the later parallel in *Acts of Philip* 135: "Behold, the dinner is prepared, and blessed is the one who has been invited." While the wedding banquet of the Lamb is mentioned only in the Apocalypse, the imagery would have been immediately evident to the competent reader.

This command is followed by John's awestruck prostration before the angelic revealer, who immediately forbids him to do so, but rather enjoins him to worship God alone (v. 10b), a reference to the Shema. The whole subunit is introduced with the phrase "And the angel said to me" (v. 9a). But which angel? Upon reflection, this can only refer to one of the seven bowl angels who provided John with a revelatory visit to the wilderness in 17:1–3a. For the first time it becomes clear that 17:1–19:10 is

---

29. Robert H. Gundry, "The New Jerusalem: People as Place, Not Place for People," *NovT* 29 (1987): 254–64.

30. J. Priest, "A Note on the Messianic Banquet," in *The Messiah: Developments in Earliest Judaism and Christianity* (ed. James H. Charlesworth; Minneapolis: Fortress, 1992), 222–38.

not just an unconnected series of textual units. The author has formed an *inclusio* by mentioning the *angelus interpres* at the beginning and end of the larger unit. Yet this unit is not simply a way of linking a group of subunits together but also introduces new and proleptic information, namely the reference to the invitation to the marriage supper of the Lamb (19:7, 9).

19. The next literary unit is *Rev 19:11–21:8*, which consists of three constituent subunits: (1) a description of the divine warrior and his conquests (19:11–21), (2) the defeat of Satan (20:1–10), and (3) the vision of the judgment of the dead (20:11–15). The first subunit has two parts and opens with a clear marker of a new episode: "Then I saw heaven opened" (19:11); the second part of the passage is introduced with the phrase "then I saw an angel standing in the sun" (19:17). The reader is scarcely prepared for the introduction of the main character in this section, the rider on the white horse who rides out from heaven clad in blood-stained garments at the head of a heavenly army (19:11–14). Despite the mysterious character of this new figure, the author links him with familiar titles, such as "Faithful and True" (v. 11; cf. 1:5; 3:14), "the Word of God" (v. 13; reminiscent of the Johannine Logos in John 1:1–2, 14; 1 John 1:1), and "King of kings and Lord of lords" (v. 16; 17:14 where it is a title of the Lamb). In v. 15, the warrior is further described as having a sharp sword proceeding from his mouth with which to strike down the nation, a metaphor for judgment found earlier in the Apocalypse (1:16; 2:12, 16) and clearly associated with the exalting Christ. The allusion to Ps 2:9 in v. 15, "he will rule them with a rod of iron," is a messianic passage already mentioned twice earlier (2:26; 12:5). These titles and descriptions leave little doubt in the reader that the heavenly warrior is none other than the exalted Jesus Christ who leads an eschatological assault against the enemies of God.

The second part of 19:11–21 is found in vv. 17–21, which begins with the angel's proleptic announcement of victory over the kings and mighty men of the earth, using the negative image of "the great supper of God" at which the birds of heaven are invited to feast on the corpses of the defeated enemies of God (vv. 17–18). The "great supper of God" is therefore the antithesis of "the marriage banquet of the Lamb," since the latter is a metaphor of salvation while the former is a metaphor of divine judgment. It is typical of the Apocalypse that scenes of conflict are described in the briefest possible way, if they are mentioned at all, and that is true of this passage as well. In v. 19, we learn that the enemies of God are gathered to make war against the divine warrior and his army, and abruptly in v. 20, the beast and the false prophet are captured and cast into the lake of fire. The episode concludes with the grisly scene of the birds feasting on the flesh of the defeated army.

The second subsection is the capture and ultimate defeat of Satan (20:1–3, 7–10), which frames an enigmatic "judgment scene" (in which no one is actually judged and the judges are never identified) in which the martyrs come to life and reign with Christ for a thousand years (vv. 4–6), labeled "the first resurrection" (v. 6). The motifs of this section consist of (1) an imprisonment of the malefactors followed by (2) a long interval and concluding with (3) the end of the period of imprisonment with a final punishment. This same sequence is described protologically as the imprisonment and final punishment of Azazel and his associates in 1 Enoch 10:4–14. In the opening scene the enemy is described with many of his aliases as "the dragon, that ancient serpent, who is the Devil and Satan" (these same aliases are used as a fulsome way of identifying the dragon in 12:9), leaving no doubt in the mind of the reader the identity of this great enemy of God. The millennial reign of the resurrected martyrs with Christ underscores the high value that God puts on those who die for their faith, underscored by the beatitude in v. 6: "Blessed and holy are those who share in the first resurrection; over these the second death has no power, but they will be priests of God and of Christ, and they will reign with him a thousand years."

The third and final scene in Rev 20:1–10 narrates the release of Satan from prison, his role in deceiving the nations and raising up armies to march on "the camp of the saints and the beloved city" (v. 9). The author has deftly combined a reference to Jerusalem besieged by her enemies that is now understood metaphorically as followers of Jesus who are persecuted for their faith. The motif of a repulsed attack upon Jerusalem is a part of a Zion theology that frequently surfaces in the OT (Pss 46, 48, 76; Isa 17, 29; Joel 2, 4; Zech 12, 14). Similarly, the attempt of kings and their armies to surround and conquer Jerusalem and the temple is a motif found frequently in Jewish and early Christian literature (*Sib. Or.* 3.657–58; *1 En.* 56:5–8; 4 Ezra 13:5–11, 33–38; Luke 19:43–44; 21:20).[31] The allusion to these nations under the names "Gog and Magog" would remind the competent reader of the prophetic narrative in Ezek 38–39,[32] where a hostile nation from the north will attack the peaceful and unsuspecting inhabitants of Palestine "in the latter days" (Ezek 38:8–16), but this nation will be completely defeated. The reader would naturally regard the event narrated in 20:7–10 as the fulfillment of an ancient prophecy of the defeat of God's enemies at the end of days. Oddly, the destruction of the hostile nations mentioned in 19:17–21 has been forgotten. The destruction of this hostile force by fire from heaven, a metaphor with OT antecedents, including the defeat of Gog and Magog (Ezek 38:22; 39:6; cf. Zeph 1:18; 3:8), underscores God's direct involvement from heaven in destroying his enemies.

The third subsection, Rev 20:11–15, which centers on the final judgment, is introduced with a magnificent theophanic scene: "Then I saw a great white throne and the one who sat on it; the earth and the heaven fled from his presence, and no place was found for them." This single verse is an excellent example of the theophany form,[33] which consists of just two parts, the coming of the deity and the reaction of na-

---

31. Lars Hartman, *Prophecy Interpreted: The Formation of Some Jewish Apocalyptic Texts and of the Eschatological Discourse Mark 13 par.* (Lund, Sweden: Gleerup, 1966), 77–101 ("The Tumult and Assault of the Heathen").

32. Sverre Bøe, *Gog and Magog: Ezekiel 38–39 as Pre-text for Revelation 19,17–21 and 20,7–10* (WUNT 2/135; Tübingen: Mohr Siebeck, 2001).

33. Jörg Jeremias, *Theophanie: Die Geschichte einer alttestamentlichen Gattung* (Neukirchen-Vluyn: Neukirchener, 1965).

ture. The frequency with which this form is found in the OT and early Jewish literature would mean that the competent reader would be very familiar with it (Judg 5:4–5; Pss 18:7–15; 68:7–8; Amos 1:2; Micah 1:3–4; Sirach 16:18–19; 43:16–17; 1QH 3.32–36). The focus of this judgment scene, introduced with an "And I saw" (v. 12), is on the opening of the heavenly books, including the book of life, which are then used as a basis for judging the dead. The author has used the traditional Jewish apocalyptic image of the opening of the books (Dan 7:10; cf. Ps 56:8; Isa 65:6; Jer 22:30; Mal 3:16; *Jubilees* 30:22; 36:10; *Ascension of Isaiah* 9:22), presumably one book for recording the deeds of the righteous and the other for recording the deeds of the wicked, and juxtaposed these books with the book of life (v. 12). The book of life has already been mentioned in the Apocalypse (3:5; 13:8; 17:8). In some way, the book of life is the decisive record, for the passage concludes with the statement that "anyone whose name was not found written in the book of life was thrown into the lake of fire."

20. The primary focus of the Apocalypse is introduced in *Rev 21:1–22:9*, which consists of an elaborate descriptive vision of the results of the transformation of the world centering on the New Jerusalem that descends from heaven to earth. This passage consists of an introductory subsection (21:1–8) followed by a relatively long subsection focusing on the New Jerusalem (21:9–27); it concludes with a subsection focusing on the river of the water of life flowing from the throne of God and the Edenic trees on each side of the river. Revelation 21:1–8 is an introductory subsection that first describes the transition to the new world order complete with the replacement of the first heaven and the first earth by a new heaven and a new earth and the descent of the New Jerusalem to earth (vv. 1–4), followed by a section containing a speech of God, which effectively summarizes the message of the entire book: how God sovereignly rewards the righteous and judges the wicked (vv. 5–8):

> And the one who was seated on the throne said, "See I am making all things new." Also he said, "Write this for these words are trustworthy and true." Then he said to me, "It is done!"
> I am the Alpha and the Omega, the beginning and the end. To the thirsty I will give water as a gift from the spring of the water of life. Those who conquer will inherit these things, and I will be their God and they will be my children. But as for the cowardly, the faithless, the polluted, the murderers, the fornicators, the sorcerers, the idolaters, and all liars, their place will be in the lake that burns with fire and sulfur, which is the second death.

Since elsewhere in the book God speaks only in 1:8, this relatively lengthy divine pronouncement is extremely important. The competent reader will recognize the fact that this speech is a summative pastiche of phrases and motifs found earlier in the book. That God makes all things new is a clear allusion to Isa 43:19, anchoring the transformation of the world in Old Testament prophecy. The divine title "the Alpha and the Omega," suggesting God's sovereign control over all creation, was mentioned in 1:8a and will be referred to in 22:13, where is a title belonging to Christ, not God.

The title "the Beginning and the End," essentially synonymous with "the Alpha and the Omega," will occur again in 22:13, where it too will be used to refer to Christ. The motif of providing the thirsty with the water of life was referred to in 7:17 as the eschatological role of the Lamb. The motif of conquering is of course a central emphasis in each of the seven proclamations to the church in Rev 2–3. The concluding list of sinful practices has numerous parallels with the ten commands that the competent reader would not miss.

Revelation 21:9–22:9 is dominated by the guided tour that the interpreting angel gives to the author. The passage begins in 21:9–10 when one of the seven bowl angels offers to show John "the bride, the wife of the Lamb," clearly a metaphor for the New Jerusalem, which is in turn is a metaphor for the people of God.[34] This passage is clearly reminiscent of Rev 17:1, where another (or the same?) bowl angel offers to provide a guided tour of the harlot seated on the beast with seven heads and ten horns. This literary clue signals the structural parallelism between 17:1–19:10 and 21:9–22:9, cleverly designed by the author to frame the passages of battle, destruction, and judgment in 19:11–21:8.[35] Among the finds from Qumran is a number of fragments of several copies of a document that has been called "Description of the New Jerusalem." The parallels between these texts and Rev 21:9–22:9 are so striking that it seems quite likely that the author of the Apocalypse was familiar with something very similar to these apocalyptic texts.[36] The heavenly or eschatological Jerusalem and the temple were, of course, very important motifs in early Judaism. These two motifs were closely related. In the wake of the destruction of Jerusalem in 586 B.C.E., Ezekiel envisioned the reconstruction of an eschatological temple in Ezek 40–48. In yet another strand of expectation, according to the scenario imagined in *1 Enoch* 90:28–29, the existing temple is razed and replaced with a new one built by God himself (cf. *2 Apoc. Bar.* 31:5–32:4). The New Testament contains a critique of the "temple made with hands" (Acts 7:48–50; 17:24), which is juxtaposed to the temple "made without hands," that is, built by God (Mark 14:58; Heb 9:11, 24; Philo *Spec. Leg.* 1.66–67). The New Jerusalem is mentioned once earlier in the Apocalypse, in 3:12, where it is a metaphor for the full attainment of salvation: "I will write on you [the one who conquers] the name of my God, and the name of the city of my God, the new Jerusalem that comes down from my God out of heaven." While the expectation of an eschatological temple (the core, after all, of Ezekiel's vision in Ezek 40–48) would be traditional in early Judaism, a new and unexpected element in John's vision is his insistence that there is no temple in the eschatological Jerusalem (21:22–27). Regardless of the various reasons scholars have given for the absence of the temple in John's vision of the eschatological Jerusalem, it is clear that

---

34. Gundry, "The New Jerusalem."
35. C. H. Giblin, "Structural and Thematic Correlations in the Theology of Revelation 16–22," *Biblica* 55 (1974): 487–504.
36. David E. Aune, "Qumran and the Book of Revelation," in *The Dead Sea Scrolls after Fifty Years: A Comprehensive Assessment* (ed. Peter W. Flint and James C. VanderKam; 2 vols.; Leiden: Brill, 1998–99), 2:622–48, esp. 629–36.

the author envisages a totally new reality, namely that the Lord God Almighty and the Lamb constitute the true temple of the New Jerusalem (21:22). Temples symbolize both the distance and the proximity of the worshiper and his or her god or gods. This dichotomy is shattered by the continuous presence of God and Christ with their people, making temple imagery unnecessary and outmoded.

The third subsection within Rev 21:9–22:9 centers on the river of the water of life flowing from the throne of God and watering the miraculous trees along its banks. The reason that heaven is referred to as Paradise is based on the widespread belief in early Judaism that the Garden of Eden, from which Adam fell, was not in fact a mysterious place on earth, but rather a heavenly realm (Paul, for example, reflects the belief that Paradise was in the third heaven; see 2 Cor 12:1–4). Since human beings were expelled from Paradise at the beginning of human history, the expectation that admission would again be granted to Paradise by a restored human race became a widespread element of Jewish apocalyptic thought.

21. The concluding section of the Apocalypse is the very complex composition found in *Rev 22:10–21*, often colorlessly identified as the epilogue. Unlike the references in Dan 8:26 and 12:4, 9, where the seer is told to seal up the book, John is commanded to do precisely the opposite: "Do not seal up the words of the prophecy of this book, for the time is near" (v. 10). Contradicting this ancient apocalyptic motif, the author emphasizes the immediate and timely relevance of the revelatory visions he has just described, and in so doing emphasizes the nearness of the end. The words that follow seem to be a clumsy concatenation of statements with no clear indication of who is speaking and why. One suggestive solution proposed by Ugo Vanni and reiterated by his student M. A. Kavanaugh is that this concluding section of the Apocalypse represents a liturgical sequence with an antiphonal character, that is, a liturgical dialogue.[37] Ancient readers would have picked up the literary clues immediately and understood that this concluding section of the Apocalypse was carefully designed to fit into a worship setting. That is, the author designed the book to cohere with current liturgical practices in order to secure a hearing for his revelatory vision. Part of an introit liturgy has been detected in 22:10–21, with parallels in similar introit liturgies in Didache 10:6 and 1 Cor 16:22.

Toward the end of this section, a complex text occurs that should apparently be considered the words of the exalted Christ (22:18–20):

> I warn everyone who hears the words of the prophecy of this book: if anyone adds to them
> God will add to that person the plagues described in this book;
> If anyone takes away from the words of the book of this prophecy,
> God will take away that person's share in the tree of life and in the holy city,
> which are described in this book.

---

37. Ugo Vanni, *La struttura letteraria dell'Apocalisse* (Brescia: Morcelliana, 1980), 109–15, 298–302; M. A. Kavanaugh, *Apocalypse 22:6–21 as Concluding Liturgical Dialogue* (Rome: Pontifical Gregorian University, 1984).

This final substantive paragraph in the Apocalypse consists of three literary forms crafted into a unity: (1) the integrity formula (don't add, don't take away, don't change), which is phrased as (2) two conditional curse formulas combined with the *lex talionis*, the principle of retributive justice (if anyone does *x*, God will repay him or her with *y*), and (3) a liturgical invocation ("Amen! Come Lord Jesus!"). Each of these literary forms, taken separately, was widely known throughout the ancient Mediterranean world. The integrity formula was typical of treaties between nations and cities, used in the covenant (or treaty) language of Deut 4:2: "You must neither add anything to what I command you nor take away anything from it, but keep the commandments of the Lord your God with which I am charging you." John was trying to copyright his Apocalypse, fearing that someone would be tempted to fiddle with the written account of his revelatory visions. The importance that he placed on the revelation that he had received from God through Jesus Christ was underscored by the curse formulas juxtaposed with the integrity formula. Finally the liturgical invocation, "Amen! Come Lord Jesus!" (v. 19), sounds a note that the author has underscored throughout his book: Jesus is coming soon! (1:7; 2:16; 3:11; 16:15). The concluding verse reminds us that the lengthy composition we have just read is a letter: "The grace of the Lord Jesus be with all the saints. Amen" (22:21), the salutation of which occurs in 1:4–6.

4. Conclusion

After this guided tour through the literary forms of the Apocalypse with suggestions regarding the intertextual associations that formed the context within which it might have been read and understood by the original readers, it is time to ask whether anything of significance has been learned, or whether you, dear reader, have not been led down the garden path (where angels fear to tread) by a *magister interpres*.

From the perspective of the original reader, it has become obvious that the sequence of literary forms in the Apocalypse conforms to no known ancient literary conventions.[38] Since the author rarely provides signals anticipating what he will do next, the readers either had no way to anticipate what would occur next or were in fact as surprised as we are by new turns in the narrative. Since the Apocalypse, whatever else it may be, is certainly an example of ancient revelatory literature, it is worth wondering whether the original readers would have thought that such abrupt literary moves were consonant with their understanding of the appropriate ways of narrating divine revelation.

Perhaps the most interesting result of our survey is the phenomenon that, in the Apocalypse, literary forms that had come to be associated either with apocalyptic or prophetic literary traditions (but not general enough to be associated with both) have been synthesized through juxtaposition. It is critical at this juncture to define what

---

38. This statement must be qualified by the admission that the problem of the literary patterns evident in the sequence of constituent literary forms in apocalypses is a subject which has not been investigated.

I understand by "prophecy" and "apocalyptic." Perhaps the most significant way in which prophecy can be differentiated from apocalyptic is *sociologically*. In contrast to apocalypticism, prophecy does not rigidly distinguish between the righteous and the wicked, but rather assumes that the wicked may repent and change their ways, and that the righteous require admonition, censure, and exhortation to encourage them to remain faithful or to repent and return to the fold. Apocalypticism, on the other hand (i.e., the religious ideology within the context of which apocalypses were written), is a perspective generally thought to have been espoused by an oppressed minority that clearly distinguished the righteous from the wicked and anticipated an eschatological denouement, in which they would be rewarded and the wicked punished.

By placing apocalyptic traditions within a prophetic framework (Rev 1–3 and 22:6–20), and by juxtaposing apocalyptic with prophetic elements throughout the composition, the author appears to have attempted to give a new lease on life to apocalyptic traditions that could not and did not long retain their vitality in early Christianity because of their indissoluble association with nationalistic myths connected with the royal ideology of ancient Israel. Apocalypses, the primary repository of apocalyptic traditions, were largely a scribal phenomenon perforce divorced from real settings because of their pseudepigraphical character. This suprahistorical perspective of apocalyptic literature generally appears to have been mitigated in the Apocalypse of John through the incorporation of prophetic concerns that have a historical orientation. The Apocalypse of John is one of the only apocalypses for which the author, audience, and setting are generally known because they are not concealed in the work itself, although that setting is not reflected in the hard-core, genre-bound apocalyptic sections of the work.

BEYOND GENRE: THE EXPECTATIONS OF APOCALYPSE

David L. Barr

According to Eusebius, the second-century writer Papias had approached Revelation with the wrong set of expectations:

> He says that after the resurrection of the dead there will be a period of a thousand years, when Christ's kingdom will be set up on this earth in material form. I suppose he got these notions by misinterpreting the apostolic accounts and failing to grasp what they had said in mystic and symbolic language. For he seems to have been a man of very small intelligence, to judge from his books. (*Hist. Eccl.* 3.39.11-13)

Such basic disagreements about the meaning of the Apocalypse have continued to plague the book throughout its history. And while contemporary scholars seldom adopt a materialistic reading, they still do not agree on how we should interpret the symbolic language.[1]

One important aspect of this problem is the question of the genre of the work, and on this issue important progress has been made.[2] This chapter will briefly review the discussion of genre and suggest one important modification to the current view, namely a consideration of the effect of the writing on the audience. But first a preliminary word about the dynamics of reading any ancient text.

WHEN WORLDS COLLIDE

A common and helpful metaphor to guide interpretation of a text is to reflect on the three worlds implicit in every text. There is the world within the text, the world behind the text, and the world in front of the text. Of course the one most apparent

---

The substance of this chapter was presented at the annual meeting of the Society of Biblical Literature in Nashville, Tennessee, 2000, as a multimedia presentation on the genre of the Apocalypse, sponsored by the Endowment for Biblical Research, Frontiers in Biblical Scholarship Series.

1. For an excellent history of the interpretation of the Apocalypse, both historically and in contemporary scholarship, see Arthur Wainwright, *Mysterious Apocalypse: Interpreting the Book of Revelation* (Nashville: Abingdon, 1993), 21–103 and 107–158, respectively.

2. For a discussion of the meaning and significance of genre, see pp. 12–14 in chapter 1 of this volume.

to us is the world contained within the text—a world of images, characters, actions, and devices. And indeed, the world of the Apocalypse is mysterious and exotic, with Lambs and dragons, beautiful women and beasts, heavenly messengers and human observers. There are wars and earthquakes, cosmic catastrophes and heavenly liturgies, and blood as high as the horses' bridles. It is a world in which we must learn to find our way around. It is in this world within the text that we meet the Great Red Dragon:

> Then another portent appeared in heaven: a great red dragon, with seven heads and ten horns, and seven diadems on his heads. His tail swept down a third of the stars of heaven and threw them to the earth. Then the dragon stood before the woman who was about to bear a child, so that he might devour her child as soon as it was born. (12:3–4; all citations are from the New Revised Standard Version unless otherwise noted.)

So there is a dragon in the text, but there were no dragons in the world of the audience. To understand the dragon in the text, we need to explore the world behind the text, the historical and social world that generated these images, characters, and actions. Early on scholars used history primarily to illustrate Revelation, such as the fabulous proposal that Laodicea's judgment for being "neither hot nor cold" was suggested by the water supply of that city, which could deliver neither hot water (as at Hieropolis six miles to the north) nor cold water (as at Colossae, six miles west).[3] But scholars have moved beyond this illustrative mode to show how the actual history of the time is embodied in the word.[4] Most of the essays in this volume engage the dialectic of the world within the text and the world behind the text. Indeed, on every page of the Apocalypse there are images and events that need to be understood (indeed, that can only be understood) by drawing on our information about the world behind the text.

In the world behind the text the dragon was the emperor—just the opposite of imperial propaganda (see especially chapter 9 in this volume). A common motif in portrayals of the emperor was to show him as victor and conqueror, being crowned with a victory wreath with a forlorn captive woman sitting on the ground beside him. But all you have to do to get quite a different view of the emperor is to imagine how he looked through the eyes of the captive woman at his feet. John adopts this perspective from below and much of what we find in the world in the text must be understood in terms of this world behind the text.

---

3. The background of this view is traced by Colin Hemer, *Letters to the Seven Churches of Asia in Their Local Setting*. (JSNTSup 11, Sheffield: JSOT, Sheffield Academic Press, 1986), 186–91, who largely carries forward the work of William M. Ramsay, *The Letters to the Seven Churches of Asia and Their Place in the Plan of the Apocalypse* (New York: Hodder and Stoughton, 1906). For a critique of this approach, see Steven J. Friesen, "Revelation, Realia, and Religion: Archaeology in the Interpretation of the Apocalypse," *HTR* 88 (1995): 291–314; and Craig R. Koester, "The Message to Laodicea and the Problem of Its Local Context: A Study of the Imagery in Rev 3.14–22," *NTS* 49 (2003): 407–24.

4. See the excellent commentary of J. P. M. Sweet, *Revelation* (Philadelphia: Westminster, 1979; repr., Trinity Press International, 1990).

And there is a third world, too often overlooked, the world in front of the text. If the expression "the world behind the text" is an apt metaphor for history before the writing of the story, then "the world in front of the text" serves to symbolize history since the writing of the story. This is the world of interpreters and interpretations that stand between us and the original text.

Now without question, this world in front of the text can distort our reading. We have a whole series of best-selling novels called the "Left Behind" series, imagining what will happen on earth after the "Rapture."[5] This apparently makes good sense to people even though Revelation makes no mention of a rapture, and in fact the notion was invented only in the nineteenth century.[6] But because it has become such a part of our world in front of the text, people see it in the text. In the same way, most of my students are so immersed in readings like Hal Lindsay's *The Late Great Planet Earth* that they think that that is what the story says. But of course it is not. While claiming to be a literal reading, this modern interpretation engages in the most outlandish allegorization of the text: the Beast is Russia (or China), the Ten Kings are the European Union, Babylon was, according to Lindsey, a code for a "one world religion".[7]

On the other hand, this world in front of the text is our only approach to the text. We cannot go to the world behind the text without the modern disciplines of history and the social sciences. We are always reading the text through ideas and methods from later times: the world in front of the text. Ideas and interpretations from this world make the text appear with different meanings, some valid, some distorting, some both at once.

We can never eliminate this world in front of the text, but one of the primary tasks of any interpreter is to be conscious of it and to criticize it. My task in this chapter is to take account of this third world, to make some sense of the world in front of the text, and, if possible, help us imagine what it was like to hear an apocalypse in its antique setting. More specifically, I will focus on just one issue, usually labeled as the *genre* of the work. I will first sketch what I take to be some of the major insights of current scholarship on the question of the genre of the Apocalypse, and then raise a few questions.

---

5. Tim LaHaye and Jerry B. Jenkins, *Left Behind: A Novel of the Earth's Last Days* (Wheaton, Ill.: Tyndale House, 1995); other volumes in the series include *Tribulation Force, Nicolae, Soul Harvest, Apollyon, Assassins, The Indwelling, The Mark, Desecration, The Remnant, Armageddon, Glorious Appearing*.

6. For a good discussion see Richard G. Kyle, *The Last Days Are Here Again: A History of the End Times* (Grand Rapids: Baker, 1998), 99–113; or David S. Katz and Richard Henry Popkin, *Messianic Revolution: Radical Religious Politics to the End of the Second Millennium* (New York: Hill and Wang, 1999), 142–69. See also the more technical work of Mark Patterson and Andrew Walker, "'Our Unspeakable Comfort': Irving, Albury, and the Origins of the Pre-tribulation Rapture," in *Christian Millenarianism from the Early Church to Waco* (ed. Stephen Hunt; Bloomington: Indiana University Press, 2001), 98–115.

7. Hal Lindsey with C. C. Carlson, *The Late Great Planet Earth* (New York: Bantam, 1970), 103–23.

The Idea of Genre

One curious note is that no one seems to have raised the issues of the genre of the Apocalypse until the modern period. So far as I can discover the first person to suggest that John's Apocalypse belongs to a distinctive literary type was by Friedrich Lücke in 1832.[8] Earlier interpreters seem to have simply equated it with prophetic works, whether they saw it predicting actual events to occur in (or at the end of) history or whether they saw it speaking symbolically of spiritual things.[9] Lücke's twofold recognition (that the Apocalypse is not like other prophetic works and that it is like a body of other writings from antiquity) is without doubt the most important scholarly contribution to the modern understanding of the Apocalypse. But it was only the beginning.

The first attempt to define the genre sought to list the typical traits of this kind of writing. This was a very useful exercise, if eventually unsuccessful. D. S. Russell noticed that such writings differed from the classical prophets in two important ways: they were pseudonymous (usually written in the name of someone long dead) and they were constructed in writing (whereas the classical prophets delivered their oracles in speech, later reduced to writing).[10] In addition, he argued that these writings were more thoroughly symbolic and esoteric—correlated features, both related to the sectarian nature of such writings. Others had somewhat different lists.[11] There is widespread agreement today on these five traits:

1. The claim that a secret revelation has been given to some seer or prophet. (1:1–2)
2. This revelation is imparted either in a dream, a vision, or a transportation of the seer to heaven—though often the three means are combined.
3. The revelation is usually mediated by some figure, such as an angel, who acts as guide and interpreter to the seer. (21:9–10)
4. The revelation is usually not self-explanatory, but consists in a variety of arcane symbols involving animals (often composites of different animals, with multiple heads), mythological figures, and numbers.
5. The reception of the revelation is often attributed to some figure from the past: Isaiah, Zephaniah, Enoch, Daniel, Ezra, Adam, Peter, Moses.

---

8. F. Lücke, *Versuch einer vollständigen Einleitung in die Offenbarung Johannis und in die gesamte apokalyptische Literatur* (Bonn: Weber, 1832); but see the discussion in chapter 1, p. 33.

9. For a concise overview of the interpretation of Revelation, see part one of Wainwright, *Mysterious Apocalypse*.

10. D. S. Russell, *The Method and Message of Jewish Apocalyptic, 200 B.C.–100 A.D.* (Old Testament Library, Philadelphia: Westminster, 1964).

11. Philipp Vielhauer, for example, included pseudonymity, accounts of visions (a picture), surveys of history in future-form (universal or particular), and the use of combined forms, including prayers and paraenesis; see Edgar Hennecke et al., eds., *New Testament Apocrypha* (Philadelphia: Westminster, 1964), 2:581–87.

If we were to try now to define the genre by these traits, we might say that:

> An Apocalypse is a secret revelation given to some seer or prophet in a dream, a vision, or a transportation to heaven and mediated by some heavenly guide and interpreter, using a variety of arcane symbols and often attributed to some figure from the past.

We have pretty clear evidence in art that these traits were felt by ancient readers, even if not articulated. For example, the illustrations in the Cloisters manuscript show John suspended on his island, with the ship of the church below and the angel above.[12] The angel brings him a message from above and John receives it in a trance or dream. So, visually, we have traits 1, 2, and 3: Secret message via an angel to seer in a trance.

Other pages in the same manuscript show the exotic figures that the angel must interpret for John (trait 4). So just because earlier generations did not articulate and list such traits, it does not mean they did not notice them. Identifying and understanding such traits are important and useful activities. I use them constantly with my students. However, there are two problems with such a list.

The first problem concerns the nature of genre definition, which requires more than just listing traits. Any attempt to define genre by listing common traits runs into two contradictory truths: No work of literature is unique (each is related to others by a series of interlocking traits); but none of these works to which it is related is exactly alike. Each shares numerous traits with the others; but not all share all the traits. So the issue in defining a genre is one of boundaries: is the definition broad enough to take in all the exemplars and still narrow enough to exclude works that are clearly of a different kind? And probably the answer must always be "no."

Let me illustrate with a crude analogy to dogs. We might define a dog as a four-legged animal with pointy ears that wags its tail and barks. But if we look at some specific dogs, problems arise. A beagle has most of these traits, but with long floppy ears. And then there is the basenji, the African barkless dog. And the Boston terrier might be a happy little fellow but it has no tail to wag. So notice what happens when we try to overlap the traits. They overlap in several ways (some share barking, some share tail wagging, some share pointy ears), but the only trait they all share is being four legged, hardly distinctive. Attention to traits might help us understand what something is like, but no accumulation of traits will be adequate to define the kind.

A significant advance on this listing of traits technique was made by members of the SBL Genres Project, who published a more systematic definition in *Semeia* 14 in 1979. While scholars have continued to tweak the definition put forward in that volume, most today build on it. It is the best definition so far put forward, both comprehensive and precise. But it is a scholar's tool, not a reader's aid. And the very

---

12. See folio 3r, Cloisters Manuscript of the Apocalypse, Metropolitan Museum of Art. See folio 16r for the angel interpreting the strange beasts.

quality that makes it so useful to the scholar, its precision, makes it ineffective for the reader. Here is definition as articulated by John Collins, the editor of the volume:

> "Apocalypse" is a genre of revelatory literature with a narrative framework, in which a revelation is mediated by an otherworldly being to a human recipient, disclosing a transcendent reality which is both temporal, insofar as it envisages eschatological salvation, and spatial insofar as it involves another, supernatural world.[13]

Thus Collins defined the genre both in terms of form (a narrative of a revelation) and of content (a disclosure of eschatological salvation), each of which he elaborates in the full essay. The narrative may describe a vision, an epiphany, or an otherworldly journey and it will include auditory revelations, cast either as a discourse or a dialogue. This all seems largely correct to me.

But let me work it around to my concerns by briefly reviewing three critiques of this definition made by others.

First, David Hellholm has argued that an adequate definition must include some description of the function of the genre.[14] He sees the general function of apocalypses as giving comfort to an oppressed minority. While I disagree with the notion that apocalypses are responses to oppression, I wholeheartedly agree that we need to consider social function if we expect to understand the genre. Second, E. P. Sanders sought to simplify the concept of apocalypse by describing its "essential" character, which he proposed was "the combination of revelation with the promise of restoration and reversal."[15] This is too brief to be useful, for this troika of revelation, reversal, and restoration occurs in a greater variety of literature than apocalypses. Still, Sanders points in a valuable direction, for he raises the question of why such works were written in the first place. And third, Christopher Rowland has protested that there is no common content to apocalypses, more specifically, he would exclude any set ideas about the future or the end of the age (eschatology) as an element of the genre (even while admitting that it is an important component of many apocalypses).[16] I believe Rowland is right in each of these points. There is no more reason to think that all apocalypses would share a common idea than there is to think that all sonnets must praise a lover. Many do; some do not. Further, the degree to which a particular apocalypse proposes to reveal the future (rather than the present) is open to debate, a point to which I will return. Collins has answered each of these critics,[17] and has further

---

13. John J. Collins, "Apocalypse: The Morphology of a Genre," *Semeia* 14 (1979): 9.
14. "The Problem of Apocalyptic: Genre and the Apocalypse of John," in *SBL 1982 Seminar Papers* (Atlanta: Scholars Press, 1982), 167.
15. "The Genre of Jewish Apocalypses," in *Apocalypticism in the Mediterranean World and Near East* (ed. David Helholm; Tübingen: Mohr Siebeck, 1983), 456.
16. Christopher Rowland, *The Open Heaven: A Study of Apocalyptic in Judaism and Early Christianity* (New York: Crossroad, 1982), 71.
17. John J. Collins, *The Apocalyptic Imagination: An Introduction to the Jewish Matrix of Christianity* (Los Angeles: Crossroad, 1984), 8.

refined his working definition to include attention to the function of apocalypses.[18] I will return to some of this in a moment, but I will leave the working out of these details to another occasion; my purpose here is different.

My purpose is to try to advance the conversation some small bit. I do not wish to debate the traits, or to suggest that I now have the list of traits that is better than all previous lists. They have guided us well and I find sound insights in the various contributions to this discussion. Rather I want to do two things. I want to think about the concept of genre (theory) and then I want to reconsider the question of genre from the perspective of the audience rather than the perspective of the author; that is, I want to consider the social function of apocalypses.

I said a moment ago that there were two problems with defining genres by listing traits but I have only articulated one problem, the problem of the diversity and the lack of universals.

The second problem can be stated thus: even if we could define a set of universal traits, we would not thereby provide adequate insight on the significance of the genre. If genre theory is to be more than just a convenient way to organize the closet, picking up the things history has simply left on the floor and putting them in their place, there needs to be some attention to the audience.

When we consider genre from an audience perspective rather than an author perspective, the question shifts from what are the common traits to what do various combinations of these traits signal to the audience. It is not a question of how to write but of how to read—or, more accurately in the case of the Apocalypse, how to listen. To use a modern example, when we hear a story that starts "once upon a time" that single trait signals us that we are hearing a fairy tale, even though not all fairy tales start that way. And we know how to listen to a fairy tale. We know how to listen to a great variety of writings. But how are we to listen to an apocalypse? Or, more accurately, how did an ancient audience listen? To consider that question we need to be conscious of ideas from the world in front of the text.

Apocalypse Then and Now

When we hear the word *apocalypse*, we think of disaster: *Apocalypse Now* was a fitting title for a film about the devastation caused by our war in Vietnam. And it seems to fit much of what we read in apocalypses, where battles and blood, monsters and demons, fear and carnage are on every side. For us it may appear to be the "Nightmare of God" (as Daniel Berrigan titled his reading of Revelation).[19] Or per-

---

18. John J. Collins, *Seers, Sibyls, and Sages in Hellenistic-Roman Judaism* (Leiden: Brill, 1997), 25–36.
19. Daniel Berrigan, *The Nightmare of God* (Portland, Oreg.: Sunburst, 1983).

haps, as Tina Pippin would have it, it seems like a horror show: "less like the shower scene in *Psycho* than the all-out killing in the *Texas Chain Saw Massacre.*"[20]

Now our response to the word *revelation* is quite different, though in fact this is only the Latin translation of the Greek word *apocalypsis*. But this modern notion of revelation leads to its own problems, including fantasies about streets of gold and lakes of fire, to say nothing of the many—indeed universal—failures to predict the future based on a reading of Revelation as revelation.

Both our modern notions of "revelation" and of "apocalypse" are culturally conditioned by our setting today; they are of no use to us in reading this ancient genre. They are all part of that world in front of the text through which we must look. Of course, in some real measure, so is the academic definition of the apocalypse genre I have been discussing. The genre "apocalypse" was invented in the nineteenth century, as noted above.[21] So I propose a little detour. Let us suspend the literary question of genre and ask what folks in Roman Asia Minor might have conjured up in their minds when they heard about an "apocalypsis". Just what was a "revelation"?

First let me say that the ancients seem rather taken with revelations; they found them in all sorts of settings, some obvious, some obscure (to us). Oracles, both verbal and written, omens, astrology, dreams, necromancy, empyromancy, examining the entrails of sacrifices, seeing unusual sights, casting of lots, even things like sneezing or random speech could be deemed to reveal hidden things.[22]

Decisions were often made by drawing lots. For example, a lot from an Isis temple reads, "Mistress Isis, if my illness has come from you and you will give me my healing, make this token come out for me." The companion lot would read in the negative: if my illness does not come from you and you will not be the source of my healing, make this token come out for me.[23] While there was some debate about the reliability of revelations (Stoics defending them; Epicureans attacking them), most seemed to have believed such revelations occurred. As Cicero observed:

> There is an ancient belief, handed down to us even from mythical times and firmly established by the general agreement of the Roman people and of all nations, that divination of some kind exists among men.... Now I am aware of no people, however refined and learned or however savage and ignorant, which does not think that signs are given of future events.... (*Div* I.1.1)

Most were convinced that the divine world was willing to communicate with the human world, either through some natural phenomenon that revealed the divine

---

20. Tina Pippin, *Apocalyptic Bodies: The Biblical End of the World in Text and Image* (London: Routledge, 1999), 78–116.

21. One could, of course, argue that there was a recognized genre on the basis of the fact that many ancient works are titled "the apocalypse of" so-and-so. But this is more likely a claim to a certain kind of experience: they have had an apocalypse/revelation.

22. For a nice survey, see Robert Flaceliere, *Greek Oracles* (London: Elek Books, 1965).

23. David S. Potter, *Prophets and Emperors: Human and Divine Authority from Augustus to Theodosius* (Revealing Antiquity 7; Cambridge: Harvard University Press, 1994), 28. For an early Christian example, see Acts 1:24–26.

mind or through the direct divine inspiration of some special person. Whether by signs, omens, or direct speech humans could glimpse divine mysteries.[24] The basic presupposition of all revelation is the idea that there is another world where mysteries can be discerned if we but had eyes to see.

This idea is captured nicely on the right panel of the St. John's Altarpiece by Hans Memling (ca. 1475). The artist portrays John gazing into the upper world where he sees himself observing the throne of God (and includes an angel mediating the throne scene and the four horsemen).[25] This idea of a world hidden from our ordinary sight is as old as Homer, whose *Iliad* shows that the real battle for Troy is fought by the Gods. Virgil, that prophet of the reign of Augustus, imitated this view in his story of Aeneas. He shows the battle of Troy raging and Aeneas raging mad, when suddenly his mother Venus appears to him, causing him to pause:

> Thus while I rave, a gleam of pleasing light
> Spread o'er the place; and, shining heav'nly bright,
> My mother stood reveal'd before my sight
> Never so radiant did her eyes appear;
> Not her own star confess'd a light so clear:
> Great in her charms, as when on gods above
> She looks, and breathes herself into their love.
> She held my hand, the destin'd blow to break;
> Then from her rosy lips began to speak:
> 'My son, from whence this madness, this neglect
> Of my commands, and those whom I protect?

She then proceeds to show him that it is not the apparent historical forces at work—it is not because of Helen or Paris that this disaster has fallen. It is the work of the Gods:

> Not Helen's face, nor Paris, was in fault;
> But by the gods was this destruction brought.
> Now cast your eyes around, while I dissolve
> The mists and films that mortal eyes involve,
> Purge from your sight the dross, and make you see
> The shape of each avenging deity.
> Enlighten'd thus, my just commands fulfill,
> Nor fear obedience to your mother's will.

She then showed him behind the scenes of the battle, showed him Neptune, Juno, Athena, and Jove, all fighting in the battle with the invading Greeks. He sees the fall of Troy and recounts both his vision and his own sense of powerlessness, and then uses the symbol of a fallen tree to seal the point:

---

24. This interaction is vividly drawn by Patricia Cox Miller, *Dreams in Late Antiquity: Studies in the Imagination of a Culture* (Princeton: Princeton University Press, 1998).

25. The altarpiece is in the Memlingmuseum, Sint-Janshospitaal, Bruges, and can be seen online at http://www.wga.hu/frames-e.html?/html/m/memling/2middle2/13john3.html.

> Troy sunk in flames I saw (nor could prevent),
> And Ilium from its old foundations rent;
> Rent like a mountain ash, which dar'd the winds,
> And stood the sturdy strokes of lab'ring hinds.
> About the roots the cruel ax resounds;
> The stumps are pierc'd with oft-repeated wounds:
> The war is felt on high; the nodding crown
> Now threats a fall, and throws the leafy honors down.
> To their united force it yields, tho' late,
> And mourns with mortal groans th' approaching fate:
> The roots no more their upper load sustain;
> But down she falls, and spreads a ruin thro' the plain.[26]

Now this is no apocalypse, yet it is an apocalypse—a pulling aside the covering to let us see behind the veil of human limits to what is really going on. Such unveiling is the root meaning of the word *apocalypsis*. Just how might we "dissolve the mists and films that mortal eyes involve" and so see clearly what is going on in our world? There were many attempts to pierce this mist.

Some of the modes of revelation were informal and intuitive: you see or hear something and have a hunch, a revelation. Examples of intuitive revelations include the significance attached to certain animals, involuntary speech or sneeze, the color and shape of inner organs of sacrificed animal, casting of lots, even observing the weather: it bodes an ill night. Other modes of revelation were more formal, more specialized, more professional, based on direct divine contact in inspired utterances, dreams, or visions. Let's review how some of these more formal revelations worked.

Oracles are at the heart of Greek religion, so closely intertwined that Sophocles can see only ruin if they are abandoned:

> No longer to the holy place,
> To the navel of the earth, I'll go
> To worship, not to Abae
> Nor to Olympia,
> Unless the oracles are proved fit,
> For all men's hands to point at.
> O Zeus, if your are rightly called
> The sovereign lord, all-mastering,
> Let this not escape you nor your ever-living power!
> The oracles concerning Laius
> Are old and dim and men regard them not,
> Apollo is nowhere clear in honor; God's service perishes.[27]
>
> *Oed. Tyr.* 897–910

---

26. The translation is that of John Dreyden, from the Perseus project at http://www.perseus.tufts.edu/cgi-bin/ptext?doc=Perseus%3Atext%3A1999.02.0052&layout=&loc=2.604 (*Aeneid* 2.604–631).

27. Sophocles, *Oedipus the King* (trans. David Green; New York: Washington Square, 1954).

Without regard for oracles, there will be no honor for the divine; God's service perishes.

Greece was dotted with oracular shrines (we know of at least 20) with the most important being the shrine of Apollo at Delphi.[28] Such oracles were often connected to a cave, a sort of hole or doorway into another reality. In this older conception it is the underworld where secrets lie hidden, not the overworld of apocalyptic, but the paradigm of information from another level of reality is similar. Oracles were responsive; people consulted oracles. The questions they brought were varied. Individuals asked about their health, about the chances for success in a new venture (work, marriage, journey), about whether they would have a child (or whether the child expected was really his), about how to obtain divine favor, and such. Cities also consulted oracles about major decision: war, establishing a new colony, causes of crop failure, and most especially guidance on how to conduct certain rites.

Oracles gave their responses by various means, some mechanical (casting lots), some psychological (dreams), and some verbal (trance-like pronouncements from an inspired priest or, more commonly, priestess). The verbal and the psychological are most interesting for our purposes. In addition to oracular shrines, these techniques were used in many temples. The temple is by definition a gateway to the God. Some statues were even rigged with hollow tubes so that the inspired priest would appear to speak through the very mouth of the God. More interesting, however is dream divination common in the temples of Asclepius, who made revelations about health into a major industry.

In a typical Asclepium the supplicants would enter through a sacred way and descend into an underground chamber and first be purified by water from a sacred spring. They would then proceed by underground passage to the main temple chamber. The supplicant would spend the night sleeping in the temple, hoping for a visitation from Asclepius. Many reported that the God appeared to them in a dream, either in human or animal form, and touched or massaged the afflicted area, perhaps giving additional instructions for health (like eating and exercising). Some report being healed immediately, others report slow progress toward health. We see in these healing that the power of revelation was thought to penetrate even the human body, purging it of its afflictions. No wonder people sought such revelations.

No doubt the quest for such divine knowledge made some folk gullible. Lucian tells us of the charlatan seer who grew rich with his false oracle of the python. It seems that one Alexander got himself a large python (sacred form of Apollo) and had a puppet head constructed. He would then sit in the dimly lit chamber with the python draped around him, with its head concealed under his arm. Using the puppet head, he would give oracles to inquirers, who in turn gave offerings to him.

Oracles were primarily living events. One went to the shrine, asked a question, and received an answer (usually yes/no, but often ambiguous). But there were also

---

28. On Greek oracles, see H. W. Parke, *Greek Oracles* (London, Hutchinson, 1967), and Potter, *Prophets and Emperors*.

collections of oracles, some from specific shrines, some from specific seerers, and some literary productions in the name of the famous. A vast collection of literature was produced in the name of the Sibyl of Apollo, called conveniently the *Sibylline Oracles*. The ones we have are largely Jewish and Christian imitations, though clearly there were collections of Greek and Roman oracles in antiquity.[29] One such collection was officially consulted by the Senate in times of crisis; unfortunately it perished when the temple of Jupiter, where it was housed, burned down in 83 B.C.E.

The oracles we have do not seem to be of this type; that is, they are not the sort of oracular pronouncement one might consult in a time of crisis. They seem more an amalgamation of Greek mythology, the stories of Genesis, and the moral preaching of the Hebrew prophets, all wrapped in the mantle of the pagan priestess. Sometimes an oracle might sound like the book of Daniel:

> Also at a certain time there will come to the prosperous land of Asia a faithless man clad with a purple cloak on his shoulders, savage, stranger to justice, fiery. For a thunderbolt beforehand raised him up, a man. All Asia will bear an evil yoke. . . . (3:388–392).

In fact some oracles speak of a succession of worldly kingdoms (sometimes four; more often ten), leading inevitably to the present time when Rome rules.[30] Other oracles sound more like sermons than predictions:

> But urge on your minds in your breasts, and shun unlawful worship. Worship the Living one. Avoid adultery and indiscriminate intercourse with males. Rear your own offspring and do not kill it, for the Immortal is angry at whoever commits these sins. (3:762–766).

What ties these two kind of oracles together is the notion that they come from God through the Sibyl: both are revelations of the divine will. Such oracles of the Sibyl continued to be produced well into the Middle Ages.

Another sort of literary production of revelation was the scribal skill of mining ancient sacred writings for new revelations, an art well exemplified in the scriptural commentaries from the Dead Sea Scrolls. These commentaries take the technical name *pesher*, meaning interpretation, because of their pattern of taking a biblical sentence and then commenting "being interpreted, this means." The meaning was some situation of the interpreter's time, completely unrelated to the historical sense of the work.

For example, the commentary on Hab 1:4 reads thus, first quoting Habakkuk (which I italicize) then interpreting it:

> *So the Law is weak and justice never goes forth.* Interpreted this concerns those who have despised the Law of God. . . . *For the Wicked encompasses the righteous.* The

---

29. See the introduction by John J. Collins in *The Old Testament Pseudepigrapha* (ed. James Charlesworth; Garden City, N.Y.: Doubleday, 1983), 1:313–26.

30. Book Four speaks of four kingdoms. Books One and Two speak of ten generations.

wicked is the Wicked Priest, and the righteous is the Teacher of Righteousness. (1QpHab)

In fact the scribal interpreter understood more than the original prophet, for the real meaning of the revelation was hidden until God has revealed it to the new Teacher:

> God told Habakkuk to write down that which would happen to the final generation, but He did not make known to him when time would come to an end. And as for that which He said, That *he who reads may read it speedily*: interpreted this concerns the Teacher of Righteousness, to whom God made known all the mysteries of the words of His servants the Prophets. (1QpHab 7:1)

We find a similar view among early Christians, as when Peter is reported to have explained the exuberance of those inspired by the spirit on the day of Pentecost by claiming that this is what the prophet Joel was speaking about (Acts 2:15). So by oracles old and new, it was widely believed that God spoke.

In addition to these supposed direct words from the divinity, there were many other ways of discovering the secrets of the world above. There is an interesting example of empyromancy in the romantic tale of Apuleius, whereby the seer looks into a fire and foretells the future. He explains it thus:

> It is not so very mysterious that this Flamelet, trivial as it is, and produced by human agency, should yet possess an awareness of that greater and celestial Flame as of its Sire, and that it should know and announce to us by divine intuition what the latter will be doing up on the crest of the sky. (*The Golden Ass*)[31]

Since the fire below corresponds to the fire above (the sun), it can reveal divine mysteries, for surely the sun sees all that happens on earth. The notion of the all-seeing heavens is part of a larger conception, whereby the heavens are conceived of as personal forces directing the affairs of earth: astrology.

The stars not only saw all that transpired on earth; they controlled what happened. This could be scientifically shown in observable effects on tides, seasons, and weather. What appeared to be chance events when viewed from below could be shown to be ordained when viewed from above. Those with the skill to interpret, and it was an increasingly specialized task in this era, could read the heavens and reveal their secrets.

We see then that there was both a thirst for revelations and a ready supply of the intoxicating wine of secret divine disclosures. Now to push this just one step further, we must emphasize the conceptual model of the cosmos that makes sense of all this, a dualistic model of an above and a below wherein the two worlds are distinct yet linked, with multiple channels of communication, whether in the physical world (omens), in the hidden depths of earlier revelations (scribal activity), or in the living words of priests, sibyls, and prophets (inspiration). Notice that John uses all three

---

31. Quoted from Jack Lindsay, *Apuleius' The Golden Ass* (Bloomington: Indiana University Press, 1962), 57.

channels in his Apocalypse. All apocalypses are built on this schema, whether one gets the secret knowledge by visiting the other realm or by a messenger descending to reveal these truths in visions, words, or dreams. This is not to say that apocalypses are just the same as these other forms of divination.

I want to be clear that I am not questioning two of the greatest advances in thinking about apocalypses over the past century. I am not arguing that prophecy is an adequate generic identifier. In spite of arguments to the contrary,[32] apocalypses are a new kind of writing with a rich heritage in the prophetic and mythological traditions.[33] Nor am I abandoning the useful distinction between apocalypse as a literary type, apocalyptic as a worldview, and apocalypticism as a social movement. These distinctions, suggested by Klaus Koch[34] and developed by Paul Hanson,[35] are enormously helpful. But the categories do overlap, and we can learn something by considering that overlap.

Nor am I arguing that an apocalypse is simply the same thing as an oracle or omen. Obviously not. But I do think we can refresh the current definition by reconsidering these other cultural artifacts. Current definitions of apocalypse are focused too much on literary traits and worry too much about being inclusive and definitive. Without rejecting these definitions, I want to look at the social reality embedded in the apocalypses.

What I am arguing is that we can get some sense of the expectations of the audience of an apocalypse when we understand the broader social role of means of revelations in that culture. Now it is time to end our detour and focus more specifically on the literature.

---

32. Frederick David Mazzaferri, *The Genre of the Book of Revelation From a Source-Critical Perspective* (BZNW 54; Berlin and New York: de Gruyter, 1969). The more careful work of Elisabeth Schüssler Fiorenza relates John's work to the phenomenon of early Christian prophecy without claiming that it is generically related to prophetic writings: "Apokalypsis and Propheteia: The Book of Revelation in the Context of Early Christian Prophecy," in *L'Apocalypse Johannique et l'Apocalyptique dans le Nouveau Testament* (ed. Jan Lambrecht; Louvain: Louvain University Press, 1980), 105–27.

33. Clearly demonstrated by Paul D. Hanson, *The Dawn of Apocalyptic: The Historical and Sociological Roots of Jewish Apocalyptic Eschatology* (rev. ed.; Philadelphia: Fortress, 1979); Richard J. Clifford, "The Roots of Apocalypticism in Near Eastern Myth," in *The Origins of Apocalypticism in Judaism and Christianity* (ed. John J. Collins; New York: Continuum, 2000), 3–38. See also John J. Collins's article in the same volume, "From Prophecy to Apocalypticism: Expectations of the End," 129–61, and Robert R. Wilson, "From Prophecy to Apocalyptic: Reflections on the Shape of Israelite Religion," *Semeia* 21 (1982): 79–95. On the genre of John's Apocalypse, see the discussion and bibliography in David E. Aune, *Revelation: Word Biblical Commentary* (Dallas: Word, 1997), 1:xxv–xc.

34. Klaus Koch, *The Rediscovery of Apocalyptic* (SBT 2/22; London: SCM, 1972).

35. See Paul Hanson, "Apocalypses and Apocalypticism," *ABD* 1:279–80.

Literary Expectations

Aristotle taught us that tragedies function to produce pity and fear in the audience; this is generally accepted.[36] Adela Yarbro Collins has argued that apocalypses pursue a related catharsis, which she suggested was fear and resentment.[37] This is a very important idea; it is, I think, exactly the right question, even if it is the wrong answer. What did reading/hearing an apocalypse do to the audience?

One suggestion, articulated by David Aune[38] and endorsed by John Collins,[39] is that apocalypses function to interpret present circumstances in light of supernatural realities and to show that this interpretation has divine authority. By showing how events in this world correspond to realities in the other world, an apocalypse establishes the validity of certain ideas or practices. Thus much apocalyptic literature is about social issues: Who is the true prophet? (*Ascension of Isaiah*); How should we behave (*Apocalypse of Peter*); or How should we fast and who is the true martyr (*Apocalypse of Elijah*).[40] This is a good suggestion and no doubt true, though perhaps a bit too conceptual, too abstract, too academic. It calls our attention to social forces at work in the community, but it does not tell us what happens to the audience by the very hearing of the apocalypse.

Aune made a second suggestion, which Collins does not seem to have picked up but which I find very important. Aune points out that the literary product as an autobiographical narrative functions to "mediate a new actualization of the original revelatory experience."[41] Now Aune makes a very daring suggestion here. The audience does not just learn about the experience of the seerer, they also experience that original revelation as it is "re-presented" and "re-actualized" for them. Exactly so.

I have pursued the idea of the social function of John's apocalypse before,[42] but I have never approached it though the idea of genre. Thinking through this again for this article has both expanded and simplified my thought. Let me clarify my suggestion by distinguishing it from a third suggestion from Aune. He argued that apocalypses encourage "cognitive and behavioral modifications based on the message communicated from the transcendent world" (90). Probably so, at least from the

---

36. Though the meaning and means of catharsis are disputed; see Leon Golden, "The Clarification Theory of Katharsis," *Hermes* 104 (1976): 437–52.

37. Adela Yarbro Collins, *Crisis and Catharsis: The Power of the Apocalypse* (Philadelphia: Westminster, 1984), 152–54.

38. David E. Aune, "The Apocalypse of John and the Problem of Genre," *Semeia* 36 (1986): 89.

39. John J. Collins, *Seers, Sibyls, and Sages in Hellenistic-Roman Judaism* (Leiden: Brill, 1997), 33.

40. Examples from David Frankfurter, "Early Christian Apocalypticism: Literature and Social World," in *The Origins of Apocalypticism in Judaism and Christianity* (ed. John J. Collins; New York: Continuum, 2000), 1:433.

41. Aune, "Problem of Genre," 89.

42. David L. Barr, "Blessed Are Those Who Hear: John's Apocalypse as Present Experience," in *Biblical and Humane: A Festschrift for John Priest* (ed. Linda Bennett Elder, David L. Barr, and Elizabeth Struthers Malbon; Atlanta: Scholars Press, 1996), 87–103.

perspective of a modern university professor. I quite agree that the apocalypse aims to transform the audience, but I do not think it worked in quite this rationalistic a fashion.

Rather, I suggest an apocalypse functions to transform the audience by their experience of the other reality of the apocalypse. The closest analogy I can suggest is the transforming power of religious rituals. Such rituals do not merely communicate information, though they may be built on an accompanying story that is told in the process of celebrating the ritual.

Rituals are of two kinds. Some rituals serve to confirm the world as it is, to preserve the present order. Examples include holiday celebrations and acts like pledging the flag. This would be the function of various rites connected with the emperor: they reaffirm the rightness of Roman rule. Other rituals serve to transform, to change the world and one's place in it. Examples of such rites would be weddings, puberty rites, and college commencement rituals. The process of ritual transformation is seen most clearly in rites of passage, which involve a three-stage process, according to anthropologists.[43]

The ritual participant moves from stage A to stage B through a transitional stage of vague and ill-defined boundaries (for example, from childhood to adulthood through a puberty ritual wherein one might be alternately taught the secrets of adulthood and terrorized with the fears of childhood). This transitional stage or state is a time-between, related to both but like neither. Anthropologists refer to it as a liminal state—a boundary crossing. It is a time when the world is reordered and the participant achieves a new place in it.

It is the dynamics of this liminal state that interests me, for here a person passes through a temporary experience and is permanently changed as a result. This model allows us to avoid undervaluing the imaginative experience of hearing the Apocalypse. Writers who interpret this experience as merely a denial of reality[44] or as a temporary, ephemeral event soon to be eclipsed by life in the real world,[45] fail to appreciate the transformative function of language. One passing through this rite, this liturgy, can be permanently altered.

This leads me back then to the issue mentioned earlier: are apocalypses designed to tell the audience about the end of the world? Of course. This brief survey of the range of apocalypsis in the ancient world (from omens to oracles to astrology) suggests that those who consulted them were looking for clues about the future: should I marry? Should I travel? Should we go to battle? Still, I would ask you to consider if this is not primarily information about the present. The marrying, traveling, or fight-

---

43. Arnold van Gennep, *The Rites of Passage* (Chicago: University of Chicago Press, 1960), and Victor W. Turner, *The Ritual Process: Structure and Anti-structure* (Ithaca, N.Y.: Cornell University Press, 1969).

44. So Adela Yarbro Collins, *Crisis and Catharsis: The Power of the Apocalypse* (Philadelphia: Westminster, 1984), 155.

45. So John G. Gager, *Kingdom and Community: The Social World of Early Christianity* (Englewood Cliffs, N.J.: Prentice-Hall, 1975), 56.

ing is what is at issue: things to do today. What one hopes to find in the revelation is whether one's activity corresponds to the will of heaven. As a recent study of Greco-Roman prophecy suggests, "In antiquity, as now, prophecy was only rarely concerned with the future."[46]

Just so, the apocalypse takes the audience behind the veil of limited human experience to the secret world where all meaning becomes clear. So the vision in Rev 12, about the Heavenly Woman about to give birth to the messiah but being pursued by the Dragon, is a visionary telling of a past event, the birth of Jesus. Still, its focus is on the present: the Dragon makes war on the rest of the Woman's children: John's community. It is a revelation of why the community can expect opposition.

The vision in Rev 13, about the two beasts who rule the world and demand divine honors, is a visionary telling of past events when Rome rose to world domination; its purpose is not to reveal that past but to explain the present experience of Roman power. Its purpose is to unveil that power in its naked totalitarian domination and so energize the community to live free lives. It is a revelation of how the followers of Jesus are expected to live.

Just so, I argue, the vision in Rev 19, about the rider on the white horse, is a revelation of present reality. Now it is common for interpreters to speak of this rider coming from Heaven and to relate him to the second coming of Jesus. I have so spoken myself, but that is not quite what the story says. In the story John sees "heaven opened, and behold, a white horse! He who sat upon it is called Faithful and True, and in righteousness he judges and makes war." Notice the present tense verbs. I find it striking that the only future tense verb in this scene is that he "will rule" (or will shepherd) the nations. All other action is either past or present. What does this mean? If one could but see behind the scenes, as John does, Christ would appear as conqueror, ruler, and one who can slay all the wicked with the sword of his mouth. This is a visionary telling of the life, death, and resurrection of Jesus, as well as the present experience of the community of those who keep his testimony. Its purpose is to reveal the present reality of those who follow Jesus: they have conquered Satan "by the blood of the Lamb and by the word of their testimony, for they loved not their lives even unto death" (12:11). Only people who love something "more than life" can ever be free.

Now that last sentence attempts the difficult task of slipping the bounds of Roman Asia Minor and seeing Revelation in our terms. I am not good at this. I can only make some crude analogies to our modern experience. We do not live in a two-story world like the ancients, so we don't expect revelations of this sort. If I told you about my trip to heaven, you would wonder about my sanity (or about my choice of mind-altering substances). We live in a scientific world, so we expect to understand things by seeing behind their appearances to their "reality" in quite a different way than did the ancients.

But we do still believe that what you see on the surface is not necessarily the

---

46. Potter, *Prophets and Emperors*, 2.

reality (as anyone who follows politics knows). Like the ancients we have developed various techniques for seeing behind the veil of ordinary perception. In some way scientific instrumentation provides an analogy.

Is it too metaphorical to say that the discovery of germ theory was a revelation? The invisible had been made visible. And it is one thing to learn about germs; it is quite another to look through the microscope and see them for yourself. Sharing the vision will change the way you live in the world more surely than just knowing the facts.

We have other ways of seeing behind the surface; whole disciplines are devoted to the task: political science, sociology, psychology, even religion studies. In my own personal biography, reading Reinhold Niebuhr was a revelation. His sociological unpacking of morality (*Moral Man and Immoral Society*) came to me with the force of insight (if not revelation). I had grown up in a Christian community where concern for social justice was limited to changing the hearts of individual. All social ills would be solved, we thought, if everyone were a Christian. But when I saw "behind the scenes" at how social institutions actually work, how even the best of people will act unjustly for the good of the social group (the CEO *must* lay off a couple of thousand workers to protect the profits of the investors), I began to live in a new way.

My third analogy emphasizes the experiential aspect of apocalypse, the analogy of the arts. When we sit in the theater and the stage goes dark, we cross a border into another reality. When we stand before a painting or sculpture we have the potential to be transformed. When we hear a poem or a song, or maybe just music, we sense another world. Our ability to cross such boundaries, to perceive other worlds, provides some analogy by which we can better grasp what the ancient audience heard when they heard an apocalypse.

These may not be very good analogies, but they are analogies. What we see when we "see through" the world of our ordinary perceptions is a reality we take to be more real, more true. It is not the future, though it may predict the future (once you see through the apparently democratic nature of modern politics to the control exerted by international business, you have a pretty good idea of what the future holds).

So too, I suggest, when John saw Jesus enthroned in heaven, when he saw him standing on Mount Zion with 144,000 faithful, when he saw him mounted on a white horse, what he has seen is not the future but the present. The present as it exists in heaven and thus the actual reality of the world in which he lived. Like Aeneas before, once he sees the gods on the battlements, he knows the war is over.

So in addition to the traits that scholars have isolated and in addition to the conceptual model of the genre of an apocalypse, we need to understand what the audience expected when they were presented with a revelation, an apocalypsis. This study suggests that they expected to see beyond and behind the world of ordinary sense to a more real world. A world that already existed and that would thus control both the future and the present.

This understanding of how revelations work explains how John can claim that these thing must happen soon (1:1), how Jesus comes "soon" (22:6–7), and how

"There will be no more delay" (10:5–7). For there was no delay. Hearing John's Apocalypse as apocalypse, as an unveiling of the mists and films that cloud our mortal eyes, transforms the world in which we live. Hearing John's Apocalypse allows us to gain a whole new perspective on the world and to the extent that the performance of the work reproduces the experience in the audience, they experience the coming of Jesus and the presence of God's rule. Hearing the Apocalypse as apocalypse transforms it from a materialistic and unbelievable schema for the future into a serious reflection on how to live in a world of oppression and domination.

Hearing and Seeing but Not Saying: A Rhetoric of Authority in Revelation 10:4 and 2 Corinthians 12:4

Jean-Pierre Ruiz

Interpreters as early as Origen have compared the prohibition in Rev 10:4, "Seal up what the seven thunders have said and do not write it down," with 2 Cor 12:4, where Paul tells of someone who "heard things that are not to be told, that no mortal is permitted to repeat." Origen linked the puzzle of Rev 10:4 with the equally vexing enigma of the unutterable utterances of 2 Cor 12:4 and with Mark 4:34. Recognizing the allusion to Ezek 2:8–3:3 in Rev 10:8–11, he arrived at the following reading:

> Ezekiel receives a roll of a book with writing within and without, in which there was mourning, lamentation, and woe; and when the Word commanded him he ate the book lest he should write it down and betray its contents to people who were unworthy. John is also recorded to have seen and done a similar thing. Moreover, Paul heard unspeakable words which it is not lawful for a human being to utter. Jesus, who was superior to all these men, is said to have spoken the Word of God to his disciples privately, and especially in places of retreat. But what he said has not been recorded. . . .
>
> John teaches us the difference between matters that may and that may not be written down when he says that he heard seven thunders teaching him about certain subjects, and forbidding him to commit their words to writing.[1]

While subsequent interpreters have not accepted Origen's suggestion that Ezekiel's consumption of the scroll served to safeguard the contents of the scroll from unworthy eyes,[2] the link he drew between Rev 10:4 and 2 Cor 12:4 has remained intriguing. In this study I will neither presuppose nor demonstrate any literary inter-

---

An earlier version of this chapter appeared in the *SBL Seminar Papers, 1994* (SBLSP 33; Atlanta: Scholars Press, 1994), 182–202.

1. *Contra Celsum* 6:6. Translation adapted from that by Henry Chadwick (Cambridge: Cambridge University Press, 1965). Also see Origen, *In Ioannis Evangelium* 13:5, where Rev 10:4 and 2 Cor 12:4 are brought to bear on John 21:25.

2. See E. F. Davis, *Swallowing the Scroll: Textuality and the Dynamics of Discourse in Ezekiel's Prophecy* (Bible and Literature Series 21; Sheffield: Almond, 1989).

dependency between Rev 10 and 2 Cor 12:1–10, and I do not intend to suggest that both texts reflect a common underlying source.[3]

I seek to understand the prohibition in Rev 10:4 by reading it side by side with 2 Cor 12:4, insisting on this undertaking despite Jurgen Roloff's dismissive verdict that "it is too simple to see an analogy here with the heavenly visions that were imparted to Paul and whose contents he consciously set aside from his preaching to the churches as religious encounters that concerned him only in a very personal way."[4] Andre Feuillet leaves the door to a juxtaposition of Rev 10 and 2 Cor 12:1–10 just barely open, clarifying Rev 10:4 by pointing to Dan 8:26 and Rev 22:10 with the claim that

> The sense of these two texts is so clear that it should be unnecessary to look any farther for the sense of our passage. The idea of the communication of heavenly messages which must not be revealed until a long time after they are read, and to be kept secret in the meanwhile, is a common feature of the Apocalyptic literature in general. Commentators of this passage have often suggested some sort of divine revelation of a particularly unspeakable nature, such as those which St. Paul describes in 2 Cor. XII:4. We would not wish to exclude this last explanation . . . given the fact that John, unlike Daniel, is commanded not to seal what has been written, but to seal and not to write.[5]

I want to pry the door just a bit further open than Feuillet leaves it, allowing movement in both directions by suggesting that the grounds for studying Rev 10 and 2 Cor 12:1–10 side by side are more substantial than the secrecy motif and Paul's use of *apokalypsis* in 2 Cor 12:1, 7.[6] It may be worth noting that while interpreters of Rev 10 occasionally refer to 2 Cor 12:1–10, interpreters of 2 Cor 12 only rarely make any mention of Rev 10. My study will indirectly suggest that this oversight is unfortunate, because a comparison of the two texts also substantially clarifies Paul's argument in 2 Cor 12.

Important studies have already investigated dream, vision and heavenly ascent narratives in the Greco-Roman context, and in the literature of both Second Temple Judaism and early Christianity.[7] Several more specific studies have focused on 2 Cor

---

3. The background and context of 2 Cor 12 have been the focus of extensive study. See, for example, J. W. Bowker, "'Merkabah' Visions and the Visions of Paul," *JSS* 16 (1971), 157–73; H. J. Klauck, "Die Himmelfahrt des Paulus (2 Kor 12,2–4) in der koptischen Paulus-Apokalypse aus Nag Hammadi (NHC V/2)," *Studien zum Neuen Testament und seiner Umwelt* 10 (1985): 151–190; P. Schafer, "NT and Hekhalot Literature: The Journey into Heaven in Paul and the Merkavah Mysticism," *JJS* 35 (1984): 19–35; J. D. Tabor, *Things Unutterable: Paul's Ascent to Paradise in its Greco-Roman, Judaic, and Early Christian Contexts* (Studies in Judaism; Lanham, Md.: University Press of America, 1986).

4. *The Revelation of John* (Continental Commentaries; Minneapolis: Fortress, 1993), 124.

5. "The Value of the Apocalypse for the Solution of the Eschatological Problem," in *Johannine Studies* (Staten Island, N.Y.: Alba House, 1965), 219.

6. Thanks to Michael F. Hull, whose insightful suggestions prompted me to investigate these texts more closely.

7. See M. Dean-Otting, *Heavenly Journeys: A Study of the Motif in Hellenistic Jewish Literature* (Judentum und Umwelt; Frankfurt: Lang, 1984); J. S. Hanson, "Dreams and Visions in the Graeco-

12.[8] With that in mind, this paper has limited goals and advances modest claims, also hoping to steer clear of the peril of what Samuel Sandmel called "parallelomania."[9] Gershom Scholem yielded to this temptation, comparing 2 Cor 12:1–4 with the story of the four rabbis in *pardes,* a comparison judged methodologically inconsistent by Peter Schäfer.[10]

Hoping to avoid this danger and others that might arise from embarking on a comparative study in the strict sense, I prefer to identify what follows as a juxtapositional study. It will proceed according to the following itinerary. After presenting a broad overview of the context and organization of Rev 10 and then of 2 Cor 12:1–10, I will offer a series of three progressive juxtapositions: (1) knowing and not telling; (2) the scroll and the thorn; (3) contests of authority in context. At each point I will present material from Rev 10 and then from 2 Cor 12:1–10, juxtaposing these texts in order to see what can be teased out at the end.

Reflection on Waldemar Janzen's "Withholding the Word" provided the catalyst that set the present study in motion. Commenting on Jer 42:1–6, Janzen focuses on v. 4, the prophet's response to the people's request for prayer. Jeremiah replies, "Very well, I am going to pray to the Lord your God as you request, and whatever the Lord answers you I will tell you; I will keep nothing back from you." Janzen hypothesizes that these words of reassurance reflect a "century-old tension between prophet and community" and that "In this tension the prophet's strength lay solely in the access to the divine word, and to pronounce it or to withhold it was the only leverage he could exert."[11]

Both Rev 10 and 2 Cor 12 present tensions between disclosure and non-disclosure: the narrator withholds information he has received during an ecstatic audition and informs the audience in writing that he knows more than he is permitted to divulge.[12] Much effort has been expended in satisfying scholarly curiosity over what

---

Roman World and Early Christianity," *ANRW* 23.2: 1395–427; M. Himmelfarb, *Ascent to Heaven in Jewish & Christian Apocalypses* (New York: Oxford University Press, 1993); A. F. Segal, "Heavenly Ascent in Hellenistic Judaism, Early Christianity, and Their Environment," *ANRW* 23.2:1333–94.

8. See Tabor, *Things Unutterable.* Also see Klauck, "Die Himmelfahrt des Paulus," 151–190; and B. H. Young, "The Ascension Motif of 2 Corinthians 12 in Jewish, Christian, and Gnostic Texts," *GTJ* 9 (1988): 73–103. In *Paradise Now and Not Yet: Studies in the Role of the Heavenly Dimension in Paul's Thought with Special Reference to His Eschatology* (Cambridge: Cambridge University Press, 1981), 71–86, A. T. Lincoln devotes a section of his chapter on 2 Corinthians to the third heaven in 2 Cor 12.

9. "Parallelomania," *JBL* 81 (1962): 1–13.

10. G. Scholem, *Jewish Gnosticism, Merkabah Mysticism, and Talmudic Tradition* (2d rev. ed.; New York: Jewish Theological Seminary of America, 1965), 14–19; Schafer, "New Testament and Hekhalot Literature," 19–35. Like Scholem, J. W. Bowker ("'Merkabah' Visions and the Visions of Paul," *JSS* 16 [1971]: 57–73) is drawn too easily into comparisons of Paul's visions with rabbinical materials.

11. "Withholding the Word," in *Traditions in Transition: Turning Points in Biblical Faith* (ed. B. Halpern and J. D. Levenson; Winona Lake, Ind.: Eisenbrauns, 1981), 100.

12. Such literary tensions between disclosure and non-disclosure are by no means confined to biblical literature. In Apuleius's *The Golden Ass* (XI, 23), Lucius only reluctantly provides partial satisfaction for readers curious to know what transpired and what he saw during his initiation in the temple.

the seven thunders might have said in Rev 10:3 and just which things are "not to be told, that no mortal is permitted to repeat" in 2 Cor 12:4, yet little has been made of these texts as expressions of the connection between narrative control and rhetorical strategy. I will propose that, in different ways, the apostle Paul and the prophet John exploit the tension between disclosure and non-disclosure of heavenly information to reassert their authority in crisis situations where they perceive threats to that authority. In response to such dangers, the restriction of access to information is an exercise of the power which Paul claims as an apostle and which John claims as a prophet.

In both texts, disclosure follows nondisclosure. John is forbidden to write what the seven thunders said, yet he must then take the open scroll from the angel's hand, swallow it and embody its contents in prophetic proclamation. Paul stands under the prohibition to reveal the *arrēta rēmata* but receives instead the *skolops tē sarki* by which he is enabled to pronounce a more appropriately apostolic proclamation of Christ's power perfected in weakness.

REVELATION 10 AND 2 CORINTHIANS 12:1–10 IN CONTEXT

REVELATION 10

Formally, Rev 10 is commonly understood as a prophetic commissioning or commissioning scene. With Rev 11:1–14, it falls between the sounding of the sixth trumpet (9:13–21) and the seventh trumpet (11:15–19), constituting the second of three so-called intercalations (7:1–17; 10:1–11:14; 12:1–14:20).[13] In addition, Rev 10:1–11:13 falls between the announcement in 9:12, "The first woe has passed. There are still two woes to come" and the announcement in 11:14 that the second woe has passed and that the third is imminent.[14] What follows Rev 10 is the symbolic measuring of the sanctuary (11:1–2) and a narration of the activity and the fate of the two prophetic witnesses (11:3–13), a description that maintains a thread of thematic continuity with the order John receives in 10:11 to "prophesy again about many peoples and nations and languages and kings."[15]

Lucius then requires that his readers hold the disclosure in confidence: "Ecce tibi retuli quae, quamvis audita, ignores tamen necesse est: ergo quod solum potest sine piaculo ad profanorum intelligentias enuntiari, referam."

13. See J. Lambrecht, "A Structuration of Revelation 4, 1–22, 5," in *L'Apocalypse johannique et l'Apocalyptique dans le Nouveau Testament* (ed. J. Lambrecht; BETL 53; Gembloux, Belgium: J. Duculot, 1980), 95–99. I agree with C. H. Giblin, who contends that the first two intercalations are better understood as enlargements of the sixth seal and the sixth trumpet, not interludes or intercalations (*The Book of Revelation: The Open Book of Prophecy* [GNS 34; Collegeville, Minn.: Liturgical Press, 1991], 90, 108).

14. See U. Vanni, *La struttura letteraria dell'Apocalisse* (Aloisiana 8a; Brescia: Morcelliana, 1980), 131–33; Giblin, *Book of Revelation*, 116–17.

15. On Rev 11, see C. H. Giblin, "Revelation 11.1–13: Its Form, Function, and Contextual Integration," *NTS* 30 (1984): 433–59. E. Lohmeyer is among those who maintain that Rev 11:1–14 presents the contents of the open scroll of Rev 10 (*Die Offenbarung des Johannes* [HNT 16; Tübingen: Mohr Siebeck, 1970], 87).

As a commissioning scene, Rev 10 builds on the inaugural vision of 1:9–20 and introduces a new element, an open scroll in the hand of a mighty angel (10:2) which is mentioned again in 10:8 and once again in 10:9–10.[16] Mention of a scroll links this chapter with the seven-sealed scroll in Rev 5, a scroll which is progressively unsealed by the Lamb beginning in 6:1. The angelic command to swallow the scroll and John's execution of that order in 10:8–11 recalls Ezek 2:8–3:11, in which the same symbolic gesture forms part of Ezekiel's commissioning vision. The ingestion of this document underscores and amplifies the command John receives from the risen Christ during his inaugural vision: "Write in a book what you see and send it to the seven churches" (1:11).[17]

Revelation 10 falls fairly neatly into three sections: vv. 1–4, 5–7 and 8–11. Verses 1–4 introduce the vision of a powerful angel's descent from heaven, describing that angel's appearance (v. 1) and his position straddling land and sea (v. 2). The seer mentions the open scroll in the angel's right hand without further comment on its significance, moving quickly to mention the angel's outcry like a lion's roar (v. 3). The voice of the seven thunders follows (v. 3), with the seer's attempt to record this audition and the double imperative pronounced by a heavenly voice demanding that the seer seal up what the seven thunders said and not write it down (v. 4).

The angel of 10:1 is reintroduced in v. 5, a reintroduction which repeats the earlier description of the angel's position. This angel's solemn oath (v. 6) looks ahead to the seventh trumpet and, with an allusion to Amos 3:7, declares God's announcement of the divine *mystērion* to the prophets. It is significant that the second (10:5–7) and third (10:8–11) sections conclude with references to prophecy, the second focusing on the prophets as privileged recipients of divine disclosures (10:7) and the third focusing on John's prophetic activity.

In 10:8–11, the heavenly voice of v. 4 is reintroduced with specific reference to its previous hearing. In v. 8 the narrator tells us, "the voice I heard from heaven spoke to me again." Once again a two part imperative is issued: the heavenly voice commands the seer to take the scroll from the angel's right hand, and the angel orders the seer to ingest the scroll (v. 9). As he does so, and as the scroll's sweet taste in his mouth gives way to bitterness in his stomach (v. 10), the seer's renewed prophetic obligations are disclosed (v. 11).

2 Corinthians 12:1–10

Despite the notorious difficulties involved in understanding the composition history of Paul's correspondence with the Corinthians, nearly all scholars acknowledge a dramatic change in tone from 2 Cor 9 to 2 Cor 10–13, a shift that suggests the original independence of these latter four chapters from the preceding chapters. Regardless of how they address the problem of the literary integrity of 2 Corinthians,

---

16. The three occurrences of *biblaridion* in Rev 10:2, 9, 10 are the only NT instances of this expression. It is clear that the *biblion* of 10:8 is the same document.

17. See Vanni, *La Struttura letteraria*, 134–40.

most interpreters recognize the integrity of chapters 10–13 as polemical chapters in which Paul engages in an energetic self-defense of his apostolic mission against those whom he brands as "false apostles" (2 Cor 11:13).[18] Formally, these chapters can be classified as ironic apology.[19]

Second Corinthians 12:1–10 must be understood within the context of the "fool's speech," 2 Cor 11:1–12:13, in which Paul sets aside the reticence of chapter 10. There he expresses unwillingness to engage in boastful self-promotion in response to his opponents' claims and justifies this reluctance in 10:17, "Let the one who boasts, boast in the Lord."[20] In 11:1 Paul introduces his change in strategy by asking the indulgence of his readers: "I wish you would bear with me in a little foolishness. Do bear with me!" In 11:16–21, he moves on to establish safe rhetorical distance between the modest Paul of 10:17, who would only boast in the Lord, and a Paul who finds himself compelled to engage in spirited boasting. He does so by playing the fool, and by boasting in character as such to match his opponents' claims with even stronger counterclaims (11:21b–33). The "fool's speech" proper, introduced in 11:1–21a, extends from 11:21b through 12:10. Second Corinthians 12:11–13 serves as the conclusion of the "fool's speech" (12:11: "I have been a fool!),[21] and in 12:14–13:10 Paul warns the Corinthians of his imminent return to their city.[22]

As for 2 Cor 12:1–10, Paul's "fool's speech" continues there under a new heading, "I will go on to visions and revelations of the Lord."[23] This pericope itself can be subdivided into two sections, vv.1–4 and 5–10.[24] Each section begins with a mention of boasting: *kauchasthai dei* (v. 1) and *hyper tou toioutou kauchēsomai* (v. 5). Both sections mention revelations: v. 1 *apokalypseis kyriou*; v. 7: *tōn apokalypseōn*.[25] The

---

18. See V. P. Furnish, *II Corinthians* (AB 32A; Garden City, N.Y.: Doubleday, 1984), 30–54; R. P. Martin, *2 Corinthians* (WBC 40; Waco, Tex.: Word, 1986), xl–lii.

19. On the genre(s) of 2 Cor 10–13, see J. W. McCant, "Paul's Thorn of Rejected Apostleship," *NTS* 34 (1988): 551–52.

20. Furnish suggests that this may be Paul's adaptation of Jer 9:24 (LXX) (*II Corinthians*, 474).

21. Martin (*2 Corinthians*, 430) notes that *gegona afrōn* in 12:11 is the terminus of the inclusion that opens in 11:1 (*afrosynes*).

22. On the organization of 2 Cor 10–13, see Ulrich Heckel, *Kraft in Schwachheit: Untersuchungen zu 2. Kor 10–13* (WUNT 2/56; Tubingen: Mohr-Siebeck, 1993), 6–50.

23. Against Windisch and Bietenhard, Furnish sides with R. Bultmann and D. Georgi in suggesting that "the absence of articles and the use of the plural indicate only that Paul is taking up a general topic, not that he has numerous and specific visions and revelations in mind" (*II Corinthians*, 524).

24. J. A. Crafton follows a different approach, suggests that at this point Paul's fool's speech includes three anecdotes that parody his opponents' strategy: the story of Paul's escape from Damascus as a parody of heroism in battle (11:32–33), a heavenly ascent in which no revelation is received (12:2–4), and in 12:7–9 a failed prayer for miraculous healing (*The Agency of the Apostle: A Dramatistic Analysis of Paul's Responses to Conflict in 2 Corinthians* [JSNTSup 51; Sheffield: JSOT Press, 1991] 129).

25. The plural is found only here in the NT, whereas Paul uses the singular quite frequently and in several different senses. For example, according to Furnish (*II Corinthians*, 524), it occurs in Rom 2:5; 8:19; 1 Cor 1:7 referring to the manifestation of eschatological events; in Gal 1:12 to refer to the revelation by which Paul received the Gospel; in Gal 2:2 to describe divine instruction regarding his

turn from third person description to the first person singular in 12:5 also marks the distinction between the first section and the second.[26]

Focusing still more closely, commentators who note the parallelism in 2 Cor 12:2–4 come to very different conclusions about its significance. Some have taken the parallel descriptions of heavenly ascent together with the plural *optasias kai apokalypseis kyriou* in v. 1 and the plural *apokalypseōn* in v. 7 as indications that Paul is describing more than one heavenly ascent.[27] J. D. Tabor suggests that Paul presents a two stage ascent with the third heaven as an intermediate goal and Paradise as its summit.[28] However, most interpreters hold that these verses describe one experience, and that the parallelism can be successfully explained as something other than redundancy.[29] A. T. Lincoln offers a psychological explanation for the literary parallelism, opining that Paul, reluctant to reveal such an intimately personal experience, "has to repeat himself before he can bring himself to conclude the account."[30] A more likely solution is offered by Josef Zmijewski, who recognizes vv. 2–4 as an instance of synthetic parallelism whereby the second description takes up and advances what is presented in the first description of the same event.[31]

THE FIRST JUXTAPOSITION: KNOWING AND NOT TELLING

REVELATION 10

In the transition from vision to audition that takes place in 10:3, John moves from detailing the mighty angel's appearance and position to a description of the angel's outcry. He writes that the angel's loud cry sounds like a lion's roaring, but fails to indicate whether the angel is saying anything, whether this outcry is articulate speech.[32] This is not the Apocalypse's only comparison of a voice or a loud voice with

---

itinerary; and in 1 Cor 14:6, 26 to indicate revelation which took place during the public worship of the Corinthian church.

26. For a review of the various explanations of why Paul uses the third person to describe what commentators agree is a report of personal experience, see Furnish, *II Corinthians*, 543–44.

27. Martin, himself convinced that these verses refer to one experience, lists several patristic commentators (Clement of Alexandria, Irenaeus and Tertullian) and several modern authors (Denney, Plummer, Filson, Schlatter) who maintain that Paul presents two separate events here (*2 Corinthians*, 403). An even more complete presentation of the various positions is presented by Heckel, *Kraft in Schwachheit*, 57–58.

28. *Things Unutterable*, 115–21. C. Rowland also holds that Paul presents a two-stage ascent (*The Open Heaven: A Study of Apocalyptic in Judaism and Early Christianity* [London: SPCK, 1982], 381–82).

29. *II Corinthians*, 542. Also see J. Zmijewski, *Der Stil der paulinischen "Narrenrede": Analyse der Sprachgestaltung in 2 Kor 11,1–12,10 als Beitrag zur Methodik von Stiluntersuchungen neutestamentlicher Texte* (BBB 52; Cologne and Bonn: Peter Hanstein, 1978), 331–35.

30. "'Paul the Visionary:' The Setting and Significance of the Rapture to Paradise in 2 Cor 12:1–10," *NTS* 25 (1978–79): 204–20; also idem, *Paradise Now and Not Yet*, 77.

31. Ibid., 335.

32. On the use of *mykatai* in 10:4, see P. Prigent, *L'Apocalypse de Saint Jean* (CNT 14; Lausanne: Delachaux & Niestlé, 1981), 152.

some imposing sound from the natural realm. In 1:10, John describes "a loud voice like a trumpet" which addresses him, a voice John turns to face and to recognize as one "like the Son of Man," the risen Christ whose voice is then compared to the sound of many waters in 1:15. John's heavenly ascent in Rev 4 is introduced in v. 1 by a reference to the same voice described according to its first articulation as "the first voice, which I had heard speaking to me like a trumpet."

In Rev 14:1–5, John's vision of the Lamb standing on Mount Zion together with the 144,000 is accompanied by an audition where a triple comparison describes the sound John hears: "I heard a voice from heaven like the sound of many waters and like the sound of loud thunder; the voice I heard was like the sound of harpists playing on their harps." Several chapters earlier, the description of the voice in Rev 6:1 is even closer to what we find in 10:3. There the opening of the first seal is followed by the articulate speech of one of the four living creatures, "calling out, as with a voice of thunder" to summon forth the bow-wielding rider on a white horse.

In the context of Rev 10, then, it would be consistent with what we find elsewhere in the Apocalypse that sounds made by an angel would represent articulate speech, whether or not the contents of that articulation are specified. However, elsewhere in the Apocalypse, *phōnē* is also used to denote inarticulate noise rather than the sound of coherent speech. In several instances, these noises are likened to other and presumably somewhat more familiar sounds. For example, in Rev 9:7 the wings of the locusts unleashed at the sound of the fifth trumpet make a noise like that "of many chariots with horses rushing into battle." It is possible, then, that Rev 10:3 presents a tension between the articulate and the inarticulate, a tension that is highlighted by the distinction between the angelic shout and the utterance of the seven thunders. This ambiguity is underlined by the way in which the auditory sequence is presented: "when he shouted, the seven thunders sounded their voices."[33]

In the Apocalypse, thunder is mentioned in four instances as a member of the formula *astrapai kai phōnai kai brontai* (4:5; 8:5; 11:19; 16:18), a formula that signals theophanies and their effects.[34] The common contention that the sevenfold *qôl YHWH* of Ps 29 furnishes the background for the seven thunders of Rev 10:3 does not simplify matters.[35] While the psalm provides the right number and the right connection between thunder and divine speech, the *qôl YHWH* of the psalm does not *say* anything intelligible. That does not mean this voice is without effect: the thunderous sound has a profound, all-encompassing cosmic impact that manifests the power of its speaker.

What does establish the sound of the seven thunders as articulate speech is their

---

33. To Lohmeyer, the angel's outcry cannot be limited to words because of its divine nature. The angel's shout and the reply of the seven thunders is an ineffable divine dialogue to which only John is privy (*Die Offenbarung des Johannes*, 85).

34. See Vanni, *La Struttura letteraria*, 141–48; R. Bauckham, *The Climax of Prophecy: Studies on the Book of Revelation* (Edinburgh: T&T Clark, 1993), 199–209; Lambrecht, "Structuration of Rev 4, 1–22, 5," 93–95.

35. See H. B. Swete, *The Apocalypse of St. John* (London: Macmillan, 1909), 127–28.

hearer's act of writing down their utterance. Though aborted by the intervention of a heavenly voice in 10:4, this writing can be understood as an instance of the sort of prophetic activity that is called for in 10:11. It might be said that an allusion to Amos 3:7–8 frames Rev 10:4, beginning with the comparison of the angel's cry to a lion's roar in Rev 10:3 and concluding with same angel's first articulate utterance in Rev 10:7. If this is so, the seer's action in Rev 10:4a can be understood in the light of Amos 3:8 "The lion has roared; who will not fear? The Lord God has spoken; who can but prophesy?" Let us take this one step further: if John's activity in Rev 10:4a can be understood as appropriate submission to the prophetic impulse, then the prohibition that follows in 10:4b becomes that much more puzzling, since it short-circuits a prophetic undertaking that Rev 1:3, 11 has specifically qualified as a matter of writing, a literary undertaking.

Unannounced, a disembodied heavenly voice interrupts John's writing of the utterance by the seven thunders. The voice pronounces a twofold prohibition: *sphragison ha elalēsan hai hepta brontai, kai mē auta grapsēs*. Ugo Vanni points out that the two imperatives are not synonymous: the first, *sphragison*, implies that something has already been written; the second, *mē grapsēs*, forbids writing.[36] The order to seal up what the seven thunders said reflects Dan 12:4, "But you, Daniel, keep the words secret and the book sealed until the time of the end." As Roloff points out, this is an instance of a motif common in the apocalyptic literature: the visionary seals the written disclosure of the divine plan in order to conceal it in the present and to preserve it intact for the eschatological generation to read.[37]

Revelation 22:10 takes up this apocalyptic motif: the order not to seal up the "the prophetic words of this book" is explained, "for the time is near." The command to leave the book unsealed indicates the proximity of the end time, a proximity proclaimed from the very beginning of the Apocalypse (1:3). From 6:1 to 8:1, the unsealing of the seven-sealed scroll introduced in 5:1 indicates the progressive movement towards that goal. The seven-sealed scroll is described in 5:1 as *gegrammenon esōthen kai opisthen* and the "prophetic words" in 22:10 have already been written in "this book." Yet, in the case of Rev 10:4, H. B. Swete notes that in Rev 10:4, "the application of the metaphor to unwritten utterances is a bold innovation."[38]

G. R. Beasley-Murray minimizes the impact of this innovation, arguing that while *sphragison* should mean "Don't make known what you have written," in the context of Rev 10 it means "Don't reveal what you have heard."[39] A closer look at

---

36. *La Struttura letteraria*, 137–38. Here Vanni takes issue with W. Bousset, who argued that the two imperatives function all but synonymously here (*Die Offenbarung des Johannes* [MeyerK 16; Göttingen: Vandenhoeck & Ruprecht, 1906], 309). R. H. Charles, while recognizing that *sphragizein* is "a technical apocalyptic term," nevertheless holds that *sphragison* and *mē grapsēs* "are practically synonymous" (*A Critical and Exegetical Commentary on the Revelation of St. John* [ICC; Edinburgh: T&T Clark, 1920], 1:262).

37. *Revelation*, 124.

38. *Apocalypse of St. John*, 128.

39. *Revelation* (rev. ed.; NCB; Grand Rapids: Eerdmans, 1978), 172.

seals and sealing in the Apocalypse suggests that this suggestion is at least slightly overcasual. The noun *sphragis* and the verb *sphragizō* appear in connection with written documents that are to be unsealed or sealed, and with reference to the marking of the faithful with "the seal of the living God" (7:2). This feature of the Apocalypse's symbolic grammar makes it safe to suggest that the heavenly voice's command in 10:4, *sphragison ha elalēsan hai epta brontai* identifies the utterance of the seven thunders as an intelligible divine pronouncement. In contrast to the divine seal that marks the faithful, those who belong to the Beast are distinguished by its mark (*charagma*) on their right hands or foreheads (13:16), imposed by the beast from the land, which is identified in 19:20 as the "false prophet."

Vanni suggests the likelihood that the aorist *mē grapsēs*, the second part of the voice's command in 10:4, has a punctual sense, "do not write (for the moment)." To Vanni, this indicates that the seer is to remember what he has heard (sealing it securely in his memory) in order to communicate it at the appropriate moment in the future.[40] This understanding is reinforced by the connection between Rev 10:4 and the eschatological sealing motif of Dan 12:4.[41] According to Rev 10:7, the appropriate eschatological moment during which prophetic transmission of the divine *mystērion* is called for will come with the sound of the seventh angel's trumpet.[42]

All of this frames the question of the purpose and place in Rev 10 of the angelic shout, the response of the seven thunders and the prohibition against recording that utterance in vv. 3–4. Charles Homer Giblin has proposed that "God's silencing (10:4) the noisy thunders, which replied to the angel's roar (10:3), enables the angel articulately to proclaim (10:6–7) the document which he holds (10:6–7)."[43] This strikes me as somewhat reminiscent of suggestions offered by early twentieth century commentators, including W. Bousset and R. H. Charles, according to whom 10:3–4 is something of an interruption.

Bousset believed that the order to seal up the pronouncement of the seven thunders served to justify John's omission of what must have been a well-known septenary sequence.[44] That is based on the view that the presence of the article in 10:3, *hai hepta brontai*, means that the utterance of "the seven thunders" was an extant source with which John's audience would have been familiar. Charles labeled these verses an intermezzo that interrupts the Dan 12–inspired vision of the mighty angel, and that vision resumes in v. 5 with the reintroduction of the angel and the subsequent report of his oath. Rejecting Bousset's hypothesis, Charles argues that if the aim of the intermezzo were "purely literary," this would suggest that John had stepped aside from

---

40. *La Struttura letteraria*, 138.

41. On this motif in Daniel, see J. J. Collins, *Daniel* (Hermeneia; Minneapolis: Fortress, 1993), 341–42, 399; A. Lacocque, *Le Livre de Daniel* (CAT 15b; Neuchatel: Delachaux & Niestle, 1976), 181.

42. Vanni, *La Struttura letteraria*, 138.

43. *Book of Revelation*, 109 n. 85.

44. *Die Offenbarung des Johannes*, 309. Also see I. T. Beckwith, *The Apocalypse of John: Studies in Introduction with a Critical and Exegetical Commentary* (New York: Macmillan, 1919), 577–78.

his visionary experience to take up the work of an editor. Charles proposes instead that we "treat the statement as a bona fide one, and view it in the same light as St. Paul in 2 Cor xii. 4."[45]

It is precisely at this point that we must be especially cautious about falling into the kind of facile comparison of Rev 10:4 and 2 Cor 12:4 that preconceives the "things that are not to be told, that no mortal is permitted to repeat" of 2 Cor 12:4 as matters too sacred to be repeated and as the equivalent of what the seven thunders said.

2 CORINTHIANS 12:1–10

Paul's rapture into Paradise yields only an audition report: no vision report is provided, in striking contrast to other accounts of heavenly ascent, which contain extensive reports of disclosures are made to the visionary.[46] Further, 2 Cor 12:4 gives no specific account of what was heard, except for the twofold description *arrēta rēmata ha ouk exon anthrōpō lalēsai*. Both peculiarities make sense if 2 Cor 12:1–4 is to be understood in the context of Paul's "fool's speech" as a parody of a heavenly ascent, as H. D. Betz has indicated.[47]

The scanty double designation of what Paul heard warrants a closer look. First, the compound expression, *arrēta rēmata*, is a NT *hapax*. Outside the NT, *arrētos* refers to that which is not to be spoken either because it is beyond human powers or because it is too sacred to be divulged.[48] The second phrase, *ha ouk exon anthrōpō lalēsai*, indicates that the *arrēta rēmata* are neither ineffable nor unintelligible, since they are the object of a prohibition. Whatever they may have been, Paul is forbidden to divulge the unutterable utterances he heard.[49]

Paul's own nondisclosure of the *arrēta rēmata* has not prevented both ancient and more recent readers of 2 Cor 12:1–4 from speculating about what Paul heard and about its significance both as an experience and an account. In antiquity, Irenaeus testified to gnostic conjectures about and elaborations of Paul's heavenly ascent (*Adv. Haer.* II.30.7), of which the Nag Hammadi *Apocalypse of Paul* (NHC V/2) is the clearest extant example.[50]

The positions of recent interpreters can be located along two axes, either suggesting Paul's reticent reluctance to share what must have been an intimately personal

---

45. *Revelation*, 1:261–62.
46. See Himmelfarb, *Ascent to Heaven*, 72–94; Rowland, *Open Heaven*, 75–189, "The Content of the Heavenly Mysteries"; M. E. Stone, "Lists of Revealed Things in the Apocalyptic Literature," in *Magnalia Dei: The Mighty Acts of God. Essays on the Bible and Archaeology in Memory of G. Ernest Wright* (ed. F. M. Cross, W. E. Lemke, and P. D. Miller Jr.; Garden City, N.Y.: Doubleday, 1976), 414–52.
47. *Der Apostel Paulus und die sokratische Tradition: Eine exegetische Untersuchung zu seiner "Apologie" 2 Korinther 10–13* (BHT 45; Tübingen: Mohr Siebeck, 1972), 84–92.
48. BAGD, s.v. *arrētos*. Also R. P. Spittler, "The Limits of Ecstasy: An Exegesis of 2 Corinthians 12:1–10," in *Current Issues in Biblical and Patristic Interpretation* (ed. G. F. Hawthorne; Grand Rapids: Eerdmans, 1975), 263–64; Tabor, *Things Unutterable*, 122.
49. See Martin, *2 Corinthians*, 405–6.
50. See Klauck, "Die Himmelfahrt des Paulus"; Young, "Ascension Motif," 95–99.

experience, or else emphasizing the irony of this heavenly ascent narrative in the context of the "fool's speech."

Along the first axis of investigation, C. K. Barrett suggests that, "far from cultivating this kind of experience," Paul "rather disparaged it, and laid no weight on it in his exposition and defence of the Gospel."[51] Noting that comments like Barrett's are typical of the majority opinion, Tabor champions a different view, denying that Paul disparaged ecstatic experience and contending instead, "his recounting of his ascent to heaven is his way of affirming in the boldest possible manner that he is one commended by the Lord."[52] In a somewhat similar vein, Martin writes "Though we may come away somewhat frustrated and disappointed at the lack of information given here . . . perhaps Calvin's dictum is right in that this experience was 'to strengthen Paul by special means that he might not give way, but might persevere undaunted'."[53]

Along a second axis, Betz holds that the heavenly ascent narrative belongs entirely to the role of the boasting fool that Paul takes on here for the sake of the argument against his opponents. To Betz, this leaves open the question of whether 2 Cor 12:1–4 actually represents an incident in Paul's own life.[54] The emphasis Betz has placed on situating the argument of 2 Cor 12:1–4 in the context of Paul's argument in 2 Cor 10–13 represents a fundamental reorientation of attention from historical and biographical concerns to rhetorical and literary questions. More typically, historical critical efforts had been directed toward unearthing the autobiographical substratum of this heavenly ascent narrative, seeking to establish the precise reference of details like "fourteen years ago" in 12:2 and searching for some correlation of this account either with the descriptions of Paul visionary experience in Acts (especially the accounts in Acts 9; 22; 26 of the Damascus road experience), or with the autobiographical material in Gal 1–2 and 1 Cor 15.[55]

THE SECOND JUXTAPOSITION: A SCROLL AND A THORN

REVELATION 10

Commands are addressed to the visionary in two closely interrelated instances, the first negative and the second positive. The first is the order pronounced by a heavenly voice in 10:4 to seal up what the seven thunders said, to refrain from writing down their pronouncement. In 10:8 the same voice issues another order. It commands John to take the open scroll from the hand of the mighty angel whose descent from heaven was announced in 10:1, whose outcry in 10:3 was followed by the

---

51. *The Second Epistle to the Corinthians* (HNTC; New York: Harper & Row, 1973), 34.
52. *Things Unutterable*, 38.
53. *2 Corinthians*, 406.
54. *Der Apostel Paulus*, 89.
55. Lincoln, who accuses Betz of going "too far in subordinating content to form" (Lincoln, "Paul the Visionary," 209), himself regards 2 Cor 12 as a "valuable glimpse into the life of Paul the visionary" (ibid., 204).

utterance of the seven thunders, and on the basis of whose oath in 10:5–7 the eschatological import of prophetic revelation is made clear. That angel itself addresses John in 10:9, specifying the voice's command in v. 8 by ordering John to ingest the scroll. Once John obeys this command, he experiences the effects the angel warned him to expect: "it was sweet as honey in my mouth, but when I had eaten it, my stomach was made bitter" (10:10). At that point, *both* the angel and the heavenly voice address John, insisting that he prophesy again.[56]

In Ezek 2:8—3:3, from which Rev 10:8–11 draws its principal metaphor, the scroll which the prophet is to eat "had writing on the front and on the back, and written on it were words of lamentation and mourning and woe" (Ezek 2:10). In Rev 10:2 John tells us that the scroll the angel holds is open, and in v. 8 its openness is mentioned by the heavenly voice that tells John to take it from the angel. Despite this emphasis on the scroll's openness, there is no mention of its contents, and commentators have been quick to seek to fill the gap by supplying what the text does not. Suggestions range from Victorinus' identification of the scroll as the Apocalypse itself, to Feuillet's suggestion that while the scroll of Rev 5 is the Old Testament, the little scroll contains the New Testament.[57] Alongside efforts that correlate the open scroll of Rev 10 with the sealed scroll of Rev 5, others take the diminutive designation of this document as a *biblaridion* (10:2, 9, 10) as an indication of its modest extent.[58] Many have suggested that the contents of the little scroll are disclosed in 11:1–13, while some suspect that the little scroll includes all of Rev 12–22.[59] Richard Bauckham straddles the fence: "11:1–13 contains the revelation of the scroll *in nuce*. Later chapters of Revelation will greatly expand on it, but the central and essential message of the scroll is given most clearly here."[60]

Like the utterance of the seven thunders, the contents of the little scroll remain indeterminate: John refrains from writing what he has heard, and refrains from reading the contents of the scroll he ingests into the Revelation. The tension between disclosure and nondisclosure established in 10:4 persists here. In 10:4 John writes

---

56. Swete holds that *legousin* in v. 11 is "the plural of indefinite statement," and so "whether the words come from the heavenly voice (vv. 4, 8) or from the angel (v. 9), or from some unknown source, is not obvious or material" (*Apocalypse of St. John*, 131). After admitting, "The plural *legousin* is difficult," Charles also suggests that it is a plural of indefinite statement (*The Revelation of St. John*, 1:269). I am more sympathetic to Lohmeyer's suggestion that the plural unites the angel and the heavenly voice in a more emphatic pronouncement (*Die Offenbarung des Johannes*, 87). Giblin also recognizes that the plural is significant, for the mention of both voices together focuses attention on the prophetic task they outline in v. 11 (*Book of Revelation*, 109, 111).

57. Victorinus of Pettau, *Commentarii in Apocalypsin* (CSEL 49); Feuillet, "Value of the Apocalypse," 217–18, 227. So also Sweet, *Revelation*, 176.

58. Also see R. Bergmeier, "Die Buchrolle und das Lamm (Apk 5 und 10)," *ZNW* 76 (1985): 225–42.

59. For example, Charles (*Revelation of St. John*, 1:269) and Lohmeyer (*Die Offenbarung des Johannes*, 87) hold that the scroll contains chapter 11. Bousset holds that the scroll contains all of chapters 12–22.

60. *Climax of Prophecy*, 266.

that he has heard what the seven thunders said, that he was about to inscribe their pronouncement, and that he refrained from doing so in obedience to the command of a voice from heaven. John first mentions the open scroll in his description of the angel's appearance in 10:2, just before angel and the seven thunders speak. Then the scroll does not figure any further until vv. 8–11, where he takes it from the angel's hand, swallows it, and experiences the effects about which he had been warned. Thus the mention of the scroll in vv. 2 and 8–11 frames two angelic utterances (the outcry "like a lion's roar" in v. 3 and the oath in vv. 6–7), and the utterance of the seven thunders.

On this basis it might perhaps be concluded that Rev 10 makes the point that eating is more important than writing. That point need not be passed over lightly: I am suggesting that the order to refrain from writing what the seven thunders said is understandable in the light of the subsequent command to ingest the scroll. In other words, John's prophetic attention is redirected from the seven thunders to the scroll. This suggestion finds support in 10:7, where the angel's oath announces that "in the days when the seventh angel is to blow his trumpet, the mystery of God will be fulfilled, as he announced to his servants the prophets." Prevented from writing by a heavenly voice, John's prophetic activity is rechanneled by the very same voice.

This disclosure answers the nondisclosure of 10:4: by taking and swallowing the scroll in 10:10, John becomes the recipient of the *mystērion tou theou* announced by God to *this* prophet. He is the recipient of this disclosure, not its author, and the manner of its reception guarantees the authority and integrity of the disclosure *and* of its prophetic vessel. The scroll John swallows is preserved from the sort of tampering against which 22:18–19 guards the Apocalypse, while John and the scroll become indistinguishable. Once swallowed, the scroll is no longer open or accessible: the disclosure or nondisclosure of its contents depends entirely on the prophet who contains it. Once he has swallowed the scroll, John must prophesy: *dei se palin prophēteusai* (10:11).

2 CORINTHIANS 12:1–10

Most interpreters hold that 2 Cor 12:1–4, 7–10 refer to two distinct incidents, events which fall under the general heading of *optasias kai apokalypseis kyriou*. For example, we have seen that Betz identifies vv. 1–4 as a parody of a heavenly ascent. Betz likewise identifies vv. 7–10 as a parody of an aretalogy that takes the form of a (failed) healing miracle.[61] It might thus be seen as the third member in a series of foolish boasts that begins with the parody of military victory in 11:32.[62]

Robert Price offers a very different understanding of the relationship between vv. 1–4 and 7–10, contending "that the 'revelations' of verse 7 have a more immediate antecedent, i.e., the 'unutterable utterances' . . . of verse 4. Thus the thorn will have

---

61. "Eine Christus-Aretalogie bei Paulus (2 Kor 12,7–10)," *ZTK* 66 (1969): 288–305.
62. See E. A. Judge, "The Conflict of Educational Aims in New Testament Thought," *Journal of Christian Education* 9 (1966): 44–45.

been inflicted in direct connection with the heavenly secrets disclosed to Paul on the particular occasion described in our passage."[63] Price attempts to demonstrate that 2 Cor 12:1–10 portrays a single incident, proposing the following reconstruction: Paul finds himself caught up into heaven. There he is treated to ineffable revelations. Waxing proud over his enviable position, Paul suddenly finds himself the object of attack by a punishing demon or angel. Paul appeals thrice to the exalted Lord on the heavenly throne before him, who finally declares that Paul must learn his lesson, that is, "My grace is sufficient for you, for my power is made perfect in weakness."[64]

Even Price admits, "This picture may seem to some readers a bit too outlandish to be plausible."[65] Yet the effort to salvage some connection between vv. 1–4 and 7–10 may actually be worth exploring. That is because we can identify at least four features which establish a literary bridge between the two sections of 2 Cor 12:1–10, whether or not Paul is referring to a single experience. This remains possible despite Jerry McCant's observation that "Making a transition from the rapture story (12. 1–5) to the thorn in the flesh (12. 7–10) is difficult because of text-critical and stylistic problems in v. 6."[66] The four "bridge" features are:

(1) the reference to boasting in v. 1, in vv. 5–6 (transition) and in v. 9;
(2) the mention of revelations in v. 1 and in v. 7;
(3) the mention of the Lord in v. 1 and in v. 8;
(4) the mention of Christ in v. 2 and in vv. 9–10.

Using these four features, Paul establishes a consistent argument by carrying vocabulary introduced in vv. 1–4 into vv. 7–10. The careful transition from the third person to the first person in v. 5 helps to confirm this. While Price's conclusion that 2 Cor 12:1–10 presents one experience is highly unlikely, these features give evidence that the juxtaposition of the two incidents in 2 Cor 12 is not casual, and that it is not merely a matter of cataloguing parodies that counter the boasts of Paul's opponents.

On the contrary, in v. 7 Paul indicates that the *skolops tē sarki* was given *tē hyperbolē tōn apokalypseōn dio hina mē hyperairomai*. He further qualifies the *skolops tē sarki* as *aggelos Satana, hina mē kolaphizē* and repeats the purpose of this affliction, *hina mē hyperairomai*. 12:7 is notoriously difficult, prompting Barrett to write that it "can hardly be in the form that Paul intended it to have, though it may possibly be in the form in which he wrote, or dictated, it."[67] One of the key issues in translating the verse is the question of its connection with the previous verse. On the one

---

63. "Punished in Paradise (An Exegetical Theory on II Corinthians 12:1–10)," *JSNT* 7 (1980): 35.
64. Ibid, 37.
65. Ibid. Price's theory is rendered more implausible by its uncritical reliance on Scholem's *Jewish Gnosticism, Merkabah Mysticism, and Talmudic Tradition*.
66. "Paul's Thorn of Rejected Apostleship," 564. On the text-critical and stylistic issues involved, see Furnish, *II Corinthians*, 527–28; and also B. M. Metzger, *A Textual Commentary on the Greek New Testament* (n.p.: United Bible Societies, 1971), 585.
67. *Second Epistle to the Corinthians*, 313.

hand, Barrett decides that v. 7a should not be attached to v. 6, and offers "what it is perhaps hardly fair to call a translation, but does represent Paul's meaning and uses his words as far as possible," that is "And because the revelations were so marvellous, that I might not be unduly exalted there was given me a thorn in my flesh, and angel of Satan sent to beat me, that I might not be unduly exalted."[68]

Furnish, on the other hand, follows Zmijewski and links vv. 6 and 7a, and offers the following rendering of vv. 6–7:

> For should I wish to boast, I will not be a fool, for I shall be telling the truth. But I am declining to do this, so that no one can credit me with something beyond what one may see me doing or hear from me, specifically, because of the extraordinary character of the revelations. For this reason, that I not be overly exalted, there was given to me a thorn in the flesh, an angel of Satan to abuse me, that I not be overly exalted.[69]

This version more adequately links the two portions of Paul's boasting in 12:1–10, clarifying the nondisclosure of the *arrēta rēmata ha ouk exon anthrōpōo lalēsai* of 12:4 by redirecting the attention of his audience to the embodied disclosure of Paul's weakness. While the *arrēta rēmata* remained inaccessible, lying "beyond what one may see me doing or hear from me," Paul's weakness was obvious to the Corinthians. Limiting ourselves to evidence of this from chaps. 10–13, in 10:10 we find Paul's quotation of an accusation leveled against him by his opponents at Corinth: "they say, 'His letters are weighty and strong, but his bodily presence is weak, and his speech contemptible'."

12:1–10 paradoxically undoes the contradiction of which the "super-apostles" (11:5) accuse him: by refusing to disclose the unutterable utterances, Paul disarms himself, basing the credibility of his apostolate instead on the weakness of which the *skolops tē sarki* is a token. Whatever the "thorn in the flesh may have been," it occasions Paul's insistent prayer for deliverance. That prayer results in the oracular response, "my grace is sufficient for you, because power is made perfect in weakness," (10:9) that leads to the New Testament's archparadox in v. 10b, "When I am weak, then I am strong."[70]

It is also possible that 12:7–10 sheds a different light on the confessions of ignorance in 12:2–3 about whether the heavenly ascent of the "person in Christ" was in the body or out of the body. Paul professes no such uncertainty in 12:7–10, where

---

68. Ibid., 314–15.
69. Furnish, *II Corinthians*, 513, 528; Zmijewski, *Der Stil der paulinischen "Narrenrede"*, 354–55.
70. See the overview of major proposals about the "thorn in the flesh" provided by Furnish (*II Corinthians*, 548–550), and also K. Prümm, *Diakonia Pneumatos. Der zweite Korintherbrief als Zugang zur apostolischen Botschaft. Auslegung und Theologie* (Rome: Herder, 1960–67), 1:660–64. On 12:9–10, see Heckel, *Kraft in Schwachheit*, 112–20, and Heckel's treatment of the resolution of the paradox in 13:3–4 (ibid., 121–42); G. G. O'Collins, "Power Made Perfect in Weakness: 2 Cor 12:9–10," *CBQ* 33 (1971): 528–37.

the *skolops tē sarki* yields knowledge of weakness.⁷¹ Uncertainty about embodiment accompanies the nondisclosure of what was heard during the heavenly ascent, while the insistent torment of the thorn in the flesh yields embodied certainty about the message of the paradoxical power of weakness. Thus 2 Cor 12:1–10 presents more than a juxtaposition of two narratives of extraordinary experience: an ironic contrast is established whereby the humiliation of the thorn in the flesh is revealed to be more important for the apostle than the exaltation of the heavenly ascent.

The Third Juxtaposition: Contests of Authority in Context

Revelation 10

Revelation 11:7–10 graphically depicts the ghastly fate of the two prophetic witnesses, "because these two prophets had been a torment to the inhabitants of the earth."⁷² In 19:20, the beastly pair first introduced in chapter 13 meet their fate, "thrown alive into the lake of fire that burns with sulfur." One of these, the wonder-working beast from the land, first introduced in 13:11–18, is identified in 19:20 as "the false prophet."

On the heavenly level and on the earthly level, the Apocalypse involves a duel over authority, and, more specifically, over prophetic authority. In the messages to the seven churches (2:1–3:22) it becomes clear that John's voice is not uncontested. The Ephesian church receives praise from the risen Christ because it "tested those who claim to be apostles and found them to be false" (2:2) The Thyatiran church is criticized by the risen Christ for its tolerance of "that woman Jezebel, who calls herself a prophet and is teaching and beguiling my servants to practice fornication and to eat food sacrificed to idols" (2:20).⁷³

John employs three key strategies to defend the prophetic authority of the Apocalypse. The first strategy involves the vilification of opponents, using insults drawn mainly from the biblical repertory. For example, John's opponent at Pergamum is labeled "Balaam, who taught Balak to put a stumbling block before the people of Israel, so that they would eat food sacrificed to idols and practice fornication" (2:14).⁷⁴ Another opponent at Thyatira is labeled "Jezebel," and is accused of the same offense (2:20).

---

71. See E. Schweizer, "σάρξ," *TDNT* 7:125–35; E. Schweizer and F. Baumgartel, "σῶμα κτλ." *TDNT* 7:1024–94. Noting that *sōma* and *sarx* are sometimes equivalent for Paul, Schweizer writes, "In Corinth, Paul came up against a piety in which the chief concern was the spirit.... In contrast Paul speaks of the body. For him this is in the first instance sheer corporeality and as a close equivalent of *sarx* it can denote the concrete presence of the apostle," as it does in 1 Cor 5:3 and 2 Cor 10:10" (ibid., 1063).

72. On the two prophetic witnesses of 11:3–13, see Bauckham, *Climax of Prophecy*, 273–83.

73. See the approach to the messages to the seven churches presented in J.-P. Ruiz, "Betwixt and Between on the Lord's Day: Liturgy and the Apocalypse," *SBL Seminar Papers, 1992* (SBLSP 31; Atlanta: Scholars Press, 1992), 666–71.

74. See Prigent, *L'Apocalypse*, 52.

A second strategy involves John in unmasking the links between his human opponents and God's demonic opponents, and depicting the cosmic battle against God in which they are engaged: "Then I saw the beast and the kings of the earth with their armies gathered to make war against the rider on the horse and his army" (19:19). Just as John's opponents are portrayed as soldiers in the service of demonic powers bound for ultimate defeat, those who side with John are enlisted in the ranks of a heavenly army that is bound for victory.

A third strategy involves John in demonstrating the divine authorization of his own mission and the authority of the text which is its result. This strategy comprises claims in defense of the book itself, including the blessing pronounced on the reader and the audience (1:3), the blessing pronounced on those who heed its prophetic message (22:7), and the curses that threaten those who might add to the book or subtract anything from it (22:18–19). This third strategy also includes John's demonstration of his own divine authorization, and the description of John's specific prophetic portfolio.

This strategy is deployed from the outset: the Apocalypse's very first verse identifies John as the last link in the chain of transmission of disclosure that moves from God to Christ to his angel, and to "his servant John." This is reconfirmed in Jesus' words to John at the end of the book: "It is I, Jesus, who sent my angel to you with this testimony for the churches" (22:16a). During the inaugural vision (1:9–20), John is twice commanded by the "One like the Son of Man" (1:13) to write what he sees (1:11, 19), and the command to write is repeated at the beginning of each of the seven messages to the churches in Asia (2:1, 8, 12, 18; 3:1, 7, 14). John's mission is to transcribe the edicts of the risen Jesus to the churches.

If John's job description were to be surmised exclusively from the data furnished in 1:9–3:22, he might be classified more accurately as a scribe or a secretary than as a prophet. In fact, nowhere in the Apocalypse is John himself directly identified as a prophet. By juxtaposing the interrupted transcription of the seven thunders' utterance with the ingestion of the open scroll, Rev 10 might well function to correct the misperception that prophetic activity was exclusively a scribal undertaking.

Such mid-course corrections are not unusual in the Apocalypse: the two occasions on which John attempts to worship an angel (19:10; 22:8–9) provide another example.[75] On both occasions, the angel redirects John's gesture of reverence away from himself and towards God, who is its only appropriate object. That is not all: in both cases the angel identifies himself as John's fellow servant, and in both cases the angel makes reference to prophecy. In 19:10 the angel tells John, "the testimony of Jesus is the spirit of prophecy," linking testimony of/to Jesus to the prophetic spirit. In 22:9, the angel redirects John's worship by clarifying his relationship to John: "I am a fellow servant with you and with your brothers the prophets, and with those who keep the words of this book." John's gesture of obeisance is inappropriate because he and the angel are of equal dignity as "fellow servants" of God. The angel's reference

---

75. See Bauckham, *Climax of Prophecy*, 120–40.

to "your brothers the prophets," clearly implies that John himself is a prophet, and it follows from 1:1 that the mediation of *apokalypsis* is a task in which both angels and prophets are involved.

As a prophetic commissioning scene, Rev 10 is a definite instance of the third strategy by which the Apocalypse demonstrates and describes the authority of its bearer. When the mighty angel cries out and the seven thunders speak, John sets about the task of writing, clearly established in 1:9–3:22 as the characteristic activity by which his inaugural commission is exercised. Yet John is prevented from transcribing the thunders' voices, and the juxtaposition of that prohibition with the ingestion of the open scroll redefines his prophetic authority. This revision, drawing on Amos 3:7–8, underlines the prophet's privilege as divine confidant, as recipient of the eschatological *mystērion*.

In effect, Rev 10:3–4 decenters the text in order to relocate authority in the person of the prophet. This is striking and surprising in a document that consistently claims its own authority, but not entirely contradictory. The swallowing of the scroll indicates that the authority embodied in the prophet John is itself inscribed authority. That is true even though the open scroll once ingested can no longer be read. The difference between the absolute nondisclosure of the seven thunders' utterance and the message of the open scroll is that this embodied text remains accessible in the person of the prophet and in his proclamation. However, even that authority is decentered by the distance between the prophet on Patmos and the churches of Asia, a distance that is bridged only by the text of the Apocalypse.

This instance of the third strategy is not undermined by its apparent circularity. The displacement of authority from a text that is never begun (the transcript of the seven thunders' utterance) to a text that is never read but ingested (and which therefore becomes coextensive with the prophet and his activity), with the geographical distance of the prophet from the churches, ultimately serves to validate the text of the Apocalypse as an effective literary link between the churches and the prophet-author. Thus the displacement of authority from a text never begun leads to the conferral of authority on the text of the Apocalypse as the document through which access is granted to the *mystērion tou theou* disclosed to the prophets.

2 Corinthians 12:1–10

Debate over the identity of Paul's opponents in 2 Corinthians has drained many an academic inkwell, and there is no reason to add to that excess here.[76] More pertinent for our purposes is the question of how Paul's juxtaposition of the heavenly ascent and the thorn in the flesh in 2 Cor 12:1–10 contributes to the argument he mounts against these opponents. Furnish points out that Paul's strategy involves countering "each of his rivals' claims with claims of his own: (1) he, too, is of Jewish stock (11:22); (2) his career as an apostle distinguishes him as a better minister of Christ than his rivals are (11:23–29); and (3) he himself is no stranger to extraor-

---

76. See the treatment in Furnish, *II Corinthians*, 48–54.

dinary religious experiences (12:1–4)."[77] The added twist in these counterclaims is the role Paul adopts in stating them. This is not a conventional *synkrisis*, but, as Betz has helped us to understand, a deliberate parody of this Hellenistic rhetorical convention.

This counterstrategy subverts the self-promotion of Paul's opponents, whom he ridicules as "super-apostles" (11:5), according to the exaggeration of their claims, to expose them as "false apostles" (11:13). In the epilogue to the "fool's speech," Paul restates his strategy and its purpose: "I have been a fool! You forced me to it. . . . I am not at all inferior to these super-apostles, even though I am nothing. The signs of a true apostle were performed among you with utmost patience, signs and wonders and mighty works" (12:11–12).

Paul's distance from the Corinthian community heightens the credibility gap and threatens to give his opponents on the scene the upper hand. Paul brings that very point to the attention of his readers in 10:10 by repeating the charge that the boldness of his letters is undermined by the weakness of his bodily presence. The juxtaposed incidents of 12:1–10 are key elements of Paul's response to this charge.

Recalling Janzen's remarks concerning the leverage a prophet could exert by pronouncing or withholding the word to which he had exclusive access, something analogous might be said of the apostle Paul's strategy in 2 Cor 12. Whereas a vividly detailed report of heavenly ascent might have been put to powerful use in a bold letter, Paul provides the emphatic opposite of such a report. He distances himself from the incident in time (v. 2, "fourteen years ago"), and in the repeated confession of ignorance as to whether or not the rapture was bodily.[78] The third-person account of the rapture into paradise yields no vision report, and the audition report is a hollow nondisclosure. This is not a matter of protecting the privacy of an intimate religious experience. If it were, Paul might well have omitted the report altogether. The apostle reclaims the power of written communication by withholding information to which he had access (the unutterable utterances) and by boasting in writing of the thorn in the flesh, the embodied *semeion* of the weakness that is a paradoxical authenticating mark of his apostleship. Far from denying the weakness of his bodily presence, Paul capitalizes on it.

Conclusion: Beyond Juxtaposition

If I have tested my reader's patience with a series of jarring juxtapositions, it is because I have sought to suggest that placing Rev 10 and 2 Cor 12 side by side allows us to attend to significant juxtapositions *within* these texts. In Rev 10, the unwritten utterance of the seven thunders is juxtaposed with the swallowed scroll; in 2 Cor

---

77. Ibid., 532.

78. While claiming ignorance on his own part as to whether or not the rapture was bodily, Paul ascribes this knowledge to God, repeating "God knows" in vv. 2 and 3.

12:1–10 the unutterable utterances are set beside the thorn in the flesh. We find more than juxtaposition: both texts present carefully articulated contrasts.

By presenting contrasts between what the seven thunders said and the swallowed scroll, and between the unutterable utterances and the thorn in the flesh, Rev 10 and 2 Cor 12 generate tensions between document and author/narrator, tensions that are resolved in favor of the author/narrator. What the seven thunders may have said is immaterial: what does matter is that the scroll-swallower *must* prophesy. What the unutterable utterances may have been is unimportant: what does matter is that Paul *must* boast of his weakness. Moving one step further, the tensions within these texts reveal tensions between their authors and their addressees. John, at a distance from the seven churches of Asia, faces challenges to his prophetic authority on several fronts. Paul, far from the Corinthian community, faces challenges to his apostolic authority. Both authors confront these challenges by subverting the conventions of textuality. John does not write what he heard the seven thunders say, and Paul does not disclose the unutterable utterances that he heard. John eats a document, experiences discomfort, and becomes an embodied prophetic document. Paul, afflicted by the thorn, embodies the weakness that proclaims the power of Christ.

Neither text allows attention to remain focused on the author-prophet or the author-apostle for very long. In both instances, authority is redirected from the narrator to the narration. The shift from the seven thunders to the scroll and from the unutterable utterances to the thorn replaces authority in the text of the Apocalypse and in the text of Paul's letter to the Corinthians. John's defense of his prophetic mission rests on the testimony of the document in which that mission finds expression among the churches in Asia, while Paul's defense of his apostolic mission relies on the proclamation of the power of weakness which takes written form in the text of his correspondence with the Corinthian church.

To Rejoice or Not to Rejoice? Rhetoric and the Fall of Satan in Luke 10:17–24 and Revelation 12:1–17

Edith M. Humphrey

Their Dark and Involv'd Sentences, their Figurative and Parabolical Discourses; their Abrupt and Maimed Way of expressing themselves which often leaves much place to Guesses at the Sense; and their neglect of connecting Transitions, which often leaves us at a loss for the Method and Coherence of what they Write; are Qualities, that our Rhetoricians do not more generally Dislike, than their Practice.... [1]

In this way the seventeenth-century chemist and defender of Christianity, Robert Boyle, depicted the common disdain for Hebrew oratory in a day when classical rhetoric was emulated—depicted it, so as to go on and exonerate the "Scriptural Style" as "not Eloquent Now" but "excellently suited [to] the Genius of Those Times."[2] Considering the instinctive judgement of many biblical critics, before and after Boyle, that Scriptural discourse (especially the prophetic and apocalyptic) breathes a different air than that of classical rhetoric, is it at all appropriate to approach oracles or visions in terms of classical models? Certainly classical rhetoric has been applied to NT argumentative discourse, on the grounds that Hellenistic rhetoric was widely known and used (if perhaps adapted) by numerous first-century audiences, including those that were Jewish and Christian.[3] Even in these cases, however, there have been those who demur,[4] or consider the Aristotelian categories inadequate: how much more

---

1. Robert Boyle, *Some Considerations Touching the Style of the Holy Scriptures* (London, printed for Henry Herringman, 1661), 158–59, in *The Holy Bible in Literary Criticism* (ed. Alex Preminger and L. Greenstein; New York: Ungar, 1986), 215–16.
2. Ibid.
3. See G. A. Kennedy, *New Testament Interpretation through Rhetorical Criticism* (Chapel Hill: University of North Carolina Press, 1984), 8–12; Burton L. Mack and Vernon K Robbins, *Patterns of Persuasion in the Gospels* (Literary Facets; Sonoma, Calif.: Polebridge, 1989), 2–11; C. Clifton Black II, "The Rhetorical Form of the Hellenistic Jewish and Early Christian Sermon: A Response to Lawrence Wills," *HTR* (1988): 1–18, esp. 5–6.
4. For a helpful discussion of the problem, see W. Wuellner, "Jesus' Sermon in Luke 12.1–13.9," in *Persuasive Artistry: Studies in New Testament Rhetoric in Honor of George A. Kennedy* (ed. Duane F. Watson; JSNTSup 30; Sheffield: JSOT Press 1991), 93–111. Wuellner seeks here to consider a sermonic

doubt might be raised concerning a rhetorical analysis of symbolic, narrative passages which might better be grist for a study in poetics? After all, evocative visionary language seems far removed from the rational, discursive mode found in, for example, Paul's letters, where the application of classical rhetorical theory was first observed by NT scholars.

1. Visions within New Testament Argumentation

The rhetorical dimension of visionary genres such as the apocalypse, however, has been demonstrated, at least initially, in such studies as E. Schüssler Fiorenza's commentary on Revelation[5], or J. J. Collins' articulation of apocalypses as having an illocutionary function[6]. More recently, scholars collaborating in a Society of Biblical literature group have been bold enough to investigate the "rhetorical dimensions of apocalyptic discourse."[7] Apocalypses, at least, are not well comprehended as sheer artefacts, since they possess a suasive dimension. So too with shorter vision-reports in the NT. Such passages, framed by narrative, and replete with symbolism, are by no means devoid of rhetorical strategy. Moreover, where such visions occur as part of an argument, they do not seem to be easily dismissed as unusual examples of "uninvented proofs" (to use classical categories) within a Christian polemic. Even the framing of the vision report by those who used them as an integral part of argumentation had to be artfully performed, so as to have the desired effect: the vision has its impact as a nontechnical proof, a fact of the case, while the report requires invention.

Generally, in doing a rhetorical analysis of other vision-reports in the NT, I have considered the vision-report in terms of the *demonstratio*,[8] an ancient rhetorical move in which the argument is vividly depicted before the eyes of the audience. My initial analyses, however, concentrated upon passages in Luke, Acts, and 2 Corinthians,[9] where constraining arguments can be made for a self-conscious use of classical devices and rhetorical forms on the part of the authors. One of the passages considered in the present study, Luke 10:17–24, fits this mould; the second, however, Rev 12:1–17, is somewhat different. Most would assume that the Apocalypse displays either a natural or contrived Semitic atmosphere, and so must be considered in terms of Hebrew models of disputation and proclamation. Two contrasting points may be made here:

---

passage in terms of rhetoric, without ignoring the literary genre, and without specific reference to "Aristotelian" rhetoric. He finds promising the "motivational" categories of Walter R. Fischer, "A Motive View of Communication," *QJS* 56 (1970): 131–39.

5. E. Schüssler Fiorenza, *Revelation: Vision of a Just World* (Proclamation Commentaries; Minneapolis: Fortress, 1991).

6. J. J. Collins, *The Apocalyptic Imagination* (New York: Crossroad, 1987), 32.

7. Greg Carey and L. Gregory Bloomquist, eds., *Vision and Persuasion: Rhetorical Dimensions of Apocalyptic Discourse* (St. Louis: Chalice, 1999); Duane F. Watson, *The Intertexture of Apocalyptic Discourse in the New Testament* (Atlanta: Society of Biblical Literature, 2002).

8. *Ad Herrenium* IV.55.68. See also Quintilian on *visio*, 9.2.40, and Cicero's *De orat.* 3.202.

9. See Edith M. Humphrey, "I Saw Satan Fall . . ."—The Rhetoric of Vision," *ARC: The Journal of the Faculty of Religious Studies, McGill University* 21 (1993): 75–88, and "Collision of Modes?—Vision and Determining Argument in Acts 10:1–11:18," *Semeia* 71 (1995): 65–84.

first, it has been argued that the classical species have a heuristic value, even when applied to "alien" texts: see the practice of Yehoshua Gitay[10] in analysis of Hebrew prophecy, where he cites Quintilian:[11] "men [sic] discovered our art before ever they proceeded to teach it" (*Institutio Oratiora* 7.10). Second, although classical strategies may illuminate an alien text, it is important to ask which critical spectacles are more suited to a particular job of observation. For the sake of symmetry, the classical model will be applied to both passages (Luke 10:17–24 and Rev. 12:1–17) but care will be taken to consider other ways of understanding the rhetorical strength of the Apocalypse passage. Analysis can in fact show that classical categories are not incongruent in a study of the Apocalypse's rhetoric. Rather, the Apocalypse is revealed as a work characterized by cultural syncretism, and as such it demonstrates competence in both Hebrew and Greco-Roman conventions.

Both Luke 10:17–24 and Rev 12:1–17 center on a similar figure and event—that is, the vision of the fall of Satan. Yet each narrative is performed in a distinct manner. Differences are to be seen in the relationship of narrative to discourse, in the overall species of speech, in the formation of the discourse, in the place that the vision occupies within the argument at hand, and in the collision or merging of polyvalent language and deductive speech. In the analysis of narratival vision-reports within argumentation, a delicate balance of rhetorical and literary analysis is called for: so much the more with a piece of such polyvalent potential as the Apocalypse. It is hoped that this paper will be able to demonstrate, in at least a preliminary way, an interaction between Jewish and Greco-Roman rhetoric.[12] However, the problematic of such rhetorical distinctions will be highlighted, where NT passages are concerned: although the Lukan passage is largely informed by classical rhetoric, its tropes are informed by the Biblical tradition as a whole; as for Rev 12, it appears to be a more deliberately hybrid production.

2. Luke 10:17–24, an Epideictic Chreia?

We begin with the structure of Luke 10:17–24, which treats the joyful return of the seventy(two), offers Jesus' enigmatic response, and adds a rather extended discourse concerning authority, power, revelation and blessedness. Earlier analyses of the passage have tended to be atomistic, separating off Semitic and Hellenistic thought forms, and appealing to the appearance of parallel portions in Matthew.[13] Our interest is in the logic of the passage as it stands, and how this fits into the overall aim of the

---

10. Yehoshua Gitay, *Prophecy and Persuasion: A Study of Isaiah 40–48* (FOTL 14; Bonn: Linguistica Biblica, 1981).
11. Gitay, *Prophecy and Persuasion,* 39.
12. For a more concentrated analysis of the Revelation passage alone (set in a larger literary context), see "In Search of a Voice—Rhetoric through Sight and Sound in Revelation 11:15–12:17," in *Vision and Persuasion,* 141–60.
13. E.g., Bultmann, *Die Geschichte der synotischen tradition* (Göttingen: Vandenhoeck & Ruprecht, 1958), 171ff.

Lukan narrative. The reader has been made aware of the importance of the mission through an earlier extended dialogue, complete with dramatic contrasts (10:13–16); as a sympathetic reader, she or he is likely to enter into the joy of the disciples in v. 17. The disciples' introductory declaration sets up their master as an authority (*Kyrie*) whose word has power (*en tō onomati sou*). Jesus' response, enigmatic although not exactly irrelevant, is arresting: "I saw Satan fall as lightning from heaven." Much ink has been spilt regarding what Bultmann calls a "dark word" and what Samuel Vollenweider calls "this remote word of Jesus."[14] These discussions debate its intent as a vision or as a description of the work of the seventy(-two) in apocalyptic imagery. Although we are not given other visions of Jesus in this gospel, the concept of Jesus seeing ecstatically is consonant with the overall portrait that Luke paints: a Jesus who is personally addressed at the baptism, a Jesus who prays prior to the Transfiguration and enters into conversation with the supernaturally present Moses and Elijah, a Jesus who knows that his lieutenant has been demanded for by the Arch-Enemy, and (if we accept 22:43–4) a Jesus who is ministered to by an angel in Gethsemane.

Even if the vision were intended as artificial[15] (which seems unnecessarily subtle) the effect of Jesus' strange statement is to add to the *ethos* already established by the disciples. We are reminded of John Diefenbaker's or Martin Luther King's "I have a dream/vision. . . ." The very style of Jesus, "I saw," establishes his words as ones that must be carefully heeded. He speaks as prophet, not simply as teacher. And yet, he is also the teacher, responding to his disciples. If there is usually a bifocal (or even poly-focal) aspect to Luke's audience, here the words are manifestly addressed to the seventy(two) and to readers who share their identity. Like the speech of the Cynic,[16] Jesus' address to followers is friendly, though somewhat corrective—this in contrast to his debates with the Pharisees *et al.* In terms of Fischer's motivational modes, the discourse is at this point "reaffirmatory" or even "purificatory" rather than affirmatory or subvertive.[17] Jesus has a word for them, a word that will both praise and redirect. The vision stands as an explanation of their success and is thus an interpretation of the activity they have experienced. Yet the interpretive word itself requires interpretation: it is a vision to be revealed or unpacked in the following elaboration. Jesus' gnomic visionary word in verse 18, then, can be taken as an unusual type of *chreia*,[18] with the following discourse (vv. 19–24) as its elaboration.

---

14. "'Ich sah den Satan wie einen Blitz vom Himmel fallen' (Lk 10:18)" *ZNW* 79 (1988): 187–203.

15. Max Turner, "The Spirit of Prophecy and the Power of Authoritative Preaching in Luke-Acts: A Question of Origins," *NTS* 38 (1992): 71. Turner insists that the verse is "much more easily interpreted as the use of apocalyptic *metaphor* to describe the disciples' success than as a literal description of a vision."

16. Burton L. Mack, "Elaboration of the Chreia in the Hellenistic School," in Mack and Robbins, *Patterns of Persuasion in the Gospels*, 48.

17. Fisher, "Motive View of Communication," 131–39.

18. Heinz O. Guenther, "Early Christianity, Q, and Jesus," *Semeia* 55 (1991): 41–76, describes a chriea as "a brief, succinct rational saying, disinclined toward the world of the miraculous" (64).

As the larger narrative unfolds, Jesus' first word links the earthly success of his followers to events (whether past, present or future) in the heavens. Like Jesus, the disciples cast out demons by the finger of God—evidence that the Kingdom has arrived. This emotive and mysterious word, "I saw Satan . . . ", standing at the head of the unit, establishes the visionary's ethos, places earthly events in a larger, more mysterious context, and cries out for further explanation. The high style of Jesus' vision is continued in the words that follow. The word *idou* (19) gives his bestowal of authority a performative ring; Jesus' public prayer in verse 21 is declared "in the Holy Spirit;" his words in verse 22 are so exalted that they have been called an "aerolite" from John's gospel; and his private word in 23–24 extends the privilege of the seer to a group of initiates through striking parallelism and contrast. Jesus' extended discourse, then, is framed so as to assure the seventy(two) that they, like Jesus, have had their *apokalypsis* (v. 21) even though (or perhaps because) they are infants and not "the wise." At verse 19, Luke's Jesus turns from the role of seer to that of interpreter: it is their revelation, as well as his own, that he is explaining. From the viewpoint of a reader who considers himself or herself in solidarity with the seventy(-two), what Jesus says to the disciples, he says to other infants "whose names are written in heaven."

A comparison of the structure of this argument may be fruitfully made to the parts of the elaborated *chreia*, or complete argument—that exercise given to schoolboys in classical times in which a memorable saying by an authority was expanded according to various pre-set patterns:

Introduction (with a hint of encomium, "Lord")	v. 17
Chreia ("I saw Satan fall . . . ")	v. 18
Rationale ("I have given you authority")	v. 19
Opposite ("Nevertheless, do not rejoice")	v. 20
Example (He rejoiced in the Holy Spirit . . .)	v. 21
[no Analogy here]	
Authority ("for so it seemed good in Your sight . . . ")	v. 21b
("All things have been given . . . ")	v. 22
Conclusion ("Blessed are the eyes . . . ")	vv. 23–24
[Contrast analogy included here]	

It will be noted that all of the parts of the elaborated *chreia* are present, with only the analogy missing from its normal position. However, example, analogy, and authority all work toward the same end in an elaboration and correspond to what might be called "the argument" in a full-blown speech. Since the example and the authority are well developed, analogy is bypassed without weakening the argument. Further, a kind of contrasting analogy is imported into the actual conclusion, where the disciples are favourably compared to great figures of the past. This displacement makes for an emotive and striking ending.

A question that arises naturally at this point is whether the argument redirects or furthers the vision. It has been seen that Jesus' response to the seventy(-two) is a kind of apocalyptic redirection of the disciples' words, while it picks up on the idea of demons who have been overpowered. Standing on its own, the vision has a polyvalent power, which is taken down only a few paths by the discussion that follows. This is the logic: the disciples rejoice that the demons have been subject to them in Jesus' name; Jesus' vision explains why; he goes on to assert that they have been given power over the enemy; however, they should not focus on this, but on their participation in heaven; Jesus rejoices, as an example to them of the correct perspective, while extending the idea of revelation to the simple and the Father's authority; the line of authority from Father to Son to the recipient is traced; a word of blessing is conferred on the disciples' eyes and ears.

The structure of Luke 10:17–24, then, is such that an embryonic but striking vision is used in the initial position to arrest the questioners within the text, and the reader of the text, so that their attention can be redirected and deepened along certain lines. In Rev 12:1–17, however, the vision-narrative and the discourse are quite differently related.

3. Revelation 12:1–12, Subversive Advent

In terms of the overall structure of the book of Revelation, the passage has (on all accounts) been considered as a central and key sequence.[19] Adela Yarbro Collins[20] and H. B. Swete[21] see the chapter as the beginning of the second half of the drama, whereas N. W. Lund[22], John G. Gager,[23] Beagley,[24] and Schüssler Fiorenza[25] place it in the center of a series. My preference for an overall structuring is that of Schüssler Fiorenza, who sees the chapter as the central episode of the "little scroll" (chapters 10–14). This little scroll itself stands in the middle of the larger epic flow of the Apocalypse, interrupting its action, so as to comment, from a heavenly perspective, upon the implications of God's dealings with enemies, with the earth, and with those who remain faithful. Chapter 12 then takes on a structural as well as a thematic centrality. Its own structure can be outlined as follows:

---

19. For a charted schemata of several representative structurings, in which the prominence of chapter 12 becomes apparent, see Edith M. Humphrey, *The Ladies and the Cities: Transformation and Apocalyptic Identity in Joseph and Aseneth, 4 Ezra, the Apocalypse, and the Shepherd of Hermas* (JSPSup 17; Sheffield: Sheffield Academic Press, 1995), 82–83.

20. *The Combat Myth of the Book of Revelation* (HDR 9; Missoula, Mont.: Scholars Press, 1976).

21. *The Apocalypse of John* (London: Macmillan, 1922).

22. *Chiasmus in the New Testament* (Chapel Hill: University of North Carolina Press, 1942), 327–28.

23. J. G. Gager, "The Attainment of Millennial Bliss through Myth and the Book of Revelation," in *Visionaries and Their Apocalypses* (ed. P. D. Hanson; Philadelphia: Fortress, 1983), 146–55.

24. Alan James Beagley, *The "Sitz im Leben" of the Apocalypse with Particular Reference to the Role of the Church's Enemies* (Berlin and New York: de Gruyter, 1987).

25. "The Composition and Structure of the Book of Revelation," in *The Book of Revelation: Justice and Judgment* (Philadelphia: Fortress, 1985), 159–80.

Introduction	Two portents	vv. 1–3
a	Woman persecuted and flight	vv. 4–6
b	War in heaven	vv. 7–9
c	Declaration	vv. 10–12
a′	Woman persecuted and flight	vv. 14–16
b′	War on earth	v. 17

As in the Lukan passage, earlier commentators on this passage considered the various cultural sources used by John, including the presence of the Apollo-Leto motif juxtaposed with the Hebraic myth of the expulsion of Satan. Our concern here is with the juxtaposition, and the overall effect. The modified chiasmic structure of the entire chapter has the effect of linking imaginatively the primordial battle and the plight of God's people. Even John's manner of introducing the narrative suggests that this is not simply a personal vision vouchsafed to the seer, but an indication of the way things stand in the cosmos. That is, the sequence begins with the impersonal passive *"There was seen* a sign in Heaven," unlike other visionary sequences that are prefaced by the words "I saw (and behold)."[26] Notice, too, how at the end of the passage (b′) the war motif is imported into the struggle between the dragon and the woman, thus firmly linking the two sequences: "Then the dragon was angry with the woman, and went off to *make war* on the rest of her children, those who keep the commandments of God and hold the testimony of Jesus" (12:17).

In the middle of this complex narrative comes the Declaration (c). The declaration itself unfolds in a threefold structure of statement, explanation, and response. God's reign has come, since the accuser has been conquered. *How* has this happened?—through the blood of the Lamb and the word of testimony. So then?—rejoice, or be woeful, depending on one's stance "in heaven" or "on earth." The odd interaction of this victorious declaration with the surrounding rehearsal of visionary conflict is notable. Two visionary sequences, the dragon and the woman, and the heavenly conflict with Satan are skilfully spliced together, and sandwiched around the declaration. Moreover, the conflict leads to victory, where it is followed by a declaration of victory; the declaration itself is slightly bifurcated by the concluding woe, and the conflictual imagery is resumed in the narrative, leaving a sense of open-endedness. The open-endedness is accentuated by the sequences that follow the chapter under discussion. The dragon takes his stand on the shore (v. 18), so as to superintend the events of chapter 13, that is, the ravages of the dragon's beast from the sea, and the deceit of the beast from the earth. We are led to ask: why this sequence? What is the

---

26. David E. Aune suggests that the passage is not to be understood as a vision because of this change in introductory formula. ("Intertextuality and the Genre of the Apocalypse," *SBL Seminar Papers, 1991* (SBLSP 30; Atlanta: Scholars Press, 1991), 156; see ch. 2 above, p. 58. This conclusion seems rather to ignore the overall framework of the Apocalypse, that these are things seen by John from his heavenly perspective established at Rev 4, and reaffirmed at 10:1. Nevertheless, the "appear" formula is not indifferent, and has a particular rhetorical effect. See also Leonard Thompson (*The Book of Revelation* [Oxford: Oxford University Press, 1990], 38), who notes the difference but considers these as visions nonetheless.

relationship of the declaration of victory and the interconnected description of conflict? What is the effect of this juxtaposed ongoing war and confident declaration of closure? Clearly, the "victory song" of verses 10–12 is no simple declaration. Through its structure and careful interweaving with the narrative, the declaration is rendered a commentary upon the ongoing war: there is an argument implied through the unusual juxtaposition and the chiasm.

How, then, should the words of the loud voice be understood and heard? Is this a victory song? Should it be compared to victory hymns of the Hebrew Bible? Notable similarities to this form would include the key word "for" (*hoti* like *ki* in the Hebrew psalms) which introduces the reason for rejoicing, followed by a description of the mighty deeds, and the summons to rejoice. Compare, for example, Psalm 98: "Sing to the Lord a new song, *for* he has done marvellous things. His right hand and his holy arm have worked salvation for him. . . . Shout for joy to Lord, all the earth. . . ." This psalm, like many of those found in the Hebrew Bible, is one of unqualified joy. We have seen already that the positioning of the declaration suggests a more ambiguous function within John's rhetoric. Moreover, the declaration itself concludes with a woe, unlike victory songs which may warn[27] the enemies of the Victor against resistance, but do not highlight the power of the vanquished, even in a limited capacity.

Analysts have, of course, pointed out this anomaly. Those concerned to fit the declaration into a particular hymnic form have adopted Procrustes' method by lopping off verse 12b. See, for example John J. O'Rourke, who assumes that the passage was an original Semitic hymn, a pure paean of joy and praise, modified by John for his purposes.[28] Other analogies to the declaration might be drawn with profit. We think particularly of similarities to the songs of Zion, or enthronement songs of Israel; such parallels, however, have the same drawback, in that the common flavour of such songs is one of security, of the on-going settled rule of Yahweh. The quest of this study is not, of course, for oral or literary forms, but rather for rhetorical technique, organization, and effect. The original oral form of a piece, however, is not irrelevant in deciding its rhetorical power. Hymns, for example, might be classed as epideictic in force, whereas songs of Zion combine epideictic praise with deliberation—a call to agree with the speaker, and join in praise as well.

The impact of Rev 12:10–12 is not so clearly defined. Perhaps some insight may be gleaned by discussing the source of the declaration, that is, the identity of the loud voice in heaven. Klaus Peter Jörns considers that the voice is identical with the loud voices heard already at 11:15, 11:19 and so on—the choir of the martyred under the throne who unendingly praise God and the Lamb.[29] Such a view leads us back to the hymn hypothesis, without deepening our understanding. Another more compelling

---

27. Leonard Thompson (*Book of Revelation*, 61) includes warnings as typical of victory hymns, but does not comment on the difference here.

28. John J. O'Rourke, "The Hymns of the Apocalypse," *CBQ* 30 (1968): 409.

29. Klaus Peter Jörns, *Das hymnischen Evangelium: Untersuchungen zu Aufbau, Funktion und Herkunft der hymnischen Stücke in der Johannesoffenbarung* (Gütersloh: Mohn, 1971), 91.

suggestion is that the voice functions *alongside* the voices of the elders and other speakers in the heavenly throne-room, playing out the ceremonial of the court in a way that ascribes ultimate power to the King of Kings.[30] David E. Aune, in offering this hypothesis, links the voices to the ceremonial prostrating of the elders, the decision-making function of the Ruler when called upon by plaintiffs, and the argument *e consensu omnium* made by the throngs of beings who concur in the acclamation of the King. Aune's argument is that the effect of this court ceremonial, pure panegyric in the heavenly throne-room, is to render the earthly imperial ceremony a mere parody of the real thing. The acclaiming words of the attendants comment upon the action of the Ruler, as well as upon the events that are taking place.[31] Thus they perform a similar function to the Chorus in a Greek drama,[32] a chorus comprised of a single leader and multiple voices speaking antiphonally.

While Aune does not deal specifically with this passage, he does connect with the throne room-visions of the Apocalypse the rites of *consecratio* (the deification of a ruler), *accessio* (the enthronement) and *adventus* (the visitation of a subject people by the ruler or his emissaries)—all of which would have been well known to the audience of Asia Minor. Shouts of acclamation, both spontaneous and ritualistic, accompanied such rites, and would include the naming of the ruler, reasons for his greatness (which included, by the way, "salvation" of those visited), and the recital of his mighty deeds. How is our understanding of the passage enriched if chapters 11 and 12 are read in the light of the drama of the *adventus*?

In chapter 11, after the sounding of the seventh trumpet, we hear an announcement of victory from heaven and the answering acclaim of the elders addressed in second person to God. In a piece that sounds remarkably like the *adventus* welcome speech,[33] the elders thank the ruler (in a second-person address) on behalf of a larger group of subjects, eager for benevolent rule and judgement. Again, in chapter 12, the same expectation is orchestrated. In place of a direct second-person address to the ruler (God), we visualize an attendant announcing to all, with a mighty voice, the ruler's actual visitation: "Now have come the salvation and the power and the kingdom and authority" (12:10). He then goes on to explain the benefits of this rule (in this case, the emancipation of the subjects) and describes the heroism of the king and his army. All of these are typical topics of the *adventus* speech, but are here offered in third person, and directed towards the subjects, rather than paying homage in the second person to the ruler, as is usually the case in the *adventus*. This is a proclamation, or heralding of an *adventus* that has just occurred, explaining to the whole community what a few have been privileged to witness as they rushed to greet

---

30. David E. Aune, "The Influence of Roman Imperial Court Ceremonial on the Apocalypse of John," *BR* 28 (1983): 5–26, esp. 15–20.

31. Ibid., 14.

32. This is pointed out elsewhere by Aune, "Intertextuality," 155; see ch. 2 of this volume, pp. 43–44.

33. See Sabine MacCormack, *Art and Ceremony in Late Antiquity* (Berkeley: University of California Press, 1981), 8, for a description of the *adventus* or *parousia*.

the conqueror outside the city wall. Fittingly, the general proclamation closes in a call to rejoice. In like manner, and with the similar result of an encomium, this epideictic declaration introduces the matter, narrates the reason for it, praises the achievements of the ruler and concludes with a call to honour him:

Introduction	"I heard a loud voice"	10a
Narration	Proposition and reason	10b, c
Achievements	Victory (*felicitas*)	11a
	Humility (*pietas*)	11b
Conclusion	Call to rejoice	12a
	(*Problem: woe contrast	12b)

The heralding of the *adventus* has a greater explanatory power than the victory hymn in working through the function and impact of this passage. However, there is a problem that remains. It cannot account for the problematic mood of 12b, the dark accent of "woe" any more coherently than the hymn hypothesis. Moreover, the reader meets this declaration of victorious presence in a strange context! Surrounding the joyful passage (whether hymn or heralded *adventus*) are those poignant battle/persecution narratives with which it interacts. Ambivalence is hardly the natural stuff of either hymn or encomium. Yet the seer presses these to his service in his inimitable fashion. As is frequently the case in the Apocalypse, the imagery is used not simply in a direct, but also in an oblique manner. At the same time as the seer tunes his voice with the heavenly heralds to acclaim the true divine Ruler, he sounds an ironic undertone with regards to human power. So he works towards the disestablishment of the pretending earthly empirical powers, "rehearsing empire so as to expose it."[34] Court ceremonial and symbolism is used both to undercut their imperial correlates, and to establish the One who is King of kings. Within such a complex schema, the logic of 12b is flawless. To recognize God's rule is to understand that the fury of the dragon and his imperial representatives is inevitable, but short-lived. The establishment of the true arriving Ruler involves the judgement of the pretender and his minions. So the epideictic tenor of the declaration takes on forensic overtones.

This double direction of the symbolism and echoed rhetorical forms help us to make sense of the visions as they come to us, taking full account of both their celebratory function and their critical acuity. If the declaration and other such passages were to be seen as projections of Christian worship or simple reapplications of Hebrew praise songs upon the events of heaven, then we would be are hard-pressed to explain the thrust of 12b and the place of the *adventus* within a scene of cosmic and earthly terror. The credulous would be likely to dismiss the vision as incoherent, while the suspicious might detect a dark, triumphalist comedy. John is, however, nei-

---

34. For a careful and perceptive disclosure of this ironic mode, see Harry O. Maier, *Apocalypse Recalled: The Book of Revelation after Christendom* (Minneapolis: Augsburg, 2002).

ther strumming in "scripture song" while Rome burns, nor is he simply confused.[35] Rather, he is plying his art in two directions at once: Behold (he says with directness) the Ruler of all! There (he says, in irony) is your short-lived despot! This dual use of imagery discloses the "subtlety and deftness of John's . . . design."[36]

To return again to Fischer's motivational modes, this declaration, as it stands in its completeness, and in connection with the surrounding narrative, is affirmatory, as well as subvertive. In distinction from the Lukan elaboration following Jesus' brief vision, the overall direction of the rhetoric is not to re-affirm nor re-direct hope, but to establish it, while subverting usual categories. John speaks to those who see themselves as marginalized, and puts a megaphone to the heavenly heralding of a Kingdom; at the same time, he intimates the just condemnation of the pretender. We are hard-pressed to find a structure that fits his purposes, though the heralded *adventus* may come close. The Lukan passage, on the other hand, aptly may be compared to an elaborated chreia, epideictic in direction, but speaking with a deliberative accent. It fits more easily into the classical rhetorical mould, but warps or alters it just enough to fit into the ethos of earliest Christianity, which is seemingly embarrassed by outright praise of anyone but the Lord.

Burton Mack speaks about early Christian speech as frequently having a "bifocal address," as using "negative contrast throughout entire argumentations" and as raising "the issue of authority" in a marked manner.[37] If this is true of the more classically-informed Lucan passage, it is even more demonstrable in the rhetorical use of the Satanic fall motif in John's vision. The loud voice in heaven, as a component within the twin narratives of the woman and the war, enacts an *adventus*. This declaration, both hymnic and arresting in tone, also argues in encomium style for the honor of God, the Lamb and his martyrs. At the same time it intimates judgement for the accuser and for those linked to him in woe. In a cosmic perspective where the natural "home" of every actor is not yet revealed, the rhetorical effect remains complex. Some readers will be uncertain as to the appropriate response, and will find themselves abandoned, as the visionary intends, in a painful moment. They are, for the moment, with the refugee, in the wilderness. Yet her place of origin was the heavens. Are they, then, to join the herald and hymners, or are they to begin the strains of

---

35. The interplay between direct and indirect rhetoric is persistent throughout this chapter, it would seem. Another curious detail frequently noted in chapter 12 is the assumed child-Messiah, whereas John is clear at 12:10 and elsewhere that the death of Jesus is key to salvation. Is he simply confused? Or has he misappropriated the ancient theme of apotheosis (classical texts) or assumption (Jewish texts). This is hardly likely. What if John presents his curious vision of assumption so as to uproot both classical and Hebraic assumptions, and then corrects the visionary picture with a word about the slaughtered Messiah? So, in the *vision* (vv. 1–6) the child is assumed without dying, and thus presented to the ancient reader as the hero or eschatological martyr, the candidate *par excellence* for divine protection and honorific status; but in the *oracle* that interprets the vision (vv. 10–12), we hear neither of apotheosis nor iron rule. Instead, the voice proclaims that the Lamb's "rule" of vulnerability is shared by the martyrs, and that salvation is won through Messiah's "blood."

36. Aune, "Influence," 5.

37. *Rhetoric and the NT* (Minneapolis: Fortress, 1990), 96.

woe? It is perhaps typical of early Christian rhetoric that the answer to this quandary is not given in an absolute way.

4. Ratios of Space and Time

There are, then, two different ratios of the heavenly and earthly in these passages. The Lukan vision links the victory of the seventy(-two) in a *direct* way with the vanquishing of Satan, as its elaboration directs them to see the larger picture and rejoice aright. The Apocalypse's vision-plus-declaration argues for the establishment of the kingdom, and uses the fall of Satan as its rationale; then it links that fall *inversely* to the blood of the Lamb and the martyrdom of the faithful. If the Lukan passage says, "yes, things are as they seem" (but even greater than you can imagine), the Apocalypse passage argues that things are *not* as they seem. Contrary to the usual perspective, martyrdom and death equal victory in the Apocalypse. Again, the very fury of Satan's earthly activity signals that God is already the Victor. The sign of God's rule is in Luke's passage a successful and dramatic apostolic ministry (but this is only a sign of the great drama, and not the whole show); the sign of God's rule in the Apocalypse is a fugitive and exiled Queen, or, if we prefer, a host of martyrs, protected by God, and promised glory.

In the first case, the rhetorical logic is: Do rejoice, but rejoice in *this*, which is even greater than *that*. Discourse prevails, and the strange visionary word of Jesus is bent to the service of teaching. In the second case, the logic is more convoluted, but perhaps more powerful: Rejoice *because* of your seeming failure; Rejoice in spite of death, for death implies life. The Lamb is a Lion, the fugitive is a queen, and the dragon is already judged. An even darker note is intimated, for those who need to hear it. This note sounds the insistent question: to rejoice or not to rejoice? Where are you standing, where are your loyalties?—have you a part of those in the heavens or on the earth? Are you called to rejoice or to woe? In the words of Leonard Thompson, with the Apocalypse, the boundary markers are "soft,"[38] and so the question of identity is an ever-present one. In the Apocalypse, polyvalence (rather than discourse) prevails: the oracular but argumentative declaration interacts equally with the narrative to make its mark. Just as the prophet is given in chapter 11 a bitter-sweet scroll to eat, the faithful are given a bitter-sweet word, and left to sort out the issues. Atypically for an apocalypse, there is no interpretation of the vision, except that offered by the declaration. The voice from heaven gives its oblique commentary, and accentuates the conflictual symbolism.

Intriguing similarities are to be found in these texts, as well. Both passages have a deep concern for authority: the Lukan passage offers a corrective to the ideal reader's idea of where authority lies and how it is expressed; the Apocalypse stories-plus-oracle declare that the authority of God is secure, despite appearances. Perhaps, if we were to engage in mirror reading, we could imagine Luke addressing a group that sets too

---

38. Thompson, *Book of Revelation*, 100.

much stock by miracles, whereas the group addressed by the Apocalypse yearns to hear that the day of miracles is not over. Another significant similarity between the two passages is the dualism found at the conclusion of each argument: the contrast of the blessed eyes of the disciples with those who did not see in past times; the rejoicing of those in the heavens over against the woe to those on earth and sea. In the first case, the dualism is a temporal one, emphasizing the *kairos* of God's action in Jesus; in the second case, the dualism is spatial, contrasting and linking the state of affairs in the heavenly and earthly places of God's rule. This, it seems, is a distinctive Christian aspect to argumentation, and in both cases (but more extremely in the Apocalypse) the classical forms are modified to allow for the transcendent. The double statements afford the conclusion of these speeches an air of solemnity and mystery, and as such are consonant with the visionary words that are so vital to their arguments: we have to do here with that which is greater than ages, or worlds.

Sarcasm in Revelation 2–3: Churches, Christians, True Jews, and Satanic Synagogues

Steve Friesen

The author of the Apocalypse can be terribly offensive. While this endears his text to some readers, scholars tend to be put off by the abrasive character of these visions. Denunciations are not fashionable in the academy unless the slander includes footnotes and full bibliography. In the case of Revelation, however, the discomfort is not just a matter of academic taste. There are more serious issues at stake. The rhetoric of Revelation has been wielded in a bewildering array of settings over the centuries, and a disturbingly high percentage of these have been lethal. Christian hostility toward Jews, Christian imperialism, and Christian sectarian violence are a few of the examples that spring to mind.

Adela Yarbro Collins wrestled with these topics by treating the aggressive character of Revelation under the rubric of "vilification."[1] Vilification in Revelation can be offensive, she noted, but it also had positive functions in the emerging Christian movement. Denunciations of other Jews facilitated boundary formation as the churches tried to distinguish themselves from the synagogues. The condemnation of Rome and of imperial cults helped define the congregations as groups that did not acknowledge the divinity of the emperor or the emperor's universal claims to lordship. Vilification of rival Christian leaders, on the other hand, helped establish the boundaries between Christian gentiles and the non-Christian gentiles of mainstream culture. The joy of vilification was mostly for that early period in the history of the movement, according to Yarbro Collins. Now that Christian self-identity and power are well-established, the practice of vilification should be put away for more mature strategies.

Peder Borgen addressed the same set of issues under the rubric of "polemic,"[2] and his argument came to a similar conclusion: the polemic of Revelation had the

---

[1]. Adela Yarbro Collins, "Vilification and Self-Definition in the Book of Revelation," *HTR* 79 (1986): 308–20.

[2]. Peder Borgen, "Polemic in the Book of Revelation," in *Anti-Semitism and Early Christianity: Issues in Polemic and Faith* (ed. Craig A. Evans and Donald A. Hagner; Minneapolis: Fortress, 1993), 199–211.

character of an intramural skirmish. The synagogues and the *ekklesiai* ("churches") were both claiming to be the rightful heirs of Israel's traditions, and the polemic resulted from the tensions between competing Jewish groups. The denunciations by John are understandable in that first century setting where the churches were small and vulnerable to persecutions. In later historical settings—that is, when churches became powerful and distinctly non-Jewish—such denunciations are no longer excusable. They are now extramural and anti-Semitic.

It is a salutory development that Christian anti-Semitism is finally becoming an important topic in New Testament studies, and Revelation is certainly one place where the issues need to be aired. It seems to me, however, that studies like the two mentioned above are too concerned with making John's Revelation palatable. The effort to exonerate or rehabilitate the text has distracted us from the logically prior task of describing the text. In other words, the primary question should not be, "Are the denunciations anti-Semitic?" We should start by asking, "What kind of denunciations are found in the text?" Our answers to this question might not be so reassuring, but they should bring us closer to understanding the text and the first-century communities that listened to it.

When we take this approach, we find the categories vilification and polemic too vague.[3] We can be more precise. Harry Maier has shown that the text of Revelation as a whole is permeated by ironic strategies. Dealing with the whole text (not just the messages of Rev 2–3), Maier defended Revelation not against the charge of anti-Semitism, but rather against the accusation that John's anti-Roman visions trafficked in the same ideology of domination that the text claimed to oppose. Maier's rebuttal was that the dramatic irony in John's text was a destabilizing strategy that ultimately undercut all notions of power based on conquest.[4]

I find Maier's argument about irony in Revelation convincing. In regard to the messages to the seven churches, however, I think we can be even more precise. These messages are certainly ironic but the element of sarcasm is particularly strong in these chapters. The distinction is important for two reasons. One is that the recognition of sarcasm in the text tends to undermine efforts to exonerate Revelation and its author. The author blended sarcasm and satire into a volatile form of vilification that I will not defend. Second, the distinction leads to the conclusion that the author did not claim that members of his churches were true Jews or the true Israel. In order to make this argument, I first need to define my terms. I then review examples of sarcasm from Rev 2–3, focusing especially on the references to synagogues of Satan. I conclude with observations on the relationship of synagogues and churches in Revelation.

---

3. "Polemic" has the added liability of suggesting an argument at the level of ideas and principles. "Vilification" at least allows for the personal attacks in Revelation. For definitions here and elsewhere in the paper, see Merriam-Webster Online (http://www.m-w.com/home.htm).

4. Harry O. Maier, *Apoclaypse Recalled: The Book of Revelation after Christendom* (Minneapolis: Fortress, 2002), 164–97.

Irony, Satire, and Sarcasm

The denunciations in Rev 2–3 are best described by as irony, satire, and sarcasm. These terms overlap, but each describes a particular kind of language practice that can be isolated conceptually for the purpose of analysis. The choice of these terms makes analysis more complicated, however. Many disciplines deal with these topics and I have to decide how they will be defined in this study. Are these literary terms? Social strategies? Psychological maneuvers? Linguistic figures? Speech acts?

I propose to deal with the irony, satire, and sarcasm of Revelation at a general level. I consider them to be language practices that can be manifested in personal relations, in public statements, and in written texts for a variety of strategic purposes. This allows me to draw on theories from literary studies, psychology, linguistics, and elsewhere. There is a good deal of similarity in the various disciplinary discussions of these topics. So they should complement each other, if we treat the theories at a general level and pay attention to their particular disciplinary contexts.

In broad terms, irony is normally treated as a statement in which there is both a surface meaning and another contradictory meaning at some other level. Theorists tend to discuss two formats for the phenomenon. One format is verbal irony, a statement that says less than is meant or even the opposite of what is meant. In such cases, the speaker creates an inconsistency that requires the audience to consider whether some meaning other than the literal meaning might better explain the statement. For example, after reading this chapter you might say to someone, "Friesen wrote the best chapter on sarcasm in the whole book." Your intonation might suggest to your listener that you meant to communicate something other than the literal meaning of the sentence.[5] Or your hearer might calculate the actual number of sarcasm chapters in this book and conclude that what sounded like praise actually implied disapproval or criticism. These inconsistencies in your statement at the level of intonation and context alerted your confidant that a second, contradictory meaning was actually intended. Inconsistencies at the level of words or clauses can serve the same purpose.[6]

But why did you phrase the original statement in a way that said something other than what you meant? It would have been simpler and clearer if you had simply declared, "Friesen's chapter sucked." By framing your criticism ironically, however, you gave yourself plausible deniability because you never actually criticized my work. At the same time you gave your hearer the opportunity to acknowledge the criticism or to ignore it. This double defense mechanism would not be available to either of you if you simply vilified my paper.[7] Other motives for irony beyond deniability are also possible. Experimental studies suggest that ironic insults cut deeper than plain

---

5. For a discussion of the six basic markers used by speakers to signal their sarcasm, see John Haiman, "Sarcasm as Theater," *Cognitive Linguistics* 1 (1990): 181–205.
6. Kathrina Barbe, *Irony in Context* (Pragmatics and Beyond, n.s., 34; Philadelphia: John Benjamins, 1995), 29–31.
7. Ben R. Slugoski and William Turnbull, "Cruel to be Kind and Kind to be Cruel: Sarcasm, Banter, and Social Relations," *Journal of Language and Social Psychology* 7 (1988): 105–6.

insults.[8] Or perhaps your dismissal of my paper was an attempt to attract attention to your own cleverness. Maybe you wanted to entertain. Maybe my paper threatened your own reading of Revelation. Without more context, it is difficult to be sure of your motives.[9]

A second, broader format for irony is described as structural. Structural irony requires a narrative setting and communicates an experience of the world as paradoxical. A hero might set out to accomplish a task only to be confounded by the actual course of events. Or a narrator might set out to tell a story using a worldview that the audience knows to be contrary to fact.[10] In either case, the machinations of experience overcome the intentions or assumptions of the actor. The world is shown to be contradictory to human aspirations. The mood of structural irony might be humorous or tragic, depending on the way the author shapes the narrative. In either case, the strategy is not as defensive as in verbal irony. Structural irony allows the one composing the narrative to flatter the audience for their ability to discern the true state of things, while simultaneously promulgating a view of human experience that highlights the inconsistencies and frustrations of life.

These two formats for irony have at least one feature in common: they exploit the gap between appearance and reality, between words or events and the context of those words or events.[11] At first glance this dissonance seems fruitful for the analysis of Rev 2–3, for John traffics in unfulfilled expectations. A closer look suggests otherwise. Simple verbal irony does not take us far enough: John does not dissemble, as though he would hide his true intentions behind a facade of subtlety. Nor does structural irony describe accurately the heart of the issue. Examples of structural irony can be found in the text, but it is not John's preferred strategy in the messages of Rev 2–3.[12] In general, John makes a clear connection between the choices made by people and the resulting consequences. The issue in Revelation is not the paradoxical character of existence. The issue is whether hostile powers will deceive humans into making eternally fatal choices.

Satire also appears often throughout Revelation. Satire is normally considered a special form of irony. Satire is ironic because it operates in the space between pretense and actual experience. Three of its characteristics make it particularly appropriate for a discussion of Revelation. First, satire manifests a particular intolerance for personal

---

8. Penny M. Pexman and Kara M. Lineck, "Does Sarcasm Always Sting? Investigating the Impact of Ironic Insults and Ironic Compliments," *Discourse Processes* 33 (2002): 214–15.

9. For a survey of theories about the usefulness of ironic insults, see Maggie Toplak and Albert N. Katz, "On the Uses of Sarcastic Irony," *Journal of Pragmatics* 3 (2000): 1469–70.

10. Chris Baldic, ed., *The Concise Oxford Dictionary of Literary Terms* (New York: Oxford University Press, 1990), 114.

11. Roger Fowler, ed., *A Dictionary of Modern Critical Terms* (rev. and enlarged ed.; New York: Routledge, 1987), 128; also Sachi Kumon-Nakamura, Sam Glucksberg, and Mary Brown, "How about Another Piece of Pie? The Allusional Pretense Theory of Discourse Irony," *Journal of Experimental Psychology* 124 (1995): 4.

12. For examples, see the survey in Maier, *Apocalypse Recalled*, 176–97.

or institutional folly. The distance between intent and practice forms the basis for denunciation.[13] Second, satire does not require the suppression of the values of the implied author as is the case with most other forms of irony. The author embraces an implicit or overt moral standard and uses it in his[14] vilification of the victim.[15] Third, satire demands a fantastic or even grotesque element as it displays the absurdity of people, situations, or organizations.[16] The fantastic element often results from the satirist's effort to portray some aspect of life as an absurdity.[17]

These features of satire lend themselves to several kinds of strategies. Satire might be employed to destroy an opponent. Satire's reliance on a moral standard can also lead to a corrective function. It can also have great entertainment value. In general, though, a satirical strategy subjects vice, folly, arrogance, or injustice to ridicule for the purpose of exposing unacceptable practice or even changing it.[18] In Revelation, however, we are not dealing with a satirical genre of literature. Satire does not provide a unifying aspect for the visions of Revelation. Nor would anyone mistake the Seer for Juvenal or Horace.[19] I am suggesting here, and argue below, that satire and sarcasm describe many of the important features of John's denunciations.

The other crucial aspect of John's vilification is *sarcasm*, which can be defined as "a sharp and often satirical or ironic utterance designed to cut or give pain," or "a mode of satirical wit depending for its effect on bitter, caustic, and often ironic language that is usually directed against an individual."[20] Academicians argue whether or not sarcasm should be classified as a form of irony.[21] I side with those who define sarcasm as a special form of irony, for without some ironic dimension a denunciation is simply abusive. The element common to irony, satire, and sarcasm is that all of

---

13. Fowler, *Critical Terms*, 214.
14. Satire appears to be especially a male activity since there are far fewer examples of female satirists; J. A. Cuddon, ed., *A Dictionary of Literary Terms* (rev. ed.; London: Andre Deutsch, 1979), 599.
15. Northrop Frye, *Anatomy of Criticism: Four Essays* (Princeton: Princeton University Press, 1957), 223–25. The author's values, however, need not be espoused openly in satiric texts. Swift's *Modest Proposal* relies on a recognition by the audience of the barbarity of his proposal's content to communicate his values.
16. Frye, *Anatomy*, 224.
17. I use "satire" here for a phenomenon that is also known as "parody": Maier, *Apocalypse Recalled*, 166–70; John Haiman, *Talk Is Cheap: Sarcasm, Alienation, and the Evolution of Language* (New York: Oxford University Press, 1998), 21–22.
18. Linda Hutcheon, *Irony's Edge: The Theory and Politics of Irony* (New York: Routledge, 1994), 52–53.
19. Roman satire, understood as a genre of literature, can encompass a variety of practices and strategies that go beyond the definition of satire as I have laid it out here. In other words, an exemplary text of Roman satire might include ironic or sarcastic features that are intended to attack, entertain, or correct. See Niall Rudd, *Themes in Roman Satire* (London: Duckworth, 1986), 1–39.
20. Merriam-Webster Online.
21. Barbe, *Irony*, 27–29. "So, while we do not want to exclude sarcasm from the realm of irony, we need to see it as a limiting case on the very border of the ironic" (Frank Stringfellow Jr., *The Meaning of Irony: A Psychoanalytic Investigation* [Margins of Literature; Albany: State University of New York Press, 1994], 17).

them deal with unattained aspirations. The salient characteristic of sarcasm, however, is that it is a bitter, caustic, personal, and painful form of verbal aggression. Here's how Haiman contrasted irony and sarcasm.

> First, situations may be ironic, but only people can be sarcastic. Second, people may be unintentionally ironic, but sarcasm requires intention. What is essential to sarcasm is that it is overt irony *intentionally used by the speaker as a form of verbal aggression*, and it may thus be contrasted with other aggressive speech acts, among them the put-on, direct insults, curses, vituperation, nagging, and condescension."[22]

For example, after finishing this chapter, you might employ satirical sarcasm by e-mailing me with the advice, "Stick to archaeology and leave Revelation to the experts." Such a statement would be sarcastic since it is caustic and personal. The ironic element satirizes my arrogance in claiming to be an authority on Revelation. The satire functions at a secondary level, though, providing the irony for what is essentially a sarcastic rejection of my writing, my competence, and indeed my vocation.

The choice to use sarcasm calls certain features into play that are missing in verbal and structural irony. Sarcasm is seldom ambiguous. The subtle inconsistencies of irony are usually replaced by a frontal attack that is transparent to the audience. Artistry is unnecessary. The audience is not left to wonder about the values of the speaker or about which level of meaning to take seriously.[23] Thus the speaker's deniability normally disappears, although the hearer can still choose to ignore the sarcasm.[24] For instance, I might reply to your e-mail by saying, "Thanks for the advice. Fortunately, my spam filter didn't prevent your note from reaching me." The characterization of your e-mail as spam signals that the entire message means something different from what the words say: my gratitude is actually insincere and I consider your opinion to be of no more value than unsolicited, computer-generated advertising. I have renounced plausible deniability in order to strike back with sarcasm, but you might still choose to ignore my real message in a way that would not be possible if I renounced sarcasm and simply demeaned your family lineage.

To sum up, we need to be aware of three related language practices as we read Revelation: irony, satire, and sarcasm. I define them as follows. Irony is the broadest term, indicating a statement or narrative that exploits the gap between appearance and reality. It comes in two major formats: verbal irony (utterances that mean some-

---

22. Haiman, *Talk Is Cheap*, 20; emphasis in original.
23. Stringfellow, *Meaning of Irony*, 16–17.
24. Barbe, *Irony*, 27–29. Deniability is sometimes retained, however, even with sarcasm (Haiman, "Sarcasm as Theater," 202–3). For example, consider the following abstract and see if you can determine whether the author has absolutely no appreciation for sarcasm, or is a sarcastic genius. "In an empirical study of ironic sarcasm and banter, Brown and Levinson's model is found to require an additional relationship parameter, 'relationship affect', to account for the ways in which neutral observers interpret counter-to-fact insults and compliments. As predicted, the literal meanings of utterances are also found to influence observers' cognitive representations of the relationship between speaker and hearer. However, unexpected correlations among the relationship variables suggest that the model's additivity assumption may need to be relinquished" (Slugoski and Turnbull, "Cruel to Be Kind," 101).

thing other than what is literally stated); and structural irony (narratives in which the course of events frustrate the intentions of characters). Satire can be viewed as a less obtuse form of irony that ridicules vice or folly. It holds its opponents up to a moral standard of some sort and highlights their shortcomings. Sarcasm is often satirical or ironic, but is characterized especially by bitter personal attack. With these overlapping phenomena defined, we can return to Rev 2–3 and highlight certain aspects of the text.

The Sarcastic Christ

The messages of the risen Christ to the seven churches in Rev 2–3 make extensive use of satire and sarcasm, and also employ irony at certain important points. Three groups bear the brunt of this verbal aggression in this section: congregations, church leaders, and synagogues. The sarcasm directed at congregations is normally expressed as criticism of the angel of the church. In the message to Sardis, the church's angel is told that it has the reputation of being alive but it is actually dead (3:2–3). The sarcasm is moderate (by the standards of the Apocalypse), and the satirical aspect is strong. The shocking revelation that the congregation's actual status is the opposite of its reputation is followed by imperatives aimed at reforming the situation. "Wake up and strengthen the rest of the things that are about to die!" The angel of the church in Laodicea, on the other hand, comes in for a stronger dose of sarcasm. First comes a condemnation for lukewarmness (3:16), then comes the revelation of the angel's mistaken opinion. "For you say, 'I am wealthy and have enriched myself and I have no need,' and you do not realize that you are wretched and pitiful and poor and blind and naked" (3:17).

The ultimate recipients of the satirical sarcasm directed at the angels are actually the congregations, of course. Through the logic of apocalyptic symbolism, the verbal abuse ends up as a denunciation of, and appeal to, the saints. The whole purpose of these messages is, after all, that all the churches should know that Christ is the one who searches their hearts and minds, and the one who repays to all according to their deeds (2:23).

Certain church leaders qualify for special sarcastic attention in the text. The Ephesians had encountered individuals who called themselves apostles. These were probably itinerant saints similar to those discussed in Didache 11:3–6. In Rev 2, the Ephesian congregation–through the angel of the church–was commended for testing these alleged apostles and for discerning that they were liars (2:2). In this case there is no discernible satirical motif regarding the self-proclaimed apostles, only sarcastic denunciation against them in a third person reference.

Not so with certain prophets in the churches. One or two in particular take the brunt of sarcastic satire that is based on scripture. The existence of the first victim is actually questionable: the name Balaam might refer to a particular prophet from Pergamum, but this is not certain since the message technically objects to "those who hold to the teaching of Balaam" (2:14), which might not necessarily refer directly to a contemporary church prophet. The ancient Balaam was a foreign prophet credited with causing the Israelites to worship foreign gods and with convincing the Israelite men to have illicit sexual relations with Moabite women (Num 22:1–25:3). If a contemporary individual prophet is meant in Rev 2:14, the comparison with Balaam suggests that he was male and was promoting a more lenient attitude than John toward polytheistic sacrificial practices. If the phrase does not refer to a contemporary church prophet, the phrase may simply be a way of satirizing certain members of the church through biblical allusion. The satire suggests they participated in gentile sacrifices to some extent, at least by John's definition, and so were unfaithful to God. In either case, scriptural allusion becomes the means by which pretense is exposed.

The second prophetic example is clearly an individual from the congregation in Thyatira. She is satirized as a latter-day Jezebel. The basis for the satire is the Biblical figure of Jezebel, the Phoenician queen who promoted Canaanite worship in Israel during the reign of her husband king Ahab.[25] The extent to which this imagery informs our understanding of the Thyatiran situation is unclear. The satire would be appropriate if used against a gentile woman who was an influential leader in the congregation,[26] one who used her influence to move the congregation closer toward participation in sacrificial activity. It does not allow us to speculate about what influence she might have had in the wider community. The satirical element is stronger than the sarcastic in this instance, and there is a hint of reserve in the satire, as though Christ were pulling his punches. Note that Jezebel's status as a prophet is not rejected like the status of the so-called apostles of Rev 2:2. Moreover, Jezebel is not personally demonized; rather, her *teaching* is rejected and equated with knowing the "deep things of Satan" (2:20, 24).[27] The satire is accompanied by threats against those who do not repent and exhortations to the innocent.

This brings us to the harshest sarcasm from the risen Christ, which requires more extensive comment. In the messages to Smyrna and Philadelphia he refers to synagogues of Satan, people who call themselves Jews but are lying (2:9; 3:9). Most scholars conclude that the "synagogue of Satan" epithet was aimed at the mainstream Jewish communities of Smyrna and Philadelphia, and I agree with them.[28]

---

25. She plays a role in the narratives of 1 Kgs 16:31–2 Kgs 9:37.

26. At least some of the saints from the Thyatiran congregation were not in agreement with her, according to 2:24.

27. The meaning of "the deep things of Satan" is unclear, but it is probably a sarcastic satire of the claims of "Jezebel." Aune noted that the phrase ὡς λήγουσιν ("as they say") indicates that we are dealing with some sort of assertion or slogan from those who agree with Jezebel. The original assertion may have been that they knew "the deep things of God," or simply "the depths," which John has turned into a sarcastic inversion. David E. Aune, *Revelation 1–5* (WBC 52; Dallas: Word, 1997), 207–8.

28. For surveys of other identifications of the "synagogues of Satan," see Adela Yarbro Collins, "Insiders and Outsiders in the Book of Revelation and Its Social Context," in *"To See Ourselves as Others See Us": Christians, Jews, "Others" in Late Antiquity* (ed. Jacob Neusner and Ernest S. Frerichs; Chico, Calif.: Scholars Press, 1985), 205–6; and Borgen, "Polemic," 200. Paul Duff agrees that the opponents were members of the local Jewish communities, but argues that John was trying to generate tension with them rather than responding to existing tensions (*Who Rides the Beast? Prophetic Rivalry and the*

One other alternative to this identification in recent scholarship is that the synagogue of Satan referred not to Jews but rather to church members who had moved back toward Jewish synagogue practice.[29] This alternative position was championed by Heinrich Kraft. He asserted that the synagogue of Satan had to refer to church members who had adopted a synagogal identity for three reasons: because "satanic" in Revelation describes someone who entices others away from faith and confession; because one cannot imagine John denying that the Jewish communities were God's people; and because John was concerned about Christians and not about Jews. None of these arguments is convincing: the first could be true of Jews or of anyone else; and the last two cannot be supported from Revelation. Nevertheless, Kraft invoked a hypothetical scenario in which Christians might have abandoned the churches to seek refuge in the legal status of the Jewish community. To the Jews these would have appeared as God-fearers. To John they would have been a syncretistic group, ready to compromise with polytheistic and imperial cult institutions, and capable of diluting the commitment of the churches.[30]

More recently, David Frankfurter has made the case that the synagogue of Satan could have referred to post-Pauline gentile saints who followed Paul's instructions to exercise cautious freedom in eating meat sacrificed to other deities (1 Cor 10:23–30) and who thought of themselves as the true Jews (cf. Rom 2:28–29).[31] In order to make his case, Frankfurter rightly pointed out the diversity among Jews of the Diaspora in western Asia Minor, but then argued that John's sectarian criticism had to be directed at insiders within the Jesus movement, and that John's own halakhic practices could be characterized as a form of hyperpurity. While it is true that John's opponents could have shared Paul's view on sacrificial meat, "synagogue" and *Ioudaios* are not attested as popular self-designations in Pauline or post-Pauline churches. Moreover, it is highly unlikely that John was scrupulously concerned with purity or Jewish halakhic practice. In fact, John seems completely unconcerned about Sabbath observance, food regulations (beyond the topic of sacrificial meat), ablutions, or circumcision.[32]

Rhetoric of Crisis in the Churches of the Apocalypse [New York: Oxford University Press, 2001], esp. 43–47 and 49–51); also see ch. 7 of this volume.

29. Stephen G. Wilson ("Gentile Judaizers," *NTS* 38 [1992]: 614) suggested that the synagogue of Satan might refer to non-Christian Gentiles who had joined the synagogues and were harassing the churches with the zeal that tends to characterize converts. Wilson offered no arguments for this position, however, and immediately shifted to speculation that they could also be Gentile church members who had moved toward the synagogues, which is the position of Kraft.

30. Heinrich Kraft, *Die Offenbarung des Johannes* (Handbuch zum Neuen Testament 16a; Tübingen: Mohr Siebeck, 1974), 61.

31. David Frankfurter, "Jews or Not? Reconstructing the 'Other,'" *HTR* 94 (2001): 403–25.

32. John Marshall argued for a similar identification: the synagogues of Satan were gentile God-fearers who joined the churches and claimed the identity of *Ioudaios* for themselves (John W. Marshall, *Parables of War: Reading John's Jewish Apocalypse* [Studies in Christianity and Judaism 10; Waterloo, Ontario: Wilfred Laurier University Press, 2001], 13–16, 133–34). His argument was based not on John's alleged halakhic concerns but rather on a straightforward, referential understanding of the

It is much easier to accept the majority opinion on this matter: the synagogue of Satan references were directed at some members of the Jewish communities in Smyrna and Philadelphia. The message to the Smyrniote church suggests that the synagogue of Satan would be responsible for tensions with the authorities. The double reference to Satan and the devil makes the connection,[33] and it is more likely that some members of the Jewish community (rather than former church members) would be in a position to carry out such activities against churches.[34]

The problem with the conclusion that John was calling synagogues satanic, however, is that it makes John's message extremely distasteful nowadays. Nineteen centuries later, with a long history of Christian oppression of Jews to take into account, such a statement cannot pass without comment. Some have pointed to mitigating circumstances. The synagogues may have been under great pressure after the Jewish War with Rome (66–70 C.E.) to define themselves as loyal, stable institutions in the Roman world and may have been more aggressive toward the churches for this reason.[35] Or perhaps the denunciation of these particular synagogues was a part of John's larger bias against anyone with high social standing in the cities of Asia.[36]

A consensus also appears to be forming that the synagogue of Satan references should be understood as an intramural Jewish skirmish between the synagogues and the churches, both of which were claiming the right to be called the true Israel. The studies by Yarbro Collins and Borgen mentioned at the beginning of this paper explained the "synagogue of Satan" vituperation as an argument between competing groups who both claimed the exclusive right to call themselves "Jews." Yarbro Collins focused on the social function of John's denunciation, describing it as an attempt to claim the term "Jew" for the churches. John, according to Yarbro Collins, considered the churches to be the true Israel.[37]

Borgen argued the case somewhat differently. He agreed that the "question behind the phrase 'synagogue of Satan' is: where are the true Jews to be found, in the *ekklesia* or in the synagogue?"[38] He placed this specific polemic about those who falsely claim to be Jews (Rev 2:9; 3:9) in a broader context of Jewish intramural arguments. A survey of relevant texts from Philo and from the Dead Sea Scrolls led

---

phrase Καί οὐκ εἰσίν ("but they are not") in regard to "those who call themselves Jews." I do not agree that we are dealing with referential language here because the general and immediate contexts are full of irony, satire, and sarcasm.

33. Note the equation of Satan and devil in Rev 12:9.

34. Yarbro Collins, "Vilification," 312–13. Both Marshall (*Parables of War*, 133) and Frankfurter ("Jews or Not?" 406) point out that the second-century Martyrdom of Polycarp has played too large a role in the reconstruction of first-century tensions in Smyrna between churches and synagogues. Their point is well-taken.

35. Elisabeth Schüssler Fiorenza, *Revelation: Vision of a Just World* (Proclamation Commentaries; Minneapolis: Fortress, 1991), 55.

36. Leonard Thompson, *The Book of Revelation: Apocalypse and Empire* (New York: Oxford University Press, 1990), 174.

37. Yarbro Collins, "Vilification," 314, 319.

38. Borgen, "Polemic," 204.

him to conclude that John built on Jewish traditions, especially those dealing with the denunciation of pagan worship, national priesthood, and proselytism. Borgen concluded that John was reworking these traditions to support the idea that the church was the true Israel founded on the salvific death of Jesus, the eschatological community in which were found the true Jews.[39]

One problem with this argument is that it does not sufficiently account for the ethnicity of John's audience. It is not clear what kind of intramural argument is involved here if the churches were composed mostly of gentiles. The churches certainly drew on Israel's heritage, but what percentage of the saints came from Jewish parents? Or what percentage of the saints kept Torah to the extent that they would have been perceived by neighbors as Jewish?[40] Although it is impossible to quantify an answer, John's implied audience is mostly gentile. This is what we would expect from the earlier history of churches in western Asia Minor, and texts like Rev 5:9 provide confirmation.[41] Moreover, as stated above, Revelation does not deal with standard issues Torah observance, such as sabbath, circumcision, washings, or food regulations (except for meat sacrificed to other deities). Nor does Revelation portray civilized humanity in terms of Jews and Greeks or Jews and gentiles as in Acts or the Pauline letters. Revelation actually shows little concern for issues that would be involved in an intramural Jewish polemic.

Another problem with the idea that John was claiming that the church was the true Israel is that John never bothered to write such a thing.[42] Revelation is a long text with ample space for John to describe the churches by calling them Jews or the true Israel. But he did not do so. The synagogue of Satan references will not support such an elaborate hypothesis. A simpler solution is available. It only becomes evident once we are attuned to the sarcastic tendency of the text and begin noticing its presence in the messages to Smyrna and to Philadelphia.

One synagogue of Satan reference comes from the message to the angel of the church in Smyrna (Rev 2:8–11).

> And to the angel of the church in Smyrna write: Thus says the first and the last, who was dead and came to life. I know your oppression and your poverty—but you are rich!—and the blasphemy from those who say they are Jews and are not but are a synagogue of Satan. Do not fear the things which you are about to suffer. Behold, the Devil is about to throw some of you into prison so that you might be tested, and you will have oppression for ten days. Be faithful until death, and I will give you the

---

39. Borgen, "Polemic."
40. This is based on Shaye Cohen's argument about how one would have been classified as Jewish in a first-century urban diaspora setting. Since ethnic Jews were not distinguished by clothing, speech, names, or occupations, people would have noticed other things such as someone associating with Jews, living in a Jewish part of town, married to a Jew, integrated socially with other Jews, or performing Jewish rituals and practices. Shaye J. D. Cohen, *The Beginmnings of Jewishness: Boundaries, Varieties, Uncertainties* (Berkeley: University of California Press, 1999), 25–68.
41. See also Rev 7:1–17, discussed below.
42. This was noted in passing by Wilson ("Judaizers," 613).

crown of life. Let the one with an ear hear what the spirit says to the churches. The victor will not be harmed by the second death.

The focus in this message is on severe suffering: Christ states that he knows the angel's oppression (θλῖψις) and that more is to come. Here the second person singular address to the angel breaks down and the congregation is addressed directly through the use of plurals. Since this is obscured in standard English, I translate in standard Texan: "Behold, the Devil is about to cast some of y'all into prison that y'all might be tested, and y'all will have oppression for ten days" (2:10).

Within this general context of ongoing oppression, Christ says he also knows "the blasphemy of those who say they are Jews and are not, but (are) a synagogue of Satan" (2:9). In order to understand this phrase, it is important to note the consistent ironic tone of the message. The angel of the congregation is called poor, yet declared rich; some addressees are about to suffer but should not be fearful; whoever is faithful unto death will receive the crown of life. These statements imply a structural irony in which present "reality" is deceptive. Poverty, a gruesome future, and physical death are not what they seem to be. This ironic context makes it unnecessary to suppose that John's use of the phrase "synagogue of Satan" implied that someone else deserved the title of Jew. After all, no other congregation was truly poor in contrast to the Smyrniote congregation; no other saints were truly afraid; no other individuals were truly faithful unto death; and, I extrapolate, no one else was claiming to be the true Israel.

Thus, the sarcastic phrase "synagogue of Satan" did not question who could claim to be Jewish; it denied the opponents' allegiance to God. It satirized their probable claims to phrases like "synagogue of the Lord" (cf. Num 16:3),[43] but there are no signs that the offending phrase encapsulates an attempt to outline the relationship of Israel and the churches. In the message to the church in Smyrna we are dealing with sarcasm, not with systematic theology. Denunciation was the goal, not the by-product.

The message to the congregation in Philadelphia (Rev 3:7-13) confirms and extends this interpretation.

> And to the angel of the church in Philadelphia write: Thus says the holy one, the true one, the one who has the key of David, the one who opens and no one shall close, who closes and no one opens. I know your deeds. Behold, I have placed an opened door before you which no one is able to close. For you have little power, and you kept my word and have not denied my name. Behold, I give from the synagogue of Satan—those saying they are Jews and are not but they lie—behold, I shall make them so that they will come and will prostrate themselves at your feet and will know that I love you. Since you kept the word of my endurance, I also will keep you from the hour of testing which is about to come upon the whole world in order to test those dwelling upon the earth. I come quickly. Hold on to what you have so that no one takes your crown. The victor I will make to be a column in the temple of

---

43. Jürgen Roloff, *The Revelation of John* (CC; Minneapolis: Fortress, 1993), 48.

my God and he shall never more depart. And I will write upon him the name of my God and the name of the city of my God, the new Jerusalem which comes down from heaven from my God, and my new name. Let the one who has an ear hear what the spirit says to the churches.

It is impossible to understand this message without recognizing its ironic appropriation of Isaianic oracles. The message comprises a collage of phrases related to Isaiah that interpret the congregation's contemporary experience as the first part of a larger narrative about the congregation's eventual vindication. That larger narrative can be characterized as structural irony, that is, a story in which the intentions of certain actors are thwarted or reversed by the actual course of events. This conclusion is supported by an argument with four steps.

First, note that the message begins with a formula that is unusual. The risen Christ describes himself as the one who has the key of David. All the other messages open with descriptions that come from Rev 1, but this message uses imagery from elsewhere—an oracle in Isa 22:15–25. The Isaiah passage denounced a royal official with authority over Jerusalem and Judah, declaring that his position would be given to Eliakim.

> On that day I will call my servant Eliakim son of Hilkiah, and will clothe him with your robe and bind your sash on him. I will commit your authority to his hand and he shall be a father to the inhabitants of Jerusalem and to the house of Judah. I will place on his shoulder the key of the house of David; he shall open and no one shall shut; he shall shut, and no one shall open.[44]

The invocation of Isa 22:22 in Rev 3:7–8 thus portrays the risen Christ as the one with the key of David, that is, the new official over God's people, over Jerusalem and Judah.[45] The reuse of Isa 22 is limited, though, and not a thorough allegory. A complete allegory would be untenable because it would represent Christ as the Isaianic royal official subservient to the king, and because Isa 22 goes on to predict the downfall of this official as well. So the allusion to Isa 22 is focused on the imagery of the official. John's point is the authority of the Christ over "Jerusalem;" he is the one with authority to open and close.

Second, the ending of the message to the Philadelphian church picks up the important question about who will abide in the holy city (3:12–13). The promise at the end of the message affirms that the victor will become a permanent fixture in the temple and will never ever leave again. The name of God, the name of the new Jerusalem, and the risen one's new name will be written upon the victor/column. The text makes clear that the earthly Jerusalem is not in view here. It is the new Jerusalem, the one that comes down from God.

Third, the meaning of the open door in Rev 3:9 is crucial. What door is open

---

44. Isa 22:20–22 (NRSV).
45. Isa 22:22 MT; LXX reads καὶ δώσω τὴν δόξαν Δαυιδ αὐτῷ, "and I will give to him the glory of David." In the LXX, vv. 18 and 21 refer to the removal and bestowing of a crown, which perhaps comprises another influence on the message to the Philadelphian congregation.

before the Philadelphian congregation? It does not refer to a missionary opportunity like the open-door imagery of 1 Cor 16:9, 2 Cor 2:12, Col 4:3, or Acts 14:27. Such a reading would be foreign to Revelation's portrayal of the relations between churches and their social settings.[46] It would also be alien to this particular message in which the congregation was exhorted to hold onto what they had. They were not told to extend themselves in mission activity.

In Isa 22, the opening and shutting of the door has to do with authority over Jerusalem and the house of Judah, and this is the root meaning in Rev 3:9 as well.[47] Christ possesses authority over access to the new Jerusalem, the right of entry into the eschatological city of God.[48] The idea recurs in Rev 22:14, where a blessing is pronounced upon those who have washed their robes so that they may eat of the tree of life and so that they may enter the new Jerusalem by the gates (which are named after the twelve tribes of Israel).[49] He will guarantee their admission since the congregation had little power but had remained loyal (3:9).

Finally, one other phrase in the Philadelphia message makes an important connection with Isaiah. The one who has the key of David says he will in the future force the synagogue of Satan, the ones who say they are Jews and are not, to come and prostrate themselves at the feet of the saints. This is an extremely unusual idea in Revelation, since elsewhere bowing down to anyone but God—even to angels—is unacceptable.[50] The reason for the prostration motif in 3:9 is that Revelation here reuses a standard idea from Second and Third Isaiah to build on the allusion to the keys of David. Certain oracles late in the book of Isaiah promised that the future would bring about a great reversal. The gentiles who had destroyed and humiliated Jerusalem during the Babylonian and Persian periods would eventually come and bow down to the city in recognition of its special status. "The descendants of those who oppressed you shall come bending low to you, and all who despised you shall bow down at your feet; they shall call you the City of the Lord, the Zion of the Holy One of Israel."[51]

The poetry in Isaiah laid out a structural irony in abbreviated form: the nations that oppressed Jerusalem would someday bow down before the city they had

---

46. Robert H. Mounce, *The Book of Revelation* (New International Commentary; Grand Rapids: Eerdmans, 1977), 117; Roloff, *Revelation*, 61; contra, e.g., R. H. Charles, *A Critical and Exegetical Commentary on the Revelation of St. John* (2 vols.; International Critical Commentary; Edinburgh: T&T Clark, 1920), 1:87.

47. This may also involve a secondary allusion to Isa 45:1–2, which names Persian Cyrus as God's anointed one (לִמְשִׁיחוֹ "his anointed" in the MT; τῷ Χριστῷ μου "my anointed" in the LXX). The Gentile ruler, the anointed one, will open doors and gates; doors of bronze and bars of iron will give way before him.

48. This is approximately what Roloff suggested when he described the open door as entry into the kingdom of God or as membership in the end-time people of God (*Revelation*, 61). He did not provide an argument, however, for the conclusion.

49. Rev 21:12. More on this text below.

50. Cf. Rev 19:10; 22:8–9.

51. Isa 60:14; see also 45:14; 49:23.

despised. In the oracle of the risen Christ, the irony of the Isaianic vision turns into a double reverse. The risen Christ in Revelation promises that some Jews of Philadelphia would someday come and bow down to the (mostly Gentile) congregation. This is structural irony with a sarcastic twist.

When these several allusions to Isaiah in the message to Philadelphia are viewed together, the somewhat strained analogy embedded in the Rev 3:7–13 becomes clear. Revelation reuses Isaiah to assert the right of the mostly Gentile congregation to enter the new Jerusalem. Christ is the royal official with jurisdiction over the holy city, and the role of Isaiah's gentiles is played by the Jewish community in Philadelphia, the synagogue of Satan. This ironic imagery does not come from an unstated assumption on the part of John that the churches are the real Jews or the true Israel. In this instance, the synagogue of Satan reference is simply a satirical, sarcastic flourish embedded within the ironic reuse of scripture. As a socio-literary strategy, it explained the difficult situation of the Philadelphian saints and offered them hope for the future.

Christians? True Jews?

Two issues remain to be considered. The first is whether these messages were anti-Jewish. I understand "anti-Jewish" to mean a blanket condemnation of Jewish people or practices. In that case the answer is, "No, Rev 2–3 is not anti-Jewish." The messages are sarcastic and satirical, but their condemnations were localized and specific, not global and systematic. The ironic strategies were acts of verbal aggression aimed at particular situations about which we have precious little information.

This does not exonerate the text, in my opinion. I do not approve of vicious name-calling, even if it is practiced by an emerging religious group in a vulnerable and potentially lethal situation. But I also recognize that ancient literature, biblical or otherwise, is not subject to my values and opinions. Moreover, I speak from a protected, privileged position within American academic institutions. My knowledge of religious discrimination and social ostracism is second- and third-hand, at best. From my vantage point, however, I do not approve of such sarcasm as an ethical decision.

The second issue is whether we should describe the synagogue of Satan dispute as an intramural Jewish argument of the late first century, as nearly all recent commentators affirm. This question is more difficult and depends a good deal on how we define the terms we use. I maintain that neither "Christian" nor "Jewish" is particularly helpful in this task. Yarbro Collins noted that Ignatius of Antioch had a developed language for distinguishing between "Judaism" and "Christianity" in the early second century, and she warned against imposing that separation upon John's Revelation.[52] That warning should be heeded and developed further. At least part of our trouble in understanding the "synagogue of Satan/Jews who are not Jews"

---

52. Yarbro Collins, "Vilification," 311–12.

references is due to the fact that we have not developed an appropriate language for understanding the community addressed in Revelation.

The most glaring example of our misbegotten conceptual framework is the ubiquitous use of the term "Christian" by modern scholars to describe John, his text, and his congregations. This practice is inexcusable. Revelation is a lengthy text, with ample opportunity for John to call himself or his audience "Christian." He did not. From this I conclude that John either did not know the term, or did not like the term. Nor is there evidence for acceptance of the term by the churches before the second century CE. Granted, our evidence is spotty, but the nearly complete absence of the term Christian in early "Christian" literature is consistently overlooked in New Testament studies. Christian occurs three times in all of the New Testament, twice as a label used by hostile outsiders[53] and once as an ambiguous editorial aside indicating that the term originated in Antioch.[54] If the Gospel of Thomas and the Gospel of Peter are first century documents (which I doubt), then we have further evidence of the irrelevance of the term Christian for this period. Ironically, the terms that we know were used most frequently as self-designations in the first-century churches—saint, brother, sister—are almost never used in New Testament studies.[55]

Our use of *Christian* to describe Revelation is a powerful and pervasive retrojection that warps our analysis of the first century by subtly redefining the churches as opposed to, and superior to, Judaism.[56] Thus, the practice has clouded the debate about anti-Jewishness and synagogues in Revelation because the concept of "Christianity" is now inextricably entangled in the rejection of the concept "Judaism." The moment we introduce the foreign notion of Christianity into Revelation studies, we are forced by our inappropriate categories to import into our interpretation an asymmetrical relationship with Judaism. To put it another way, we are never going to be able to understand the relationship between synagogues and churches in Revelation if we keep calling the church members "Christian." The discussion is misdirected from the beginning by the terms that frame it.

"Judaism" as a modern term is only slightly less of a problem. In modern New Testament studies it has been cast as the foil against which one understands Christianity, the disease for which Christianity is the cure. But at least there is ancient precedent for the concept. With careful analysis of first-century usage of *Ioudaios* and *Ioudaïsmos*, we might be able to rehabilitate the vocabulary and use it in a way that does not automatically conjure up the ghosts of theological anti-Semitism.[57]

---

53. Acts 26:28 by Herod Agrippa II addressing Paul; 1 Peter 4:16 as a legal accusation about which one might be ashamed.

54. Acts 11:26 is ambiguous because the author does not say whether the term was used by insiders or outsiders or both, and because it only implies that the term goes back to the time of Paul (who never uses "Christian" in his extant letters). Perhaps the Antiochean origins of the term explains Ignatius's use of the term χριστιανισμός (e.g., *Magn.* 10:3).

55. This irony almost requires a sarcastic response, but I desist.

56. Marshall, *Parables of War*, 13.

57. Cohen (*Beginnings of Jewishness*) is a helpful resource for this task.

At the level of terminology, Revelation is clear enough. The movement in which John was a prophet was composed of churches. The churches made up some sort of network, for the text of Revelation is a communication to them all.[58] John's term for this network of churches was "kingdom."[59] The kingdom was made up of priests to God, but they are more often called saints[60] or servants of God.[61]

At the level of conceptualization, three images from Revelation help us gain some clarity on the relationship between synagogues and the kingdom of priests envisioned by John. These images suggest that John perceived a transcendent reality which he portrayed as a woman, a crowd, and a city. Some of Israel and some of the churches participated in this transcendent reality, which was in some sense their origin, their contemporary experience, and their destiny—simultaneously.

The first image is the woman of Rev 12. Without solving all the problems involved with this vision (and they are many), it is safe to say that the text suggests a connection between the churches and ancient Israel.[62] A heavenly woman gives birth to the messiah, and to other offspring as well. The other offspring are "those keeping the commands of God and having the testimony of Jesus" (12:17), so the woman is in some sense the source of the saints and their messiah. There is no talk here of Christianity, of true Jews, or of Israel, and the relationships between synagogues and churches are not defined.

The second image is the crowd from Rev 7. This double vision, interjected between the sixth and seventh seals, describes the composition of the kingdom. The first part of the vision (Rev 7:2–8) describes one part of the kingdom as the faithful 144,000 of Israel, twelve thousand from each of the twelve tribes. This is a reworking of Ezekiel's vision of the sealing of the faithful Jerusalemites before the Babylonian assault on that city (Ezek 9). According to John's vision, just as God had saved the faithful of his people in that earlier catastrophe, so God would always protect the remnant of his people. The picture is filled out with the second part of the vision (Rev 7:9–17). A multitude too large to number appears around the throne. These come "from every nation, and tribe and people and tongue" (7:9). The imagery suggests a vision of the churches as a contemporary and eschatological movement, composed of some people from the twelve tribes of Israel and a lot of people from all the other tribes of the world. Again, "Jew," "Israel," and "Christian" are not appropriate terms for this movement.

The third image is the new Jerusalem. The oblique use of this image was already highlighted from the message to the angel of the church in Philadelphia. In Rev 3:7–13, a largely Gentile congregation is guaranteed admission to the city where God

---

58. Note the plural "churches" in 1:4; 2:23; and 22:16.
59. Rev 1:5–6; 5:9–10. John did not use "church" in a universal sense for the larger movement.
60. Rev 5:8; 8:3–4; 11:18; 13:10; etc.
61. Rev 1:1; 2:20; 7:3; 10:7; etc. For more on priesthood and purity, see my *Imperial Cults and the Apocalypse of John: Reading Revelation in the Ruins* (New York: Oxford University Press, 2001), 181–82.
62. So Yarbro Collins, "Vilification," 312.

and the Lamb will dwell with humanity. Their vindication will be acknowledged by their antagonists from the local synagogue. The later vision of the new Jerusalem in Rev 21:9–22:5 is more elaborate than the image in Rev 3:7–13, and does not need to be described fully here. Two aspects touch on the character of the churches in their relationship to Israel, however, and deserve comment. One aspect is the preexistent character of the new Jerusalem, which is only "new" to humanity. The new Jerusalem is a preexistent reality which the saints encounter at the end of normal history (Rev 21:2–4). Habitation in the city entails the full, unmediated presence of God and the end of human suffering.

The second aspect of the new Jerusalem that touches on our topic is the description of the walls of the city. Revelation 21:12–14 remodels the vision of the eschatological Jerusalem found at the end of Ezekiel's oracles (Ezek 48:30–35). Ezekiel had described the future Jerusalem as having twelve gates, one for each of the tribes. In John's vision, the gates are also named after the twelve tribes of the sons of Israel, but a new feature is added. The twelve courses of foundation stones for the wall of the city are named after the twelve apostles of the lamb.

It would be disastrous to try to squeeze these several images into one schema, as if the heavenly woman, the 144,000, the unnumbered multitude, and the new Jerusalem were interlocking parts to the same puzzle. John's imagery is impressive and functional, but hardly systematic. There is a coherence to it, however, that justifies this brief review. In none of these images were the churches portrayed as Israel, as the true Jews, or as Christians. It would be more accurate to say that John's text describes Israel and the churches as participating in a larger transcendent reality. Both synagogues and churches claimed the same scriptural traditions, but according to John, the larger reality did not include all Jews nor did it include all those who called themselves saints. Christian, true Jew, and Israel are inadequate terms for its description. That reality was an eschatological kingdom, a heavenly woman, an unnumbered multitude, a heavenly city that cut across boundaries of ethnicity, language, and culture.[63]

These were grand claims, especially for a network of small vulnerable groups like the churches. From the outside, the churches hardly looked like the eschatological fulfillment of God's dealing with the world (nor do churches today). These sorts of grand claims, juxtaposed with more modest earthly appearances, provided the matrix within which the ironies of John's text flourished. The paradoxical experience made irony, satire, and sarcasm appealing strategies. The gaps between aspiration and achievement gave the prophet room to maneuver.

---

63. Cf. Friesen, *Imperial Cults*, 180–93.

PART TWO

Politics and Reality

"The Synagogue of Satan": Crisis Mongering and the Apocalypse of John

Paul B. Duff

Although the conventional wisdom has long held that the "synagogue of Satan" mentioned in the Apocalypse (Rev 2:9 and 3:9) refers to individuals outside the ἐκκλησία (specifically, Jews from the synagogues in Smyrna and Philadelphia), various alternative suggestions have recently challenged that scenario. Despite their differences, most of these more recent hypotheses have two things in common. First, they recommend that the "synagogue of Satan" was made up of insiders (i.e., members of the ἐκκλησία) and, second, almost all of them in some way tie the "synagogue of Satan" to John's other adversaries ("Jezebel" and the Nicolaitans) mentioned in chapters 2 and 3 of the Apocalypse.[1]

In the first part of this essay, I look at the difficulties that have attended the traditional identification of the "synagogue of Satan." I then focus on the recent at-

---

1. Most scholars accept that "Jezebel" and the Nicolaitans come from one group and not two. This is evidenced by the fact that the charges against the Nicolaitans in the Pergamum letter (2:14) are identical to those leveled at "Jezebel" in the Thyatira letter (2:20). See, for instance, C. K. Barrett, "Gnosis and the Apocalypse of John," *The New Testament and Gnosis: Essays in Honor of Robert McL. Wilson* (ed. A. H. B. Logan and A. J. M. Wedderburn; Edinburgh: T&T Clark, 1983), 127–28; Elisabeth Schüssler Fiorenza, *The Book of Revelation: Justice and Judgment* (Philadelphia: Fortress, 1985), 116; David E. Aune, *Revelation 1–5* (WBC 52; Dallas: Word, 1997), 149. Some scholars have also postulated another rival prophet in the figure of "Balaam," who is mentioned in the letter to the church at Pergamum. See, for instance, Adela Yarbro Collins, *Crisis and Catharsis: The Power of the Apocalypse* (Philadelphia: Westminster, 1984), 44–45; Lloyd Gaston, "Judaism of the Uncircumcised in Ignatius and Related Writers," in *Anti-Judaism in Early Christianity* (ed. Stephen G. Wilson; Studies in Early Christianity and Judaism 2; Waterloo, Ontario: Wilfrid Laurier University Press, 1986), 42; David L. Barr, *Tales of the End: A Narrative Commentary on the Book of Revelation* (Santa Rosa, Calif.: Polebridge, 1998), 50; cf. Leonard L. Thompson, *The Book of Revelation: Apocalypse and Empire* (New York: Oxford University Press, 1990), 80; Frederick J. Murphy, *Fallen Is Babylon: The Revelation to John* (New Testament in Context; Harrisburg, Pa.: Trinity Press International, 1998), 114. But this suggestion seems unlikely. John uses the name "Balaam" in the context of the Israel of the distant past in order to compare the past "teaching of Balaam" to the present "teaching of the Nicolaitans" (cf. Rev 2:6). Note the difference in John's language in the letter to Thyatira where he refers to "Jezebel." In the latter, John uses the present tense whereas in the Pergamum letter he uses the aorist tense.

tempts to tie the "synagogue of Satan" to factions inside the churches. But, as we see, although these recent suggestions initially appear attractive, ultimately they are not persuasive. Consequently, the appellation "synagogue of Satan" must be applied to the local synagogues, as interpreters have traditionally believed.[2]

But, by identifying the "synagogue of Satan" with Jews from the local synagogues, we cannot simply return to the old explanations for Jewish aggression against the churches. This is because the previous reasons given for Jewish hostility are problematic. Consequently, in the second part of this essay, I focus on the difficulties one encounters when attempting to identify the tensions that existed between the synagogues and John's churches. As we discover, the intensity of the hostility that John directs against the "synagogue of Satan" is difficult to justify based upon evidence from the text of the Apocalypse. As a result, in the final section of the essay, I suggest that John's negative comments were intended to exacerbate tensions between the churches and synagogues, tensions that were heretofore otherwise unremarkable. By fostering enmity against the synagogues and (perhaps more importantly) by promoting fear of hostility from local Jews, John intended to discourage his closest allies in the internal church struggles (i.e., the members of the churches in Smyrna and Philadelphia) from defecting to the synagogues.

Hostility from the Local Jewish Community?

Throughout much of the twentieth century, it was generally assumed that an empire-wide Roman persecution of those in the churches[3] provided the backdrop for the book of Revelation.[4] This persecution, so the assumption held, resulted from the church members' refusal to participate in the imperial cult. Many scholars identified the "synagogue of Satan" with Jews who collaborated with government officials in the

---

2. See the similar conclusion in ch. 6 above.
3. Throughout this essay, I have tried to avoid the use of the term "Christian." Although, a short time after the book of Revelation was written (depending upon when one dates this book), the terms "Christian" and "Christianity" were in use in Asia Minor as is evidenced by Ignatius's letters (Ign. *Mag.* 10:3; Ign. *Phld.* 6:1). Consequently, it is possible (and perhaps even likely) that the term "Christian" was an appropriate label in Asia Minor at John's time. Nevertheless, we cannot be certain. As a result, I will use the terms "church" or "churches" when referring to Revelation's addressees. For more on the methodological issue surrounding the use of the terms "Christian" or "Christianity" with respect to Revelation, see John W. Marshall, *Parables of War: Reading John's Jewish Apocalypse* (Studies in Christianity and Judaism 10; Waterloo, Ontario: Wilfred Laurier University Press, 2001), esp. 25–87.
4. Throughout the century, it was usually assumed, first, that the Apocalypse was written in the later years of the emperor Domitian's reign and, second, that Domitian actively persecuted the church. See, for instance, W. M. Ramsay, *The Letters to the Seven Churches* (ed. Mark W. Wilson; London: Hodder and Stoughton, 1906; repr., Peabody, Mass.: Hendrickson, 1994), 91.

persecution of the churches, whether wittingly[5] or not.[6] Others assumed that the Jews actively persecuted the churches independent of any government action.[7]

Recent years have witnessed the erosion of the theory of empire-wide Roman persecution at John's time.[8] Despite this, the notion of Jewish collaboration in Roman

---

5. E.g., R. H. Charles, *A Critical and Exegetical Commentary on the Revelation of St. John* (2 vols. Edinburgh: T&T Clark, 1920), 1.58; J. Ramsey Michaels, *Revelation* (IVP New Testament Commentary Series 20; Downers Grove, Ill.: InterVarsity Press, 1997), 74; J. P. M. Sweet, *Revelation* (Westminster Pelican Commentaries; Philadelphia: Westminster, 1979), 85; Aune, *Revelation 1–5*, 162–63 (cautiously); G. K. Beale, *The Book of Revelation: A Commentary on the Greek Text* (New International Greek Testament Commentary; Grand Rapids; Eerdmans, 1999), 240–41; Craig R. Koester, *Revelation and the End of All Things* (Grand Rapids: Eerdmans, 2001), 64–65. According to such proposals, Jews denounced church members to the authorities. These theories typically cite the *Martyrdom of Polycarp* as evidence for active Jewish participation in Roman persecutions for that text (describing the death of the Smyrnaean bishop in the mid second century) depicts the Jews of Smyrna as playing a major role in Polycarp's death. The *Martyrdom of Pionius*—probably a mid-third-century text (see Robin Lane Fox, *Pagans and Christians* [New York: Knopf, 1986], 460–92)—is also cited sometimes even though it recounts events a century after the death of Polycarp and more than a century and a half (or more) after the writing of Revelation. See, for instance, Charles, *Revelation*, 1:57.

6. Colin Hemer, for instance, suggested that the synagogues in the Asian cities unintentionally exposed church members to Roman persecution. This situation came about, Hemer maintains, because the synagogues were forced to provide lists of their bona fide members to the authorities in order that the latter could more effectively collect the *fiscus Ioudaicus* (the tax levied against all Jews by the Romans following the Roman Jewish war of 66–70 C.E.). Unfortunately, when the synagogues turned over their membership roles to the authorities, those from the churches who had previously found refuge from Roman persecution in the synagogues were exposed. See Colin J. Hemer, *The Letters to the Seven Churches of Asia in Their Local Settings* (JSNTSup 11; Sheffield: JSOT, 1986), 7–10. Hemer's proposal, though, is extraordinarily speculative for a number of reasons. There is no evidence, for instance, that the synagogues were asked for membership roles at this time. Nor is there evidence that members of the ἐκκλησία at John's time sought refuge in the synagogues. Most importantly, the assumption about the demand that all participate in the imperial cult at John's time or face persecution is particularly problematic. On the imperial cult, see, especially S. R. F. Price, *Ritual and Power: The Roman Imperial Cult in Asia Minor* (Cambridge: Cambridge University Press, 1984), 125; Thompson, *Book of Revelation*, 163–64. For an understanding of the role that the imperial cult played in the lives of the members of the ἐκκλησία, see Steven J. Friesen, *Imperial Cults and the Apocalypse of John: Reading Revelation in the Ruins* (Oxford: Oxford University Press, 2001).

7. See G. B. Caird, *The Revelation of St. John the Divine* (Harper's New Testament Commentaries; New York: Harper & Row, 1966), 35, and Henry Barclay Swete, *The Apocalypse of John: The Greek Text with Introduction, Notes, and Indices* (Grand Rapids: Eerdmans, 1954), 31. Schüssler Fiorenza (*Book of Revelation*, 194–95) suggests that the Jews were anxious to get rid of "trouble-makers" like those in the church so that the synagogues not be targeted by Rome.

8. The long-held belief that Domitian (traditionally held to be the emperor at John's time) persecuted the church was called into question due to the fact that there is little (if any) good evidence to support it. In my view, the three groundbreaking studies that fully acknowledged the lack of evidence for persecution and tried to come to terms with that are John A. T. Robinson, *Redating the New Testament* (Philadelphia: Westminster, 1976), 221–53; Yarbro Collins, *Crisis*; and Thompson, *Book of Revelation*. Robinson's strategy was to redate the Apocalypse. Yarbro Collins suggested that although the community was not, in fact, persecuted, it, nevertheless, perceived itself to be under attack. Thompson suggested that the scenario of persecution that the book of Revelation implies, is part and parcel of the genre "apocalypse." As such, persecution appears in the visions section of the text although it does not

persecution has not totally fallen out of favor. Instead, the theory has been modified somewhat. Faced with the growing difficulties that attended the assumption of an empire-wide Roman persecution, a number of scholars have suggested that localized outbreaks of persecution served as the backdrop for the Apocalypse.[9] And, according to this revised scenario, Jews participated in these localized outbreaks of violence. So, while in its reconstituted form, this theory remains viable, nevertheless, external support for localized persecution in area of the churches at John's time is difficult to produce, as is evidence for Jewish participation in such.[10] But because of its potential for explaining John's hostile remarks about the "synagogue of Satan," we will return to this possibility in the pages that follow.

While some scholars have speculated that Jews participated in localized governmental persecution, others—as mentioned above—suggested that Jews independently harassed members of the churches. G. B. Caird, for instance, appealed to Hebrews 10:34 to argue that the poverty of the Smyrnaean church members (mentioned by John in Rev 2:9) resulted from the looting of their property at the instigation of the Jewish community.[11] But Caird was clearly grasping at straws when he made this suggestion. Although the Hebrews text mentions plundering of property, it in no way connects these acts with the Jewish community.[12]

Another scholar, Adela Yarbro Collins, suggested that Jewish hostility took the

---

accurately reflect the book of Revelation's *Sitz im Leben*. For a more complete summary of these positions, see Paul B. Duff, *Who Rides the Beast? Prophetic Rivalry and the Rhetoric of Crisis in the Churches of the Apocalypse* (Oxford: Oxford University Press, 2001), 6–10. It should be noted that, although the empire-wide Roman persecution position still has a few champions, it has been fairly thoroughly discredited. For an argument supporting it, see Marta Sordi, *The Christians and the Roman Empire* (Norman: University of Oklahoma Press, 1986).

9. E.g., Sweet, *Revelation*, 27–28.

10. A good example of localized persecution comes from a time after the Apocalypse was written (in a different area of Asia Minor). Two letters of Pliny the Younger to the emperor Trajan, written in 112 from Pliny's post in Bithynia (10.96 and 10.97), depict such a situation. Some would credit the death of Antipas, mentioned in Rev 2:13, to a similar outbreak of localized hostility. For a list of texts outlining Jewish persecution of the church, see Aune, *Revelation 1–5*, 162–63. Unfortunately, the texts cited by Aune are not contemporary with John (they are mostly later) and, as Aune points out, "[I]t is important to recognize that the emphasis on Jewish hostility and persecution as a major cause of the suffering of Christians was in part a theological convention in Christian apologetics requiring little or no evidence" (163). The *Martyrdom of Polycarp*—the text frequently used to justify Jewish participation in persecution of the church—has shown itself to be historically unreliable as regards the part played by the Jews in Polycarp's death (of course, even if it were reliable, the date of the event still presents a problem since it occurred at least a half-century after Revelation was written). The antagonistic Jewish role in this text was almost certainly a literary construct that was designed to echo the role of the Jews in the various passion accounts of the Gospels. Consequently, it can be used to illuminate neither the historical events surrounding Polycarp's death nor the relations between church and synagogue at John's time. See Thompson, *Book of Revelation*, 126, and Aune, *Revelation 1–5*, 162.

11. Caird, *Revelation*, 35.

12. Likewise, there is no consensus on either the date of Hebrews or its location. As a result, there is no good reason to connect the scenario of Hebrews with that of Revelation.

form of the expulsion of church members from the synagogues.[13] The cause of the expulsions, she recommended, could be best attributed to the Christological claims of the members of the churches. Although Yarbro Collins's scenario is certainly possible, there is nothing in the text of the Apocalypse (either in chapters 2, 3, or elsewhere) that recommends that the affirmation or denial of Jesus' messianic status caused tension between the church and synagogue.[14] Nor is there solid evidence for synagogue expulsions in western Asia Minor at the end of the first century.[15]

As we can see then, even if we accept the likelihood of some kind of Jewish hostility toward the churches at John's time, establishing a specific cause for that hostility is not an easy task. If, on the other hand, we put aside the assumption of Jewish hostility, explaining John's enmity toward the synagogue is equally difficult. Perhaps, because of the challenges that attend the identification of the "synagogue of Satan" with Jews outside the ἐκκλησία, a number of scholars have instead proposed that the "synagogue of Satan" represents a faction that existed within the churches.

Was the "Synagogue of Satan" a Faction within the Ἐκκλησία?

Beginning in the late 1960s, a growing number of scholars began to suggest the possibility that the "synagogue of Satan" was John's label for a group from within the ἐκκλησία. Although there are several variations on this theory, they can, for the most part, be categorized according to two types.

The first type consists of those proposals that view the "synagogue of Satan" as made up of Judaizing gentiles from within the churches. In one form or another, this scenario has been advocated by Barclay Newman, Helmut Koester, C. K. Barrett, John Gager, Lloyd Gaston, Stephen Wilson, and J. Ramsey Michaels.[16] Of these,

---

13. Yarbro Collins, *Crisis*, 85; idem, "Insiders and Outsiders in the book of Revelation and Its Social Context," in *"To See Ourselves as Others See Us": Christians, Jews, "Others" in Late Antiquity* (ed. J. Neusner and E. S. Frerichs; Chico, Calif.: Scholars Press, 1985), 207–10. For other suggestions that Jews independently persecuted members of the churches, see also Swete, *Apocalypse*, 31, and Schüssler Fiorenza, *Book of Revelation*, 194–95.

14. Cf. Marshall, *Parables*, 48.

15. As the Gospel of John indicates (9:22), the author of that document knows of synagogue expulsions but, despite church tradition, that text was clearly not written by the author of the Apocalypse. In addition, there is no evidence that the fourth gospel was written in Asia Minor (although Raymond Brown allows for this possibility in his *Gospel according to John: A New Translation with Introduction and Commentary*, vol. 1: *John I–XII* [Garden City, N.Y.: Doubleday, 1966], ciii–iv). Most interpreters think Syria is a more likely location for the gospel. See, for instance Helmut Koester, *Introduction to the New Testament*, vol. 2: *History and Literature of the New Testament* (Philadelphia: Fortress, 1982), 185.

16. Barclay M. Newman Jr., *Rediscovering the Book of Revelation* (Valley Forge, Pa.: Judson, 1968), 48–55; Helmut Koester, "Gnomai Diaphorai: The Origin and Nature of Diversification in the History of Early Christianity," in James M. Robinson and Helmut Koester, *Trajectories through Early Christianity* (Philadelphia: Fortress, 1971), 148, C. K. Barrett, "Christianity at Corinth," in his *Essays on Paul* (Philadelphia: Westminster, 1976), 242; John G. Gager, *The Origins of Anti-Semitism: Attitudes toward Judaism in Pagan and Christian Antiquity* (Oxford: Oxford University Press, 1983), 132; Gaston, "Judaism," 42–44; idem, *Paul and the Torah* (Vancouver: University of British Columbia

Newman, Gaston, and Wilson have laid out their claims in the most systematic way.[17]

Newman's argument is by far the most problematic of the three, since it is based primarily on evidence gathered from mid to late second century Gnostic texts. Gaston and Wilson, on the other hand, have drawn their evidence from a more temporally and spatially relevant source, the letters of Ignatius of Antioch.[18] Both have paid particular their attention to Ignatius's letter to the Philadelphians, where the bishop warns:

> If anyone interpret Judaism to you do not listen to him; for it is better to hear Christianity from the circumcised than Judaism from the uncircumcised.

Gaston and Wilson each appeal to this text in order to support their suggestion that "those who call themselves Jews but are not" (i. e., the "synagogue of Satan") are, as Revelation's statement literally indicates, not Jews. They are, instead, gentiles promoting Jewish practices within the churches. As such, they can be identified with the "uncircumcised" in Ignatius's letters who "interpret Judaism." Gaston, further, links the docetism alluded to in the Ignatian letters (especially in the letters to the Trallians and the Smyrnaeans) to what he sees as the gnosticizing libertine practices of "Jezebel" and the Nicolaitans in the communities of the Apocalypse.[19] So, according

---

Press, 1987), 25, 213, Stephen G. Wilson, "Gentile Judaizers," *NTS* 38 (1992): 613–15; idem, *Related Strangers: Jews and Christians, 70–170 C.E.* (Minneapolis: Fortress, 1995), 162–63; Michaels, *Revelation*, 73–74. Shaye J. D. Cohen allows for this possibility but ultimately believes that John refers to actual Jews: "The striking phrase 'those who say they are Jews and are not' may well have been a current expression in the first century. It will have been applied to gentiles who 'act the part of Jews' but are not in fact Jews, and was deliberately and cleverly misapplied by Revelation to the Jews themselves." See his book *The Beginnings of Jewishness: Boundaries, Varieties, Uncertainties* (Berkeley: University of California Press, 1999), 187. See also Massey H. Shepherd Jr., "The Gospel of John," *The Interpreter's One-Volume Commentary on the Bible* (ed. C. M. Laymon; Nashville: Abingdon, 1971), 708; S. E. Johnson, "Unsolved Questions about Early Christianity in Anatolia," in *Studies in New Testament and Early Christian Literature: Essays in Honor of Allen P. Wickgren* (ed. David E. Aune; Leiden: E. J. Brill, 1972), 186; idem, "Asia Minor and Early Christianity," in *Studies in Judaism in Late Antiquity: Studies for Morton Smith at Sixty*, vol. 2: *Early Christianity* (ed. J. Neusner; Leiden: Brill, 1975), 111.

17. For the most part, the rest have simply made the suggestion but not argued for it.

18. Although it is difficult to date Ignatius's letters with precision, most agree that the letters were probably written in the first two decades of the second century. See William R. Schoedel, *Ignatius of Antioch* (Hermeneia; Philadelphia: Fortress, 1985), 5.

19. It should be noted that Wilson is careful not to speculate beyond what he thinks his evidence can bear. He does not try, for instance, to connect the docetic beliefs alluded to in Ignatius to the situation in John's churches. As Wilson's hesitancy suggests, there are problems with using Ignatius to flesh out the situation behind the Apocalypse. Scholars have been unable, first, to establish a consensus about who or what Ignatius was addressing when he spoke of Judaism and, second, to draw any convincing links between John's situation and that of Ignatius. Concerning the former, for instance, scholars cannot even agree whether Ignatius faced one set of opponents (docetic Judaizers or Judaizing Docetists) or two (Docetists and Judaizers). I am persuaded that Ignatius faced *both* Judaizers and Docetists. Most likely, the issue of Judaizing, as Cohen has indicated (*Beginnings of Jewishness*, 187), seems to be about Sabbath observance. Ignatius probably labels it "Judaizing" in order to more effectively condemn it

to Gaston, John faces Judaizers in a number of the churches but they are identified as Nicolaitans in some of the letters[20] and the "synagogue of Satan" in others.[21]

The second type of proposal (connecting the "synagogue of Satan" with a group within the ἐκκλησία) postulates that the "synagogue of Satan" was constituted both by Judaizing gentiles and by Jews in the churches. Variations on this theory have been proposed by Heinrich Kraft,[22] John W. Marshall,[23] and David Frankfurter.[24] The most ambitious attempt to argue this position to date has been made by Marshall. He sets the date of the book of Revelation in 69 or early 70, during the time of the disastrous Jewish revolt against Rome.[25] Marshall contends that the Apocalypse predates any formal separation of Christianity from Judaism. John, a Jew, labeled some, namely, "comfortably Hellenized Jews" and/or God-fearers in the assemblies[26] (who compromised with the larger pagan society), the "synagogue of Satan." These individuals appear in the other letters that do not mention the "synagogue of Satan"—but in the guise of "Balaam," "Jezebel," and the Nicolaitans—where they are accused of practicing πορνεία ("fornication") and eating εἰδωλόθυτα ("food sacrificed to idols").[27]

---

before his gentile audience. Concerning the difficulty in using Ignatius, Wilson himself admits that the evidence "is not unambiguous" ("Gentile Judaizers," 615).

20. As many scholars have pointed out, these are not really letters. See Schüssler Fiorenza, *Book of Revelation*, 46, and David E. Aune, "The Form and Function of the Proclamation to the Seven Churches (Revelation 2–3)," *NTS* 36 (1990): 182–204. Regardless, for the sake of convenience, I will refer to them as letters in the remainder of this essay.

21. Gaston, "Judaism."

22. Heinrich Kraft (*Die Offenbarung des Johannes* [HNT 16a; Tübingen: Mohr Siebeck, 1974], 60–61) postulated that the "synagogue of Satan" was a "Jewish Christian" group who compromised with the state and with the larger pagan culture. Kraft, though, gives little evidence for this identification.

23. Marshall, *Parables*.

24. David Frankfurter, "Jews or Not? Reconstructing the 'Other' in Rev 2:9 and 3:9," *HTR* 94 (2001): 403.

25. This date solves two problems for Marshall. First, it makes better sense of the persecution language of the Apocalypse as well as the author's antipathy for Rome than does a later date and, second, it places Revelation early enough to justify the claim that Judaism and Christianity had not yet defined themselves against one another (as seems to have been the case at the very end of the century as attested in the letters of Ignatius of Antioch). Unfortunately, the early date also causes serious problems for Marshall since most scholars believe that a later date better fits the evidence from the book of Revelation. See, for instance, Friesen, *Imperial Cults*, 136–51.

26. Since "Christianity" had yet to split from Judaism, Marshall argues against assigning any technical meaning to the terms ἐκκλησία and συναγωγή. Rather, he prefers to translate each as "assembly" or "gathering."

27. Although Marshall nowhere *explicitly* states that the "synagogue of Satan" is the very same group as the others mentioned, and although he is reluctant to put much faith in historical reconstruction based upon Rev 2 and 3, nevertheless, the identification of the Nicolaitans with the "synagogue of Satan," runs implicitly throughout the work. See especially, *Parables*, 122–34. David Frankfurter has recently argued a scenario similar to Marshall's, although, in some respects, his position lies somewhere between that of Marshall and those (mentioned above) who suggested that the "synagogue of Satan" was composed of gentiles. Although Frankfurter, like Marshall, understands the milieu of Revelation to be that of Judaism (where the issues have to do with proper observance), nevertheless, he sees the "synagogue of Satan" (in Smyrna and Philadelphia) as made up of pagan God-fearers who sided with

Rather than undertake a critique of the various incarnations of these different positions, I will instead focus on one element that almost all have in common. Although some might understand the identity of the adversaries differently, nevertheless, as I mentioned above, most advocates of these positions understand John's polemic to be directed at only one set of opponents. They tie the "synagogue of Satan" to the adversaries mentioned in the other parts of chapters 2 and 3 of the book of Revelation.[28] In fact, the validity of their theories usually depends upon that identification because the proposals appeal to the practices of "Jezebel," the Nicolaitans, and the like in order to flesh out the identity of the "synagogue of Satan."

Consequently, we can test these theories by closely examining evidence about John's opponents found in chapters 2 and 3. As we will see, such an examination suggests that the "synagogue of Satan" mentioned in the letters to Smyrna and Philadelphia should not be identified with the rivals discussed in the letters to Ephesus, Pergamum, and Thyatira for two different reasons. The first reason focuses on the differences in the structures of the seven letters. The second concerns a specific threat directed against the "synagogue of Satan," a threat delivered by the risen Jesus in the letter to the church at Philadelphia.

The Structure of the Letters to the Churches

As a number of scholars have pointed out, the so-called letters of chapters 2 and 3 share similar structures.[29] A close examination of the documents, though, shows not one but two different structures underlying the messages. Five of the letters—to the churches in Ephesus, Pergamum, Thyatira, Sardis, and Laodicea—share the first structure and two—the letters to Smyrna and Philadelphia—share the second.[30] The most significant difference between these structures, for our purposes, lies in the fact that the former set of letters includes a call for repentance (aimed at some or all of the church members) and a threat from the risen Jesus (directed against the recipients of the letter). The latter set, on the other hand, does not.

That the letters to the two churches that mention the synagogue of Satan lack a call for repentance suggests that different circumstances underlie them. This absence

---

the neo-Paulinist Jews, "Jezebel" and the Nicolaitans, mentioned in the letters to Ephesus, Pergamum, and Thyatira. See his "Jews or Not," 403–25.

28. There are two exceptions to this. The first is Wilson who does not deal with other individuals or groups beside the "synagogue of Satan" in the Apocalypse. The other exception is Frankfurter who, as mentioned in the previous note, makes a distinction between "Jezebel" and the Nicolaitans on the one hand and the "synagogue of Satan" on the other. According to Frankfurter, John objects to the neo-Pauline *teachings* of "Jezebel" and the Nicolaitans but he objects to the *practices* of the "synagogue of Satan." The former are Jews while the latter group is composed of gentiles who were merely observing some degree of Jewish practice ("acting the Jew"). We will return to Frankfurter's suggestion below. See n. 49.

29. E.g., Aune, "Form and Function"; Schüssler Fiorenza, *Book of Revelation*, 46; Duff, *Who Rides*, 32–36.

30. For a more extensive analysis of the structure of the letters, see Duff, *Who Rides*, 32–36.

seems to indicate that Smyrna and Philadelphia did not experience the same internal "heresy" found in the churches that mention "Jezebel" or the Nicolaitans (i.e., the churches at Ephesus, Pergamum, and Thyatira).[31] In sum, based upon the structural differences in the letters, it seems unlikely that the "synagogue of Satan" was an internal "heretical" faction like the Nicolaitans.

The Eschatological Fate of the "Synagogue of Satan"

When we turn to the eschatological fate of the various evil parties mentioned throughout the Apocalypse, we encounter a second, more significant difficulty in identifying the "synagogue of Satan" with John's other internal adversaries. Of course, in the visions section of the Apocalypse (chs. 4–22), the different agents of Satan, including "Babylon," the beasts of chapter 13 and 17, and the unrepentant mass of humanity,[32] all face eschatological annihilation.[33]

What about those adversaries mentioned in the letters? What is the expected fate of these characters? Since it is clear that John's major adversary in the churches is the woman that he identifies as "Jezebel,"[34] what does John see as her eschatological fate or that of her followers? What about the fate of the "synagogue of Satan?" Unfortunately, answering these questions is not as simple as one might initially presume.

The fate of "Jezebel" and her followers. In the Thyatira letter (Rev 2:21–23), John

---

31. But, of course, these structural differences are not, by themselves, conclusive. One could simply counter that the Nicolaitans and the "synagogue of Satan" were two names for the same group and that the churches at Smyrna and Philadelphia had successfully resisted the advances of this group. But, there is a problem with this counter suggestion. We can see the problem clearly by turning to the letter to the church at Ephesus. Although the Ephesian church had apparently successfully resisted the advances of the Nicolaitans (an accomplishment for which John commended them, Rev 2:6), the letter to Ephesus still includes both a call for repentance and a threat. This fact suggests to me that the mere presence of internal "heretical" factions (whether or not they have gained a following) was a frightening enough prospect for John to include in his letter the call for repentance and the threat. Since we do not see these elements in the letters to Smyrna or Philadelphia, this indicates that John did not see the "synagogue of Satan" as posing the same kind of danger to the Smyrnaean or Philadelphian communities that the Nicolaitans posed to the Ephesians (or the divided communities of Pergamum and Thyatira).

32. Described in 21:8 as "the cowardly, the faithless, the polluted, the murderers, the fornicators, the sorcerers, the idolaters, and all liars.'"

33. According to Rev 19:20, the beast from the sea and the "false prophet" will be thrown into the lake of fire.

34. In fact, the importance of the "Jezebel" can easily be confirmed by the prominence given to the letter in which she appears, the letter to Thyatira. This letter is the longest of the seven letters. According to the twenty-seventh Nestle-Aland edition of the New Testament, the letter to Thyatira has 230 words (with seventy-four of them aimed specifically at "Jezebel" and her followers). All of the other letters run between one hundred and two hundred words, although most of them have fewer than 150 words. The letter to Thyatira is also the most detailed, and it occupies the central position in chapters 2 and 3 as the fourth out of seven letters.

narrates the risen Jesus' threat aimed at "Jezebel" as well as two parties associated with her as follows:

> Beware, I will throw[35] ["Jezebel"] onto a sick bed,[36] and those who commit adultery with her I throw into great distress, unless they repent of her doings; and I will strike her children dead.

While, at first glance, "Jezebel's" fate seems easy enough to understand, nevertheless, as we will see, it is essential to look first at the fate of the other parties mentioned in this passage in order to understand her destiny correctly.

The group mentioned immediately after "Jezebel" is described as those who "commit adultery with her" and the other group is labeled "her children." The latter, "Jezebel's" children, almost certainly represents her followers, those who have acknowledged the legitimacy of her prophetic calling (most likely to the exclusion of John's prophetic claims). The fate of this group is clear and unequivocal. They will be killed (ἀποκτενῶ ἐν θανάτῳ).[37]

The text tells us that the former group, those who "commit adultery with her," will be thrown into "great distress, unless they repent." The image of adultery used here suggests divided loyalty, a party that is interested and involved with a second party (besides that to which it is legitimately tied), although not committed to that second party in any formal sense.[38] Based on the adultery imagery, the lesser punishment, and the possibility of repentance offered them, this group must represent those in the community who have been attracted to "Jezebel's" message but have not cut their ties to John.[39]

To sum up thus far then, the comments about "Jezebel's" children demonstrate that those in the community who have committed themselves to another leader

---

35. Although the NRSV translates this and the next line in the present, following the Greek, the context demands translating it in the future (as have most translations). Consequently, I have used the future tense here.

36. Although the NRSV renders κλίνη as "bed," Charles (*Revelation*, 1:71–72) and Aune (*Revelation 1–5*, 205) have pointed out that βάλλω αὐτὴν εἰς κλίνη represents a Hebrew idiom that means "to cast upon a bed of illness." As a result, "sickbed" (cf. RSV) renders the phrase more accurately than "bed" (NRSV). Of course, the bed imagery also suggests the sexual promiscuity (probably metaphorical promiscuity in the sense of idolatry) of which he accuses her.

37. Note the emphasis on death in this remark. The text literally reads "I will kill them in (with?) death."

38. An adulterer, for instance, still maintains some kind of relationship with his/her spouse. This loyalty prevents the adulterer from simply ending the marriage in order to devote all of his/her time to the new object of affection. Note that the imagery of adultery is only used here. This is significant. Typically, John uses the sexual metaphor of "fornication" (πορνεία). Whereas the adultery metaphor suggests involvement with insiders (i.e., "Jezebel" and those who "commit adultery with her are all members of the ἐκκλησία), the πορνεία metaphor is used to describe involvement with the outside (i.e., with the larger pagan society).

39. See Paul B. Duff, "'I Will Give to Each of You as Your Works Deserve': Witchcraft Accusations and the Fiery-Eyed Son of God in Rev 2.18–23," *NTS* 43 (1997): 121. This group probably represents the real audience at whom John aimed his Apocalypse. See Duff, *Who Rides*, 58–59.

within the ἐκκλησία will be dealt with in the same manner as the churches' outside enemies (such as the beasts). They will be destroyed. Those who have not yet committed themselves to that other leader (those individuals whose loyalty is divided between John and "Jezebel") will be given a chance to repent.

When we turn to the fate of "Jezebel," her destiny at first appears puzzling. According to the text, she is to be thrown "onto a sickbed." It seems, at least on the surface, that while her followers are condemned to death by the risen Jesus, their leader "Jezebel" is merely destined to fall ill. But this can hardly be possible. Although the text does not explicitly state it, logic demands that "Jezebel's" sickness result in her death. A lesser punishment than that of her "children" is inconceivable.[40] The text, therefore, should not be understood as contrasting the terminal fate of "Jezebel's" children with the less severe fate of their leader. Rather, it implies that "Jezebel" will be thrown onto a sickbed from which she will never arise. So, a lingering (and presumably painful) death is apportioned to "Jezebel" while her followers face a relatively quick dispatch.[41] If this analysis is correct, then it is clear that the harsh punishment meted out to John's opponents who we know to be within the churches corresponds to the fate of the various external evil figures mentioned in the visions of the work.[42]

The fate of the members of the "synagogue of Satan." If the "synagogue of Satan" is to be identified with John's other adversaries in the letters section of the Apocalypse as some have suggested, then we should expect the fate of the "synagogue of Satan" to conform to the fate of "Jezebel" and her followers. That is, we should expect a promise of their destruction (presumably at the eschaton).

But this is not what the text describes. In the letter to the church at Philadelphia, the risen Jesus states:[43]

> I will make those of the synagogue of Satan who say that they are Jews and are not, but are lying—I will make them come and bow down before your feet, and they will learn (γλῶσιν) that I have loved you (3:9).

This passage not only neglects any mention of the future destruction of the "synagogue of Satan" but instead it points to what I read as a rather benevolent treatment at the eschaton. Granted, the "synagogue of Satan" will be humiliated, but it will also learn (γνῶσιν) from its humiliation. The eschatological vindication of the church will result in what the Jewish tradition would call παιδεία (or *mwsr* in the Hebrew

---

40. This seems especially so in light of two facts. First, she has already refused the chance to repent and, second, John has attempted to shift much of the blame for the activities of those she "committed adultery with" onto her (see Duff, *Who Rides*, 90). In short, if anything, John has depicted "Jezebel" in as negative a light as possible.

41. I have argued previously that "Jezebel" is expected to fall victim to the powerful glance of the Son of God's fiery eyes. See Duff, " 'I Will Give,' " 121–22.

42. In John's apocalyptic world, where the battle lines between good and evil have been sharply drawn, such is to be expected. An enemy of God is an enemy of God, whether internal or external.

43. Revelation 2:9, the other passage that mentions the "synagogue of Satan," does not address the fate of this group.

Bible) for the synagogue.⁴⁴ Although the words παιδεία and *mwsr* certainly indicate punishment, nevertheless, it is the type of punishment that would be administered by a parent rather than an enemy.⁴⁵

An example of such "punishment," for instance, is alluded to in Prov 3:11 (LXX), where the text admonishes:

> My child, do not despise the LORD's discipline (παιδείας κυρίου)
> or be weary of his reproof

Although this particular text does not specifically indicate the reason that one should welcome "the LORD's discipline," other Jewish texts do. For instance, in the book of Judith, the heroine encourages the people of her town to face up to their seemingly desperate situation with the words: "the Lord scourges those who are close to him in order to admonish them" (8:27).

According to this way of thinking, then, the Jewish tradition distinguishes between two kinds of punishment. The first is directed by God at his chosen. He punishes (or "disciplines") them so that they might alter their behavior (repent, in other words) and so be reconciled to him. The second type of punishment is directed at the rest of humanity. God will punish them unmercifully because they have earned his wrath.⁴⁶

Surprisingly, there is no indication that the "synagogue of Satan" will receive the latter type of punishment. Nothing in the text suggests that it will suffer the fate of "Jezebel" and her "children." Although explicit details of the final fate of the "synagogue of Satan" are missing, the text nevertheless suggests that what awaits the synagogue is divine correction. At the eschaton, they will come to "know" (γνῶσιν) the truth, "that [God] has loved [the church at Philadelphia]" (Rev 3:9).⁴⁷ Presumably, after they have been disciplined and "know the truth," they will repent and be saved, along with the faithful of the ἐκκλησία.⁴⁸

---

44. For a few examples, of which there exist many, see Prov 3:11–12; Wisd 3:5; 11:1–14, Sir 18:13. For more on this kind of punishment, see Georg Bertram, "παιδεύω, κτλ.," *TDNT* 5:603–25.

45. This is an important idea in apocalyptic Judaism and also in some New Testament texts. For more on this idea, especially in the New Testament, see Sam K. Williams, *Jesus' Death as Saving Event: The Background and Origin of a Concept* (HDR 2; Missoula, Mont.: Scholars Press, 1975), 29–34.

46. In an apocalyptic scenario this punishment translates into their destruction at the eschaton.

47. See Rev 2:23, where there is an example of a related kind of divine correction. As a result of "Jezebel" and her "children" being struck dead and "those committing adultery" with her are thrown into "great distress," John points out that "all the churches will know that I am the one searching minds and hearts." In other words, the churches will fully recognize the power of God because of the punishment meted out to some of their members. In this case, as well as that cited in the Philadelphia letter, *paideia* serves to educate (and so reform). Unfortunately, in the case of the Thyatira letter, most of those punished will not be punished in the manner reserved for those that God loves but rather they will be destroyed.

48. Of course, it is possible that John is proposing a scenario where the "synagogue of Satan" will be forced to bow down before the faithful in Philadelphia before they are destroyed. Scenes such as these appear in some second temple literature, such as Wisd 5, *1 Enoch* 62, and *4 Ezra* 7:83–87. These

Consequently, the identification of the "synagogue of Satan" with the adversaries mentioned in the letters to Ephesus, Pergamum, and Thyatira is problematic because the eschatological fate of the "synagogue of Satan" does not seem to conform to the fate of "Jezebel" and her followers.[49] This, in turn, suggests that the "synagogue of Satan" and the other adversaries ("Jezebel" and the Nicolaitans) represent different groups.

To sum up then, there are a number of reasons to suggest that the "synagogue of Satan" not be identified with John's other adversaries mentioned in the letters. First, the different structure of the letters addressed to the churches at Smyrna and Philadelphia (the letters that mention the "synagogue of Satan") recommends a different situation. And second, the eschatological fate of the "synagogue of Satan" does not conform to the eschatological fate of John's other internal adversaries.

If the "synagogue of Satan" cannot be identified with John's adversaries in the other churches, then our best alternative is to return to the idea that it stands for the neighboring Jews in the cities of Smyrna and Philadelphia. But, as we saw above, this leaves us with the problem of explaining John's hostility. What is the reason for it? In order to answer this question, we need to examine more closely those passages that mention the "synagogue of Satan."

Relations between the "Synagogue of Satan" and the "Faithful" in the Letters to Smyrna and Philadelphia

The first passage that mentions the "synagogue of Satan" appears in the letter to the church at Smyrna and reads as follows:

> I know your affliction and your poverty, even though you are rich. I know the slander (βλασφημία) on the part of those who say that they are Jews and are not, but are a synagogue of Satan. Do not fear what you are about to suffer. Beware, the devil is about to throw some of you into prison so that you may be tested, and for ten days you will have affliction. Be faithful until death, and I will give you the crown of life. (Rev 2:9–10)

---

scenes imply the evil group's acknowledgment of their error before their destruction or punishment (probably, the closest analogy would be found in Wisd 5). But, interpreting the "synagogue of Satan's" fate in this way would be mistaken for two reasons. First, as we will see below, other scenes of divine wrath are *not* directed against the Jews in the Apocalypse (with one notable exception, in which the Jews are given a final chance to repent—and many do). Second, and more importantly, in all the scenes of judgment found in the Hellenistic Jewish texts mentioned above, the passages not only mention, but they emphasize the terror, confusion, and/or dread that falls upon the condemned at the time of their judgment. In short, these texts tend to revel in the anguish that the evil ones suffer, in anticipation of their punishment or destruction. We see nothing like this in the Apocalypse.

49. This point also raises difficulties for Frankfurter's position ("Jews or Not?") for, if, as he insists, the milieu of Revelation is Judaism, why would the Jews (i.e., "Jezebel" and the Nicolaitans) receive a harsher punishment than the gentile God-fearers in the "synagogue of Satan"? It seems that the Jews should either receive equally harsh punishment or the gentiles should receive the harsher punishment.

Assuming that the "synagogue of Satan" represents the local synagogue at Smyrna, the only unequivocal information that the text gives about its relationship to the ἐκκλησία is the charge of βλασφημία that John directs against the synagogue.[50] When applied to human beings and not God, βλασφημία is probably best rendered "slander," as in the NRSV translation.[51]

But, this charge is vague. The label "slander" obviously leaves open a couple of options.[52] For instance, as we have already seen, some scholars have argued for Jewish denunciation of the churches to the local authorities who, at the urging of the Jewish community, persecuted the ἐκκλησία. Such Jewish denunciation could certainly be understood as βλασφημία. Others, though, have recommended that the Jewish slander mentioned involved nothing more than isolated instances of verbal hostility.[53]

How should we decide which alternative is best? The letter to the Philadelphians, unfortunately, gives us little help. In fact, its information about the relations between the church and synagogue is even less specific than what we have seen in the letter to the church at Smyrna. It states:

> These are the words of the holy one, the true one, who has the key of David, who opens and no one will shut, who shuts and no one opens: Look I have set before you an open door, which no one is able to shut. I know that you have but little power, and yet you have kept my word and have not denied my name. I will make those of the synagogue of Satan who say that they are Jews and are not, but are lying—I will make them come and bow down before your feet, and they will learn that I have loved you. Because you have kept my word of patient endurance I will keep you from the hour of trial that is coming on the whole world to test the inhabitants of the earth. (Rev 3:7–10)

Here there is no reference to slander. In fact, there is no certain reference to any

---

50. Some scholars have connected the three terms θλίψις ("affliction,"), poverty (πτωχεία), and slander (βλασφημία) together and seen them as a description of that which the community endured at the hands of the Jews. Sweet, for instance, associated the first term, θλίψις, with persecution or harassment by the Jews (*Revelation*, 84–85). Caird, as mentioned above, suggested that the poverty (πτωχεία) of the community was due to looting that resulted from a result of the hostility "instigated by the Jews" (Caird, *Revelation*, 35). But these suggestions are without merit for of the three nouns θλίψις, πτωχεία, and βλασφημία, the text only directly connects the last to the "synagogue of Satan."

51. BAGD, s.v.

52. In his recent commentary, Aune (*Revelation 1–5*, 162) compares this text to other Christian texts that lodge this charge against Jews. Unfortunately, all of the texts that Aune mentions come from a later time. The earliest of these, Justin's *Dialogue with Trypho*, can be dated no earlier than the Bar Kochba rebellion.

53. Cf. Thompson, *Book of Revelation*, 126. Perhaps the "slander" consisted of name-calling or the synagogue's refusal to accept the ἐκκλησία (especially the gentiles in it) as Jews (i.e., as part of the community of the elect). In other words, maybe the synagogue members lumped the ἐκκλησία in with the unredeemed (and unredeemable) gentiles. Mark D. Nanos (*Irony of Galatians: Paul's Letter in First Century Context* [Minneapolis: Fortress, 2002]) suggests a similar scenario underlying Paul's letter to the Galatians. Or John could even have considered the members of the synagogue's claim that *they were Jews* as βλασφημια. John may have assumed that true Jews were Torah-observant *and* followers of Jesus (Yarbro Collins, "Insiders and Ousiders," 209).

interaction between the ἐκκλησία and the synagogue. The only clear reference to the "synagogue of Satan" in the passage is the prediction about its eschatological fate (along with that of the church). Although it is possible that the image of the open door that "no one can shut"[54] had some tie to the synagogue, it is impossible to say that it did for sure. Even if we could somehow prove a connection between this image and the synagogue, it would still be difficult, if not impossible, to determine its precise meaning without more evidence.[55]

So, the only thing of which we can be certain about relations between the synagogue and church is the fact of the "slander" from the synagogue at Smyrna. Of the various ways of interpreting this slander, one is fairly serious (denunciation to the authorities) while the other is fairly innocuous (e.g., incidents of name-calling, theological disagreement, etc.). Is there a way that we can eliminate either of these possibilities?

Evidence from throughout the Apocalypse indicates that it is highly unlikely that this slander refers to any Jewish denunciation of members of the ἐκκλησία to the authorities. There are two reasons for this. First, in the letters, there is virtually no evidence to support any scenario of persecution by the authorities.[56] Other than predictions (which, obviously, do not present a window into the situation of the churches at John's time), the only credible suggestion of persecution comes in the letter to Pergamum, where we are told that "Antipas, my witness, my faithful one, . . . was killed among you" (2:13). But the context of this particular passage clearly shows that Antipas's death was not a contemporary incident but, rather, an event of the past.[57] And, in addition, there is no indication that persecution (whether officially sanctioned or not) was the cause of Antipas' death.[58]

---

54. This is connected to the image of the "key of David." Both allude to Isa 22:22 ("I will place on his shoulder the key of the house of David; he shall open, and no one shall shut; he shall shut, and no one shall open").

55. Yarbro Collins, for instance, saw the promise of the open door functioning as consolation aimed at those who had been expelled from the synagogue (*Crisis*, 86). Others, appealing to Paul's use of the open door image to indicate missionary opportunity (1 Cor 16:9; 2 Cor 2:12; cf. the pseudepigraphic Col 4:3 and the non-Pauline Acts 14:27), suggested that the text predicts that the Jews will be converted (cf. Sweet, *Revelation*, 102, and Beale, *Book of Revelation*, 286–87). Neither of these suggestions, though, is persuasive. Although synagogue expulsion is a possibility, there is nothing in the text that clearly points to it. Is also seems unlikely for other reasons. For instance, a New Testament text where synagogue expulsion is clearly mentioned (John 9:22), is quite unlike what we see in the book of Revelation. In the latter, the author is, as we have seen, ambiguous in his feelings toward the Jews. Despite some hostility, he ultimately anticipates their salvation. In the Gospel of John, on the other hand, the synagogue expulsions have produced an unambiguous bitterness toward the Jews. Concerning the idea of the open door referring to the conversion of the Jews, on the other hand, there are at least two arguments against it. First, if John anticipates their eschatological enlightenment (as we saw above), he could hardly have expected successful missionary action among them in his time. Secondly (and perhaps more importantly), John's text shows no interest in missionary activities.

56. See Duff, *Who Rides*, 31–47.

57. The text mentions that the church did not deny its faith "*even in the days* of Antipas . . ."

58. For more on the ambiguity of this passage, see Duff, *Who Rides*, 38.

But there is a second reason that Jewish denunciation of church members seems unlikely. This reason can be drawn from John's attitude toward the Jews elsewhere in the Apocalypse. We have already seen that John's attitude toward the synagogues (as illustrated in the Philadelphia letter) seems sympathetic. A sympathetic attitude toward the Jews also emerges elsewhere. Probably the best example appears in chapter 11 of the Apocalypse.

In that chapter, the two witnesses are killed by the "beast from the bottomless pit" and afterwards, "their dead bodies ... lie in the street of the great city that is prophetically called Sodom and Egypt, where also their Lord was crucified" (Rev 11:8). Virtually all scholars agree that the city mentioned here is to be identified as Jerusalem (because of the reference to the crucifixion).[59] John's allusion to Judaism in this passage—in the guise of the text's reference to its holy city—at first, seems unabashedly negative. John identifies Jerusalem with Sodom and Egypt, two infamous locations in the memory of Israel. Nevertheless, the end of the episode turns this seemingly negative reference to Judaism around, for there the text concludes:

> At that moment there was a great earthquake, and a tenth of the city fell; seven thousand people were killed in the earthquake, and the rest were terrified and gave glory to the God of heaven (13:19).

Remarkably, this is the only passage in the whole of the visions section of the Apocalypse where a positive response results from divine chastisement.[60] So, in this passage, we encounter another instance of chastisement that is meant to lead to repentance. While here, as in the letter to the Philadelphians, the author makes it clear that the Jews (i.e., the inhabitants of the city of Jerusalem) will be chastised by God, he also indicates that they (or at least most of them) will ultimately be saved.

In light of the kind of sympathy that John demonstrates for Jews and Judaism in places like chapter 3 and chapter 11,[61] therefore, the possibility that the accusation of βλασφημία refers to Jewish denunciation of church members to government authorities seems highly unlikely. If Jews were participating in such denunciations (and thus

---

59. Marshall, *Parables,* 163–72, argues that this city is Rome and not Jerusalem. His argument, though, is unpersuasive.

60. Yarbro Collins, "Insiders and Outsiders," 206–7. Yarbro Collins sees it as the only passage in the *whole book* but she has not recognized the repentance implied in the letter to the Philadelphian church.

61. In order to see John's sympathy for Judaism more clearly, it is also significant to note where Jews do *not* appear in Revelation, as Marshall has pointed out. With the exception of the Philadelphia letter and chapter 11, references to the Jews or Judaism "do not occur with pronouncements of judgment, censure, or punishment" (Marshall, *Parables,* 186). These two exceptions, as we note, show the Jews in a situation of punishment, but the punishment results in their repentance and, presumably, their vindication. See also Yarbro Collins, who sees the woman "clothed with the sun" as representing Israel/Judaism. She comments on John's positive understanding of the connection between Israel (or Judaism) and the church in chapter 12 of the Apocalypse in her *The Combat Myth in the Book of Revelation* (HDR 9; Missoula, Mont.: Scholars Press, 1975), 130–35. Marshall also interprets the identity of the woman similarly in this passage. See his *Parables,* 135–37.

endangering the lives of those in the churches), we should expect a more unambiguously bitter reaction to the Jews throughout the book.

If we eliminate the option of Jewish denunciation to the authorities, then the βλασφημία must refer to some kind of verbal sparring. John's hostility, then, could perhaps be explained as a tool used by the seer to clarify the boundaries between church and synagogue. Both Yarbro Collins and Leonard Thompson have argued along these lines. They have each connected John's hostility to the issue of the community's self-identity. For instance, Yarbo Collins has suggested that:

> The polemic against "the synagogue of Satan" must be seen . . . as a passionate polemic against a sibling or parent faith, like the attacks of the Qumran community on all other Jews as virtual apostates.[62]

Although this approach makes some sense, nevertheless, the comparison with the Qumran community raises difficulties. The Qumran community's "passionate polemic" against Jews outside their community was hardly ambiguous, as is John's "polemic." The Dead Sea community made virtually no distinction between those Jews outside of their community and the "Kittim" or gentiles (at least as far as their ultimate fate was concerned). John, on the contrary, distinguishes between the synagogue and his other adversaries, as we have seen.[63] Because of the ambiguity that he demonstrates toward Judaism, it seems inappropriate to label John's comments about Judaism as a "passionate polemic." If anything, his comments seem to constitute a conflicted polemic.[64] Ultimately, it is clear that John is trying to set walls between the church and synagogue. But, his ambiguous attitude is puzzling. Is John attempting to forge a "Christian" identity for his churches over against that of the parent faith (Judaism)? If this were the case, would not John's attitude have been less ambiguously hostile?[65] There seems to be something else at work here.

In order to discover this "something else," it might be fruitful to look once again at the larger context of the Apocalypse. Regardless of whatever else might have been going on, it is apparent from the language of chapters 2 and 3 that John was competing against "Jezebel" and the Nicolaitans for the allegiance of some of the churches. The competition was clearly most fierce in the cities of Pergamum and Thyatira.

---

62. Yarbro Collins, "Insiders and Outsiders," 208. See also Thompson, *Book of Revelation*, 126.

63. It is curious that Yarbro Collins, who herself points to John's positive description of Jews and Judaism in chapter 11 and 12 (see above, nn. 60 and 61) did not acknowledge the difference between John's attitude to Judaism and the Qumran writers' attitude to Jews outside their community.

64. One can also contrast what we see here with the unambiguously hostile *Peri Pascha* by Melito of Sardis. The anti-Jewish hostility in this text does seem to focus on sharpening the distinction between church and synagogue. See T. Kraabel, "Melito the Bishop and the Synagogue at Sardis: Text and Context," *Studies Presented to George M. A. Hanfmann* (ed. D. G. Mitten, J. G. Pedley, and J. A. Scott; Mainz: Philipp von Zabern, 1971), 77–85.

65. Thompson (*Book of Revelation*, 126) talks of John "sharpening the distinction" between church and synagogue. But a truly "sharp distinction" would place the synagogue outside of the bounds of the eschatological community of the redeemed. This would be difficult to square with John's expectation of Jewish "repentance" in the Apocalypse.

Recent theories, which we have looked at above, have posited a connection between this situation and that in the churches of Smyrna and Philadelphia. Unfortunately, the connection posed by these theories (i.e., the identity of the "synagogue of Satan" with John's adversaries in the other letters) seems untenable. But it is worth asking if there might not be some other, less obvious, connection between these two sets of churches. Do John's references to the synagogues in Smyrna and Philadelphia have some bearing on his struggle with "Jezebel" and the Nicolaitans in the churches of the other cities?

A Possible Solution

Since the appearance of the works of Georg Simmel in the early part of the twentieth century[66] and Lewis Coser in its middle years,[67] it has become a well-established sociological tenet that conflict can be (and often is) used to strengthen group cohesion and to bring the aims of the community into sharper focus. Studies of religious movements and especially new religious movements have given us many examples of this principle in action.

Conflict has been shown to be especially important in societies dominated by charismatic leadership.[68] Studies of religious movements dependent on an individual charismatic leader have shown time and again that such charismatic leadership is unstable because it is entirely dependent on the fragile but exceptional "gift" possessed by the leader.[69] Because of the fragility of the source of their power, charismatic leaders throughout history have used a variety of strategies to combat the threat of their loss of control.[70] One such strategy is "crisis-mongering," that is, creating a crisis or exacerbating an unstable situation so that a crisis might result. This tactic has

---

66. G. Simmel, *Conflict and the Web of Group-Affiliations*, (New York: Free Press, 1955). The original date of this work, entitled *Der Streit* in German, was 1908.

67. Lewis Coser, *The Functions of Social Conflict* (New York: Free Press, 1956).

68. The idea of charismatic leadership goes back to Max Weber. See, for example, Max Weber, *Economy and Society: An Outline of Interpretive Sociology* (Berkeley: University of California Press, 1978), 1:242–44 and 2: 1114–15. For more recent work on charismatic religious leaders, see Roy Wallis, ed., *Millennialism and Charisma* (Belfast: Queen's University, 1982); Thomas Robbins and Dick Anthony, "Sects and Violence: Factors Enhancing the Volatility of Marginal Religious Movements," *Armageddon in Waco: Critical Perspectives on the Branch Davidian Conflict* (ed. Stuart A. Wright; Chicago: University of Chicago Press, 1995), 236–59; and Thomas Robbins and Susan J. Palmer, "Patterns of Contemporary Apocalypticism in North America," in *Millennium, Messiahs, and Mayhem: Contemporary Apocalyptic Movements* (ed. Thomas Robbins and Susan J. Palmer; New York: Routledge, 1997), 21–22.

69. The fragility of charisma can be demonstrated by the various ways that it is be threatened. For instance, it might simply dissipate, a stronger leader may emerge, or the movement may move toward institutionalization and the charisma routinized. See Roy Wallis, "Charisma, Commitment, and Control in a New Religious Movement," in idem, *Millennialism*, 73–140.

70. For a discussion of different strategies in the context of a new religious movement, see especially Wallis, "Charisma."

the potential to "accentuate the indispensability of the inspired leader."[71] In a study of charismatic leadership in recent religious movements, Frederick Bird has pointed out,

> In times of crisis people often look to an individual as savior with the hope that this person will lead them out of their troubles. Successful resolution of crises redounds to the credit of charismatic leaders, and the extraordinary trust in them appears well invested. Because of this crisis-confidence relationship, charismatic leaders often seem to court crises as opportunities for demonstrating their prowess.[72]

Courting crises, therefore, can often lead to a renewed vitality of the leader's "charisma."

In John's case, a rival prophet ("Jezebel") had gained enough popularity in several of the communities that she was able to challenge John's authority. And, if the letters to the churches in the book of Revelation are any indication, that challenge was largely successful in a number of churches.[73] In response, John tried to turn the attention of the churches to the surrounding environment and to show the danger that threatened them. As recent studies have shown, John (at the very least) exaggerated the threat that Rome presented to the communities (i.e., he "courted a crisis" between Rome and the ἐκκλησία).[74] He likely did so because, in the communities where there was competition for leadership, he hoped to encourage the churches to look to him (and not "Jezebel") to lead them through the crisis.[75]

But what has this to do with John's statements about the "false Jews" in Smyrna and Philadelphia? John's leadership seems to have been secure in those communities. He seems to have had nothing to fear from "Jezebel" in those churches. Perhaps, though, he feared something else. Perhaps, he perceived a danger of losing these communities to the synagogue. What would be the basis for such a fear?

It is beyond dispute that the conservative churches in Smyrna and Philadelphia had a close affinity to Judaism, as had John.[76] It is also likely that upon seeing

---

71. Robbins and Palmer, "Patterns," 21.

72. Frederick B. Bird, "Charisma and Leadership in New Religious Movements," in *Handbook of Cults and Sects in America* (Religion and the Social Order 3; Greenwich, Conn.: JAI Press, 1993), 80.

73. In Pergamum and Thyatira the churches were apparently split between "Jezebel" and John. The churches in Sardis and Laodicea may had already been lost to John when he wrote Revelation since he makes little effort in the work to win the churches in these cities over to his side. See Duff, *Who Rides*, 48–60.

74. If we look at the attitude that the seer displays toward Rome throughout the Apocalypse, it is clear that he has described a danger to the churches that did not seem to have existed (at least in the minds of others in the churches). See Thompson, *Book of Revelation;* Robert M. Royalty Jr., *The Streets of Heaven: The Ideology of Wealth in the Apocalypse of John* (Macon, Ga.: Mercer University Press, 1998), 27–38; and Duff, *Who Rides.*

75. As part of his strategy, John attempted to discredit "Jezebel" by closely tying her to Rome and the evil forces that appear in the Apocalypse. See Duff, *Who Rides,* esp. 83–125.

76. John's close connections with Judaism have long been touted. In fact, as we have seen above, Marshall (*Parables*) and Frankfurter ("Jews or Not?") have gone so far as to argue that we should not consider John or his church's position as lying at all outside Judaism. Although Marshall and Frank-

John's authority diminish in the face of "Jezebel's" challenge (at least in some of the churches), the churches in Smyrna and Philadelphia were suddenly faced with the possibility of trying to maintain their convictions in a larger community (i.e., the greater church in Asia Minor) which—in their view—was moving in entirely the wrong direction (i.e., in the direction of "Jezebel's" program of assimilation into what John and his allies saw as the dominant and evil culture). In light of all this, perhaps the idea of aligning themselves with their local synagogues might have seemed like a reasonable option.[77]

Because of Judaism's Torah observant behavior, on the one hand, and its accepted legal status, on the other, those in the synagogue could easily maintain high walls between themselves and the larger society (perhaps more easily than could those in the churches). The ability to maintain these high walls was obviously something that was valued by those in John's circle (i.e., in the churches of Smyrna and Philadelphia). In short, life in the synagogue might have seemed a more attractive option for some in the church than remaining with a group whose idea of "faithful" existence differed so dramatically from theirs.[78]

Of course, from John's point of view, such a migration would be disastrous. He would lose what little solid base of support that he had in his struggle with "Jezebel." A rush to the synagogue by his supporters would tip the scales totally in favor not only of his rival but also of what he saw as an aberrant form of the ἐκκλησία.

If John's response to his faithful communities could create (or exacerbate) tension between the churches and synagogues of Smyrna and Philadelphia, he could possibly shut off that option to his supporters.[79] Accordingly, in his Apocalypse, he could subtly suggest that those who might otherwise have been seen as the most sympathetic to the point of view of his "faithful" were (at least for the present) trapped in the great Satanic conspiracy against the people of God. Hemmed in on all sides, therefore, the "faithful" might feel that their only viable option was to recommit themselves to their communities, pull together, and persevere with John at their head.

Although there is no direct evidence for this scenario, there are a few things that suggest its likelihood. First, and most obvious, is the fact that John resorted to the strategy of "crisis mongering" elsewhere in the Apocalypse. As mentioned above, he

---

furter have pushed this point too far, I think that what they have to say about the communities overall might apply, to some extent, to the conservative communities at Smyrna and Philadelphia.

77. This could even have been the case if some tension (in the form of name-calling, for instance) had previously existed between the church and synagogue. As a matter of fact, there is no unequivocal evidence (either in Revelation or elsewhere) to suggest that one could not continue to follow Christ as a member of the synagogue. Although synagogue expulsions of Jesus followers are mentioned in the Gospel of John, that text is most likely from Syria and we cannot establish the date with any certainty.

78. It is quite possible that the communities in Smyrna and Philadelphia would have had more in common with those Jews in the synagogues than with "Jezebel" and her followers in the churches, especially if these churches were populated by Jews (or former Jews, if one prefers).

79. If some tension already existed then he simply would have had to exacerbate it.

largely exaggerated the danger that Rome presented to the churches at the time in order to unite the divided communities behind him.[80]

Second, in the letter to the Smyrnaean church, John sets the accusation of the synagogue's slander immediately before the prediction that "the devil is about to throw some [members of the church] into prison." Given John's attitude toward Greco-Roman society, it is highly unlikely that he would have had any social connections that would have enabled him to learn beforehand about any plans to arrest members of the ἐκκλησία. The prediction about the arrest, therefore, must be entirely John's creation. The fact that he put this prediction directly after the accusation of the synagogue's "slander" is certainly provocative, for it leads the reader to believe that the "slander" of the synagogue is related to the prediction of arrest (and possible death). John likely constructed this letter in such a way as to convince the members of the Smyrnaean community that the synagogue was an imminent threat to them.[81]

Third, we see another possible hint in the Philadelphia letter with the introduction of the image of the open door. Why did John introduce this image in a letter than mentions the "synagogue of Satan?" Perhaps its purpose was to emphasize to those in his community that the open door to salvation was through the ἐκκλησία.[82] Hence, they should not abandon it.[83]

The scenario of John intentionally setting up a somewhat artificial wall between the church and the synagogue can help us make sense of John's conflicted attitude toward Judaism in the book of Revelation. On the one hand, his condemnation of the "synagogue of Satan" was intended to drive a wedge between the local synagogues and his churches so that his allies in Smyrna and Philadelphia would not be tempted to abandon the churches for those synagogues. On the other hand, John could not completely conceal his sympathy for Judaism as evidenced by the fact that he was ultimately unwilling to postulate a scenario that depicted the Jews' eschatological annihilation.

Conclusion

In response to recent suggestion that the "synagogue of Satan" should be identified with John's other adversaries mentioned in Rev 2 and 3, I have argued instead

---

80. See above, n. 74.

81. As mentioned above, there is, in theory at least, no reason to exclude the possibility of Jews turning over members of the churches to local authorities for persecution in John's time and place. While possible though, John's sometimes generous attitude toward Judaism makes such a scenario highly unlikely in the case of John's churches.

82. It is interesting to note that one other place in the Apocalypse where we encounter an open door is in 4:1. There the open door gave the seer access to the divine realm. John, with his image of the open door in the Philadelphia letter, also promises access to the deity (conversely, the closed door in Rev 3:20 prevents the community of Laodicea from access to the risen Jesus).

83. The implication being, of course, that the direct route to salvation was not through the synagogue. Of course, as we saw above, John hints that, at the eschaton, after its "discipline," the members of the synagogue would also be saved.

that John used the appellation "synagogue of Satan" to refer to Jews from local synagogues (as the conventional wisdom has long recommended). But, in contrast to the traditional interpretations, I have recommended that John's remarks about the "synagogue of Satan" give no evidence that Jews persecuted or harassed the ἐκκλησια. Nor does a scenario that links the synagogue with Roman persecution ring true. The letters to the churches suggest little, if any, hostility on the part of the Jews.

In fact, because of John's evident sympathy for the Jews and Judaism (as can be seen in a few places in the Apocalypse), both his identification of the synagogue with Satan in 2:9 and 3:9 and his hint that the synagogue presents a danger to the ἐκκλησία are quite puzzling. I suggest that John made his negative remarks about the Jews in Smyrna and Philadelphia in order to discourage his followers from defecting from the churches in those cities and joining the local synagogues. If such were to happen, "Jezebel" and her followers could easily gain the upper hand in the struggle for the leadership of the churches in Asia.[84]

---

84. A version of this paper was first presented to the Early Jewish/Christian Relations Section of the Society of Biblical Literature at the 1988 Annual Meeting. I would like to thank members of that section for their helpful comments and suggestions. I would also like to thank in particular David Frankfurter for subsequent (and substantive) communication on this topic.

Symptoms of Resistance in the Book of Revelation
Greg Carey

For a book that blesses those who do what it says and curses those who don't, the Book of Revelation has certainly failed to cultivate submissive readers. Even its inclusion within the canon endured opposition, and it remains unclear whether the Protestant Reformers such as Luther and Calvin embraced Revelation, experienced ambivalence toward it, or functionally rejected it. Contentiousness marks Revelation's contemporary readers as well. We academicians may not find ourselves drawn to popular prophecy belief, but we do find ourselves torn between two other possibilities. Should we resist Revelation on account of its authoritarianism, violence, and misogyny, or should we embrace it as a voice that inspires resistance against injustice?

As readers line up for or against the Apocalypse, I find myself unable to identify with either side. My own attempts to achieve resolution with respect to the Apocalypse have brought frustration, while my encounters with its readers have led me to give up straightforward attempts to endorse or censure the book. I cannot sort out Revelation's liberating and dangerous "parts," for both life and death, affirmation and dehumanization, often cohabit its particular features. Instead, I find myself increasingly drawn toward the model of resistance criticism as a resource for grappling with Revelation's complexities. In my view, Revelation's moral ambiguities in large part emerge from its identity as a subversive vision; thus, some of the foremost objections against the book involve the "symptoms of resistance" it manifests.

Symptoms of Resistance in Life and in Apocalypse

As I am completing this essay, forces from the United States, the United Kingdom, and Australia, are conducting an invasion of Iraq. Global response to this conflict reflects grave ambivalence, in part because the United States is claiming to act in its own self-defense. Claiming the status of a victim that seeks justice and security, the United States appeals to the September 11, 2001, terrorist attacks as evidence of dire threats that must be averted. While it seeks to eliminate some of these threats by invading Iraq, the United States simultaneously asserts and promises that it will address the Palestinian-Israeli crisis after the current invasion. Yet the United States' efforts to foster a just peace in that conflict prior to September 11 impressed few. Not coincidentally, news reports have long emphasized widespread Arab resentment against the United States in particular. Within the United States, anti-Arab sentiment again is on the rise, as images of anti-American protests persist on the airwaves. The United States, as the dominant and perhaps imperial power of its age, has won enemies who rejoice when it suffers violence.

Perhaps one image makes the point. In the immediate wake of the September 11 attacks one particular scene splashed its way onto the television news shows: a small crowd of Palestinians who were apparently rejoicing in the United States' humiliation. For those of us who call for the recognition of Palestinian claims regarding civil rights, land and water access, and the like, the moment was at best an embarrassment, at worst the confirmation of our unspoken fears. Palestinians have been on the wrong end of the media representation wars for decades, and many Americans continue to regard all of them as anti-American terrorists: this scene only confirmed such dangerous stereotypes. Things became even more difficult when people like Pat Robertson linked the Palestinians with the attacks—even while the attacks were still unfolding! Moreover, as it has become clear that the attacks did not involve Palestinian groups, Osama bin Laden's embrace of the Palestinian cause continues to bind the Palestinians to the war of terror in the imaginations of many.

The scene, of course, invites interpretation. On close inspection, the crowd seemed awfully small and they also appeared to be performing for the cameras. Could this have been a staged demonstration, one that produced exactly the alienation for which it was designed? As one Palestinian voice after another expressed condemnation for the September 11 attacks, it seemed reasonable to ask, how exactly did Palestinians regard the attacks? How many of them celebrated them, and how many condemned them? How many thought the attacks were justified? How many would have supported the attacks if they could? And how many simply found the attacks unsurprising, seeing them as an inevitable consequence of US policy?

Ordinarily I am not quick to begin biblical interpretation with such explicit reflection upon contemporary events. Nor do I embrace autobiographical interpretation unless it somehow offers a fresh perspective that transcends one individual's experience. However, after seeing the street celebration—whatever it may have meant—I could not help but recall some of the songs one would hear in a "performance" of the Apocalypse. For example, just as the seven angels bring the seven bowls filled with the wrath of God we hear the victorious believers singing:

> Great and marvelous are your works,
> O Lord God the Pantocrator.
> Just and true are your ways,
> O Ruler of the Nations!
> Who will not fear you, O Lord,
> and glorify your name?

> For you alone are holy.
> All the nations shall come and worship before you,
> for your righteous punishments have been revealed. (15:3b–4)

And after the third bowl has been poured out, an angel speaks for all to hear:

> Righteous are you,
> the One who is and who was, the Holy One,
> for you have judged these things;
> For blood of saints and prophets have they poured out,
> and blood to them you have given to drink.
> They deserve it. (16:5b–6)

These songs manifestly reveal a desire for violent revenge. Among other things, they rejoice that the time has come for God to reward the saints and "destroy those who have destroyed the earth" (11:18). Many interpreters have sought to mitigate their offense by arguing that (*a*) only God executes these judgments, not mortals, and (*b*) only the truly oppressed have a right to express such desires. While I do not find either view entirely satisfactory,[1] the songs compel me to ask: What does it mean to defend these songs in Revelation, if one also experienced horror that people could rejoice over the events of September 11? And more to the point of this paper: Is there anything we can learn about Revelation by considering those songs in the light of those who rejoice when death strikes the United States?

If I may turn to contemporary events one more time, CBS News reporter Ed Bradley related that a trip to the Middle East in the wake of the September 11 attacks revealed few people who defended the attacks but "an extraordinary amount of anger . . . toward the United States government."[2] Bradley also reported that most Arabs believe the United States "[deserves] what happened to it," and that in a recent poll eighty percent of Arab people regarded the United States as "the" enemy.[3] In other words, while we cannot know how many Arabs in general or Palestinians in particular celebrated the events of September 11, we can say that such rejoicing emerged from the sense that the United States is their oppressor. "They deserve it" can work in many directions.

Who can look on horrific devastation—whether imagined or real, via media reports or through the medium of visionary rhetoric—and exclaim, "They deserve it!"? I believe that in one particular way students of Revelation have something to learn from those who perceived a sense of cosmic balance in the events of September 11. Structurally speaking, and without necessarily invoking the discourses of victimization and oppression, I propose that in both cases *symptoms of resistance* are evident. As

---

1. My basic objections are spelled out in *Elusive Apocalypse: Reading Authority in the Revelation to John* (StABH 15; Macon, Ga.: Mercer University Press, 1999), 171–85.
2. Transcript, "What Are They Saying about Us?" *60 Minutes* 34/2 (23 September 2001), 11.
3. Ibid., 13.

Vincent Wimbush describes it, "the realm of the imaginary, the visionary, the utopic is discovered and cultivated by those who define themselves as pressed and limited in some significant ways by power, as a means of resisting power."[4] Thus, when one group perceives that its fundamental identity and security are threatened by powerful forces and articulates how things could or should be otherwise, we have resistance discourse. And in resistance discourse, certain symptoms emerge often enough to represent recognizable patterns. As an example of resistance literature, the Book of Revelation presents a variety of such common symptoms.

The Practice of Resistance Criticism

In itself, to invoke resistance (or postcolonial) criticism as a lens through which to read Revelation is nothing new. For the most part, resistance criticisms have generated sympathetic readings of the Apocalypse, according to which Revelation embodies and empowers the voice of the oppressed.[5] Revelation may express a desire for vengeance, and it may employ negative images of women, many argue, but it does so out of a larger desire for justice.[6] Thus, resistance readings of the Apocalypse tend to generate ethically univocal conclusions.[7] Even carefully qualified positions tend to articulate a single voice: either the book includes some lamentable excesses in its

---

4. "Introduction: Interpreting Resistance, Resisting Interpretations," *Semeia* 79 (1997): 6.

5. For example, Brian K. Blount, "Revelation: The Witness of Active Resistance," in *Then the Whisper Put On Flesh: New Testament Ethics in an African American Context* (Nashville: Abingdon, 2001), 158–84; Allen A. Boesak, *Comfort and Protest: The Apocalypse from a South African Perspective* (Louisville: Westminster, 1987); Allen Dwight Callahan, "The Language of the Apocalypse," *HTR* 88 (1995): 453–70; Wes Howard-Brook and Anthony Gwyther, *Unveiling Empire: Reading Revelation Then and Now* (Bible and Liberation; Maryknoll, N.Y.: Orbis, 1999); Néstor Míguez, "Apocalyptic and the Economy: A Reading of Revelation 18 from the Experience of Economic Exclusion," in *Reading from This Place*, vol. 2: *Social Location and Biblical Interpretation in Global Perspective* (ed. Fernando F. Segovia and Mary Ann Tolbert; Minneapolis: Fortress, 1995), 250–62; Pablo Richard, *Apocalypse: A People's Commentary on the Book of Revelation* (Bible and Liberation; Maryknoll, N.Y.: Orbis, 1995); Elisabeth Schüssler Fiorenza, "The Words of Prophecy: Reading the Apocalypse Theologically," in *Studies in the Book of Revelation* (ed. Steve Moyise; New York: T&T Clark, 2001), 1–19; idem, "The Rhetoricality of Apocalypse and the Politics of Interpretation," in *The Book of Revelation: Judgment and Justice* (2d ed.; Minneapolis: Fortress, 1999), 205–36. See also ch. 12 below.

6. Jean K. Kim's assessment of Babylon the Whore represents an exception, as Kim insists that while the image participates in counter-imperial resistance, it also adapts imperial models of women's sexual subordination, advancing a masculine nationalism at the expense of women. At the end of the day, Kim's interpretation emphasizes how Revelation participates in a pattern common to many resistance movements: employing male domination as a means of sustaining group identity (" 'Uncovering Her Wickedness': An Inter(con)textual Reading of Revelation 17 from a Postcolonial Feminist Perspective," *JSNT* 73 [1999]: 61–81).

7. To date, the most notable exception to this pattern is Robert M. Royalty, *The Streets of Heaven: The Ideology of Wealth in the Apocalypse of John* (Macon, Ga: Mercer University Press, 1998). Royalty does not employ postcolonial or resistance theory explicitly, yet his work articulates how the Apocalypse at once undermines and reinscribes imperial discourses.

advocacy for justice, or, while basically well-intentioned, the Apocalypse fails to live up to its own principles.

But, generally speaking, resistance and postcolonial perspectives are far more effective in teasing out ambiguity and disrupting certitude than in assuring resolution. Not exactly a tool, or a model, or even a method, resistance theory rather evokes a discourse, an ongoing negotiation about how power—including attempts to subvert, redirect, or even capture power—relates to culture. To name Revelation as an example of resistance literature, then, does not necessarily guarantee an assessment that the book is "good" or "bad," "liberating" or "oppressive," to particular degrees. Instead, reading Revelation as resistance literature stimulates questions and invites diagnosis.[8]

Resistance criticism promises an alternative mode of analyzing Revelation and the theological and ethical debates that attend it. It does so by bringing into relief the historical, discursive, and cultural forces coursing through the Apocalypse and its readers. The resistance reading I propose, then, explores Revelation as a provocative conversation partner, perhaps even a witness from one's spiritual ancestors, but not as a prescriptive authority. Its symptoms of resistance live on in the discourse of its interpreters and spur continuing and critical engagement.

Symptoms of Resistance

Markers of identity. If Revelation reflects the sharp divisions that exist within and around its audience, it also provides one of the primary reasons for those divisions: John's attempt to create more distinct boundaries between his audience and the larger society. So complete is John's "against culture" call that a heavenly voice cries out at Babylon's destruction, "Come out from her, my people" (18:4). This is a call for the most radical of sectarian practices, an absolutely negative stance toward society at large, against the empire and its inhabitants.

This markedly sectarian identity manifests itself in several ways. For one thing, there is the call to avoid πορνεία and εἰδωλόθυτα. Many readers identify this pair as two ways of saying the same thing, for in Hebrew prophecy πορνεία is often a metaphor for participation in idolatry. If the key concern is whether members of the churches participate in idolatry by eating εἰδωλόθυτα, then Revelation is calling its audience to a demanding disidentification from the larger society. Almost all food in the ancient world was offered to the gods in some manner; to refuse food that had been implicated in some form of worship would be to avoid many sections of the

---

8. See, for example, Tat-Siong Benny Liew, "Reading with Yin Yang Eyes: Negotiating the Ideological Dilemma of a Chinese American Biblical Hermeneutics," *BibInt* 9 (2001): 309–35. Liew, by the way, developed the framework of "inter(con)textual hermeneutics," which Kim fails to acknowledge (*Politics of Parousia: Reading Mark Inter[con]textually* [Biblical Interpretation 42; Leiden: Brill, 1999]).

market and any common meals with one's neighbors. No wonder this was a divisive issue.

The symptoms of such a markedly sectarian outlook manifest themselves in Revelation's characterization of the world. While contemporary Christian groups often invoke the language of "us" against "the world," Revelation identifies its audience against "the inhabitants of the earth," who worship the Beast (13:8, 12, 14), are intoxicated by the Whore's wine (17:2), and who are responsible for the martyrs' blood (6:10). The inhabitants are hardly human, as they do not (cannot?) repent (9:20–21; 16:9–11). So thorough is their degradation that they eventually become carrion (19:18–21). There is nothing good about the earth's inhabitants, and to interact with them in any significant way is understood as defilement, literally soiling one's clothes (3:4). Revelation's gleeful violence results in part from its attempt to define such strict communal boundaries.

Of course, Revelation's boundaries define not a sectarianism of sect against church, but a sort of introversionist identity politics.[9] Admittedly, I am mixing more than metaphors here in applying categories from the sociology of religion and contemporary political discourse, but I think the point is justified. For Revelation struggles to identify a movement by constructing its identity over against neither a church nor a foreign power, but against the dominant culture of its own time and place. John's task sounds remarkably similar to Stuart Hall's identity politics:

> It isn't that the subjects are there and we just can't get to them. It is that they don't know yet that they are subjects of a possible discourse. And that always in every political struggle, since every political struggle is always open, it is possible either to win their identification or to lose it.[10]

Hall's vision illuminates the contingent dimension of Revelation's sectarianism, for we see in the Apocalypse the symptoms of conflict over identity. When John penned his vision and addressed it to the seven churches, the identity he sought to articulate was by no means assured. The seven churches were in the process of inventing a discourse in which they located themselves as collective subjects within a larger hostile world. John's task involved getting them to participate in *his* identity discourse, as opposed to the other available options.

Internal division. One structural curiosity of Revelation derives from a contrast in focus between the body of the apocalypse and its frame. While the body of the vision (4:1–22:13) looks primarily outward, away from John's audience toward the

---

9. The language of introversionism derives from Bryan R. Wilson, *Magic and the Millennium* (London: Paladin, 1975). I have found its application to early Christian sectarianism in Philip F. Esler, "Introverted Sectarianism and Qumran and in the Johannine Community," in *The First Christians in Their Social Worlds: Social-Scientific Approaches to New Testament Interpretation* (New York: Routledge, 1994), 70–91.

10. "Subjects in History: Making Diasporic Identities," in *The House That Race Built* (ed. W. Lubiano; New York: Random House, 1997), 291.

heavenly and imperial worlds, the framing material (1:1–3:22; 22:14–21) appeals most directly to John's audience, the seven churches of Asia. One could apply source-critical tools to this question, but aspects of the letters to the churches find their way into the body of the Apocalypse in such a way as to discourage simple cut-and-paste solutions. Rather, it is more likely that the concerns reflected in the letters provide the frame within which John's vision is meaningful. Nevertheless, while the literary structure of the Apocalypse has the local concerns framing the anti-imperial vision, in rhetorical and cultural terms it is the imperial presence that determines those local divisions. In other words, the divisions expressed in the letters to the churches and the other framing material are symptoms of imperial pressure.

Would not such a distinctive communal identity galvanize unity? Μὴ γένοιτο! Framing this anti-imperial attack, the letters to the churches reveal keen divisions among John's audiences. Indeed, John's condemnation of other Christian teachers—the Nicolaitans, Balaam, and Jezebel—is no less strident than that of the empire. Moreover, John attacks non-Christian Jewish communities as well, calling them the "synagogue of Satan" (2:9; 3:9) and identifying them with the martyrdom of one of his colleagues (2:13).[11] Apparently, resistance against the empire does not prevent division among its subjects.

For students of resistance literature this division presents a common scenario. Imperial pressures stress their subjects to the point of creating new fractures and exacerbating old ones.[12] *Read rhetorically, it is not the contexts of the churches that frames the anti-imperial polemic; rather, John and his audience are framed by imperial power.* It is how they respond to the empire that divides them. While John calls for resistance to the broader culture, his Christian opponents advocate a more accommodationist ethos. Moreover, it is likely that the strident counter-cultural message of John and his colleagues has created tension with the synagogue. Non-Christian Jews likely were concerned that they might be identified with people like John, a situation they could resolve by isolating John and his colleagues. In response, John resorts to intimidation by means of revelation, charging that his internal and neighborly enemies face the risen Jesus' judgment. As James C. Scott puts it, "solidarity among subordinates, if it is achieved at all, is thus achieved, paradoxically, only by means of a degree of conflict."[13]

In this context we may recall the very different impression one gets from reading

---

11. While most commentators hold to this view, see the objections raised by David Frankfurter, "Jews or Not? Reconstructing the 'Other' in Rev 2:9 and 3:9," *HTR* 94 (2001): 403–25; and John W. Marshall, *Parables of War: Reading John's Jewish Apocalypse* (ESCJ 10; Waterloo, Ontario: Wilfrid Laurier University Press, 2001), 12–16, 124–48. Cf. Stephen G. Wilson, *Related Strangers: Jews and Christians, 70–170 C.E.* (Minneapolis: Fortress, 1995), 162–65. For fuller discussion, see chs. 6 and 7 above.

12. Homi K. Bhaba, "Postcolonial Criticism," in *Redrawing the Boundaries: The Transformation of English and American Literary Studies* (ed. S. Greenblatt and G. Gunn; New York: Modern Language Assocation of America, 1992), 452–53; Barbara Harlow, *Resistance Literature* (New York: Methuen, 1987), 160.

13. *Domination and the Arts of Resistance* (New Haven: Yale University Press, 1990), 131.

Paul. In 1 Cor 8 and 10 and in Rom 14:1–15:4, Paul addresses the very issue that so concerns John–whether or not to eat food that has been sanctified in pagan contexts. And like John, Paul recognizes a variety of views on the topic. Some abstain on account of conscience, while others take advantage of their liberty and partake. Paul's counsel seems to be that whether one eats such food makes no real difference—after all, "The earth is the Lord's and everything in it" (1 Cor 10:26)—but members should subordinate their own freedom in deference to the conscience of those who might object. It is tempting to imagine: If Paul and John were in the same context, would Paul include John among the relatively ignorant "weak"? Yet we should resist this temptation, as it fosters anachronism. We cannot know how Paul's context compared with John's, which clearly reflects tension with the imperial cult. Nevertheless, Paul's case may be instructive: Perhaps John's keener sense of the imperial cult and its implications intensified the question's significance. If so, then the fractures within and around Revelation's divided audience reflect symptoms of resistance to empire, as do John's authoritarian attempts to mend those wounds.

Discursive hybridization. Resistance literatures, by their very identity, tend to communicate through discursive hybridization. Always there is a discourse of the center, and there is the discourse of the subordinates. The challenge, then, is to find the most effective discourse by which to subvert that of the center. Usually, that resistance discourse involves a measure of hybridization, a blending of the two discourses into something new. Such hybridization is to some degree both strategic and necessary: it is strategic in that it enables the margins to speak to the center while also subverting centrist discourse, and it is necessary in that the media of widespread communication are often tied to the discourse of the center. Some have called this strategy "abrogation and appropriation": one appropriates the "standard" discourse in order to abrogate its fundamental categories, aesthetic values, and syntactic rules.[14] Thus, many African poets and novelists have employed English as a vehicle for widespread publication, while many readers of Salman Rushdie find themselves "translating," as it were, his hybrid English into standard written English.

With respect to the Apocalypse, it has long been acknowledged that Revelation's Greek is often non-standard. Many have also identified what have become known as Septuaginalisms in Revelation's syntax; this "biblical" Greek has suggested to some that a Semitic *Vorlage* lies beneath parts or all of the Apocalypse or that its author's first language may have been Aramaic. Allen Dwight Callahan, however, has shown that while Revelation's Greek is often non-standard, numerous other instances reveal that its author knew and employed conventional *koine* syntax. Moreover, Callahan has pointed out that while Revelation's Greek often recalls the Septuagint, no evidence requires the judgment that John was a native Aramaic speaker–or even that he

---

14. Bill Ashcroft, Gareth Griffiths, and Helen Tiffin, *The Empire Writes Back: Theory and Practice in Post-colonial Literatures* (New York: Routledge, 1989), 38–39.

knew any Semitic language.[15] Rather, we appear to have a case of hybrid discourse as a means of subversion.

The seer, like his postcolonial anglophone counterparts in the New World order, negotiated a linguistic balancing act between decolonization and intelligibility. On the one hand, his language had to be close enough to the language of conventional discourse that he could be understood; on the other, he had to coin an idiolect sufficiently deviant to privilege effectively the subaltern voice.[16]

If the Apocalypse transgresses the standards of correct Greek syntax, it also violates the criteria of aesthetic refinement. One of the basic frameworks of elite literary and rhetorical theory was the concept of propriety, the idea that art should be suitably fitted to its subject matter. Pseudo-Demetrius's *On Style* expressed it this way: "But fitness [*prepon*] must be observed, whatever the subject; or in other words the style must be appropriate [*prosphoros*]—subdued for humble topics, lofty for high themes" (2.120). And Cicero defined the eloquent speaker as the one "who can speak of trivial things in a subdued manner, middling things in the blended style, great things with gravity" (*Orator* 100).

The concept of propriety blended well with Hellenistic notions of style and genre. At the base was the idea that art is imitation of life (see Quintilian, *Inst. Or.* 10.2.1). Most classifications of either style or genre included a hierarchy of three or four types, arranged in relation to the seriousness of their subject matter. Aristotle, for example, who wrote about tragedy, epic, and comedy, assigned heroic action to epic and tragedy (*Poetics* 5.7) and the representation of inferior people to comedy (5.1). And Quintilian emphasized that comedy should not "rise high" nor tragedy "stroll about" (*Inst. Or.* 10.2.22).

This hierarchy also applies to style, which, according to Aristotle, should be neither "mean, nor above the dignity of the subject, but appropriate to it" (*Rhetoric* 3.2.2). Style should imitate the proper emotion, character, and subject matter for its subject (3.7.1–2). So for Demetrius's four levels of style—plain, elevated, elegant, and forcible (2.36)—there correspond appropriate subjects. It is interesting to note that themes such as the heavens and the earth require the elevated style, which is animated but dignified (2.75).

With respect to imagery, the ancients valued the image that could bring its subject matter visually before the audience (Longinus, *On the Sublime* 15.1). But too much imagery resulted in excess, which took away from the effect of a piece of literature by focusing the audience's attention upon the images themselves (15.8–9). Aristotle balanced the value of "getting the picture as clear as if [the author] were at the actual event" with the fundamental requirement of clarity (*Poetics* 17.1). It was necessary that imagery be appropriate in order to be understandable.

The Hellenistic emphasis upon propriety implies an essentially conservative function. Those who discuss it are the literary elite. The idea that certain subjects de-

---

15. "The Language of the Apocalypse."
16. Ibid., 466.

mand particular styles and genres reflects a distinct status bias. Thus, when Aristotle argues that it is inappropriate to put fine language in the mouth of a slave (*Rhetoric* 3.2.4), or that "it is not appropriate for a woman to be manly or clever" (*Poetics* 21.4), he is also implying a politics: Whatever is the norm in the world should be codified in art. If art imitates life, and slaves are lower than free persons, then slaves depicted in art should also be low.

For example, parody was a recognized literary device in the ancient Mediterranean. Demetrius noted the grace of imitating another author's writing for the purpose of making fun (3.150). But Aristophanes' comedies such as *Frogs* and *Clouds*, which made fun of other figures such as Euripides, Aeschylus, and Socrates for intellectual and literary reasons, posed a form of high-brow politics. Demetrius, who noted how Aristophanes' humor was more suited to comedy with its lower subject matter than to more dignified forms (3.128),[17] would surely have noted the tension between form and subject matter in Aristophanes' work.

As resistance literature, Revelation twists the standards of propriety for its own ends, engaging the loftiest of subjects—emperor and empire—through imagery that is bizarre, even base. Its images parody Rome's pretensions to glory, as well as its imperial cult. In the weird locusts of 9:7–11, for example, Elisabeth Schüssler Fiorenza perceives a possible parody of the cult of the emperor Domitian, whose deity was Apollo (the king of the locusts is named Apollyon; 9:11), a deity for whom locusts were a symbol.[18] While this argument is tentative, there is general agreement that the beasts of Rev 13 should be taken to represent Roman imperial power. The First Beast utters "haughty and blasphemous words" (13.5), persecutes the saints (13.7), and has authority over the entire world (13.7–8), while the Second Beast makes the earth worship the image of the First Beast (13.12). These are almost surely references to the imperial cult. John also takes Roman diplomatic and commercial might and personifies it through another base image, the Whore, Babylon (Rev 17–18). Thus, in John's representation Rome becomes a beast, a whore, and possibly even ruler of a bunch of locusts.[19]

Resistance literatures challenge dominant discourses by attacking the symbolic structures of the establishment and building symbolic patterns of their own.[20] John's bizarre imagery does exactly that. He takes the language and techniques of the imperial power and twists not only the language but also the categories for discerning appropriate literature. John's bizarre imagery attacks imperial sensibilities while creating

---

17. There may be a textual problem here. Compare the LCL text with the translation of D. A. Russell and M. Winterbottom, eds., *Ancient Literary Criticism: The Principal Texts in New Translations* (Oxford: Oxford University Press, 1972), 196.

18. *Revelation: Vision of a Just World* (Proclamation Commentaries; Minneapolis: Fortress, 1991), 71–72. Cf. Sophie Laws, *In the Light of the Lamb: Imagery, Parody, and Theology in the Apocalypse of John* (GNS 31; Wilmington, Del.: Glazier, 1988).

19. See van Henten in ch. 9.

20. *Resistance Literature*, 85.

its own symbolic network. As we shall see, however, John cannot escape the imperial discourses of his day, without which his own resistance would be inconceivable.

Reinscription of "other" discourses. Beyond the matters of language and aesthetics, which by no means are merely peripheral, resistance discourses also manifest a tendency to reinscribe the very things they resist. Though asserting difference from the center may be an effective rhetorical device, difference always defines itself by what it excludes.[21] As Scott indicates, two imaginative options are available to the powerless: the reversal of present structures or their annihilation.[22] The result is what Ashcroft, Griffiths, and Tiffin call "counter-determination," the symmetry between a resistance discourse and that which it seeks to decenter.[23] The problem for resistance discourses is how to counter an imperial center without reinscribing an oppressive center of their own. In the Apocalypse we find a familiar pattern: Rome's public displays of power and status are disrupted through parody and satire.[24] But having noted these overt rhetorical strategies, let us emphasize their effects. Revelation does not abolish the trappings of Roman glory, it transfers them to Christ and his followers.

For example, Robert J. Royalty calls particular attention to the imagery of wealth in the Apocalypse. On the one hand, the Beast and the Whore are condemned in part in terms of their gaudy wealth, but on the other hand, the New Jerusalem/Bride wears white linen (19:8), its walls are "decorated with every precious stone" (21:19), and its street is of pure gold (21:21).[25] In addition to wealth, one might analyze the trappings and titles of royalty. In Revelation, the Septuagint's "Pantocrator" functions as a name for God over against imperial claims to preeminence, while God and Jesus both sit on thrones (for Jesus, see 2:21). Crown imagery also pervades the Apocalypse, as crowns belong to Jesus, to the twenty-four elders, and potentially to the audience. In Revelation, the Lamb may be a victim of imperial power, but he is also the one who creates a dominion of kings and priests (1:6; 5:10; 20:6).

The relationship between war and peace provides another instance in which Revelation transfers imperial claims. Rome promised peace to the inhabitants of its empire, though naturally it could guarantee that peace only on the basis of its military might combined with its commercial and diplomatic influence. "Who is like the Beast, and who can make war against it?" (13:4). Revelation 13:7 even claims that the Beast makes war against the saints and conquers them (cf. 11:7). And yet, of the seventeen instances in which some form of νικάω appears in Revelation, fourteen—perhaps fifteen (6:2 is the questionable case)—are assigned to Jesus and his followers. For the risen Jesus is the ultimate conqueror, and his followers may participate in his blessings if they conquer in the struggle to endure faithfully. While the

---

21. Richard Terdiman, *Discourse/Counter-Discourse: The Theory and Practice of Symbolic Resistance in Nineteenth-Century France* (Ithaca, N.Y.: Cornell University Press, 1985), 278.
22. *Domination and the Arts of Resistance*, 80–81.
23. *Empire Writes Back*, 170.
24. Cf. Scott, *Domination and the Arts of Resistance*, 105.
25. *Streets of Heaven*.

language of peace is not nearly so prominent in Revelation as that of conquest, the promise remains that those who conquer by their testimony will dwell where there is neither curse nor night, neither death nor pain. Like Rome, John promises peace through conquest.

Conclusion

In this essay I have introduced several "symptoms" of resistance in the Apocalypse. Thus far, I have invoked the language of "symptoms" in a neutral sense: these discursive signs are indeed common among resistance literatures. Yet this choice of words is not accidental, for the motivation to resist reflects actual human suffering resulting from alienation, poverty, domination, humiliation, persecution, or some other cause. Even if a given resistance discourse amplifies such injustices, the resulting disorders are no less real. As Scott has written, "The inability to defend oneself or members of one's family . . . against the abuses of domination is simultaneously an assault on one's physical body and one's personhood or dignity."[26] Scott cites Richard Wright's *Black Boy*, in which suppressed rage in one context evokes violent fantasy in the next:

> My momma says, that old white woman where she works talked about slapping her and ma said, "Miz Green, if you slaps me, I'll kill you and go to hell to pay for it."[27]

Perhaps some contemporary demonstrations of anti-United States sentiment demonstrate how such internalized rage can manifest itself in shocking ways. In Revelation such rage, whatever its etiology, sinks deep into discourse and canon, rendering even Revelation's faithful readers to some degree wounded as well. While texts do not determine the responses of their readers, still I imagine that many of the disorders we find among the Apocalypse's reading communities derive in part from the symptoms of resistance in their primary text.

---

26. *Domination and the Arts of Resistance*, 37.
27. Ibid., 39, citing *Black Boy: A Record of Childhood and Youth* (New York: Harper & Brothers, 1937), 68.

DRAGON MYTH AND IMPERIAL IDEOLOGY IN REVELATION 12–13

Jan Willem van Henten

Scholars tend to take the connection between the ideology of the emperor cult and the articulation of certain Christological views in the New Testament for granted, especially if they have their eye on the Revelation of John.[1] In this contribution I would like to discuss one aspect of this connection, namely the incorporation of mythological traditions about dragons and their slayers in the emperor's ideology and the possible implications of this incorporation for the reading of Revelation. The socio-political context of Rev 12–13 is often linked to the imperial cult and other kinds of propaganda for the emperor, no matter whether one is inclined to date Revelation around 70 C.E., at the end of the first century or in the last years of Trajan's rule.[2]

On the narrative level, the dragon and the two beasts clearly function as the antagonists of God, Jesus Christ and God's people. Attempting to contextualize Revelation in first or second century Asia Minor, it is hard to avoid relating the figures of the dragon and the two beasts of Rev 12–13 to the practice and ideology of the

---

I warmly thank Professors Henk Versnel (Leiden), David E. Aune (Notre Dame), and Adela Yarbro Collins (Yale) for their comments on earlier versions of this contribution.

1. See, e.g., A. Deissmann, *Licht vom Osten. Das Neue Testament und die neuentdeckten Texte der hellenistisch-römischen Welt* (Tübingen: Mohr, 1923), 287–324; D. Cuss, *Imperial Cult and Honorary Terms in the New Testament* (Paradosis 23; Fribourg: Editions Universitaires, 1974), 50–88. J. R. Fears, "Herrscherkult," *RAC* 14:1047–93, assumes a connection between the emperor cult and Christological passages in several New Testament writings, referring to Rom 13; 1 Cor 8:4–6; 1 Tim 2:1–6; Tit 3:1–8 and 1 Pet 2:11–17. Cf. also D. Zeller, ed., *Menschwerdung Gottes—Vergöttlichung von Menschen* (NTOA 7; Fribourg: Universitätsverlag; Göttingen: Vandenhoeck & Ruprecht, 1988).

2. Cf. E. Stauffer, *Christ and the Caesars: Historical Sketches* (London: SCM, 1955), 147–91; Cuss, *Imperial Cult*; P. Prigent, "Au temps de l'Apocalypse II: Le culte impérial au 1er siècle en Asie Mineure," *RHPR* 55 (1975): 215–35; D. L. Jones, "Christianity and the Roman Imperial Cult," *ANRW* 23.2:1023–54; E. Schüssler Fiorenza, *The Book of Revelation: Justice and Judgment* (Philadelphia: Fortress, 1985), 192–99; S. R. F. Price, *Rituals and Power: The Roman Imperial Cult in Asia Minor* (Cambridge: Cambridge University Press, 1984), 197–98. See now the sophisticated discussion in S. Friesen, *Imperial Cults and the Apocalypse of John: Reading Revelation in the Ruins* (Oxford: Oxford University Press, 2001).

Roman government in Asia Minor at the time. A simple equation of the symbolic descriptions of the dragon and the beasts with the devil, the emperor, and the high priest of the imperial cult would not do justice to the complex symbolic universe evoked by John's visions. However, and this is my first readerly step, one should assume some connection with imperial ideology if one aims at interpreting Revelation in the perspective of its ancient urban setting in the Roman province of Asia, as its first readers might have done. After all, imperial propaganda was part of the day-to-day experience of most inhabitants of this province.[3]

A second step in the attempt to read Revelation in the socio-political and religio-cultural context it may have had during the first decades of its circulation is to read it together with other texts, sacred or otherwise, that the readers and hearers might have been familiar with. For example, as many ordinary Christian readers as well as scholars have done and still do, one could interpret Revelation's visions in line with prophecies that became part of the Jewish Bible. Other interpreters, however, especially those of Rev 12, have often referred to non-Jewish traditions, oriental and/or Greco-Roman; whereas other readers turned to traditions from both sides. Earlier scholarship has devoted endless discussions to the mythological traditions that may have been taken up in John's symbolic language that describes the dragon and the beasts. Representatives of the German Religio-Historical School (*Religionsgeschichtliche Schule*), which was important at the end of the nineteenth and beginning of the twentieth centuries, have argued that John adapted and incorporated Babylonian or Greco-Roman myths about chaos monsters and the divine warrior who destroyed those monsters. Many later interpreters of Revelation have followed in their footsteps. In my contribution I will draw on the material from this discussion, but I do not aim at reviving this debate. I simply assume that such myths were part of the cultural and religious context of Revelation's first readers.

My main focus will be on the application of those myths by those who advanced the emperor's ideology, since the association of the emperor with the slayers of chaos monsters, such as the dragon Python or the partly human and partly monstrous Typhon, implied a claim that should not be misunderstood: the emperor was associated with the supreme god Zeus/Jupiter, or Apollo, or the Egyptian royal god Horus, all of whom restore order by slaying the agent of chaos. The question then arises, of course, how this claim about the emperor's role as the divine protector of order and stability fits in with the message of Revelation as a whole.

My reading assumes that the ancient readers of Rev 12–13, and especially of Rev 13:15, had every reason to connect the visions with the claim for the emperor's divine status which they encountered in their city life, since such a claim is easily refuted by the tenor of the visions. Thus, we may have a case analogous to what another apocalyptic passage, *Sibylline Oracles* 5:28–34, unmistakably suggests, despite its veiled language: a principal ruler demands divine status for himself but turns out to be the agent of chaos; his claim for divine status is false, evidenced by his deeds:

---

3. See the survey in Friesen, *Imperial Cults*, 23–131.

> One who has fifty as an initial [Nero] will be commander,
> a terrible snake, breathing out grievous war . . .
> But even when being invisible he will be destructive. Then he will return
> declaring himself equal to God.
> But God will prove that he is not. (*Sib. Or.* 5:28–29, 33–34)[4]

Assuming that it is most likely that ancient readers connected John's prophecy with current displays of a specific divine emperor, I examine how a reading of Revelation through the lens of Greco-Roman traditions about monster-slayers may have undermined the emperor's claim of divine status, certainly a blasphemous idea in Jewish and Christian circles.[5] This chapter focuses first on the mythological traditions about chaos monsters and their opponents as they may have circulated in the imperial age. It then deals with the religio-political use of such traditions in the depiction of the emperor as a divine figure who restores order by defeating chaos. Finally, it discusses the possible connections between this ideology of a divine emperor and the imperial cult. The conclusion summarizes the implications of my discussion of the Greco-Roman materials concerning chaos monsters for a contextualized reading of Rev 12–13.

Dragon, Beasts, and Combat Myths

Revelation's symbolic depictions of the dragon and the two beasts in the visions of chapters 12–13 are part of a cluster of passages about the antagonists of God, of Jesus Christ, and of the people of God. Chapters 12–13 form the core of this cluster.[6] The dragon passages of Rev 12 correspond to descriptions of dragons in Greco-Roman combat myths. He is called a snake as well as a dragon (ὄφις, Rev 12:9,

---

4. Translation (slightly revised) by J. J. Collins, "Sibylline Oracles: A New Translation and Introduction," in *The Old Testament Pseudepigrapha* (ed. J. H. Charlesworth; London: Darton, Longman & Todd, 1984), 1:393. The passage belongs to a complex of Nero passages that is associated with the figure of "Nero redivivus"; see J. J. Collins, *The Sibylline Oracles of Egyptian Judaism* (SBLDS 13; Missoula, Mont.: Scholars Press, 1974), 80–87; L. Kreitzer, "Hadrian and the Nero Redivivus Myth," *ZNW* 79 (1988): 92–115; G. C. Jenks, *The Origins and Early Development of the Antichrist Myth* (BZNW 59; Berlin: de Gruyter, 1991), 257–67; J. W. van Henten, "Nero Redivivus Demolished: The Coherence of the Nero Traditions in the Sibylline Oracles," *JSP* 21 (2000): 3–17.
5. Exod 20:3; 23:24; 34:14; Deut 6:13; 1 Cor 8:4–6.
6. See also 11:7; 14:9–12; 15:2; 16:2, 10–15; 19:19–21; 20:1–4, 7–10. Whether one advocates a concentric, cyclical or linear structure for Revelation, one has to take into account that chapters 12–13 are linked with chapters 17–18 on the whore of Babylon, joining a positive image of a woman with a negative one. The connection between these sections is supported by the corresponding motifs and similar vocabulary. The woman of Rev 17–18 sits on a scarlet beast, which is full of blasphemous names (17:3, cf. 13:1). The beast of chapter 17 has seven heads and ten horns, as does the first beast from chapter 13 (cf. 13:1; with 17:3, 9–12; also 17:8 with 11:7). See for further discussion of the cohesion in the "war scroll" of Rev 12–22, D. L. Barr, *Tales of the End: A Narrative Commentary on the Book of Revelation* (Santa Rosa, Calif.: Polebridge, 1998); for Rev 12, see Edith M. Humphrey's contribution in this book (ch. 5).

14–15; 20:2; δράκων, 12:3–4, 7, 9, 16–17; 13:2, 4, 11; 16:13 and 20:2).[7] He has a huge body (12:3 μέγας; cf. 12:4, 15), and several heads and horns (12:3). He first fights in heaven and after his fall against heaven (12:4, 7–9; cf. 13:6–7). The dragon has a destructive character and his aggression is emphasized time and again (12:7, 17; cf. 11:7; 13:4, 7; 16:14; 19:19 and 20:8). His main action in chapter 12 is his attack on the heavenly woman and her child. The imagery connected with the persecution of a woman with her infant by a dragon seems to be absent in the Hebrew Bible and parabiblical Jewish traditions.

Many commentators build on the research done by Dieterich, Gunkel and Bousset around the beginning of the twentieth century, to assume that non-Jewish mythological traditions about chaos monsters are incorporated into Rev 12.[8] Authors may differ on the details or the origin of the myths that may have been incorporated by John, but there can be no doubt that there is considerable consensus on the kind of material that seems to be important. Basically, all relevant mythological traditions have been discussed by Adela Yarbro Collins in her 1976 book *The Combat Myth in the Book of Revelation*.[9] She finds significant correspondences between the narrative of the Rev 12 vision and the pattern of non-Jewish combat myths.[10] She also argues

---

7. Cf. Fontenrose, *Python*, 10: ". . . nonhuman form: most often that of a snake . . ."
8. A. Dieterich, *Abraxas: Studien zur Religionsgeschichte des späteren Altertums* (Leipzig: Teubner, 1891), 111–26; H. Gunkel, *Schöpfung und Chaos in Urzeit und Endzeit: Eine religionsgeschichtliche Untersuchung über Gen 1 und Ap Joh 12* (Göttingen: Vandenhoeck und Ruprecht, 1895); W. Bousset, *Die Offenbarung Johannis* (KEK 16; Göttingen: Vandenhoeck und Ruprecht, 1906), 351–56. Also J. Fontenrose, *Python: A Study of Delphic Myth and Its Origins* (Berkeley and Los Angeles: University of California Press, 1980), 210, 264; H. D. Saffrey, "Relire l'Apocalypse à Patmos," *RB* 82 (1975): 385–417, esp. 410–17; A. Yarbro Collins, *The Combat Myth in the Book of Revelation* (HDR 9; Missoula, Mont.: Scholars Press, 1976), 57–100; A. Vögtle, "Mythos und Botschaft in Apokalypse 12," *Tradition und Glaube: Das Frühe Christentum in seiner Umwelt* (ed. G. Jeremias, H.-W. Kuhn, and H. Stegemann; Göttingen: Vandenhoeck und Ruprecht, 1971), 395–415; R. Bergmeier, "Altes und Neues zur 'Sonnenfrau am Himmel' (Apk 12)," *ZNW* 73 (1982): 97–109; D. E. Aune, *Revelation* (3 vols.; WBC 52a–c; Dallas: Word, 1997–98), 667–74. Survey: P. Busch, *Der gefallene Drache: Mythenexegese am Beispiel von Apokalypse 12* (TANZ 19; Tübingen: Francke, 1996). Skeptical: H. Gollinger, *Das "Große Zeichen" von Apokalypse 12* (SBM 11; Würzburg-Stuttgart: Echter, 1971), 127–33.
9. See n. 8.
10. Yarbro Collins, *Combat Myth*, 61: A. The Dragon (Rev 12:3); B. Chaos and Disorder (Rev 12:4a); C. The Attack (Rev 12:4b); D. The Champion (Rev 12:5a); E. The Champion's "Death" (Rev 12:5b); G. Recovery of the Champion (Rev 12:7a); H. Battle Renewed and Victory (Rev 12:7b–9); I. Restoration and Confirmation of Order (Rev 12:10–12a); J. The Dragon's Reign (Rev 12:12b–17).

The capitals are taken from Fontenrose, *Python*, whose pattern of the combat myth is slightly different (262–64). Yarbro Collins concludes that all elements of the pagan combat myth are present in Revelation. In her opinion, the death of the champion (E) is, however, only presupposed (12:5) and the role of victor over the dragon taken over by Michael and the element of the dragon's reign is put at the end (F). Elements G, H, and I therefore move to an earlier position. If one takes Rev 12 and 13 as well as 19:19–21; 20:1–4, 7–10 as a cohesive cluster, there is no need to change the order of the elements. Two complications of the combat myth pattern in connection with Rev 12 are that (1) the dragon seems to have more than one opponent and (2) the final victory over the dragon comes only much later in Revelation.

for a close similarity between Rev 12 and one specific type of these myths, the traditions concerning the monstrous Python's pursuit of Leto, the mother of the twin gods Apollo and Artemis, and the combat between Python and Apollo after the twins have grown up.[11] Yarbro Collins assumes that John the prophet made use of this specific combat myth: "If we ask which example of this form of the combat myth most closely resembles Revelation 12, the answer is clearly the Leto myth. . . . Revelation 12, at least in part, is an adaptation of the myth of the birth of Apollo."[12] She considers the fact that this myth circulated in Asia Minor in the time when Revelation was composed important support for her conclusion.[13]

Yarbro Collins's discussion concentrates on two types of the combat myth, which were both known in the Hellenistic and Roman worlds: the myths about the dragon Python and its slayer, the god Apollo, on the one hand;[14] and traditions concerning the Egyptian anti-god Seth, who became identified with the brutal monster Typhon from Greek mythology, on the other hand.[15] Both mythological clusters contain the motif of a woman (the goddesses Leto or Isis) pursued by a dragon figure (Python or Seth-Typhon). Yarbro Collins' conclusion that the Python-Leto-Apollo complex was tapped by John builds on the views of Dieterich, Fontenrose and Saffrey,[16] but her argument surpasses theirs because of her careful comparison of the sources on Python and Seth-Typhon with Rev 12. A survey of the mythological material discussed by Yarbro Collins shows significant correspondences between the description of the

---

11. For a description of the myths on Python and references, see G. Türk, "Python," *Ausführliches Lexicon der griechischen und römischen Mythologie* 3/2.3400–3412; Fontenrose, *Python*, 46–69. On traditions concerning Apollo in connection with Revelation, see also A. Kerkeslager, "Apollo, Greco-Roman Prophecy, and the Rider on the White Horse in Rev 6:2," *JBL* 112 (1993): 116–21.

12. Yarbro Collins, *Combat Myth*, 67; cf. 83.

13. Yarbro Collins, *Combat Myth*, 70–71, 245–52.

14. Hyginus, *Fab.* 140; Lucanus, *Bell. Civ.* 5.79–81; and Lucianus, *Dialogi Marini* 9[10]. Additional sources: Fontenrose, *Python*, 18 n. 9.

15. For descriptions of Seth-Typhon in Greek mythology, see J. Schmidt, "Typhoeus, Typhon," *Ausführliches Lexicon der griechischen und römischen Mythologie* 5:1426–54; G. Seippel, *Der Typhonmythos* (Greifswalder Beiträge zur Literatur und Stilforschung 24; Greifswald: Hans Dallmeyer, 1939); Fontenrose, *Python*, 70–93; H. Te Velde, *Seth, God of Confusion: A Study of His Role in Egyptian Mythology and Religion* (Probleme der Ägyptologie 6; Leiden: Brill, 1977); J. W. van Henten, "Antiochus IV as a Typhonic Figure in Daniel 7," in *The Book of Daniel in the Light of New Findings* (ed. A. S. van der Woude; BETL 106; Louvain: Peeters, 1993), 223–43, esp. 228–35.

16. See n. 8. Fontenrose, *Python*, 262–65 (cf. 266–73), gives patterns of the combat myth and distinguishes between several subtypes that penetrated the classical world, a "Typhon-subtype" and a "Python-subtype." These share the motif of a dragon that fights the gods, tries to disturb cosmic order and is being defeated by a ruler god. The second subtype would only differ from the first in one respect and would be present in Rev 12, too: "This differs from subtype I only in that the god is killed, and his son fights the dragon, recovering his father's life and throne, usually with actual sovereignty for himself. . . . Here belong Python, Set vs. Osiris, Satan (of Rev 12), Zu . . ." (264). Cf. p. 210 with n. 54 concerning Rev 12.

pursuit of the woman and her offspring by the dragon in Revelation and the myths concerning Python, Leto, and Apollo:[17]

Python combat myth

1. Struggle for the sanctuary of Delphi
2. Leto pregnant by Zeus
3. Python pursues Leto and tries to kill her
4. The north wind rescues Leto; help by Poseidon
5. Birth of Apollo and Artemis
6. Apollo overcomes Python
7. ———
8. Apollo establishes the Pythian games.[18]

Seth-Typhon combat myth

1. Struggle for the throne
2. Isis pregnant by Osiris
3[5]. Birth of Horus
4[3]. Seth-Typhon pursues Isis and Horus
5[4]. Ra and Thoth help Isis
6. Horus overcomes Seth-Typhon
7. Rule of Horus

It is certain that the Python myths were known in the first and second centuries C.E. in the areas mentioned in Revelation. Ephesus, for instance, was temple warden (νεωκόρος) of Artemis, Apollo's sister, as is mentioned also in Acts 19:35.[19] Coins depicting Leto fleeing from Python while her children Artemis and Apollo shoot their arrows at Python from the time of Hadrian were minted at Ephesus and Magnesia on the Meander.[20] These coins, or similar ones, may have been known to the writer and audience of Revelation.

Nevertheless, there are discrepancies between the Python myths and Rev 12 as well. The figure of Artemis as well as the Pythian games have no counterpart in Rev 12.[21] In Revelation the dragon confronts the woman *after* she has given birth to her son. This does not exactly match the Python myth, because this dragon pursues Leto *until* she gives birth to Artemis and Apollo.[22] The Egyptian combat myth fits better, because Seth-Typhon pursues Isis as the dragon pursues the woman in Rev 12 after

---

17. I present Yarbro Collins's pattern of the Seth-Typhon myth here as well, with slight modifications, which is useful for my argument below. One should note that variation in the sequence of elements of the patterns in combat myths is a common phenomenon; see H. S. Versnel, *Inconsistencies in Greek and Roman Religion*, vol. 2: *Transition and Reversal in Myth and Ritual* (Studies in Greek and Roman Religion 6/2; Leiden: Brill, 1993), 76–77, referring, among other things, to the work of V. Propp and W. Burkert.

18. See Yarbro Collins, *Combat Myth*, 66, and for her discussion of the texts, see 62–67.

19. G. Biguzzi, "Ephesus, its Artemision, its Temple to the Flavian Emperors, and Idolatry in Revelation," *NovT* 40 (1998): 276–90, esp. 279–80.

20. Apollo Pythios was worshiped at Ephesus and Pergamum; see Yarbro Collins, *Combat Myth*, 248–50; also Saffrey, "Relire l'Apocalypse," 413.

21. The element of the champion's temporary ruling-out is also missing in the myths concerning Python. Fontenrose's construction of this element (*Python*, 86–89) is unconvincing. Cf. Yarbro Collins, *Combat Myth*, 64.

22. This is also noted by Gollinger, *Große Zeichen*, 130.

the birth of the child. The rescue of Leto corresponds only in part[23] to that of the woman with the sun in Revelation. The woman is Revelation is brought to safety with the help of the great eagle's wings (Rev 12:14; cf. Exod 19:4).[24] Leto is also helped by Poseidon, the god of the sea, in contradistinction, in Rev 12:15–16 the earth assists the woman against the water sent after her by the dragon.

The pattern of the cluster of combat myths about Seth-Typhon,[25] is rather close to the pattern of Rev 12, including the central element of the pursuit of a woman and her child (Isis and Horus) by the dragon. This myth may partly originate in Egypt, but there are many attestations of the veneration of Isis in Asia Minor.[26] Isis was often represented as a Madonna, a woman holding her child Horus-Harpocrates on her knees or in her arms, and this picture appears also on coins from Asia Minor.[27] Moreover, a version of the Typhon myth, which was not affected by Egyptian traditions, was located in Asia Minor itself. According to this myth Typhon temporarily eliminates Zeus and brings him to his home in the Corycian cave at Cilicia.[28] So, there seem to be serious reasons to include the Seth-Typhon myths in the discussion of combat myths relevant for a contextualized reading of Rev 12–13.

The flight of woman and child may be less prominent in the texts on Seth-Typhon; nevertheless, this theme is present in passages from Herodotus and Plutarch.[29] In a group of texts where Seth and Typhon traditions are fused, the gods' flight before Seth-Typhon becomes an important motif. All gods fled to Egypt and changed themselves into animals to mislead Seth-Typhon.[30]

An additional point may be that the myths connected with Seth-Typhon are fre-

---

23. Cf. Yarbro Collins, *Combat Myth*, 67: "The flight of the woman in Revelation 12:14 with the two wings of the eagle is analogous to Leto's flight from Python with the help of the north wind. The aid of the personified earth in v. 16 is analogous to that afforded Leto by Poseidon, god of the sea." See Hyginus, *Fab.* 140, and Lucian, *Dialogi Marini* 9(10).

24. Leto is rescued by the north wind Βορέας (Βορρᾶς), whose name was rendered in Latin as *aquilo* (cf. Dan 11:44; Luke 13:29Vg; and Rev 21:13Vg). This word could have been associated with the Latin word for eagle (*aquila*), which supports the connection with the Python-myths. T. Zielinski, "Die griechischen Quellen der Apokalypse," *Forschungen und Fortschritte* 7 (1931): 156; Aune, *Revelation*, 705.

25. See the pattern above based on the *Hymn of Amen-Mose* (from about 1400 B.C.E.), the socalled Metternichstele (from 378–360 B.C.E.), Herodotus, *Hist.* 2.144, 156, 3.5; Plutarch, *De Iside*; Diodorus Siculus, *Bibl.* 1.21–22, 88; and Aristides, *Apol.* 12.

26. F. Dunand, *Le Culte d'Isis dans le Bassin Oriental de la Méditerranée* (EPRO 26; Leiden: Brill, 1973), vol. 3.

27. V. Tran Tam Tinh and Y. Labrecque, *Isis Lactans: Corpus des monuments gréco-romains d'Isis allaitant Harpocrate* (EPRO 37; Leiden: Brill, 1973); Yarbro Collins, *Combat Myth*, 261; for attestations from Asia Minor, see also Dunand, *Culte*, 79, 88–89.

28. See, e.g., Apollodorus, *Bibl.* 1.6.3; for further references, see Schmidt, "Typhoeus," 1432–40.

29. There are also traditions that Seth-Typhon desired and pursued goddesses such as Aphrodite, Thueris, and Isis; see Fontenrose, *Python*, 84 n. 24, 133, 143 n. 46, 180, 184, 189–91.

30. See, e.g., Apollodorus, *Bibl.* 1.6.3; Ovid, *Metam.* 5.321–331. J. G. Griffiths, "The Flight of the Gods before Typhon: An Unrecognized Myth?" *Hermes* 88 (1960): 374–76; Fontenrose, *Python*, 75–76, 177; Van Henten, "Antiochus," 230–32.

quently combined with astral imagery, which is important in Rev 12 as well, because the dragon and the woman are depicted as heavenly signs (Rev 12:1, 3). Isis as well as Seth-Typhon have been associated with stars and constellations. Isis was linked to the Dog Star[31] and to Virgo, Seth-Typhon to the polar stars and the Great Bear, and according to some scholars also to Hydra.[32] Such connections to the sky and stars are absent in the Python-Leto-Apollo material.

Thus, a reading of John's visions with an eye to contemporaneous dragon myths should not draw only on traditions concerning Leto, Apollo and Python, but also incorporate the imagery connected with Isis and Seth-Typhon. In fact, Python and Seth-Typhon may have been thought to be part of one and the same mythological cluster, because the appearances and roles of both dragons are very similar.[33] Adela Yarbro Collins supports this view of a fusion of traditions when she discusses the depiction of the woman of Rev 12 and, comparing her with three great goddesses, Artemis, Atargatis and Isis, she concludes that the iconography of Isis most closely resembles the depiction of the woman with the sun in Revelation.[34]

There seems to be one important difference between the two combat myths, though, because the sources about Seth-Typhon deal more prominently and universally with supreme power and rule than those about Python. Seth kills the royal god Osiris and is attacked by the son of Osiris and Isis, Horus, also a royal god. Typhon challenges Zeus' leadership of the gods and tries to take over his power. Diodorus Siculus interprets the myth of Seth-Typhon, Osiris, Isis and Horus as a struggle be-

---

31. Plutarch, *De Isid.* 21, 38 and 61 (*Mor.* 359D; 365F; and 376A).

32. Teucer Babylonius, see F. Boll, *Sphaera* (Leipzig: Teubner, 1903), 47; Te Velde, *Seth*, 86–87. Bergmeier, "Altes und Neues." See also F. Boll, *Aus der Offenbarung Johannis* (Stoicheia 1; Leipzig: Teubner, 1914), 98–124; W. Hadorn, *Die Offenbarung des Johannes* (THKNT 18; Leipzig: Deichert, 1928), 131–32; H. Kraft, *Die Offenbarung des Johannes* (HNT 16a; Tübingen: Mohr, 1974), 164. Mythographers presented Hydra as a daughter of Typhon (Fontenrose, *Python*, 356). See especially Bergmeier, "Altes und Neues," 101–2, who has doubts about the connection between Seth-Typhon and Hydra, but makes a reasonable case for the link of Seth-Typhon with the polar stars forming the Great Bear.

33. The traditions concerning Seth-Typhon and Python have clearly undergone a process of clustering. Fontenrose (*Python*, 77–93), among other things, points to the *Homeric Hymn to Apollo*, in which Typhon is presented as Apollo's opponent. In Plutarch's *About Isis and Osiris* (*De Iside*), Leto acts as helper of Isis against Seth-Typhon and hides Apollo-Horus on the floating island Chemmis near Buto (Plutarch, *De Isid.* 18 and 38 = *Mor.* 357F; 366A). Leto is Herodotus's *interpretatio graeca* of the Egyptian goddess Uto (*W3ḏ.t*); see Herodotus, *Hist.* 2.59, 152, 155; A. B. Lloyd, *Herodotus Book II: Commentary 1–98* (EPRO 43; Leiden: Brill, 1976), 270. Yarbro Collins (*Combat Myth*, 71–76) does not discuss Leto in this connection. See also S. J. Patterson, "A Note on an Argive Relief of Selene," *HTR* 78 (1985): 439–43.

34. With regard to Rev 12:1, lines 13–4 and 45 of the Cyme aretalogy from the first or second century C.E. say that Isis determines the paths of the stars, sun, and moon. See J. Bergman, *Ich bin Isis: Studien zum memphitischen Hintergrund der griechischen Isisaretalogien* (Acta Universitatis Upsaliensis Historia Religionum 3; Uppsala: Almqvist and Wiksell, 1968), 301–3; Yarbro Collins, *Combat Myth*, 74–75.

tween protagonists of chaos and order, whereas Osiris is presented as an ideal king.[35] Precisely because of this connection with the power of rulers the myths about Seth-Typhon were frequently taken up in political discourse (as described below).

The two beasts of Rev 13 clearly act as the dragon's agents. The location of the dragon near the sea in 12:18 and the rising of the first beast out of the sea in 13:1 suggest that the vision of the two beasts is the continuation of the vision of chapter 12.[36] The first beast derives its power, throne and authority from the dragon (13:2, 4; cf. 13:5, 7, 12) and resembles the dragon with its ten horns and seven heads (13:1; cf. 12:3). The beast rising out of the earth is closely related to the first beast and speaks like the dragon (13:11). Further on the dragon and the two beasts are again presented as a single group of antagonists (16:13; 20:10, where the second beast is called the false prophet). This cohesion of chapters 12 and 13 calls for a discussion of dragon myth materials in relation to both chapters, and not only chapter 12.[37]

Of course, my attempt to contextualize Rev 12–13 in no way excludes readings that interpret both visions in line with the ongoing use of Jewish traditions within and outside the Hebrew Bible. Daniel and other prophetic writings are echoed many times in Revelation;[38] and Jewish readers may have been inclined to interpret the dragon and the beasts as recreations of biblical chaos monsters like Leviathan, Behemoth and Rahab[39] or considered the Exodus tradition or Gen 3 as the point of departure for the interpretation of the dragon in chap. 12.[40]

My reason for linking Rev 12–13 to the Greco-Roman combat myths is that these myths continued to resonate in Asia Minor's urban culture in many ways,

---

35. Diodorus Siculus, *Bibl.* 1.21–22; cf. Herodotus, *Hist.* 2.144; Plutarch, *De Isid.* 12–13 and 49, *Mor.* 355E; 356AB; 371AB.

36. According to Kraft, *Offenbarung*, 175, the dragon mirrors itself in the sea.

37. Remarkably, most research into the mythological traditions that may have contributed to the depiction of the antagonists is restricted to Rev 12, while the dragon and its companions reoccur time and again (n. 7); see J. W. van Henten, "'En de draak werd toornig op de vrouw' (Openb. 12:17)," in *Kleine Encyclopedie van de Toorn* (ed. A. de Jong and A. F. de Jong; Utrechtse Theologische Reeks 21; Utrecht: Faculteit Godgeleerdheid, 1993), 57–75, esp. 64–65 and 73–75.

38. See, e.g., G. K. Beale, *The Use of Daniel in Jewish Apocalyptic Literature and in the Revelation of St. John* (Lanham, Md.: University Press of America, 1984); J.-P. Ruiz, *Ezekiel in the Apocalypse: The Transformation of Prophetic Language in Revelation 16,17–19,10* (European University Studies, ser. 23; Theology 376; Frankfurt: Lang, 1989); J. Fekkes, *Isaiah and Prophetic Traditions in the Book of Revelation* (JSNTSup 93; Sheffield: Sheffield Academic Press, 1994); J. Paulien, *Decoding Revelation's Trumpets: Literary Allusions and Interpretation of Revelation 8:7–12* (Berrien Springs, Mich.: Andrews University Press, 1987); S. Moyise, *The Old Testament in the Book of Revelation* (JSNTSup 115; Sheffield: Sheffield Academic Press, 1995); G. K. Beale, *John's Use of the Old Testament in Revelation* (JSNTSup, 166; Sheffield: Sheffield Academic Press, 1998).

39. This association may also be supported by the comparisons of Egypt, Babylon, and other empires with Rahab, Leviathan, or Tannin (Isa 30:7; 51:9–10; Jer 51:34; Ezek 29:3–5; 32; Ps 87:4; cf. Dan 7 and 8).

40. Cf. Gollinger, *Große Zeichen*; D. E. Guery, "Les signes de la Femme et du Dragon: Apocalypse 12," *LumVie* 45 (1996): 23–33; J. Dochhorn, "Und die Erde tat ihren Mund auf: Ein Exodusmotif in Ap. 12,16," *ZNW* 88 (1997): 140–42; J. Kalms, *Der Sturz des Gottesfeindes: Traditionsgeschichtliche Studien zu Apoalypse 12* (WMANT 93; Neukirchen-Vluyn: Neukirchener, 2001).

which may have enabled ancient readers to directly associate their internal symbolic universe as evoked by the visions with cultural symbols prominent in the external world. The seven decrees of Rev 2–3, especially those for Pergamum and Ephesus, suggest that the Roman administration and its ideology were linked up with the satanic forces of the dragon.[41]

A reading of Rev 12–13 in combination with contemporaneous combat myths helps to understand several details in their ancient context that hardly have parallels in biblical writings, or are only paralleled by Dan 7 or 8.[42] These details have striking parallels in the Greco-Roman combat myths. Revelation 12:3 emphasizes the red color of the dragon. This can, perhaps, be taken as an allusion to the depiction of Leviathan in Job 41:10–13,[43] but the association with the figure of Seth-Typhon is telling in any case, because Seth-Typhon is not only consistently depicted as a red animal, but the color red was also one of the means to identify animals or humans with this chaos monster.[44] The battle location indicated in Rev 12–13 (12:7, 17; 13:4, 7) does not fit in with the biblical chaos monsters living in the sea, but Typhon's ruinous performance can easily be associated with the heavenly battle of Rev 12:7. The sweeping down to earth of a third of the stars in Rev 12:4 may echo Dan 8:10–12, but this motif is also paralleled by Seth-Typhon's attack against heaven and his casting down of several stars and constellations.[45] According to Apollodorus, Typhon's head often brushed the stars (*Bibl.* 1.6.3). Apollodorus also says that Typhon attacked Zeus, who had just defeated the Giants and got hold of the throne of heaven and earth.[46] Typhon hurled rocks and attacked heaven with hisses and shouts,

---

41. H.-J. Klauck, "Das Sendschreiben nach Pergamon und der Kaiserkult in der Johannesoffenbarung," *Bib* 73 (1992): 153–82.

42. The first beast of chapter 13 is often interpreted as a creative combination of the four beasts from Dan 7. See, e.g., Beale, *Use of Daniel*, 229–39; A. Yarbro Collins, "The Influence of Daniel on the New Testament," in *Daniel: A Commentary on the Book of Daniel* (ed. J. J. Collins; Hermeneia; Minneapolis: Fortress, 1993), 90–112, esp. 107–9. The characterization of this beast resembles the description of the fourth beast's eleventh horn in Dan 7 because of the emphasis on its blasphemy and arrogance in combination with its warfare against God and the saints who dwell in heaven (cf. Rev 13:1, 5–7, and 17:3 with Dan 7:8, 20–21, 25 [LXX/Theod]; also the addition in Dan 7:8 [LXX], καὶ ἐποίει πόλεμον πρὸς τοὺς ἁγίους). The first beast's warfare is connected with the dragon's wars; cf. 12:7, 17. Beale (*Use of Daniel*, 231–33, 245) supposes that the dragon's giving of authority to the first beast (13:2, 4) was inspired by the bestowal of authority on the one resembling a human being in Dan 7:13–14. Many scholars have argued that Dan 7 draws on Jewish as well as non-Jewish mythological traditions. See for a synthesis J. J. Collins, "Stirring Up the Great Sea: The Religio-Historical Background of Daniel 7," in *The Book of Daniel in the Light of New Findings* (ed. A. S. van der Woude; BETL 106; Louvain: Peeters, 1993), 121–36.

43. Cf. Yarbro Collins, *Combat Myth*, 76.

44. Fontenrose, *Python*, 81, 185; Van Henten, "Antiochus," 236–38, with references. Cf. *Sib. Or.* 8:88 (possibly an allusion to Rev 12:3), referring to a purple dragon.

45. J. J. Collins, *The Apocalyptic Vision of the Book of Daniel* (HSM 16; Missoula, Mont.: Scholars Press, 1977), 107.

46. Apollodorus, *Bibl.* 1.6.3. Fontenrose, *Python*, 71, 84.

while spouting a great jet of fire from his mouth.⁴⁷ Thereafter, the gods fled to Egypt, but Zeus took up the fight against Typhon from heaven. Nonnus of Panopolis (fifth century C.E.), who combined several traditions on Seth-Typhon and elaborated them extensively, describes in the first book of his *Dionysiaca* Typhon's struggle against stars and constellations. He dragged them away from their position and even dumped the two Fishes into the sea (*Dion.* 1.165–218; cf. 2.281–90).⁴⁸ Typhon's well-known association with comets is connected with this motif. Pliny refers to a comet called Typhon after a king with this name, which was seen in Egypt and Ethiopia and considered ominous.⁴⁹ Finally, as suggested already, the combination of astral symbolism and combat myth makes the combat myth about Seth-Typhon an attractive co-text of Rev 12, where we find a similar combination. As a matter of fact, a passage of Plutarch describes three important constellations: the Dog Star, the Great Bear and Orion. It links these constellations to the three key figures of one version of the Seth-Typhon combat myth, namely Isis, Seth-Typhon and Horus respectively. These three figures can easily be compared with the mother, the child and their adversary, two of which are also introduced as constellations (Rev 12:1, 3).

POLITICAL APPLICATIONS OF THE COMBAT MYTHS ABOUT PYTHON AND SETH-TYPHON

My discussion of the combat myths about Python and Seth-Typhon has hinted already at a political use of these mythic traditions. This section will deal with the recycling of the combat myths in politics, especially as part of the propaganda for a divine emperor.

One of the pillars in the temple of Apollonis, mother to the Attalid kings Attalus II and Eumenes II, in her native town Cyzicus, showed a picture of Artemis and Apollo's fight against the dragon who threatened them (*Anth. Pal.* 3.6).⁵⁰ Other representations of the Python-Apollo-Leto-myth were found on coins of the Imperial period (above). Augustus singled out Apollo for special veneration. He made Apollo into his patron deity and presented himself, particularly before 27 B.C.E., as Apollo's

---

47. For further references, see Schmidt, "Typhoeus," 1433–34.
48. G. Braden, "Nonnos' Typhon: Dionysiaca Books I and II," *Texas Studies in Language and Literature* 15 (1974): 851–79; W. Fauth, *Eidos poikilon: Zur Thematik der Metamorphose und zum Prinzip der Wandlung aus dem Gegensatz in den Dionysiaka des Nonnos von Panopolis* (Hypomnemata 66; Göttingen: Vandenhoeck und Ruprecht, 1981), 160–66.
49. Pliny, *Nat. hist.* 2.23.91. For further references, see Boll, *Sphaera*, 164. Typhon was connected with storm winds as well; cf. Acts 27:14.
50. Türk, "Python," 3407–8.

incarnation.⁵¹ In Virgil's famous *Fourth Eclogue*, Augustus's reign is associated with a prophecy about the beginning of a new golden age and the reign of Apollo:⁵²

> The Maid returns, old Saturn's reign returns,
> Offspring of heaven, a hero's race descends.
> Now as the babe is born, with whom iron men
> Shall cease, and golden men spread through the world,
> Bless him, chaste goddess: now your Apollo reigns (lines 6–10, trans.
>   P. Alpers).⁵³

The emperor Nero founded a special corps of five thousand soldiers, who accompanied him on his participation in contests and shows. These so-called Augustiani applauded Nero's performances. Their acclamations betray divine honors and associate Nero with Apollo: "Glorious Caesar! Apollo! Augustus! Unmatched, like Pythios! By thyself we swear, O Caesar, none surpasses you".⁵⁴ After Nero's glorious return from his tour in Greece early in 68 C.E., he was welcomed with similar exclamations: "Hail, Olympian Victor! Hail, Pythian Victor! Augustus! Augustus! Hail to Nero, our Hercules! Hail to Nero, our Apollo! The only victor of the Grand Tour, the only one from the beginning of time! Augustus! Augustus! O Divine Voice! Blessed are they that hear you!"⁵⁵ Other passages and artefacts can undoubtedly be added to these references, but, already, it is obvious that Roman rulers were associated with Apollo as victor. Several instances of this triumphant role for Apollo go back to his defeat of Python.

---

51. For a survey, see P. Lambrechts, "Die 'apollinische' Politik des Augustus und der Kaiserkult," in *Saeculum Augustum*, vol. 2: *Religion und Literatur* (ed. G. Binder; Wege der Forschung 512; Darmstadt: Wissenschaftliche Buchgesellschaft, 1988), 88–107. For further literature, see P. Zanker, *Augustus und die Macht der Bilder* (Munich: Beck, 1990), 338.

52. On the *Carmen Saeculare* of Horace with a similar message, see D. Georgi, "Who Is the True Prophet?" *HTR* 79 (1986): 100–126.

53.   iam redit et Virgo, redeunt Saturnia regna,
            iam nova progenies caelo demittitur alto.
            tu modo nascenti puero, quo ferrea primum
            desinet ac toto surget gens aurea mundo,
            casta fave Lucina: tuus iam regnat Apollo.

Lambrechts ("Die 'apollinische' Politik," 95) supposes that the child is none other than Octavian-Apollo. A legend concerning Augustus's birth may have confirmed the claim of his special relationship with Apollo. Suetonius, *Aug.* 94, and Cassius Dio 45.1 say that Augustus's mother, Atia, became pregnant in the temple of Apollo after the visit of the god in the shape of a snake.

54. Cassius Dio 62.20.5: "Ὁ καλὸς Καῖσαρ, ὁ Ἀπόλλων, ὁ Αὔγουστος, εἷς ὡς Πύθιος. μά σε, Καῖσαρ, οὐδείς σε νικᾷ. See Cuss, *Imperial Cult*, 77–78. On the meaning of εἷς in this acclamation, see H. S. Versnel, *Inconsistencies in Greek and Roman Religion*, vol. 1: *Ter unus: Isis, Dionysos, Hermes. Three Studies in Henotheism* (Studies in Greek and Roman Religion 6; Leiden: Brill, 1990), 243. For the connection between Nero and Apollo, see also *Inscriptiones Graecae* 7 no. 36.

55. Dio 63.20.5. Cuss, *Imperial Cult*, 79–80. These exclamations are, of course, also inspired by the Pythian Games won by Nero and Apollo as patron god of the arts.

A search for political applications of the Seth-Typhon myths yields rich material as well. In Egypt, Ptolemaic kings as well as native Egyptians used the myth of the conflict between Horus and Seth-Typhon to blacken their opponents, be they a Seleucid king, an Egyptian rebel or the Ptolemies in indigenous texts, and to propagate their own role as Horus who restores order by overcoming Seth-Typhon.[56] The struggle between Horus and Seth-Typhon was a central theme in Ptolemaic royal ideology.[57] The ceremony of the coronation of the Ptolemaic kings at Memphis included a ritual reenactment of the killing of Seth-Typhon by Horus.[58] Annalina Levi discusses coins from the reigns of Hadrian, probably dating from 134–136 C.E., and of Caracalla (dated 215 C.E.), which seem to build on the imagery of Horus triumphing over Seth-Typhon. On these coins both emperors are depicted in military dress, standing with one foot on a crocodile,[59] matching a traditional representation of the royal god Horus, often portrayed with his feet on a crocodile or hippopotamus, or killing a crocodile.[60] The crocodile and the hippopotamus most probably represent Horus' enemy Seth-Typhon.[61] Other emperors were associated with Horus too: Domitian, for example, bears the Horus title on an obelisk, which now stands on the Piazza Navona in Rome.[62]

In the imperial period, the version of the Seth-Typhon myth that focuses on the battle between Zeus and Typhon is particularly relevant, because Zeus/Jupiter was the god with whom the emperors were affiliated most frequently.[63] Two passages from the first or early second century, a passage in Pseudo-Seneca's tragedy *Octavia* and Dio Chrysostom's first oration on kingship (*Or.* 1), draw extensively on the

---

56. Van Henten, "Antiochus," 235–42. L. V. Zabkar, "Six Hymns to Isis in the Sanctuary of Her Temple at Philae and Their Theological Significance," *JEA* 69 (1983): 115–37. The first of this series of hymns to Isis from the reign of Ptolemy II Philadelphos published and discussed by Zabkar contains the phrase: "You are the divine mother of Horus . . . who causes the rebels to fall" (118).

57. C. Onasch, "Zur Königsideologie der Ptolemäer in den Dekreten von Kanopus und Memphis (Rosettana)," *Archiv für Papyrusforschung* 24/25 (1976): 137–55; L. Koenen, "Die Adaptation ägyptischer Königsideologie am Ptolemäerhof," in *Egypt and the Hellenistic World* (ed. E. Van 't Dack, P. Van Dessel, and W. Van Gucht; Studia Hellenistica 27; Louvain, 1983), 143–90; Van Henten, "Antiochus," 224–25, 238–41. See also D. Frankfurter, "Lest Egypt's City Be Deserted: Religion and Ideology in the Egyptian Response to the Jewish Revolt (116–117 C.E.)," *JJS* 43 (1992): 203–20.

58. Nigidius Figulus, Schol. Germ. (ed. Swoboda, 1964), 123: "Typhon interficitur in templo Aegypti Memphi, ubi mos fuit solio regio decorari reges, qui regna ineunt."

59. A. C. Levi, "Hadrian as King of Egypt," *The Numismatic Chronicle* 6, ser. 8 (1948): 30–38.

60. See, besides the references of Levi (n. 59), W. Barta, "Horus von Edfu," *Lexikon der Ägyptologie* 3:34–35; B. Altenmüller, "Horus, Herr der Harpunierstätte," *Lexikon der Ägyptologie* 3:36–37.

61. Animals especially linked to Seth were the ass, crocodile, hippopotamus, fish, and pig. See T. Hopfner, "Der Tierkult der alten Ägypter nach den griechisch-römischen Berichten und den wichtigeren Denkmälern," *Denkschriften der (kaiserlichen) Akademie der Wissenschaften in Wien* 57/2 (1913), Register s.v. "Settiere," p. 198.

62. Levi, "Hadrian," 35 n. 24.

63. J. Beaujeu, *La religion romaine à l'apogée de l'Empire*, vol. 1: *La politique religieuse des Antonins (96–192)* (Paris: Belles Lettres, 1955), 71–73; C. P. Jones, *The Roman World of Dio Chrysostom* (Loeb Classical Monographs; Cambridge: Harvard University Press, 1978), 117, who refers to the impressive temple for Zeus Philios and Trajan at Pergamum.

Seth-Typhon combat myth. Pseudo-Seneca's *Octavia* depicts the sad lot of Nero's first wife and contains severe accusations of Nero. This passage is all the more fascinating, because many readers of Revelation suppose that the head of the first beast in Rev 13, which was fatally wounded but recovered, and the number of this beast as indicated in Rev 13:18, refer in some way to Nero.

Nero banished his first wife Octavia to Campania and had her killed in 62 C.E. on the island of Pandateira. The *Octavia* describes the fate of this woman, who was sadly disgraced by Nero. In the tragedy, Octavia depicts Nero as a malicious man and accuses him of all kinds of evil deeds. The emperor is consistently characterized as a tyrant (lines 33, 87, 110, 609–10, 620, 899 and 959). Traditions connected with Typhon resound in one section, which seems to allude to events in Nero's life and to his government (*Oct.* 228–41).[64] Lines 228–37 focus on the world of the gods and the stars and in lines 237–41 there follows a comparison of Nero's rule with the destructive performance of Typhon. Both passages are closely connected. Astronomic references in lines 228–37 already characterize Nero's time as a calamitous period:

> And oh that the lord of the heaven-dwellers, who often shakes hands with deadly bolt and terrifies our souls with the awful fires and portents strange, would make ready to whelm with flames this impious prince. We have seen a glowing radiance in the sky, a comet spreading its baleful trail, where slow Boötes, numb with Arctic chill, with endless, nightlong wheeling, guides his wain . . . (Pseudo-Seneca, *Oct.* 228–34; trans. F. J. Miller, LCL)

This passage aligns Zeus/Jupiter with Typhon, and recalls the combat myth. The "lord of the heaven-dwellers" (*caelitum rector*) must be Jupiter, as is confirmed by the reference to his bolt (*fulmen infestum*, line 229). The comet (line 232) and the astronomic references of lines 233–34 may be associated with Typhon. Boötes (*Bootes*, derived from Βοώτης, 'Ploughman') is a constellation under its own name or another name for Ἀρκτοῦρος or Ἀρκτοφύλαξ 'Bearward'.[65] In that case the star is connected with the constellation of the Great Bear, which was sometimes identified with Typhon (see above). The adjective *Arctous* in the ominous phrase *frigore Arctoo rigens* also points to the most northern constellations, to which the Great Bear and the Little Bear belong.[66] The association with Typhon evoked by the text is strengthened by the reference to a comet and the mention of Typhon in line 238. The passage may hint at the bolt of lightning which struck the table at which Nero was eating during a visit to a villa near the ponds of Simbruvium (near Subiaco; 60 C.E.) or the thunderbolt which melted down a statue of Nero in a gymnasium (62–63

---

64. Commentaries: G. Ballaira, *"Seneca": Octavia* (Corsi Universitari; Turin: Giapichelli, 1974), 43–44; L. Y. Whitman, *The Octavia: Introduction, Text, and Commentary* (Noctes Romanae, Forschungen über die Kultur der Antike 16; Bern: Haupt, 1978), 67–69.

65. Hipparch 1.2.5; Arratus 92. LSJ 242. H. von Geisau, "Bootes," *Der kleine Pauly* 1:928–29.

66. Draco also belonged to the northern constellations; see E. Boer, "Sternbilder," *Der kleine Pauly* 5:362.

C.E.).⁶⁷ The first event is mentioned by Tacitus in connection with the appearance of a comet (*sidus cometes*) and talk of Rubellius Plautus as a possible successor to Nero. Tacitus relates the second occurrence in a brief reference to a series of ominous events before he starts with his description of the consulate of C. Memmius Regulus and L. Verginius Rufus. Octavia had died and Nero had a daughter from Poppaea soon afterwards (*Ann.* 15.23). The magnificent gymnasium at the Campus Martius dedicated by Nero (Tacitus, *Ann.* 14.47) was struck by a bolt of lightning and Nero's statue in the gymnasium was melted into a lump of bronze. The association of these events mentioned by Tacitus with Typhon and his fate would be obvious and Pseudo-Seneca may be interpreted in this perspective as well. The Romans were familiar with the elimination of Typhon by the thunderbolts of Zeus/Jupiter,⁶⁸ and the events could easily be understood as forebodings of Nero's end.

The identification of Nero with Typhon is, in any case, explicit in lines 237–41 of the *Octavia*. After a reference to Typhon's birth because of Jupiter's neglect of Tellus⁶⁹ Nero is depicted as being worse than Typhon:

> Not such a pest was Typhon, whom wrathful mother Earth produced in scorn of Jove; this scourge, worse than he, this enemy of gods and men, has driven the heavenly ones from their shrines, and citizens from their country.... (Pseudo-Seneca, *Oct.* 237–41)⁷⁰

The passage includes several characteristics of Typhon that occur elsewhere: he is a savage beast, destructive (*ferus* and *pestis*, lines 237 and 239; cf. line 235 *saevus dux*), and the enemy of the gods. Lines 235–36 refer to Nero's pollution of heaven, which would fit in with Seth-Typhon's attack on heaven (*en ipse diro spiritu saevi ducis polluitur aether...*). The last lines of this passage (239–41) actually indicate a battle on two fronts, of the gods and of humankind. The traditional imagery connected with Seth-Typhon is expanded to the human world, which probably arises from the association of Nero with Typhon.

This is an attractive parallel to Revelation, where the combat myth is also depicted as taking place on two levels, the heavenly and the human. While Typhon

---

67. Tacitus, *Ann.* 14.22; 15.22. Whitman, *Octavia*, 67.

68. For example see Aeschylus, *Prom.* 362; Antoninus Liberalis 28.2–4; Ovid, *Metam.* 5.346–358; Hyginus, *Fab.* 196.

69. Pseudo-Seneca seems to connect Typhon with the giants, thus implying that his mother was Gaia/Tellus (Hesiod, *Theog.* 183–186; cf. 306). Other sources mention Typhon as Hera's son. According to *Hom. Hymn to Apollo* 305-55, Hera produced Typhon because of her wrath at Zeus giving birth to Athena and asked the Delphic dragoness to raise him. Gradually Typhon became associated with the giants (Hyginus, *Fab.* 151; cf. already Pindar, *Pyth.* 8.17–18).

70. Non tam ferum Typhona neglecto Iove
irata Tellus edidit quondam parens:
hic gravior illo pestis, hic hostis deum
hominumque templis expulit superos suis
civesque patria . . .

attacks the gods, Nero-Typhon is the enemy of gods[71] *and* humans. The expulsion of the gods from their temples can be connected with the pursuit of the gods by Seth-Typhon on the level of the heavenly world,[72] but easily associated with Nero's plundering of temples in Rome, Greece and Asia Minor in the human world.[73] Nero's frequent expulsion of citizens from Rome[74] can also be seen as an analogy of the pursuit of the gods by his match Seth-Typhon. No doubt *Octavia* 228–41 was grist to the mill of Nero's critics.

Dio Chrysostom's first oration may equally have served the propaganda purpose of the emperor's opponents. Domitian banished Dio Chrysostom from Italy as well as from his native Bithynia for many years. For Dio, Domitian must have been the embodiment of a 'typhonic' ruler. Dio and other contemporary writers portray Domitian as the tyrant par excellence, so that they could praise Trajan, after the brief intermezzo of Nerva, to the skies.[75]

The second part of Dio Chrysostom's most sophisticated speech on kingship (*Or.* 1)[76] is based on the legend that Hermes shows the youth Heracles the right as well as the wrong type of rule by taking the boy on a walk to a huge mountain, which appears to consist of two summits (1.58–84).[77] Heracles wants to be a ruler (1.65)[78] and Hermes leads him along a secret path to the two peaks, one of which stands high above the clouds while the other is dark and misty. On the throne of each peak sits a woman. One is called Kingship (βασιλεία, 1.73) and the other Tyranny (Τυραννίς, 1.78). The first woman is further described as a child of Zeus (like Heracles himself, 1.59), considered a god by Heracles (θεὸς ἀληθῶς εἶναι, 1.83) and is linked with the personified characteristics of virtuous kingship: Justice (Δίκη), Order (Εὐνομία), Peace (Εἰρήνη), Law (Νόμος)[79] and Friendship (Φιλία, 1.74–75;

---

71. On this epithet of Seth-Typhon, see L. Koenen, "θεοῖσιν ἐχθρός: Ein einheimischer Gegenkönig in Ägypten (132/1)," *CdE* 34 (1959): 103–19.

72. For references to the pursuit of the gods by Seth-Typhon and his attack on temples and some analogies in the human world (concerning Antiochus III and IV), see Van Henten, "Antiochus," 228–35, 242 n. 81.

73. Dio Cassius 62.11.3; Suetonius, *Nero* 32; Tacitus, *Ann.* 15.45; Whitman, *Octavia*, 68.

74. Dio Cassius 62.11.3–12.1.

75. *Or.* 40.12; 45.1; 50.8. See Jones, *Roman World*, 118; L. L. Thompson, *The Book of Revelation: Apocalypse and Empire* (Oxford: Oxford University Press, 1990), 95–115.

76. See further P. Desideri, *Dione di Prusa: Un intellettuale greco nell'impero romano* (Biblioteca di cultura contemporanea 135; Messina, Italy: D'Anna, 1978), 283–375.

77. The legend is said to be modeled on a story by the sophist Prodicus about Heracles meeting two women (Vice and Virtue). See Xenophon, *Mem.* 2.1.21–34; Cicero, *De off.* 1.118; Desideri, *Dione di Prusa*, 245 n. 6; Jones, *Roman World*, 116. See also A. Loyen, "Hercule et Typhée: A propos de Virgile, Enéide VIII, 298," in *Mélanges de Philologie, de littérature et d'histoire anciennes, offerts à Alfred Ernout* (Paris: Klincksieck, 1940), 237–45.

78. On Heracles as ideal king, see R. Höistad, "Cynic Hero and Cynic King: Studies in the Cynic Conception of Man" (diss., Uppsala, 1948).

79. Also called Λόγος Ὀρθός, Σύμβουλος, and Παρέδρος, 1.75.

82). The other woman is ugly, greedy, hated by everybody[80] and associated with Cruelty ("Ωμότης), Insolence ("Υβρις),[81] Lawlessness ("Ανομία), Rebellion (Στάσις) and Flattery (Κολακεία, 1.82). Right at the beginning of the description of the two peaks their names are given: "One of them bore the name Royal Peak and was sacred to Zeus the King; the other, Tyrannical Peak, was named after Typhon".[82] The companions of Lady Tyranny correspond to the description of Seth-Typhon in the myths. Heracles, of course, prefers the first woman, so that Zeus entrusts him with the rule over all humankind (1.83–84).

Ideology of the imperial cult and mythology

In the previous section I tried to show that combat myths of both Python and Seth-Typhon were used to endorse the association of rulers with the divine world by linking him to gods who restore order by triumphing over Python or Seth-Typhon. The Seth-Typhon complex, moreover, seems to have been used in two ways: either by constructing the emperor as the victorious Zeus/Jupiter or Horus or, by inverting the political message of the myth, by associating the emperor with the forces of chaos, i.e. the world of Seth-Typhon. Exact information about the emperor cult is missing in Rev 13 and a close connection between ruler cult and persecutions of Christians cannot be taken for granted in the first and second centuries C.E.[83] Scholars may never be able to establish the precise connection between John's visions and the practices of imperial cults in Asia Minor.[84] However, it seems at least possible to read some of the statements in chapter 13, with Revelation's ancient readers, as reflections on the emperor's claim for divine status, as articulated, among other things in the private and public bestowal of divine honors upon the emperor in Asia Minor's cities. How does

---

80. *Or.* 1.78–82; G. Mussies, *Dio Chrysostom and the New Testament: Parallels Collected* (SCHNT 2; Leiden: Brill, 1972), 250, points to the correspondence between this woman who has many sceptres, many tiaras and many diadems on her head and the diadems on the head of the dragon and the first beast (Rev 12:3; 13:1; cf. 19:12).

81. Cf. 1.76 where Dio refers to authority (or power) with folly (ἐξουσία μετὰ ἀνοίας) as the worst result of this woman's activities.

82. 1.67: ἐκαλεῖτο δὲ αὐτῶν ἡ μὲν Βασίλειος ἄκρα, ἱερὰ Διὸς Βασιλέως, ἡ δὲ ἑτέρα τυραννική, Τυφῶνος ἐπώνυμος.

83. Arrested Christians were forced to venerate the gods, sometimes also the emperor, but there was no obligation to attend provincial or municipal sacrifices or to perform rites. See D. Fishwick, *The Imperial Cult in the Latin West: Studies in the Ruler Cult of the Western Provinces of the Roman Empire* 2/1 (EPRO 108; Leiden: Brill, 1991), 530. Pliny (*Ep.* 10.96) and some martyr texts refer to the obligation for Christians to venerate the emperor or to perform acts that belonged to imperial cult (*Mart. Pol.* 8–10; *Mart. Pion.* 8; 18; Eusebius, *Hist. eccl.* 7.15.2). For a dossier of the evidence, see F. Millar, "The Imperial Cult and the Persecutions," in *Le culte des souverains dans l'Empire romain* (ed. W. den Boer; Entretiens sur l'antiquité classique 19; Vandoeuvres-Genève: Fondation Hardt, 1973), 143–65. See also P. Prigent, "Au temps de l'Apocalypse III: Pourquoi les persécutions?" *RHPR* 55 (1975): 341–63; Jones, "Christianity"; P. Keresztes, "The Imperial Roman Government and the Christian Church," *ANRW* 23.1:247–315, 375–86; Price, *Rituals and Power*, 123–26, 220–22.

84. Cf. Friesen, *Imperial Cults*, 145–47, 201–9.

such a reading fit in with the political applications of the combat myths? Whether or not John the prophet hints at the emperor cult itself, his ancient readers and listeners may have been alerted to the fatal consequences of the ideology connected with this cult. The vision of Rev 13 constructs a clash of two mutually exclusive ideologies.[85] Building on the story of the veneration of Nebuchadnezzar's statue[86] in Dan 3,[87] with the death penalty as sanction for disobedient subjects, John's vision depicts the second beast as organizing the general adoration of the first beast (13:14–15; cf. 13:8, 12; 19:20; 20:4).[88] Ancient readers may have been inclined to interpret this first beast as a symbol for Rome, perhaps an individual Roman emperor, or the emperors as a collective.[89] They may have even linked the second beast to the high priesthood of the imperial cult or—more generally—to the provincial councils who were responsible for the activities connected with the emperor cults, although the latter associations might have been less obvious.[90] Yet, in the context of early imperial Asia Minor, many ancient readers would have interpreted the blasphemous names of the first beast according to Rev 13:1 (cf. 17:3) as hints at the various honorific titles attributed to the emperor in connection with his supposed divine status (titles such as κύριος, σωτήρ, and θεός), which are, of course, blasphemous to the God of Jews and Christians.[91]

In the eastern part of the Mediterranean world the emperor's divine status was commonly acknowledged: in the provinces, in the cities and even in private life, as is apparent from provincial and local decrees and archaeological sources:[92] "Sacrifices were sometimes offered to the emperor as to a god. So too the emperor was

---

85. H. S. Versnel, "Geef de keizer wat des keizers is en Gode wat Gods is: Een essay over een utopisch conflict," *Lampas* 21 (1988): 233–56.

86. Dan 3:12, 18 reads "your image" (εἴδωλον σοῦ εἰκών σου).

87. Cf. Rev 13:15 with Dan 3:7, 10, 12, 14–15, 18 (LXX); 3:7, 11–12, 15, 18 (Theod.) with the verb προσκυνέω and εἰκών as object. Also the groups living under the authority of the first beast (Rev 13:7) with Dan 3:2, 7 (LXX): ἔθνη, φυλαὶ καὶ γλῶσσαι; Dan 3:4, 7 (Theod.): λαοί, φυλαί, γλῶσσαι (cf. also Dan 3:96 [LXX/Theod.]).

88. See S. Giet, *L'Apocalypse et l'histoire: Étude historique sur l'Apocalypse johannique* (Paris: Presses Universitaires de France, 1957), 113–45; Jones, "Christianity," 1034–35; Keresztes, "Roman Government," 271–72; Price, *Rituals and Power*, 196–98. See also S. J. Scherrer, "Signs and Wonders in the Imperial Cult: A New Look at a Roman Religious Institution in the Light of Rev 13:13–15," *JBL* 103 (1984): 599–610. According to 13:4, the dragon is venerated, too.

89. Cf. B. Reicke, "Die jüdische Apokalyptik und die johanneische Tiervision," *RSR* 60 (1972): 173–92, esp. 175.

90. Cf. Cuss, *Imperial Cult*, 20, 96–112. On provincial councils and officials of the emperor cults, see J. Deininger, *Die Provinziallandtage der römischen Kaiserzeit von Augustus bis zum Ende des dritten Jahrhunderts n. Chr.* (Vestigia 6; Munich: Beck, 1965). Friesen (*Imperial Cults*, 203) offers a brief critical summary of several proposals for referents of the symbolic second beast.

91. Cf., e.g., Bousset, *Offenbarung*, 360; H. B. Swete, *The Apocalypse of John* (London: Macmillan, 1907), 161–62; R. H. Charles, *A Critical and Exegetical Commentary on the Revelation of St. John* (2 vols.; ICC; Edinburgh: T&T Clark, 1920), 1:347–48; Kraft, *Offenbarung*, 175; Cuss, *Imperial Cult*, 50–53.

92. S. R. F. Price, "Gods and Emperors: The Greek Language of the Roman Imperial Cult," *JHS* 104 (1984): 79–95. H. Hänlein-Schäfer, *VENERATIO AUGUSTI: Eine Studie zu den Tempeln des ersten römischen Kaisers* (Archaeologica 39; Rome: Bretschneider, 1985), elaborates the differences

called *theos* (god) and the main aim of the cult was to display piety (*eusebeia*) towards him."[93] We can assume that Jewish and early Christian authors were familiar with this practice, not only in Asia Minor, but also and even in Israel/Palestine. Herod the Great felt compelled to show his loyalty to Augustus after having supported Mark Antony. Herod built a temple for Augustus and Roma in the newly founded city of Caesarea (Josephus, *J.W.* 1.414; *Ant.* 15.339). The sacrifices, statues,[94] prayers, games and other forms of worship connected with the imperial cult rendered the emperor divine honors and titles which belonged, in the perspective of Revelation, only to God and Jesus Christ.

It would not have been too difficult to fill in the roles of the combat myth pattern for John's readers who were familiar with the ideologies of what, for those readers, must have been the "outside world." The association of the emperor with Apollo was prominent during the reigns of Augustus and Nero (see above), but Zeus/Jupiter was the most important god in the provincial imperial cults.[95] There are many attestations of emperors associated with Zeus/Jupiter.[96] Gaius and Domitian even arranged to present themselves as Zeus or Jupiter. Gaius' decision to erect a statue of himself as the new Zeus Epiphanes in the temple of Jerusalem[97] is well known.[98] Because of the most commonly defended date of Revelation, the sources concerning Domitian may be especially relevant.[99] Coins from 85–96 C.E. commemorate Domitian's victory over the Chatti and suggest that he could only establish peace after defeating the agents of chaos as Jupiter had done: Zeus/Jupiter had to defeat the Giants and Typhon before he could establish his permanent supreme rule. On these

---

between provincial and municipal sanctuaries for Augustus and the different practices in provincial and local imperial cults. See also Friesen, *Imperial Cults*, 25–103.

93. Price, *Rituals and Power*, 232. Cf. 231, 233.

94. See, on the connection between the image of the first beast and statues in the imperial cult, Cuss, *Imperial Cult*, 104–12.

95. I will, therefore, concentrate on Zeus/Jupiter rather than on Apollo in the following pages. Kerkeslager, "Apollo," 119, points to a reference in Philo to an imitation of Apollo by Gaius (*Leg.* 95–96).

96. See the survey by J. R. Fears, "The Cult of Jupiter and Roman Imperial Ideology," *ANRW* 17.1:3–141. Fears considers the victorious Domitian as the viceregent of Jupiter a major *topos* of the panegyrical literature of the period (79–80). Cf. Price, "Gods and Emperors," 86: "The most common assimilation (to give the figures for the evidence from Asia Minor) was between the emperor and Zeus (26), though twelve of the instances are for Hadrian alone. Next in frequency were assimilations with Helios (12) and Dionysos (8)." See also D. N. Schowalter, *The Emperor and the Gods: Images from the Time of Trajan* (HDR 28; Minneapolis: Fortress, 1993), esp. 109–11. Scherrer ("Signs and Wonders," 605) refers to representations of emperors with symbols and insignia of Jupiter Optimus Maximus.

97. This implies that Gaius would have been considered a "god having the same temple" (*synnaos theos*) as the God of the Jews (A. D. Nock, *Essays on Religion and the Ancient World* [Oxford: Clarendon Press, 1972], 1:202–51). Second Thessalonians 2:4 has been linked to this decision of Gaius, but the connection cannot be proven.

98. Josephus, *J.W.* 2.184–203; *Ant.* 18.261–309; Philo, *Leg.* 184–388, esp. 188, 265, 346. Cf. Suetonius, *Cal.* 22; Dio Cassius 59.28; Prigent, "Culte impérial," 218–19.

99. Suetonius, *Dom.* 13, says that Domitian wanted to be called *dominus et deus noster*. Cf. Dio Cassius 67.5.7.

coins Domitian is represented as Jupiter's earthly vice-regent, and he fulfils a role like that of Hercules, who served Jupiter and the other gods. The emperor is crowned by Victory and, in his right hand, holds Jupiter's thunderbolt (*fulmen*) as the symbol of supremacy and protection. Trajan is similarly associated with Jupiter, by hurling his thunderbolt against the Dacians on the Column of Trajan in the Forum Traiani.[100]

Steven Friesen collected and analyzed the evidence of the emperor cult at Ephesus, which was initiated by Domitian, interrupted after his *damnatio memoriae*, and reintroduced by Hadrian.[101] I shall give a few examples from this material. There were 'Olympic Games' connected with the imperial cult of Domitian at Ephesus, as appears from coins from Ephesus with portrayals of Domitian and Zeus Olympios.[102] The association of the emperor with Zeus Olympios continued during the reign of Hadrian, who is presented as Zeus Olympios in six inscriptions from Ephesus. He was also hailed in acclamations as Zeus Olympios.[103] On the front of a coin with the portrait of Domitian stands *Domitianos Kaisar Sebastos Germanikos*, while the back has a picture of Zeus Olympios sitting on his throne with a sceptre in his left hand. Zeus' outstretched right hand carries the temple of the Ephesian Artemis. Friesen compares this coin with the so-called twice neokoros coins and comments: "The Zeus Olympios coin, however, made two new statements. It assimilated the emperor to Zeus, and it placed the emperor in a direct relationship to Ephesian Artemis".[104] Thus, the evidence for associating emperors with Zeus/Jupiter is surely not restricted to Gaius and Caligula.[105] In fact, in the East the propagation of the emperor as Zeus/Jupiter probably perpetuated the link between Alexander the Great's successors and Zeus.[106] An incentive to this association was provided also by the fact that Zeus/Jupiter as protector of oaths and treaties usually accompanied the goddess Roma, who was the principal goddess of the imperial cults.[107] Consequently, the emperor was often linked with Zeus/Jupiter after he joined Roma in the cults. The virtues and status of Zeus/Jupiter were thus transferred to the emperor: "Later, when the emperors were joined in cults with Roma, they often took over the characteristics of Zeus."[108]

---

100. Fears, "Cult of Jupiter," 79. See also J. R. Fears, "The Theology of Victory at Rome: Approaches and Problems," *ANRW* 17.2:736–826, esp. 816–18.

101. S. J. Friesen, *Twice Neokoros: Ephesus, Asia, and the Cult of the Flavian Imperial Family* (Religions in the Graeco-Roman World 116; Leiden: Brill, 1993).

102. M. Lämmer, "Olympien und Hadrianeen im antiken Ephesos" (diss., Cologne, 1967), 9 (further, 4–14); Friesen, *Twice Neokoros*, 114–41.

103. Friesen, *Twice Neokoros*, 118.

104. Ibid., 119. For further material concerning Domitian in this connection, see Fears, "Cult of Jupiter," 74–80.

105. According to Klauck ("Sendschreiben," 157), it is not certain that Trajan and Hadrian themselves were venerated at Pergamum as Zeus Philios and Zeus Olympios.

106. Fears, "Cult of Jupiter," 74.

107. R. Mellor, *QEA RWMH: The Worship of the Goddess Roma in the Greek World* (Hypomnemata 42; Göttingen: Vandenhoeck und Ruprecht, 1975); R. Mellor, "The Goddess Roma," *ANRW* 17.2:950–1030.

108. Mellor, "Goddess Roma," 972.

Reading the visions of Rev 12–13 together with the traditions of the combat myths about Python and Seth-Typhon and the claim for divine status for the emperor, who is also considered a personification of the dragon's opponent, would imply the utter deconstruction of this Roman imperial ideology. It would strongly suggest that this ideology was fake and that the emperor did not play the part of the restorer of order, the savior of the world,[109] or the supreme commander of humankind, as associated with Apollo, Horus and especially Zeus.[110] After recognizing the pattern of the combat myth and the association of the dragon and the beasts with the ideology of Rome, ancient readers may have realized that the visions imply a reversal of roles, turning the imperial ideology upside down. According to this reading, the emperor's part would be that of the dragon that causes chaos and destruction, the opposite of what the connection with Zeus/Jupiter implies according to such propagandists of the emperor as Aelius Aristides. In his eulogy on Roman government, Aristides presents the emperor as Zeus, the guarantor of order (*Or.* 26.32)[111] The inversion of roles in the combat myth is no scholarly construction, as is apparent from the examples of the ancient associations of the dragon with rulers or their opponents in the Ptolemaic royal ideology or the characterization of Nero as worse than Typhon in the *Octavia* discussed above. Dio Chrysostom refutes the divine status of Domitian in a comparable way with the following remark: "[T]he most powerful, most stern man, who was called by all Greeks and barbarians both master and god (δεσπότην καὶ θεόν), but who was in reality an evil demon (τὸ δ' ἀληθὲς ὄντα δαίμονα πονηρόν, *Or.* 45.1)."[112] Such a reversal of roles in the context of the combat myths was probably bound up with a conflict between two opposite and mutually exclusive ideologies, as Henk Versnel suggests in connection with the pagan accusations of Christians and their reactions: "The adherents of one utopia put the propagandists of the other in the category of the *negative* alternative, the anomic image of primeval chaos."[113]

---

109. For a fine sketch of imperial ideologies, see Versnel, *Inconsistencies*, 2:192–201. He refers (198) to an honorary decree from Halicarnassus in which Augustus is called the Zeus of our fathers (*Zeus Patroios*) and the savior of the entire human race (*Ancient Greek Inscriptions in the British Museum* 4/1 no. 894).

110. The Zeus Olympios coin with the portrait of Domitian discussed by Friesen (above) is another example of how mythical traditions about dragons and their conquerors become fused.

111. Friesen (*Twice Neokoros*, 151) points to this passage to demonstrate that the emperor was thought to accomplish the gods' work in an unparalleled manner. For a commentary, see J. H. Oliver, *The Ruling Power: A Study of the Roman Empire in the Second Century after Christ through the Roman Oration of Aelius Aristides* (Transactions of the American Philosophical Society, n.s., 43; Philadelphia: American Philosophical Society, 1953), esp. 941–42, 948–49.

112. Cf. the criticism of Roman imperial rule by Justin Martyr. See E. Pagels, "Christian Apologists and the 'Fall of the Angels': An Attack on Roman Imperial Power?" *HTR* 78 (1985): 301–25.

113. Versnel ("Geef de keizer," 255 [trans. mine]) also mentions Revelation in this connection.

Conclusion

The interpretation of Roman imperial rule as "typhonic" or "pythonic," which is implied by the inversion of the role of the victorious god into that of his monstrous opponent in this contextualized reading of Rev 12–13 fits in with two observations concerning Revelation that have been discussed by many scholars. First, the dragon and the first beast not only function in the visions' narrative as the opponents of God and Jesus Christ, but are also presented as their opposites. This is emphasized by the parallel vocabulary describing these four figures.[114] The inversion of the combat myth role models fits in well with this observation, because it supports the divine role of God and Jesus Christ, so to say, even in the propagandist terms of the non-believing outside world. Second, scholars have pointed out that Revelation incorporates Greco-Roman traditions and literary forms despite its uncompromising rejection of the outside world to which these traditions belong. This is only understandable if we assume that John the prophet radically changed these traditions and forms, honorary titles, imperial decrees, hymns, imperial court ceremonial etc, in order to make them subservient to his own proclamation.[115] David Aune even concludes that John the prophet was not afraid to turn the original meaning of such materials completely upside down: "John has consciously employed the form of the royal or imperial edict as part of his strategy to emphasize the fact that Christ is the true king in contrast to the Roman emperor who is both a clone and tool of Satan."[116]

It goes without saying that a contextualized reading of Rev 12–13, focusing on the mythological traditions about Python and Seth-Typhon and their political applications, underscores the refutation of the claim for divine status for the emperor. Foreign rulers' pretensions to divine status had been contradicted already in the Hebrew Bible (Ezek 28:2)[117] and were refuted again in post-biblical Jewish literature. The passage from the fifth book of the *Sibylline Oracles* quoted at the beginning of this contribution indicates that Nero equated himself with God (ἰσάζων θεῷ αὐτόν,

---

114. One striking example is the phrase ὡς ἐσφαγμένον in 5:6 concerning the Lamb, which is repeated in connection with the mortally wounded head of the first beast ὡς ἐσφαγμένην (13:3). See, among others, G. R. Beasley-Murray, *The Book of Revelation* (NCB; London: Oliphants, 1974), 207–8; Jenks, *Antichrist*, 241; R. Bauckham, "The Worship of Jesus in Apocalyptic Christianity," *NTS* 27 (1981): 322–41, esp. 329.

115. See, e.g., Deissmann, *Licht*, and Cuss, *Imperial Cult* (see n. 1). See also D. E. Aune, "The Influence of Roman Imperial Court Ceremonial on the Apocalypse of John," *BR* 18 (1983): 5–26; idem, "The Form and Function of the Proclamations to the Seven Churches (Revelation 2–3)," *NTS* 36 (1990): 182–204. P. Barnett, "Polemical Parallelism: Some Further Reflections on the Apocalypse," *JSNT* (1989): 111–20, offers chiefly a survey of earlier research into this parallelism.

116. Aune, "Form and Function," 204.

117. The oracle against the king of Tyre (Ezek 28:1–10) says: "Mortal, say to the prince of Tyre, Thus says the Lord God: Because your heart is proud and you have said, 'I am a god; I sit in the seat of the gods, in the heart of the seas,' yet you are but a mortal, and no god, though you compare your mind with the mind of a god" (Ezek 28:2 NRSV). An echo of this passage is found in 2 Thess 2:4; cf. also Dan 11:36 and Ps. Sol. 2:25–29.

5:34; a similar phrase occurs in 12:86).[118] Nero's claim is immediately denied by the statement that his deeds proved he was *not* equal to God. The corresponding lines in book 12 of *Sib. Or.* (12:78–94) refute a divine status even more plainly: Nero's flight and miserable death proved that he was not divine (12:93–94; cf. Pss. Sol. 2:26–27; Acts 12:22–23). Likewise, the king of Tyre comes to a sticky end: his divine ambition is punished by God and he dies through the hand of strangers (Ezek 28:6–10). In the book of Judith a similar claim of Nebuchadnezzar (3:8) is disproved in a more subtle way in Holophernes' failure and Judith's ridiculing of Nebuchadnezzar in the ambiguous phrases of chapter 11. But, of course, one reading does not necessarily exclude others. Readers of Rev 12–13 familiar with the Roman emperor's ideology may well have associated one emperor or all of them not only with Satan but also with Python or Seth-Typhon, the chaos monsters according to the emperor's own ideological frame of reference.

---

118. The phrase may be a Jewish (Christian) articulation of a platonic expression (θεοῖς ἰσάζοιτ' ἄν Plato, *Tim.* 13 41c). See for the motif of Nero's pretension to be equal to God *Sib. Or.* 5:34, 138–40 ἰσόθεος φώς; cf. 215–17). Collins, *Sibylline Oracles*, 84.

The Lamb Who Looks Like a Dragon?
Characterizing Jesus in John's Apocalypse

David L. Barr

I David was on the island called Patmos, when I had my own vision. I saw the Patriarch of Constantinople arrive in all his glory, on a large yacht, accompanied by a large retinue that included thirteen of the fourteen Orthodox patriarchs, a Roman Catholic cardinal, and a prelate of the Church of England. It was spectacular; I finally understood what the word *Parousia* means, for it looked like nothing more than the arrival of the emperor to visit the provinces. My dominant feeling at the time, and this was a time celebrating the nineteen-hundredth year of John's Apocalypse, was one of irony. What, I asked myself, would John have thought to see the representative of Jesus playing the role of the emperor?

Then it occurred to me that this was only a visible example of what we do all the time (and by *we* I mean both the religious and the scholarly readers of Revelation). We turn Jesus into the Emperor, the Lamb into the Dragon. We reverse John's own imagery, where he sees the sea beast in the guise of a lamb;[1] we want to invest the Lamb with all the miraculous authority and coercive power of the Dragon, forcing him to force the earth's inhabitants to worship the one on the throne. It is the argument of this paper that those who read the Apocalypse as predicting a second coming of Jesus wherein he will obliterate the forces of evil in some final battle and force the earth to accept God's rule are profoundly wrong. And I do not mean theologically wrong; although I am sometimes misunderstood to be speaking theologically. I lay no claim to any theological tradition; I approach this text entirely as a secular critic. I mean that such a view is wrong because it fails to pay sufficient attention to this story.

An earlier version of this paper was presented at the Society of Biblical Literature, International Meeting, Rome, 9 July 2001.

1. "Then I saw another beast that rose out of the earth; it had two horns like a lamb and it spoke like a dragon. It exercises all the authority of the first beast on its behalf, and it makes the earth and its inhabitants worship the first beast, whose mortal wound had been healed. It performs great signs, even making fire come down from heaven to earth in the sight of all; and by the signs that it is allowed to perform on behalf of the beast, it deceives the inhabitants of earth, telling them to make an image for the beast that had been wounded by the sword and yet lived" (Rev 13:11–14).

Those who hold such views fail to explore John's complex use of symbolic references. They fail to grasp John's moral undergirding of this story. They fail to engage the basic narrative dynamics of the story. The rest of the paper will examine each of these, the symbolism, the morality, and the narrative, for their bearing on the characterization of Jesus in this work.

The Symbolism

I have long argued, and become ever more convinced, that John's Apocalypse is a symbolic transformation of the world[2] and this in two senses. John transforms the world through symbols, and John transforms symbols through story. I am persuaded by those who argue that, far from reacting to Roman persecution, John is reacting to Roman seduction.[3] If it were clear to everyone that Rome was the enemy, John would not have to labor so against that prophet he calls Jezebel, who is all too ready to slip into bed with Rome.[4] That so many have been persuaded that Rome is the persecutor is testimony only to the effectiveness of John's symbolic recreation of the world.

The underlying point here is that the world is socially constructed. Indeed, all worlds are socially constructed; the world of imperial culture is just as much a fictional creation as is John's world.[5] What we call reality or the real world is merely the symbolic construction that has the power (intrinsic or extrinsic) to command the allegiance of the main stream. The power of John's Apocalypse lies in its ability to take up the symbolic forms of the Roman Imperial world and transform them into another world.

Many have explored the antithetical nature of John's alternative reality. Whereas in the imperial world the emperor is the savior, in John's world, Jesus is the savior; in the imperial world the emperor is the divine warrior who has brought peace to the world; in John's world the emperor is the beast of chaos that the true divine warrior must slay.[6] Much of the symbolism of the Apocalypse is of this antithetical kind.

---

2. David L. Barr. "The Apocalypse as a Symbolic Transformation of the World: A Literary Analysis," *Int* 38 (1984): 39–50.

3. Adela Yarbro Collins, *Crisis and Catharsis: The Power of the Apocalypse* (Philadelphia: Westminster, 1984), 84–107; Leonard L. Thompson, *The Book of Revelation: Apocalypse and Empire* (Oxford: Oxford University Press, 1990), 84–107; see also idem, "Ordinary Lives: John and His First Readers," in *Reading the Book of Revelation: A Resource for Students* (ed. D. L. Barr; Atlanta: Society of Biblical Literature, 2003), 84–107.

4. Paul Brooks Duff, *Who Rides the Beast? Prophetic Rivalry and the Rhetoric of Crisis in the Churches of the Apocalypse* (Oxford: Oxford University Press, 2001), 84–107.

5. Peter L. Berger and Thomas Luckmann, *The Social Construction of Reality: A Treatise in the Sociology of Knowledge* (Garden City, N.Y.: Doubleday, 1966), 84–107; for an adaptation of this perspective to the rhetoric of Revelation, see Elisabeth Schüssler Fiorenza, "The Followers of the Lamb: Visionary Rhetoric and Socio-Political Situation," *Semeia* 36 (1986): 84–107, and chapter 12 of this volume.

6. Nicely argued by Jan Willem van Henten in chapter 9 of this volume.

Poverty is wealth; wealth is poverty (2:9; 3:17). A slaughtered Lamb shares the throne of God (3:21; 7:17).

But just here things begin to go awry. For just as John reverses the characterization of the emperor from hero to villain, so he reverses the characterization of Jesus from the conquered victim to the conqueror: he becomes the divine warrior. To see the difficulty of this characterization, we only need to consider some of the apparent actions of this warrior:

> He exhibits wrath (6:16).
> He gathers an army (14:1) and watches the torment of the wicked who burn with fire and sulfur (14:10).
> As the warrior, he treads the wine press of God's wrath (19:15), from which comes blood "as high as a horse's bridle for a distance of 1600 stadia" (14:20).
> The warrior appears with a blood-dipped robe and slays the whole army of the beast, seemingly after the battle is over, leaving them on the battlefield so that "all the birds were gorged with their flesh" (19:21).
> He, or God, consign all not found enrolled in the book of life to the lake of fire (20:14).

Steve Moyise has put it cogently:

> The destruction brought about by the opening of the seals leads people to seek death rather than face the "wrath of the Lamb" (6.16). The beast may do all sorts of despicable things to God's people but none compares with 14.10, where God's enemies "drink the wine of God's wrath, poured unmixed into the cup of his anger, and they will be tormented with fire and sulphur in the presence of the holy angels *and in the presence of the Lamb.*" Had such a statement been written about the beast, commentators would no doubt have described it as the epitome of malice, vindictiveness and evil.[7]

While he does not elaborate on the italicized clause, he recognizes the moral issue involved in watching the suffering of others. Chris Frilingos has elaborated on this voyeuristic sadism, relating it to the Roman arena and the role of manliness in that culture.[8]

That such fiery torture can be envisioned is horrible; that the Lamb can be envisioned as a spectator to it is beyond horror. And it gets worse, for one must raise here the specter of coercion. Humanity seems left in the impossible situation that the beast will kill all those who do not worship it (13:15) and God will kill and torture

---

7. Steve Moyise, "Does the Lion Lie Down with the Lamb?" in *Studies in the Book of Revelation* (ed. S. Moyise; Edinburgh: T&T Clark, 2001), 182, emphasis in the original.

8. Chris Frilingos, "Making Males in an Unmade World: A Manly Paradise in the Book of Revelation" (unpublished paper, 2000), published in revised form as "Sexing the Lamb," in *New Testament Masculinities* (ed. S. D. Moore and J. C. Anderson; SemeiaSt 45; Atlanta: Society of Biblical Literature, 2003). See also his more comprehensive treatment in *Spectacles of Empire Monsters, Martyrs, and the Book of Revelation* (Divinations; Philadelphia: University of Pennsylvania Press, 2004), esp. 80–83.

all those who do (14:9–11). It seems a fine line between killing to induce worship and killing because of worship.

And there are other kinds of divine violence: cosmological violence directed against the earth, military violence directed against the Dragon and his armies, and judicial violence directed against both the leaders of the opposition and all who follow them. While much of this portrayal is traditional—earthquake, war, harvest, final judgment—the degree of violence, involving eternal torture, and the participation of the Lamb, at least as spectator, raises acutely the question of how John intends to characterize Jesus.

Some see this violence as quite in keeping with John's own goals. Greg Carey has made a strong case that the John engages in just the kind of domination that his book seems designed to condemn.[9] The graphic portrayal of violence thus fits John's own sociological need for control of the community, for to establish his vision he must undercut the authority of all competitors. John thus engages in verbal violence against others in the community (especially Jezebel) and demands acquiescence to his revelation, even invoking a curse on anyone who would change it.

There is much violence in John's story, but there is also opposing images. There are contradictions, or what Ron Farmer has taught me to call the *contrasts*, in the text.[10] The story is full of them. Here we have a God called Pantokrator who is never shown to act, hardly even speak, in the whole story. Here we have story of Satan bound who must yet be unbound after the thousand years. Here we have a story whose main theme is that only God is to be worshipped that yet ends with a double scene of John worshipping at the feet of an angel. Here we have a story where evil is obliterated in the lake of fire where yet the final city of the new creation is one into which nothing unclean will enter.[11] Here we have a story designed to stand against Roman oppression and domination that yet portrays the domination over evil. It is a story of contrasts.

These contrasts exist even within individual symbols, for the violence attributed to the Lamb is always equivocal. He slays all the wicked, but by the sword of his mouth (not his hand). He gathers an army but never leads a charge. Earth's inhabitants cry out to be preserved from the "wrath of the Lamb" but it is important to see that this wrath is never portrayed. From the very first introduction of the Lamb it is presented as the very antithesis of the conqueror, for John is told to look at the con-

---

9. Greg Carey, *Elusive Apocalypse: Reading Authority in the Revelation to John*, (Macon, Ga.: Mercer University Press, 1999).

10. Ron Farmer, "Divine Power in the Apocalypse to John: Revelation 4–5 in Process Hermeneutic," in *SBL Seminar Papers, 1993* (SBLSP 32; Atlanta: Scholars Press, 1993), 70–103.

11. On the open ending of the Apocalypse, see David L. Barr, "Waiting for the End That Never Comes: The Narrative Logic of John's Story," in *Studies in the Book of Revelation* (ed. Steve Moyise; T&T Clark, 2001), 101–12.

quering Lion of Judah, but what he sees is the slaughtered Lamb (5:5–6).[12] I argue that the Lamb functions in this story in contrast to the Dragon; while the Dragon coerces humanity to worship and service (13:15), the Lamb only seduces (22:12–17).

Of course, John would never have introduced the Lion if it did not serve some purpose, but that purpose has nothing to do with the exercise of violence. Providing the Lion as the foil for the Lamb accomplishes two purposes in my view. First it says what the Lamb is not; the symbolic and emotional contrast could not be stronger. But second, it says what the Lamb is; that is, the Lamb is the Lion, the one who conquers Israel's foes. But this conquest is not through violence inflicted; rather it is through violence suffered. The two images meld, like one of those spinning child's toys that have pictures on both sides that, when spun, merge together. So in the Apocalypse, the Lion shows what Jesus did and the Lamb shows how he did it. As John explicitly says:

> Worthy is the Lamb who was slain to receive power. . . . (5:12)

I take it as absolutely fundamental to the Apocalypse that the violence through which Jesus is said to conquer evil is the violence done to him. The character of Jesus, his ethos, is the Lamb slain.

What truly shocks me is how few readers actually believe John; they insist that the lion remain a lion.[13] Now this may be partly John's fault, as Patricia McDonald has argued.[14] John's choice of the Holy War paradigm to structure the last segment of his vision may have been a mistake; the paradigm is so strong and so violent that readers have trouble remembering that John reverses even these symbols.

Take, for example, the miniature scene in chapter 12 where we are told the story of a war in heaven:

> And war broke out in heaven; Michael and his angels fought against the dragon. The dragon and his angels fought back, but they were defeated, and there was no longer any place for them in heaven. (12:7–8)

This is the traditional language of holy war; but the symbolic force of that language is inverted by John's coda to the story:

> But they have conquered him by the blood of the Lamb and by the word of their testimony, for they did not cling to life even in the face of death. (12:11)

It is poor reading to overlook this inversion and to read as if the Lamb has not replaced the Lion in this story. Similar inversions occur at every point in the story—

---

12. For an argument that sees this and other symbolic inversions as key to John ethical stance, see David L. Barr, "Doing Violence: Moral Issues in Reading John's Apocalypse," in *Reading the Book of Revelation: A Resource for Students* (Atlanta: Society of Biblical Literature, 2003), 97–108.

13. Or perhaps turn him into a ram; see J. Massyngberde Ford, *Revelation* (AB 38; Garden City, N.Y.: Doubleday, 1975), 31.

14. P. M. McDonald. "Lion as Slain Lamb: On Reading Revelation Recursively," *Horizons* 23 (1996): 29–47.

even in the climactic scene in which the Heavenly Warrior kills all his enemies, for his conquest is by means of a sword that comes from his mouth, not by the power of his arm (19:21).

Careful reading will show that at every point where John introduces images of violence and conquest, he undermines the symbols with images of suffering and conquering testimony. This is why there can be no final battle or final victory in this Apocalypse; or to be more accurate why there are five final battles none of which ever involves a battle scene.[15]

Viewed at the level of symbolism, the Apocalypse indulges in images of great violence and oppression, with a good deal of the imagery being built on the ancient myth of a good war in which the forces of order destroy the forces of chaos. Careful reading will show that John always subverts these images, but the Apocalypse is not always carefully read. And we must ask, even if we read John's images carefully, can we ever overcome their sheer brutality? Can any amount of hermeneutical legerdemain ever hide the naked, brutalized, cannibalized woman whom John uses as the symbol for imperial evil? Such images remain morally deficient whatever interpretation we attach to them. That is, I can understand the meaning of the scene. The woman is not really a woman, but the "great city" that is Rome (and before that Jerusalem) and she is destroyed not by God but by human agency (the ten kings and the beast). One way to understand this would be to say that just as Jerusalem was cannibalized by Rome, so Rome will fall victim to the same powers of evil. I understand that. What I cannot understand is how John could use such violent images to demonstrate this justice.

Perhaps in his desire to free his readers from the domination of the Roman imperial system, he has merely substituted the domination of Jesus.[16] Before considering the narrative directly, it will be useful to look at the system of morality in the Apocalypse.

The Morality

D. H. Lawrence called the Apocalypse "a rather repulsive work" not content till the whole world be destroyed, or worse than destroyed, confined to that lake of fire in which those who fail to get in line might suffer eternally.[17] What Lawrence and countless other readers, including me, share is revulsion to the images of violence and coercion in this story. We decry the Beast's vicious destruction of the Whore (17:16); God's ultimate consignment of most of humanity to the Lake of Fire (20:15); the Warrior's defeat of the armies of the nations with its gory feast where the birds of

---

15. Stephen Moore show how timid the Revelation is compared to real war stories like the *War Scroll* or the ancient Irish war cycle the *Táin* in "Revolting Revelations," in *The Personal Voice in Biblical Interpretation* (ed. Ingrid Rosa; London: Routledge, 1999), 191.

16. See the essay by Greg Carey in chapter 8 of this volume.

17. D. H. Lawrence, *Apocalypse* (New York: Penguin, 1976), 103.

prey are invited to "gather for the great supper of God, to eat the flesh of kings, the flesh of captains, the flesh of the mighty, the flesh of horses and their riders—flesh of all, both free and slave, both small and great." (19:17). The ultimate value in this story seems to be power, power exercised ruthlessly. One even has the sense that God is willing to engage in torture in an effort to induce humanity to repent; notice how John describes the final torments:

> The fourth angel poured his bowl on the sun, and it was allowed to scorch them with fire; they were scorched by the fierce heat, but they cursed the name of God, who had authority over these plagues, and they did not repent and give him glory. The fifth angel poured his bowl on the throne of the beast, and its kingdom was plunged into darkness; people gnawed their tongues in agony, and cursed the God of heaven because of their pains and sores, and they did not repent of their deeds. (16:9, 11; see also 9:21)

Suffering does not lead to repentance, so it seems inevitably to lead to destruction. There can be no question that this is a war story and that John uses the conventions of war, with all their repulsive details. This is disconcerting, but the moral problem goes deeper.

In an earlier consideration of John's ethics I discussed two major ethical problems that every reader of the Apocalypse must consider: the problem of the use of force and the problem of the delay in stemming evil.[18]

First, if God triumphs over evil only because God has more power than evil, then power—not love or goodness or truth—is the ultimate value of the universe. The basic Christian rationale for suffering is that it is our fault. God created humans with free will and cannot (or at least will not) violate that free will; hence God cannot be held accountable for suffering in the world. The cogency of this argument is our recognition that it is never right to use coercion, especially physical coercion and torture, to force someone to be good. The Inquisition is morally indefensible.

Second, if God has the power to quell evil and end suffering and plans one day to use that power, then by what logic can God allow innocent suffering to continue? John is not unaware of these issues and in fact consciously raises this issue of delay within the story. The martyrs whose lives have been poured out on the altar call out:

> "Sovereign Lord, holy and true, how long will it be before you judge and avenge our blood on the inhabitants of the earth?" (6:10)

The divine delay John imagines here is best understood as awaiting the outworking of the destructiveness inherent in any system of domination, what Pablo Richard calls the "violence of the system, which is then turned against the system itself."[19] The

---

18. David L. Barr. "Towards an Ethical Reading of the Apocalypse : Reflections on John's Use of Power, Violence, and Misogyny," In *SBL Seminar Papers, 1997* (SBLSP 36; Atlanta : Scholars Press, 1997), 358–73. See also Barr, "Doing Violence."

19. Richard, Pablo, "Plagues in the Bible: Exodus and Apocalypse," in *The Return of the Plague* (ed. José Oscar Beozzo and Virgil Elizondo; London: SCM, 1997), 50.

judgments of the Apocalypse are never arbitrary; never do they rest on simple power. There is a logic of judgment finally articulated by the angel of the waters when the third bowl causes the earth's water to turn to blood.

> [B]ecause they shed the blood of saints and prophets, you have given them blood to drink. It is what they deserve! (16:6)

I have argued that we must understand both the appropriateness/justice of the retribution (blood because of blood) and also the inevitability of the retribution. As we might say today: we pour contaminants into our waters and we have contaminated water to drink.[20] So the martyrs have to wait till their "number would be complete" (6:11), because in John's story God acts *through* the process of suffering.

We see then that John's own moral system is consistent with his symbol system: the world is transformed and evil is destroyed "by the blood of the Lamb and by the word of their testimony" (12:11). But what of the lake of fire? As the American philosopher C. S. Peirce once wrote:

> But little by little the bitterness increases until in the last book of the New Testament, its poor distracted author represents that all the time Christ was talking about having come to save the world, the secret design was to catch the entire human race, with the exception of a paltry 144,000, and souse them all in brimstone lake, and as the smoke of their torment went up for ever and ever, to turn and remark, "There is no curse any more." Would it be an insensible smirk or a fiendish grin that should accompany such and utterance? I wish I could believe St. John did not write it. . . .[21]

We can grant this wish; St. John surely did not write it. But can we do more? Where does the brimstone lake fit into John's story? Before plunging directly in the lake, let's look a little more carefully at the narrative.

The Narrative

Narrative analysis discovers meaning in the dialectical interaction between the words of the text and the scenarios of the reader.[22] Meaning is a cooperative venture of author and audience; different audiences with different experiences and different concerns will discover different meanings in a work of literature. That is what we

---

20. Barr, "Doing Violence," 101.
21. Charles S. Peirce, "Evolutionary Love," in *The Essential Peirce: Selected Philosophical Writings*, vol. 1: *1867–1893* (ed. Nathan Houser and Christian Kloesel; Bloomington: Indiana University Press, 1992), 365–66.
22. For an introduction, see Mark Allan Powell, *What Is Narrative Criticism*? (Minneapolis: Fortress, 1991). For a more advanced analysis and demonstration of the interaction between narrative and other criticisms, see Janice Capel Anderson and Stephen D. Moore, *Mark and Method: New Approaches to Biblical Studies* (Minneapolis: Fortress, 1992). For an application, see David M Rhoads, Joanna Dewey, and Donald Michie, *Mark as Story: An Introduction to the Narrative of a Gospel* (2d ed.; Minneapolis: Fortress, 1999).

expect. Now some have gotten carried away with this observation on the role of the reader and declare all readings valid. I reject this view, for the text constrains our readings.[23] Still we must not underestimate what the reader/audience brings to the table.[24]

Understood as a narrative, the Apocalypse is not simply a war story. In fact, it consists of three interrelated stories, with overlapping characters and repetitious events.[25] The first story tells what happened to John on Patmos, where Jesus appears to him in the character of a noble human being. This character then dictates seven messages to the seven churches. John next tells how he was called to ascend to heaven, where he saw God on the throne, followed by a drama of opening a sealed scroll, with trumpets and the announcement that the world's kingdom now belongs to the Christ. Jesus here appears as a slaughtered-standing lamb and John appears as a character in the story. The war motif is foreshadowed in this second story, when John is told the fate of the two witnesses who, when they finish their testimony, will be attacked by "the beast that comes up from the bottomless pit" who " will make war on them and conquer them and kill them" (11:7). The narrative of this war will constitute the third act of this drama, but we note in passing that this is a defensive war; the attack originated with the other side.

The war stories themselves are fairly repetitious, following the general pattern: the two armies are introduced, they gather for battle; victory is announced, followed by the partial or complete destruction of the enemy. The destruction of Babylon is woven into these stories, repeated three times (it is abandoned, 18:2; burned, 18:8 & 19:3; and symbolically thrown into the sea, 18:21). This section contains some of the goriest scenes of the book, with rivers of blood and a messianic banquet on the corpses left on the battlefield (14:20; 19:17–21).

Surely this story is built on the mythology of Holy War (and that itself is ethically problematic), but just as surely John consistently demythologizes the war—or perhaps more accurately, remythologizes the warrior with the image of the suffering savior so that the death of the warrior and not some later battle is the crucial event.[26]

---

23. For a careful articulation of this viewpoint, see Wolfgang Iser, *The Implied Reader: Patterns of Communication in Prose Fiction from Bunyan to Beckett* (Baltimore: Johns Hopkins University Press, 1974), and especially idem, *The Act of Reading: A Theory of Aesthetic Response* (Baltimore: Johns Hopkins University Press, 1978).

24. For an interesting attempt to encompass both authorial intent and reader relevance, see Stephen Pattemore, *The People of God in the Apocalypse: Discourse, Structure, and Exegesis* (Cambridge: Cambridge University Press, 2004), esp. 13–31.

25. David L Barr, "Using Plot to Discern Structure in John's Apocalypse," *Proceedings of the Eastern Great Lakes and Midwest Biblical Societies* 15 (1995): 23–33. Further, I argue that all three stories are finally the same story (27–28).

26. *Tales of the End: A Narrative Commentary on the Book of Revelation* (Storytellers Bible 1; Santa Rosa, Calif.: Polebridge, 1998), 146.

At every juncture in this story where good triumphs over evil a close examination will show that the victory is finally attributed to the death of Jesus.[27]

There are, then, three scenes (Letter Writing, Heavenly Worship, Holy War) and three corresponding characterizations of Jesus in the Apocalypse: The majestic, human-like figure; the slaughtered-standing Lamb; and the heavenly warrior. These fit their stories, for the story of the last section is one of cosmic war; the story of the middle section is one of worship in the heavenly sanctuary (where the lamb's sacrificial significance is clear); and the story of the first section is one of issuing imperial decrees (the so-called seven letters). If these characterizations remained constant the traditional reading might be defensible; but they do not. Once introduced, the Lamb dominates the rest of the action. It is the Lamb who gathers the 144,000 holy warriors on Mount Zion (14:1); it is the Lamb on whom the armies of evil make war (17:14); it is even the Lamb who marries and rules after the war (19:7; 22:3). My point is that this symbolic inversion is also a narrative inversion and that the narrative inversion is also a moral inversion: in this story evil only appears to be conquered by power. In this story, evil is conquered by the death of the Lamb. This does not entirely resolve the problem.

Two issues need to be considered separately here: John's use of violent images and the structural role of violence in the story. I have already argued that this story regularly inverts the images of violence, so that what at first appears to be coercive power (Jesus slays all his enemies) turns out on closer examination to be something else (he slays them with the sword of his mouth). Those who see nothing but contradictions between John's story and the Gospel story of Jesus engage in too naïve a reading of these images.

This does not, in my mind, justify the violent images. I find them repulsive and morally inadequate; but I suspect that is because I read from the perspective of an educated Western person in a secure social and economic situation. John and his situation were quite different. While I do not wish to excuse John by saying he was a man of his time, nor do I wish to judge him by the standards of our time. It seems to me that these images of violence remain morally problematic whatever interpretation we might offer for them. Still, careful reading is called for.

Thus in the scene of the destruction of the Whore of Babylon that Tina Pippin laments,[28] it is human brutality that is portrayed. The Ten Kings and the Beast destroy her. Even so, this is because "God has put it into their hearts to carry out God's purpose" (17:17). Thus in some way God must be held accountable for all the violence in the world, even human violence, for God is responsible for creation. But this is surely morally different than imagining divine violence. In fact, John signals

---

27. For a consistent reading of Revelation as narrative, see my *Tales of the End*. For a rather different reading, see James L. Resseguie, *Revelation Unsealed: A Narrative Critical Approach to John's Apocalypse* (Biblical Interpretation 32; Leiden: Brill, 1998).

28. Tina Pippin, *Death and Desire: The Rhetoric of Gender in the Apocalypse of John* (Louisville: Westminster John Knox, 1992), 105.

this dialectical tension by immediately adding, "The woman you saw is the great city that rules over the kings of the earth" (17:18). Those who seek to dominate others will themselves by devoured by the process; it is, John says, what God has ordained. While the image of violence is problematic for me, the understanding of violence is not.

This leads to a second consideration, to what degree does this story portray violence as the means to renew the earth? Pippin sees war and disasters as the means whereby the reign of God comes.[29] I see the reverse: wars and calamities are human endeavors to avoid God's new world. In the vision of the Seven Seals, for example, John is clear on the cause of war, famine, and death (seals two, three, and four); it is the human conqueror of the first seal (6:1–8). These are not the means to heavenly city but obstacles on the way. Seal five then shows the innocent lives under the altar crying out for justice but being comforted and told to wait "until the number would be complete." Then follows seal six, complete with all the traditional apocalyptic signs (black sun, bloody moon, falling stars, etc), and the terrible cry to the rocks and mountains:

> "Fall on us and hide us from the face of the one seated on the throne and from the wrath of the Lamb; for the great day of their wrath has come, and who is able to stand?" (6:16–17)

But instead of the wrath of the Lamb (what we hear is coming), what we see is a vision of the preservation of those who receive the mark of God (7:1–17). Renewal comes after violence but not through violence.

Yet violence is at the heart of the holy war mythology. And the focal point of that mythology is the appearance of the divine warrior, John's third major characterization of Jesus:

> Then I saw heaven opened, and there was a white horse! Its rider is called Faithful and True, and in righteousness he judges and makes war. (19:11)

I do not know how many times I have read that passage—or rather misread it—as the return of Jesus to earth. But there is no return here; this scene does not occur on earth; John sees it by peering into the opened heaven. And notice: the rider is already mounted on the white horse, a sign of victory: the battle has already been won and what you see is the victorious general. This is no Parousia in spite of the nearly uniform interpretation of the commentators and in spite of the fact that the Parousia is always associated with coming "on the clouds" and never on horseback.[30] What John sees in heaven is already happening, hence the present tense verbs. John's divine warrior is not some evil twin of the savior Jesus who conquered by his own death. He is the same person, and the battle has already been won.

We have all the paraphernalia of Holy War, but no war. The story leads us on

---

29. *Death and Desire*, 96–103.
30. As David Aune recognizes but nevertheless clings to the Parousia interpretation; *Revelation 17–22* (WBC 52; Dallas: Word, 1998), 1053.

but then deceives us. As a general rule when a narrative betrays the reader, the reader is forced to reconsider the scenario guiding the interpretation of the narrative. This is how a joke works: the audience is led down a trail, expectations are built and then undermined, leading to a moment of humor.

> An explosion killed a navy boilerman and he wound up in Hell. Being used to stoking fires and extremely hot temperatures, he found Hell actually quite comfortable. When Satan went to check out the new arrival, he found him sitting in his room smiling.
> "You like this?" Satan asked. "Yes, Sir," said the sailor, "this feels like a spring day to me."
> Not wanting the new guy to be too comfortable, Satan turned up the heat a lot. When he went back to see how his new arrival was doing, the sailor was still happy. He hadn't even broken a sweat.
> "I like this kind of weather," he told Satan.
> Satan decided to try something different. Rather than turn up the heat, he turned it off. He made the sailor's room so cold icicles formed. When he checked on the guy, the room was icy and he was shivering, but he had a grin from ear to ear.
> "Why are you still so happy?" Satan demanded. "Its freezing in here!"
> "Well that's the point, I was a really big Cubs fan . . . I figure they must have won the pennant."

The only way a joke can work is to betray the audience. If you see it coming, it isn't funny. So I argue if you don't see both the violence and the subversion of violence in this story, you won't get it. The Lamb is the Lion, but the Lion is not the Lamb.

What is the impact of this subverted violence on the audience? If the Apocalypse provides a story "in and through which the people of God discover who they are and what they are to do"[31] what does John accomplish with this portrayal of subverted violence?

I agree with those who conclude that what John calls for is not violence but consistent resistance to the dominating ethos of Roman imperial power.[32] But a narrative reading insists that we refine that a bit, for we have to ask more carefully who is being addressed in this narrative. Now every narrative has a narrator, the one who tells the story, but just as surely there must be a listener, which narrative critics have taken to calling the narratee.[33] Like the narrator, the narratee is a fictional construct found within the story. Now John's story is complex.

I see John's story moving at three basic narrative levels, each with its own narrator and narratee. The three levels of narration are the telling of the whole work by a public reader (1:3); the telling of the stories by John on Patmos (1:9); and the telling of specific information by characters in these stories (for example, the voice addresses

---

31. Adela Yarbro Collins, "Reading the Book of Revelation in the Twentieth Century," *Int* 40 (1986): 229–42, here 242.
32. See the provocative study of Pattemore, *People of God in the Apocalypse*.
33. See, for example, Seymour Chatman, *Story and Discourse: Narrative Structure in Fiction and Film* (Ithaca, N.Y.: Cornell University Press, 1978), 253–62.

the souls under the altar in 6:11). To whom does the narrator speak at each level; who are the narratees?

At the outermost level the narrator is the public reader and the narratee is the audience gathered to hear the reading (1:3). This narratee corresponds most closely to the implied audience of the work, but we know almost nothing about it. The story leaves this narratee largely undefined.

The second-level narratee, however, is carefully defined, for that is the listener to whom John narrates his vision of the risen Christ. This narratee is explicitly named as the seven churches and extensively characterized in the messages to the churches (chapters 2–3).[34] This narratee is a complex group, both rich and poor, both zealous and lax, both loving and cold. They are carefully distinguished from the people John calls Jezebel and Balaam, precisely because they are folk who might be tempted to follow such accommodating leaders.[35]

At the third narrative level, the narratees are the people addressed in the stories told to these second-level narratees—that is, the saints and martyrs who struggle to conquer the beast (see 6:10, 15:2, and the constant references to saints and servants). They are characterized as suffering and oppressed. These saints and martyrs are the focal points of the story and both the second and first level narratees are encouraged to identify with them, leading one narrative critic to assert that ideal audience takes on the role of the martyr.[36] This is something of a poetical exaggeration, but it is clear that by telling the story through the point of view of those abused by Roman power, the discourse persuades the audience to resist such power.[37]

The purpose of the Apocalypse is to remind the first level narratee of the vile things Rome has done and is doing. It was Roman power, after all, that crucified Jesus; it was Roman power that constituted the totalitarian state in which they lived. If, as the saying goes, politics makes strange bedfellows, John wanted his audience to know just whom they were getting in bed with. John's apocalypse is a revelation of the true nature of Roman power and Roman culture. Seeing Rome in this light could lead to despair, but it is a measure of John's achievement that he has created a story that both reveals the mistake of accommodating to Rome and provides a rationale for

---

34. The narratee at level 1 is clearly a much broader group than this, including more than the seven churches.

35. I do not regard Jezebel and Balaam as part of the intended naratee because John's characterization of them is through insult and name-calling, devices designed to make them appear as outsiders. See Adela Yarbro Collins, "Vilification and Self-Definition in the Book of Revelation," *HTR* 79 (1986): 308–20; and Steven Friesen's essay in chapter 6 of this volume.

36. See the excellent, if technical, discussion of the reader as martyr in chapter four of Michael A. Harris, "The Literary Function of the Hymns in the Apocalypse" (Ph.D. diss., Southern Baptist Theological Seminary, 1989), 227–301. For a somewhat similar conclusion, see Pattemore, *People of God in the Apocalypse*, 68–116.

37. So powerful has been this characterization that commentators have regularly assumed that it describes the actual audience, who must be suffering persecution and martyrdom, in spite of the strong evidence to the contrary; see Thompson, *Book of Revelation*, 253–62.

resistance. For the prayers, the patience, the persistent resistance of the saints overthrow the powers of evil and bring God's kingdom into reality.

This overthrow is portrayed violently. There is much violence in the Apocalypse, including violence against mythic characters, violence against humans allied with these characters, and verbal violence against other community members. But there is also a subversion of violence, especially in connection with the Lamb. This subversion is not complete, however, and we are left with the question of what to do with this surplus of violence. And this leads us back inevitably to the lake of fire.

We can count on Stephen Moore to cast the moral issue in blunt terms:

> Whether or not Jesus is literally whacking off heads with his sword in 19:21 is a moot point, given the frightful fate of the owners of those heads: eternal death, or worse, in the lake of fire that burns with sulphur.[38]

Now I want to take this seriously, but at the same time I think Moore misstates the case, committing the fallacy of inconsistent reading. He is willing to take the head-whacking as symbolic, but the lake must be literal—though it is a little hard to say just what literal should mean here. In what kind of lake do you burn a dragon anyway? I fail to see how one decides where in Revelation to move to a non-symbolic reading, so I refuse to make that move.

What then of that brimstone lake? I offer three observations. First, if the rider on the white horse is not a reference to some future coming of Jesus, then the lake of fire is not some future event. Second, John's own interpretation of the lake of fire, while not perfectly clear, identifies it with "the second death" (20:14; see also 20:6). And third, I note that within the story four characters are consigned to this fate: the two beasts (19:20), the devil (20:10), death and hades (20:14), and all those not written in the lamb's book of life (20:15). What these four share is their utter incompatibility with the followers of the Lamb who share his testimony.

Thus understood as a present experience of a second kind of death, experienced by those who refuse to be redeemed, the lake of fire symbolizes what we all know. There are some evils in this world that are beyond hope of repair. There are evils that cannot be changed. There are people who refuse life; they will be cast (alive) into the lake of fire.

Some, like Steve Moyise, see this violence as real and would hold John accountable. And his reading is supported by much that we see in the popular reading of Revelation in our culture, as both Greg Carey and Tina Pippin have shown in their different ways. I agree that this is true of the popular reading of Revelation, and it is true at some level within the story itself.

Others, like me and Ron Farmer, see the countercurrent as more basic. For myself, I argue that John teaches the reader how to read violence by repeatedly showing its inverted meaning: violence inflicted must always be read as violence endured. We

---

38. Moore, "Revolting Revelations," 192.

read "war in heaven" but we must understand "blood of the Lamb" and "testimony" of the faithful. Obviously I agree with this too.

I recognize that these two views are at odds but I do not hold that there is only one, or even a best, interpretation of a work of literature. However, I do hold that there are wrong interpretations and worse interpretations. Three factors separate a stronger from a weaker reading; I will cast them as questions: Does the reading open the work or close it down? Does the reading extend our understanding, both comprehensively to the whole of the work and specifically to other aspects of the work? Do other interpreters find the reading interesting and compatible with their readings?[39]

It is in fact the readings my colleagues that have caused me to rethink my own understanding of violence and ethics in the Apocalypse. I have struggled to see how I can accommodate their insights. At the least, seeking to grasp the whole range of violence in the Apocalypse has caused me to take the surface level violence more seriously. Still I find a basic contradiction between this surface reading and the basic actions and symbols of the story, especially in the character of the Lamb. Thus I propose a reading where the Lamb conquers, where there is no violent "second coming," and where the only violence that can destroy evil is the violence of evil itself.

This is what I, David, have seen. I do not claim it to be the only right reading of this story. But it is a good reading, faithful, I think, and true to the symbolism, the ethics, and the narrative of John's story. There are other readings, powerful readings, important readings. But this is the one I choose. And while it may seem aberrant in the current setting, it is not as radical as it may at first appear. Let me summarize with two basic points.

First it is John's clear conviction that the slaughtered-standing lamb has power over the powers; he alone can open the scroll (5:2–6). While the imagined mechanism for this power is debated, Jesus' death seems to represent for John the defeat of Satan (12:11).

Second it is clear that John thinks that all who join their testimony to that of Jesus, even to the point of dying like him, share in that power (12:11; 6:10; 17:6). Further, each of the letters to the seven churches contains a promise for those who conquer, so such conquest is both possible and necessary. And so there is the paradox: Victory is won. Victory remains to be won.

A similar paradox exists in Paul's thought. In a convoluted argument about the nature and reality of the resurrection, Paul embraces two contradictory points: Christ reigns; the powers still reign: "For he must reign until he has put all his enemies under his feet. The last enemy to be destroyed is death" (1 Cor 15:26)."

Christ is reigning, according to Paul, and will do so until all enemies are defeated (thus they are still in power). The reign of Christ must eventually destroy all the powers. Those who swear allegiance to Jesus' kingdom stand opposed to the rule of those powers.

---

39. For a fuller discussion, see David L. Barr, ed., *Reading the Book of Revelation: A Resource for Students* (Atlanta: Society of Biblical Literature, 2003), 163–72.

In John's Apocalypse even more than in Paul's letters, those powers are incarnate as the beast of Roman rule (13:1–18) and a central part of John's purpose in writing is to persuade the audience to resist those powers. Stephen Moore asks, "If the slaughter of the 'ungodly' should be permissible at the Parousia, then why not before?"[40] But we can easily ask the obverse question, if violence is not acceptable now how can it be acceptable at the Parousia?

No, in John's Apocalypse evil is now and ever defeated only through keeping the word of God and the testimony of Jesus. Force is never an option. In this story the Lamb is ever a Lamb. We must not, through our reading, see him as a dragon.

---

40. Moore, "Revolting Revelations," 192.

Betwixt and Between on the Lord's Day: Liturgy and the Apocalypse

Jean-Pierre Ruiz

Methodological differences among practitioners of historical critical, literary and social scientific approaches to the Apocalypse of John have not kept them from converging to find features which they have described as cultic, liturgical, or ritual. Not far beneath the surface of this apparent accord lurk disagreements about the provenance and function of these features about what they may disclose about the Apocalypse and its social world, and about how they affect the reading of the Apocalypse itself.

The ritual setting of the Apocalypse has been invoked by a number of studies that share a broadly literary orientation, studies that range from the effort to understand the Apocalypse as oral enactment, to the suggestion that the ritual setting gave rise to liturgical dialogue as a characteristic literary form in the Apocalypse.[1] Elisabeth Schüssler Fiorenza offers a succinct statement of the growing consensus: "[M]ost exegetes stress the liturgical setting and forms within Rev[elation], but concede that liturgical symbols and forms are structural component forms of the book and are combined with other component types and forms in the composition of Rev[elation]."[2]

This essay makes a case for considering the ritual features of the Apocalypse as a point of productive contact between literary and social scientific approaches. Exploring the potential of ritual theory for directing traffic safely through this hazardous intersection, I draw upon the work of ritual theorists whose intercultural and inter-

---

An earlier version of this chapter appeared in *SBL Seminar Papers, 1992* (SBLSP 31; Atlanta: Scholars Press, 1992), 645–72.

1. David L. Barr, "Apocalypse as Oral Enactment," *Int* 40 (1986): 243–56; Ugo Vanni, "Un esempio di dialogo liturgico in Ap 1, 4–8," *Bib* 57 (1976): 453–467; idem, "Liturgical Dialogue as a Literary Form in the Book of Revelation," *NTS* 27 (1991): 348–72.

2. *The Book of Revelation: Justice and Judgment* (Philadelphia: Fortress, 1985), 166.

disciplinary work has left some social scientists queasy about crossing the border into the territory of literature.³

The working hypothesis that the Apocalypse is a script for oral performance in a ritual setting will set the stage for a rehearsal toward a ritual theoretical approach to the book of Revelation.⁴ It will first be necessary to identify several major traffic patterns in prior study of the ritual features of the Apocalypse, and to consider key issues of definition. In that way, this study represents an initial effort to organize a discourse that has been scattered and diffuse until now.

Traffic Patterns

Notably different paths have been trod by interpreters curious about the ritual features of the Apocalypse. The variety of perspectives represented within this convergence of attention provides a stimulus for examining the conclusions of a few especially prominent studies.⁵

---

3. For an orientation of ritual studies, see Ronald Grimes, *Beginnings in Ritual Studies* (Lanham, Md.: University Press of America, 1982); idem, *Research in Ritual Studies: A Programmatic Essay and Bibliography* (ATLA Bibliography Series 14; Metuchen, N.J.: American Theological Library Association; London: Scarecrow Press, 1985); idem, *Ritual Criticism: Case Studies in its Practice, Essays on Its Theory* (Columbia, S.C.: University of South Carolina Press, 1990); Catherine Bell, *Ritual Theory, Ritual Practice* (New York and Oxford: Oxford University Press, 1992).

4. By appropriating the phrase "rehearsal toward" from the title of John J. MacAloon, ed., *Rite, Drama, Festival, Spectacle: Rehearsals Toward a Theory of Cultural Performance* (Philadelphia: Institute for the Study of Human Issues, 1984), I am indicating the experimental and exploratory nature of this study, suggesting that it may leave us with more provocative questions than definitive answers.

5. Treatments of ritual features and traces in the Apocalypse include B. Brinkmann, "De visione liturgica in Apocalypsi S. Johannis," *VD* 11 (1931): 335–42; Allen Cabaniss, "A Note on the Liturgy of the Apocalypse," *Int* 7 (1953): 78–86; Edouard Cothenet, "Earthly Liturgy and Heavenly Liturgy according to the Book of Revelation," in *Roles in the Liturgical Assembly* (New York: Pueblo, 1981), 115–35; idem, "Le symbolisme du culte dans l'Apocalypse," in *Le Symbolisme dans le Culte des Grandes Religions* (ed. Julien Ries; Homo Religiosus 11; Louvain-la-Neuve: Centre d'Histoire des Religions, 1985), 223–38; Gerhard Delling, "Zum gottesdienstlichen Stil der Johannes-Apokalypse," *NovT* 3 (1959): 107–37; J. A. Draper, "The Heavenly Feast of Tabernacles: Revelation 7:1–17," *JSNT* 34 (1988): 135–43; Samuel Läuchli, "Eine Gottesdienststruktur in der Johannesoffenbarung," *TZ* 16 (1960): 359–78; Lucetta Mowry, "Revelation 4–5 and Early Christian Liturgical Usage," *JBL* 71 (1952): 75–84; Josef Pescheck, "Der Gottesdienst in der Apokalypse," *TPQ* 73 (1920): 496–514; Otto Piper, "The Apocalypse of St. John and the Liturgy of the Church," *CH* 20 (1951): 250–65; Pierre Prigent, *Apocalypse et Liturgie* (CahT 52; Neuchatel: Delachaux & Niestlé, 1964); Massey H. Shepherd, *The Paschal Liturgy in the Apocalypse* (Ecumenical Studies in Worship 6; London: Lutterworth, 1960); Håkan Ulfgard, *Feast and Future: Revelation 7:9–17 and the Feast of Tabernacles* (ConBNT 22; Stockholm: Almqvist & Wiksell, 1989).

The hymns of the Apocalypse have been objects of particular attention; for example, see Michael Harris, "The Literary Function of Hymns in the Apocalypse of John" (Ph.D. diss., Southern Baptist Theological Seminary, Louisville, 1988). Earlier treatments of this material include John J. O'Rourke, "The Hymns of the Apocalypse," *CBQ* 30 (1968): 399–409; Klaus Peter Jörns, *Das hymnische Evangelium: Untersuchungen zu Aufbau, Funktion und Herkunft der hymnischen Stücke in der Johannesoffenbarung* (SNT 5; Gütersloh: Mohn, 1971); David R. Carnegie, "Worthy Is the Lamb: The Hymns

Dealing with the Apocalypse under the heading of "The Attainment of Millennial Bliss through Myth," John G. Gager's *Kingdom and Community* contributes two important connections: first, the power of myth over time; second, the setting of myth in liturgy.[6] Presupposing a social situation in which the experience or the threat of persecution enforced unwelcome tensions and even contradictions between hope and reality, Gager argues that the Apocalypse functioned as a Christian myth which offers a foretaste of future relief: "consolation not simply as the promise of a happy fate for the martyrs in the near future, but through the mythological enactment of that future in the present."[7] Though he is reluctant to define the place of the Apocalypse in the worship of the churches of Asia Minor, Gager shares the prevailing view that the book was meant to be read aloud during the liturgy. This is the second key connection, that between myth and liturgy: suppression of time through myth, says Gager, occurred as the book was read in the worshiping assembly.[8]

Gager diminishes the power of myth over time by rendering that power transitory: "For hearers of this book, even a fleeting experience of the millennium may have provided the energy needed to withstand the wrath of the beast."[9] It follows that this passing experience of an ideal world evaporated when the recitation of the book came to an end and the reality of persecution resumed its unrelenting course. Yet, because the end was considered imminent, the Christian myth of the Apocalypse would only have had to perform its palliative task a very few times.

The connection between myth and time is further weakened by Gager's borrowing of a psychotherapeutic analogy from Claude Lévi-Strauss to describe the function of the Apocalypse as myth. As the therapeutic situation of psychoanalysis effects a suppression of the present time by bringing the past into the present, the Apocalypse effects a suppression of time by bringing the future into the present.[10] This analogy breaks down on at least two counts. The first is the implication that the Apocalypse's mythic suppression of time only altered perception and only altered it temporarily: the illusion of change was shattered when the grim realities of persecution and oppression resumed. A second weakness of the analogy between psychoanalysis and the mythic therapy of the Apocalypse is that while psychoanalysis focuses on the individual, the Apocalypse is addressed to a group.[11]

This weakness may account for the turn to the connection between myth and

---

in Revelation," in *Christ the Lord: Studies in Christology Presented to Donald Guthrie* (ed. Harold H. Rowdon; Leicester, U.K.: Inter-Varsity Press, 1982), 243–56.

6. *Kingdom and Community: The Social World of Early Christianity* (Englewood Cliffs, N.J.: Prentice-Hall, 1975), 49–57.

7. Ibid., 51, 50.

8. Ibid., 50, 56–57. Gager borrows "suppression of time" from Claude Lévi-Strauss, *The Raw and the Cooked* (New York: Harper & Row, 1969), 16.

9. *Kingdom and Community*, 56.

10. Ibid., 50, 55. Lévi-Strauss builds the analogy between myth and psychoanalysis in *Structural Anthropology* (Garden City, N.Y.: Doubleday, 1967), 181–201. Gager also cites Mircea Eliade's essay, "Time Can Be Overcome," in Eliade's *Myth and Reality* (New York: Harper & Row, 1963), 75–91.

11. See Eliade, *Myth and Reality*, 78.

liturgy, Gager's identification of ritual as the setting in which the Apocalypse was to be recited. Even so, the lack of an adequate ritual theory prevents Gager from suggesting how the liturgical setting affects the interpretation of the Apocalypse and how the recitation of the Apocalypse in a ritual setting might have affected the communities in whose liturgical assemblies it was heard.[12]

Realized eschatology is the theological heading under which Leonard Thompson and David Aune consider hymnic material in the Apocalypse and in other early Christian literature. Focusing on the relationship between cult and eschatology in the Apocalypse, Thompson points out the balance between dramatic narrative and scenes of hymnic heavenly worship, discovering "that scenes of cult and its liturgy realize eschatological realities prior to their presentation in dramatic narrative form."[13] The tension between present and future is mediated in the Apocalypse by the juxtaposition of hymnic material and narrative.

Beyond the Apocalypse, David E. Aune discovers hymnic expression of realized eschatology in the Odes of Solomon.

> Christian worship functions in such a way that paradigmatic events and conditions of the past, as well as particular anticipated events and conditions of the future, are spoken of *as if* the temporal boundaries between past and future had become collapsed into an eternal present.[14]

In this context he discusses the phenomenon of the prophetic hymn, a feature which the Odes of Solomon have in common with the Apocalypse. The oracular quality of such hymns is linked with the congregational character of prophecy suggested by the Odes.[15] Aune argues that prophetic hymns like those found in the Odes, which served as vehicles for the expression of realized eschatology within a rit-

---

12. This deficiency is pointed out by Jonathan Z. Smith, "Too Much Kingdom, Too Little Community," *Zygon* 13 (1978): 129. Smith's own effort to apply a "more complex mode of analysis" to Jewish and early Christian apocalyptic movements can be found in his "A Pearl of Great Price and a Cargo of Yams: A Study in Situational Incongruity," in *Imagining Religion: From Babylon to Jonestown* (Chicago: University of Chicago Press, 1982), 90–101. Smith sets forth his own theory of ritual in *To Take Place: Toward Theory in Ritual* (Chicago: University of Chicago Press, 1987). In addition to Smith's review, see David L. Bartlett, "John Gager's 'Kingdom and Community': A Summary and Response," *Zygon* 13 (1978): 109–22. Also see Wayne Meeks, "Social Functions of Apocalyptic Language in Pauline Christianity," in *Apocalypticism in the Mediterranean World and the Near East* (ed. David Hellholm; Tübingen: Mohr Siebeck, 1983), 688. Bruce J. Malina has critiqued Gager's cognitive dissonance model by contending that cognitive dissonance was the norm rather than the exception ("Normative Dissonance and Christian Origins," *Semeia* 35 [1986]: 35). For evaluations of Gager's hypothesis among interpreters of the Apocalypse of John, see David L. Barr, "The Apocalypse of John as Symbolic Transformation of the World," *Int* 38 (1984): 46–48; Schüssler Fiorenza, *Justice and Judgment*, 167–68.

13. "Cult and Eschatology in the Apocalypse of John," *JR* 49 (1969): 331; idem, "Hymns in Early Christian Worship," *ATR* 55 (1973): 458–72.

14. "The Odes of Solomon and Early Christian Prophecy," *NTS* 28 (1982): 446; idem, *The Cultic Setting of Realized Eschatology in Early Christianity* (NovTSup 28; Leiden: Brill, 1972).

15. Aune, "Odes of Solomon," 446, 453–55.

ual setting, supply further evidence for the connection between prophecy and ritual in early Christianity.

In *The Book of Revelation: Apocalypse and Empire*, Leonard Thompson argues that "the language of worship plays an important role in unifying the book, that is, in making it a coherent apocalypse in both form and content."[16] Taking us beyond Gager's extrinsic identification of ritual as the setting within which the Christian myth of the Apocalypse was pronounced, Thompson shows that the unifying function of the Apocalypse's language of worship on the literary level extends to the community gathered for worship. The language of worship affected the worshiping community by shaping participants into an egalitarian *communitas*.[17]

Joining rhetorical analysis with hermeneutical practice, Elisabeth Schüssler Fiorenza identifies power and justice as the issues which are the heart of the Apocalypse's concerns. In this light, "The heavenly liturgies and celestial hymnody of Revelation serve rhetorically to elaborate God's power and might. They do not have liturgical but political-theological functions."[18] Because John lacked developed and specifically Christian cultic traditions and institutions on which to ground his appeal, he drew upon Jewish cultic symbolism, and adapted material from local practices in Asia Minor, from Roman imperial ceremonial and from elsewhere.[19] Schüssler Fiorenza underlines the urgency of this rhetorical strategy: "Since Roman political power was ratified in cultic terms, the symbolic universe of Revelation must appropriate cultic-religious symbols in order to draw its audience away from the magnificent symbols and cultic drama of the imperial cult."[20]

This political analysis of the rhetorical function that ritual symbolism performs in the Apocalypse, with the conclusion that the purpose of the Apocalypse's heavenly liturgies and hymnody is political rather than liturgical, calls for closer attention to the nature and function of ritual.

Some Definitions

Disagreement about what ritual is and what it does has not kept interpreters from continuing to insist that such features are prominent in the Apocalypse and that

---

16. (New York: Oxford University Press, 1990), 53.

17. Ibid., 71. Thompson relies on the concept of *communitas* developed by Victor Turner. See Turner, *The Ritual Process: Structure and Anti-Structure* (Chicago: Aldine, 1969), esp. 94–130, "Liminality and Communitas," and 131–65, "Communitas: Model and Process."

18. *Revelation: Vision of a Just World* (Proclamation Commentaries; Minneapolis: Fortress, 1991), 117, 122.

19. For evidence of the Apocalypse's borrowing from Roman imperial ceremonial and Hellenistic magic, see Aune, "The Influence of Roman Imperial Court Ceremonial on the Revelation of John," *BR* 28 (1983): 5–26; idem, "The Apocalypse of John and Graeco-Roman Revelatory Magic," *NTS* 33 (1987): 481–501. See also Steven J. Scherrer, "Signs and Wonders in the Imperial Cult," *JBL* 103 (1984): 599–610. Among the studies of the Apocalypse's reappropriation of Jewish cultic festival symbolism, see Ulfgard, *Feast and Future*.

20. *Revelation: Vision of a Just World*, 122.

they need to be reckoned with.²¹ If the search for common ground leaves us eager to scurry to the social sciences in search of clarity, we are more likely to be challenged than satisfied. Social scientific definitions of ritual are numerous, and there is a growing preference for inclusive and flexible description instead of exclusive and restrictive definition.

In his 1968 article on ritual in the *International Encyclopedia of the Social Sciences*, anthropologist Edmund Leach describes the range of definition from the narrow understanding of ritual as "a body of custom specially associated with religious performance" to its broader application "to denote any noninstinctive predictable action or series of actions that cannot be justified by a 'rational' means-to-ends type of explanation."²²

The following definitions are offered by way of illustration, without pretending to represent the entire spectrum. According to Victor Turner, ritual is "prescribed formal behavior for occasions not given over to technological routine, having reference to beliefs in mystical beings or powers."²³ In *Ritual, Politics, and Power*, David I. Kertzer defines ritual as "symbolic behavior that is socially standardized and repetitive."²⁴ This definition takes care to avoid restricting ritual to religious activity alone. Bruce J. Malina describes rites as "time-out activities" which break the flow of normal social interaction. Within such time-out activities, Malina distinguishes between ceremonies and rituals, so that ceremonies are predefined, regular breaks in the action and rituals are irregular breaks that occur only when needed by a person or group.²⁵ For Roy A. Rappaport, ritual refers to forms or structures which he characterizes as "the performance of more or less invariant sequences of formal acts and utterances not encoded by the performer."²⁶

Ronald L. Grimes turns from defining ritual to the identification of its characteristics and qualities, explaining that "Ritual is not a 'what,' not a 'thing.' It is a 'how,' a quality, and there are 'degrees' of it. Any action can be ritualized, though

---

21. Terms like *worship, liturgy, cult,* and *ritual* have been used more or less interchangeably and more or less informally by interpreters of the Apocalypse. Ritual is the expression most frequently used in current social-scientific discourse.

22. "Ritual," in *International Encyclopedia of the Social Sciences* (ed. David L. Sells; New York: Free Press, 1968), 13:520–21. Also see Jack Goody, "Religion and Ritual: The Definitional Problem," *British Journal of Sociology* 12 (1961): 142–64, and his later article, "Against 'Ritual': Loosely Structured Thoughts on a Loosely Defined Topic," in *Secular Ritual* (ed. Sally Falk Moore and Barbara Myerhoff; Amsterdam: Van Gorcum, 1977), 25–35.

23. *The Forest of Symbols: Aspects of Ndembu Ritual* (Ithaca, N.Y.: Cornell University Press, 1967), 19. See Ronald L. Grimes, "Victor Turner's Definition, Theory, and Sense of Ritual," in *Victor Turner and the Construction of Cultural Criticism: Between Literature and Anthropology* (ed. Kathleen M. Ashley; Bloomington: Indiana University Press, 1990), 141–46. For another recent overview of Turner's ritual theory, see Mathieu Deflem, "Ritual, Anti-structure, and Religion: A Discussion of Victor Turner's Processual Symbolic Analysis," *JSSR* 30 (1991): 1–25.

24. (New Haven: Yale University Press, 1988), 9.

25. *Christian Origins and Cultural Anthropology: Practical Models for Biblical Interpretation* (Atlanta: Knox, 1986), 139–43.

26. "Concluding Comments on Ritual and Reflexivity," *Semiotica* 30 (1980): 187.

not every action is a rite."²⁷ These qualifications draw attention away from particular rites and toward the process of ritualization. In an approach that focuses on practice, Catherine Bell prefers to speak of ritualization as "a way of acting that is designed and orchestrated to distinguish and privilege what is being done in comparison to other, usually more quotidian activities." In this light, "it becomes clear that formality, fixity and repetition are not intrinsic qualities of ritual so much as they are a frequent, but not universal strategy for producing ritualized act."²⁸

Drama

As a heading under which both interpreters of the Apocalypse and ritual theorists have sought occasional shelter, drama has been as versatile as it has been troublesome. With regard to the Apocalypse, the notion of drama has been invoked in efforts to impose (somewhat arbitrarily) a dramatic structure on the book, and in comparisons between the hymns in the Apocalypse and the chorus in classical Greek theater.²⁹ Adela Yarbro Collins traces an analogy between the cathartic effect of Greek tragedy and the ways of Apocalypse affects its audience.³⁰ Speaking more broadly, several interpreters draw attention to the links between drama and ritual so as to consider the Apocalypse cultic drama.³¹

---

27. *Ritual Criticism*, 13. Grimes himself charts an extensive (but not comprehensive) list of the qualities of ritual, a pool of characteristics.

28. *Ritual Theory, Ritual Practice*, 74, 92.

29. For example, John Wick Bowman, "The Revelation to John: Its Dramatic Structure and Its Message," *Int* 9 (1955): 436–53; idem, *The First Christian Drama: The Book of Revelation* (Philadelphia: Westminster, 1968). Harris's review of such efforts concludes by denying that the Apocalypse depended on Greek drama and by denying that the hymns of the Apocalypse were directly influenced by the chorus (*Literary Function of Hymns*, 8, 10–11). A more sympathetic evaluation of these hypotheses is offered by Elisabeth Schüssler Fiorenza (*Justice and Judgment*, 166–67).

30. *Crisis and Catharsis: The Power of the Apocalypse* (Philadelphia: Westminster, 1984), 152–53. See Barr, "Apocalypse as a Symbolic Transformation," 49–50; Richard L. Jeske and David L. Barr, "The Study of the Apocalypse Today," *RelSRev* 14 (1988): 341–42.

31. For example, Rudolf Halver seeks to identify the "elements of cultic drama" in the Apocalypse (*Der Mythos im letzten Buch der Bibel: Eine Untersuchung der Bildersprache de Johannes-Apokalypse* [TF 32; Hamburg: Herbert Reich, 1964], 118–26). In terms of the Apocalypse's "dramatic form," Halver argues that myth and cult are inseparable (ibid., 118–19). Schüssler Fiorenza writes, "The liturgical interpretation is often linked with the understanding of Rev[elation] as a drama, since in Greek tragedy the roots of drama and cult are closely interconnected" (*Justice and Judgment*, 166). She has also written about the "cultic drama" of the imperial cult as a force with which the Apocalypse reckons by resorting to the use of borrowed ritual symbolism (*Revelation: Vision of a Just World*, 122). A genetic connection between ritual and drama in Greek antiquity was suggested by classicists of the Cambridge school, beginning with James B. Frazer's *The Golden Bough* (3d ed.; London: Macmillan, 1935) in the first decades of the twentieth century. Among them were Jane Ellen Harrison, *Ancient Art and Ritual* (Oxford: Oxford University Press, 1951; repr., New York: Greenwood Press, 1969); Gilbert Murray, "Excursus on the Ritual Forms Preserved in Greek Tragedy," in *Themis: A Study of the Social Origins of Greek Religion* (Cleveland and New York: Meridian Books, 1962), 341–63; Francis Macdonald Cornford, *The Origins of Attic Comedy* (Cambridge: Cambridge University Press, 1934; repr., Garden City,

In social-scientific discourse, Turner's concept of social drama brought ritual and drama together in functionalists terms as a metaphor for social process. Turner uses the concept to explain patterns of conflict and its resolution in Ndembu village life, identifying a fourfold social dramatic process involving (1) breach, (2) crisis, (3) redressive action, (4) reintegration or schism.[32] Ritual is one of the several ways in which crises that threaten the social structure can be resolved. Besides ritual, the range of redressive strategies includes everything from informal negotiation and arbitration to formal juridical processes.[33]

Turner's analysis of ritual modes of redressive action according to the terminology of van Gennep's *Rites of Passage* sharpened the focus on ritual while tracing a connection between ritual and drama. The recognition that both represent modes of performance led to the extension of ritual theory into a more comprehensive performance theory.[34]

Despite the features that ritual and drama may have in common (formality, fixity and repetition, to name a few), there are evident pitfalls in aligning them too closely. Among these is the risk of reducing diverse social phenomena to a least common denominator. Treating a riot, a burial, a Latin American *quinceañera*, a Sinhalese demon exorcism, a Broadway musical and a Catholic mass as though all were the same would provide us with relatively little information about any of them. Another danger involves the temptation to treat ritual or dramatic doing simply as modes of telling, as discrete containers of cultural meaning available to the interested observer. A third weakness of the dramatic analogy has to do with its location of the observer

---

N.Y.: Doubleday, 1961). Also see Theodor H. Gaster, *Thespis: Ritual, Myth, and Drama in the Ancient Near East* (New York: Anchor, 1961; repr., New York: Norton, 1970).

The conclusions of this movement have largely fallen into disrepute. See the critique by Joseph Fontenrose, *The Ritual Theory of Myth* (Folklore Studies 18; Berkeley: University of California Press, 1966). Also see Richard F. Hardin, "'Ritual' in Recent Criticism: The Elusive Sense of Community," *Proceedings of the Modern Language Association* 98 (1983): 846–62. Most recently, see William M. Calder, ed., *The Cambridge Ritualists Reconsidered* (Illinois Classical Supplements 2; Atlanta: Scholars Press, 1992). I am grateful to Oliver Phillips of the Classics Department at the University of Kansas for bringing several of these references to my attention. Connections certainly exist between the Cambridge ritualists and the "Myth and Ritual School," which drew its title from the collection of essays edited by S. H. Hooke, *Myth and Ritual* (London: Oxford University Press, 1933). The movement was shepherded along through two subsequent volumes under Hooke's editorship, *The Labyrinth* (London: SPCK, 1935) and *Myth, Ritual, and Kingship* (Oxford: Clarendon Press, 1958).

32. *Schism and Continuity in an African Society: A Study of Ndembu Village Life* (Manchester: Manchester University Press, 1957) 91–130.

33. See the analysis of Turner's theory of social drama in Grimes, *Ritual Criticism*, 174–90: "Drama and Ritual Criticism."

34. See Geertz, "Blurred Genres," 171–75; Turner, *From Ritual to Theatre: The Human Seriousness of Play* (New York: Performing Arts Journal Publications, 1982); idem, "Are There Universals of Performance in Myth, Ritual, and Drama?" in *By Means of Performance: Intercultural Studies of Theatre and Ritual* (ed. Richard Schechner and Willa Appel; Cambridge: Cambridge University Press, 1990), 8–18; Richard Schechner, "Magnitudes of Performance," in Schechner and Appel, *By Means of Performance*, 19–49.

as a passive audience member, whereas ritual emphasizes involvement and participation on some level.[35]

INTERSECTION

Turner writes that both ritual and literature "provide 'metalanguages' for discussing sociality, special ways of talking about general ways of talking and acting.... Ritual and literature, in a way, are society talking about itself, the reflexivity of society."[36] It may be that the intersection between literary and social scientific approaches to the Apocalypse can profit from the blurring of genres taking place in the design of social scientific models. According to Clifford Geertz, "[A]nalogies from the humanities are coming to play the kind of role in sociological understanding that analogies from the crafts and technology have long played in physical understanding." To demonstrate this, Geertz illustrates the deployment by social scientists of three metaphors—game, drama, and text—drawn from the humanist domains.[37]

Commenting on Geertz's observations, Catherine Bell discerns a propensity among social scientists to treat the objects of their research, including rituals, as through they were texts. Her critique of this trend goes on to say that "We textualize . . . not because rites are intrinsically like texts, but because we approach both looking for meaning as something that can be deciphered, decoded, or interpreted."[38] This general trajectory finds a particular reflection in ritual theory, where Bell detects a dichotomy between thought and action underlying much theoretical discourse about ritual. Initially deployed as a heuristic distinction in order to isolate ritual-as-

---

35. See Bell, *Ritual Theory, Ritual Practice*, 37–46. Also Grimes, *Ritual Criticism*, 174–90: "Drama and Ritual Criticism."

36. "African Ritual and Western Literature: Is a Comparative Symbology Possible?" in *The Literature of Fact* (ed. Angus Fletcher; New York: Columbia University Press, 1976), 51. The intersection appears in Turner's own intellectual itinerary, beginning with the concept of "social drama," coined in his *Schism and Continuity in an African Society*, extending to his focused reconfiguration of elements from van Gennep's "rites of passage" in *The Forest of Symbols*, to the homecoming of the dramatic metaphor in *From Ritual to Theatre*, and even to ritual theoretical analysis of the Japanese Noh theater and the *Tale of Genji* ("Liminality and the Performative Genres," in *Rite, Drama, Festival, Spectacle*, 19–41). The social-drama metaphor has proven to be far more serviceable than Turner envisioned it as its beginnings within the framework of functionalist British social anthropology. Through it ritual theory has generated an actively interdisciplinary performance theory. Examples of such energetically interdisciplinary efforts can be found in Ashley, *Victor Turner and the Construction of Cultural Criticism*. Also see Lawrence E. Sullivan, "Sound and Sense: Toward a Hermeneutics of Performance," *HR* 26 (1986): 1–33. In a review of Turner's *Dramas, Fields, and Metaphors* (Ithaca N.Y.: Cornell University Press, 1974), Raymond Firth gave voice to the uneasiness British social anthropologists felt in the 1970s regarding Turner's forays across the social scientific border into the humanities. Firth suggested that "the aesthetic components . . . should be watched rather than wooed," a caution prefaced by a disclaimer: "I am not maintaining that anthropology, a science, involves no art" ("Society and Its Symbols," *Times Literary Supplement* [London], 13 September 1974, 2).

37. "Blurred Genres: The Refiguration of Social Thought," *American Scholar* 49 (1980): 165.

38. *Ritual Theory, Ritual Practice*, 165.

activity for the sake of theoretical clarification, the dichotomy between thinking and doing develops its own momentum on a second level, so that ritual then comes to be viewed as means by which the reintegration of thought and action takes place. On a third level, "the activities of the object," that is, those engaged in ritual activity, "and the concepts of the subject (the theorist) are also integrated by means of a discursive focus on the integrative function of ritual."[39]

Bell does not share the enthusiasm of those who suggest that the study of ritual (and its extension into the study of performance) provides common ground for the social sciences and the humanities. Instead, she warns,

> The construction of ritual as a decipherable text allows the theorist to interpret simply by deconstructing ritual back into its prefused components. The theoretical construction of ritual becomes a reflection of the theorist's method and the motor of a discourse in which the concerns of theorist [sic] take center stage.[40]

It is useful to outline three distinct directions in the consideration of texts and ritual by social scientists and humanists, directions which differ mainly in the ways in which they identify the object of their attention.[41]

1. Textualizing ritual: dealing with rituals as if they were texts.[42] In this approach, ritual is the main object of attention, and textualization is the heuristic strategy by which the observer seeks to discern the meaning of the rite.

2. Applying ritual theory to texts that do not reflect the textual codification of ritual procedures.[43] Here the text is the main object of the interpreter's attention. An example of this sort of metaphoric extension of ritual theory is Mieke Bal's study of the two accounts of the murder of Sisera by Jael (Judg 4–5). Bal exploits Turner's concept of ritual "solely in its problem-solving capacities for the specific purpose of interpretation, and secondarily for the explanation of problems of interpretation."[44]

3. Applying ritual theory to texts that do encode ritual. Here, depending on the interests of the interpreter, the object of attention can be the text itself or the ritual encoded in the text. Bal writes that "A second level or ritualistic interpretation is at

---

39. Ibid., 47–48.
40. Ibid., 54.
41. See Grimes, *Ritual Criticism*, 158–73: "Narrative and Ritual Criticism."
42. For example, see Turner, "African Ritual and Western Literature," 51.
43. Bell, *Ritual Theory, Ritual Practice*, 8.
44. "Experiencing Murder: Ritualistic Interpretation of Ancient Texts," in *Victor Turner and the Construction of Cultural Criticism*, 3. Though Bal chides Richard F. Hardin for arguing that the concept of ritual is becoming blunt from overgeneralization by overuse (Harden, "'Ritual' in Recent Criticism: The Elusive Sense of Community," 846–61), her argument for the versatility of the concept of ritual for the study of ancient texts includes the proviso that one must carefully distinguish among the levels of meaning (semantic, structural, pragmatic) on which the concept is operating (Bal, "Experiencing Murder," 19).

stake when one claims that a given text is *about* ritual, that there is ritual in a text."⁴⁵ We are operating on this level of ritualistic interpretation in approaching the Apocalypse, since Revelation implies and presupposes a ritual setting for its reception.

The evidence of Rev 1:3 and 1:10 makes it clear almost beyond dispute that John's Apocalypse was destined for oral recitation in a ritual setting, specifically, in the setting of late first century Christian worship in the Roman province of Asia.⁴⁶ This calls for attention to the relationship between text and ritual and then to the way that relationship unfolds in the Apocalypse, preceded by two necessary qualifications. First, a ritual theoretical approach to the Apocalypse must avoid reducing ritual to text. By doing so, following Bell, we might be accused of burying treasure in a field so as to feign surprise when we discover it there later, that is, creating just the sort of evidence which our method might dispose us to encounter. Second, it should not be assumed that the text of the Apocalypse ever served as a script that provided a step by step liturgical order of service for ritual action.

While it can never be claimed that there is a strict and unmediated relationship between the text of the Apocalypse and the socio-historical context of its enunciation, the intratextual evidence itself is quite significant.⁴⁷ This is because, from a reader response perspective, "the narratees are inscribed in the text as saints and servants within a worship context in the churches."⁴⁸

Of the relationship between ritual and text, Bell writes:

> The codification of ritual procedures in textual form involves strategies of ritualization different from those effective in primarily oral societies. Indeed, the very act of putting ritual practices into such a format constitutes a tactical recasting of the source and type of authority involved in ritualization. In general, such textual codification involves a shift from the authority of memory, seniority and practical expertise . . . to the authority of those who control access to and interpretation of the texts.⁴⁹

Strictly speaking, the Apocalypse does not represent a codification of ritual

---

45. Ibid., 18.
46. See Barr, "Apocalypse of John as Oral Enactment," 243–56.
47. Meir Sternberg proclaims, "The text's autonomy is a long-exploded myth: the text has no meaning, or may assume every kind of meaning, outside those coordinates of discourse that we usually bundle into the term 'context'" (*The Poetics of Biblical Narrative: Ideological Literature and the Drama of Reading* [Bloomington: Indiana University Press, 1987], 11). Furthermore, "The relationship between a literary work and a social and historical reality," Jonathan Culler says, "is not one of reflected content but of a play of forms. . . . [T]he interplay between a literary work and its historical ground lies in the way its formal devices exploit, transform and supplement a culture's way of producing meaning" (*The Pursuit of Signs: Semiotics, Literature, and Deconstruction* [Ithaca, N.Y.: Cornell University Press, 1981], 12–13).
48. Harris, *Literary Function of Hymns*, 303. Ugo Vanni underlines the importance of the ritual context in a different way ("L'assemblea ecclesiale 'soggetto interpretante' dell'Apocalisse," in *L'Apocalisse: Ermeneutica Esegesi, Teologia* [RivBSup 17; Bologna: Edizioni dehoniane, 1988], 73–86). See the critique of Vanni's position by Harris (*Literary Function of Hymns*, 228–29).
49. *Ritual Theory, Ritual Practice*, 10.

procedures in textual form, so that we should not seek to reduce this text to some underlying ritual.[50] However, the ritual setting which this text presupposes as the context for its oral recitation, which sets the Apocalypse betwixt and between orality and textuality, suggests that the dynamics of authority are bound up with the ritualizing strategy of the writing of the Apocalypse. Several key features help to illustrate how this works in the Apocalypse.

First, by its appropriation of epistolary conventions, the Apocalypse is configured as a prophetic letter.[51] Bell tells us that writing fixes things in time, and the textual codification involved in the writing of ritual is a matter of fixing the past in writing.[52] On the other hand, letter writing is less a matter of fixing things in time than of fixing persons in space, of locating sender(s) and recipient(s) at a distance from each other. Using epistolary conventions which both establish and mediate that distance and which bring sender(s) and addressee(s) into contact, the Apocalypse establishes the authority of sender(s) over its addressee(s).[53]

Second, as revelatory literature which narrates visionary experience, the Apocalypse establishes John's authority as the privileged recipient of visionary experience. This is reinforced by the setting of the inaugural vision (Rev 1:9–20) in the ritual time of the Lord's Day (1:10) and at a significant physical distance from the addressees.[54] Wherever else the setting on Patmos may imply, John's presence there "because of the word of God and the testimony of Jesus" suggests that this location is not neutral, for this "word" and this "testimony" are what John's text is all about.

In this particular time and in this particular space, John receives the command to write what he sees and to send the resulting document to the seven churches. The repetition of the command to write at the beginning of each of the seven messages in 2:1–3:22, together with the other commands to write (14:13; 19:9; 21:5) establishes John's authority as a matter not of ritual expertise or mastery over a collection of ritual texts, but of control over the production of a text. In two instances (19:9; 21:5) the command to write is combined with guarantees of the truth and trustworthiness of that which is to be written.

Revelation 10 provides two further expressions of the sort of control exercised in and by this text. In 10:4, John is commanded "Seal up what the seven thunders have

---

50. This position can be maintained in spite of the many studies which have sought to trace the influence of particular rituals, Jewish, early Christian and otherwise, on portions of the Apocalypse.

51. See Martin Karrer, *Die Johannesoffenbarung als Brief: Studien zu ihrem literarischen, historischen und theologischen Ort* (FRLANT 140; Göttingen: Vandenhoeck & Ruprecht, 1986).

52. Ibid., 136. David Hellholm speaks of the Apocalypse's encoding the *future* in writing ("The Visions He Saw Or: To Encode the Future in Writing. An Analysis of the Prologue of John's Apocalyptic Letter," in *Text and Logos: The Humanistic Interpretation of the New Testament* [ed. Theodore W. Jennings Jr.; Atlanta: Scholars Press, 1990], 109–46).

53. "A textually constituted tradition must continually and simultaneously create both the gap *and* the authority structures that can bridge it" (Bell, *Ritual Theory, Ritual Practice*, 137).

54. On "the Lord's Day" in the Apocalypse, see Ugo Vanni, "L'Assemblea liturgica si purifica e discerne nel'giorno del Signore' (Ap 1,10)," in *L'Apocalisse Ermeneutica, Esegesi, Teologia*, 87–97, with the bibliography indicated there.

said, and do not write it down." In 10:8–11, the complete identification of prophet and text is symbolized by the swallowing of the scroll, followed by the command to prophesy (10:11).[55] Text and narrator become inseparable in the symbolic act of ingestion.

A third feature illustrating the dynamics of authority is the blessing pronounced on the lector and readers at the beginning of the Apocalypse (1:3) together with the warning against altering "the words of the prophecy of this book" in 22:18–19 reinforce the authority which this text claims over its audience. The blessing in 1:3 establishes the context of ritual recitation which the book presumes, while the warning in 22:18–19 underlines the fixity that frequently characterizes the process of ritualization.

Betwixt and Between

The concepts of liminality and reflexivity are crucial to Turner's understanding of what ritual does and how its ends are achieved within the social drama. The concept of liminality furnishes us with a ritual theoretical perspective on questions which have more often been treated under the theological heading of realized eschatology, and which Gager addressed in terms of the suppression of time.

Liminality is drawn from Arnold van Gennep's division of rites of passage into three consecutive phases: "separation from antecedent mundane life;" "liminality, a betwixt-and-between condition often involving seclusion from the everyday science;" and "reaggregation to the daily world."[56] Turner contends that the liminal phase of ritual is pivotal:

> It is often the scene and time for the emergence of a society's deepest values in the form of sacred dramas and objects—sometimes the reenactment periodically of cosmogonic narratives or deeds of saintly, godly, or heroic establishers of morality, basic institutions, or ways of approaching transcendent beings or powers. But it may also be the venue and occasion for the most radical skepticism . . . about cherished values and rules. Ambiguity reigns: people and public policies may be judged skeptically in relation to deep values; the vices, follies and stupidities, and abuses of contemporary holders of high political, economic or religious status may be satirized, ridiculed or contemned in terms of axiomatic values, or these personages may be rebuked for gross failures in common sense.[57]

As a betwixt-and-between condition which enables ritual participants to stand

---

55. See Ellen F. Davis, *Swallowing the Scroll: Textuality and the Dynamics of Discourse in Ezekiel's Prophecy* (JSOTSup 78; Sheffield: Almond, 1989).
56. "Liminality and the Performative Genres," in *Rite, Drama, Festival, Spectacle*, 21. See Arnold van Gennep, *The Rites of Passage* (Chicago: University of Chicago Press, 1960), 10–11. In "Le symbolisme ritualiste de l'Apocalypse," *Revue de l'histoire des religions* 89 (1924): 163–82, van Gennep himself suggested that the book of Revelation was an initiation manual for the Jewish Christian sect in Asia Minor led by an otherwise unknown figure named John.
57. "Liminality and the Performative Genres," 22.

apart from the everyday scene, liminality furnishes a hospitable climate for reflexivity, which can be understood as "that capacity of human beings to distance themselves from their own subjective experiences, to stand apart from them and to comment on them."[58] According to George Herbert Mead, who was responsible for bringing reflexivity into social scientific discourse, "it is by means of reflexiveness . . . that the whole social process is thus brought into the experience of the individuals involved in it."[59]

The open-ended quality of such descriptions would appear to confirm the view that reflexivity is "a concept with blurred edges," and Barbara Babcock's observation that it "appears in many different costumes on many different stages."[60]

Ritual is the particular stage and costume which concerns us here, the occasion which provides a suitable climate for reflexive engagement by participants. Citing Mihaly Csikszentmihalyi's description of "flow" as a "state where action and awareness merge," Barbara Myerhoff points to a paradox whereby rituals often

> induce reflexive awareness just as they invite the fullest participation and concentration that brings about flow. Rituals' perpetual play . . . with borders and transitions, make self-reflection nearly inevitable, telling the individual what s/he is and is not at once.[61]

Defining ritual as "the performance of more or less invariant sequences of formal acts and utterances not encoded by the performer," Rappaport explains that the formal acts and utterances of ritual are intrinsically reflexive. Reflexivity in ritual is a function of its quality as performance involving participation: "To participate is, by definition, *to become part of* something larger than the self. When one performs a ritual, one not only constructs oneself but also participates in the construction of a larger pubic order."[62]

A Road Less Traveled: The Messages to the Seven Churches

Given the amount of attention which the hymnic scenes of heavenly worship have attracted the messages to the seven churches in Rev 2:1–3:22 might seem an

---

58. John J. MacAloon, "Introduction: Cultural Performances, Cultural Theory," in *Rite, Drama, Festival, Spectacle*, 11. Also see Jay Ruby, ed., *A Crack in the Mirror: Reflexive Perspectives in Anthropology* (Philadelphia: University of Pennsylvania Press, 1982).

59. *Mind, Self, and Society from the Standpoint of a Social Behaviorist* (Chicago: University of Chicago Press, 1962), 134.

60. "Reflexivity: Definitions and Discriminations," *Semiotica* 30 (1980): 2, 5. She includes the following possibilities and combinations among the modalities of reflexivity: private / public; singular and individual / plural and collective; internal / external; implicit / explicit; partial / total.

61. Mihaly Csikszentmihalyi, *Beyond Boredom and Anxiety* (San Francisco: Jossey-Bass, 1975), as cited in Barbara Myerhoff, "The Transformation of Consciousness in Ritual Performances: Some Thoughts and Questions," in *By Means of Performance*, 247. On Csikszentmihalyi's concept of flow as applied to the performative genres, see Turner, "Liminality and the Performative Genres," 27.

62. Rappaport, "Concluding Comments on Ritual and Reflexivity," 187.

unlikely focus for ritual theoretical attention. The messages to the seven churches contain none of the hymnic material on which many other studies of ritual in the Apocalypse have concentrated. Yet, if we continue to operate under the working hypothesis that the Apocalypse served as a script for oral proclamation, there are good reasons for choosing this promising path.

The very distinctiveness of Rev 2:1–3:22 proves troublesome to many commentators, J. P. M. Sweet writes, "These chapters differ so obviously in manner and matter from the rest that many have thought that they were written at a different time."[63] Aune notes "widespread agreement that the seven proclamations never existed independently of Rev, but were designed specifically for their present literary setting by the author-editor at a final stage in the composition of the entire work."[64] The messages never existed as separate documents: they are intratextual intertexts designed to be read and heard together with the rest of the Apocalypse.

Aune has argued convincingly that 2:1–3:22 represents a mixed genre unique in apocalyptic literature and original to the Apocalypse: "The literary *genre* or *kind* to which the seven proclamations belong is that of the *royal* or *imperial edict*, while the *mode* is that of the prophetic form of speech called the *parenetic salvation-judgment oracle.*"[65]

Given the peculiarity of this unit, the question of how 2:1–3:22 fits into the rest of the book, as a question of borders and transitions, warrants a particular look from literary and ritual theoretical standpoints. The links between 2:1–3:22 and the inaugural vision which precedes it are unmistakable, so that the continuity of 1:9–3:22 is commonly recognized.[66] Two examples suffice to illustrate this. The particular command to write to the angel of each church is repeated at the beginning of each message, and the messages are presented in the order specified in 1:11. The chistological predicate which introduces the sender of each message (2:1, 8, 12, 18; 3:1, 7, 14) links each of them with the figure in the inaugural vision (1:9–20), from whom John receives the command to write (1:11). In this way, the messages are bound up with the execution of John's inaugural commission.

The connection of 2:1–3:22 with what follows as of 4:1 is more troublesome than its connection with what precedes this unit, as the following comment of G. B. Caird suggests. Arriving at Rev 4:1, he declares, "We now come to the apocalypse proper," explaining:

---

63. *Revelation* (Westminster Pelican Commentaries; Philadelphia: Westminster, 1979), 77.

64. "The Form and Function of the Proclamations to the Seven Churches (Revelation 2–3)" *NTS* 36 (1990): 183. Also see Pierre Prigent, *L'Apocalypse de Saint Jean* (Commentaire du Nouveau Testament 2/14; Lausanne: Delachaux & Niestlé, 1981), 36–39.

65. "Form and Function of the Proclamations," 183. Also see Aune, *Prophecy in Early Christianity and the Ancient Mediterranean World* (Grand Rapids: Eerdmans, 1983), 326.

66. Even so, Aune observes, "By the time the reader has finished the vision of the commission narrated in 1:9–20, there is no reason to expect that the exalted Christ will dictate seven individual messages to each of the seven congregations" ("Intertexutality and the Genre of the Apocalypse," *SBL Seminar Papers, 1991* (SBLSP 30), 148; see chapter 2 of this volume..

Structurally the first three chapters are a covering letter to accompany and introduce the account of John's apocalyptic visions, which begins here in chapter iv. But John intended his readers to come to the visions with their minds prepared by what they have read in the letters.[67]

The concept of reflexivity sheds light on the relationship between the messages to the seven churches and the chapters which follow. Bruce Kapferer points out two particular ways in which ritual facilitates reflexivity. On one level, ritual can make it possible for individuals and groups "to objectify their action and experience in the context of the rite, and to stand back or distance themselves from their action within the rite so they can reflect upon their own and others' actions and understandings." On a second level, "rites promote reflexivity to the degree that they reflect back on other contexts of meaning in the performance setting or in the social and cultural world out of which ritual emerges."[68]

Following upon what has been said about the relationship between text and ritual, Kapferer's description of these two ways in which ritual facilitates reflexivity suggests a new avenue of approach to the relationship between the messages to the seven churches in Rev 2:1–3:22 and the rest of the book, and to the function of the messages. On the first level of reflexivity, the messages can be understood as devices that enable the seven churches to engage their experience reflexively, to hear "what the Spirit says" in ritual time on "the Lord's day" and in the ritual space of their gathering for worship. What follows in 4:1 can then be understood as the transition to a second level of reflexivity. This understanding of two levels of ritual reflexivity effectively accounts for the literary distinction between 2:1–3:22 and what follows it.[69]

Commentators invariably note the close parallelism which exists among the seven messages, mentioning the stereotypical expressions arranged in similar order in each of them.[70] Yet they ignore the connection between the features and the ritual setting of the Apocalypse.[71] The pattern of the seven messages gives clear evidence of the

---

67. *A Commentary on the Revelation of St. John the Divine* (Harper's New Testament Commentaries; New York: Harper & Row, 1966), 60.

68. "The Ritual Process and the Problem of Reflexivity in Sinhalese Demon Exorcisms," in *Rite, Drama, Festival, Spectacle*, 180–81.

69. See Vanni, "L'assemblea ecclesiale 'soggetto interpretante' dell'Apocalisse," 77–79. Vanni recognizes both the ritual context and the connection between the level of (reflexive) engagement which the messages to the seven churches elicit from the interpreting subjects and the engagement called for beginning with 4:1. Jeffrey Vogelgesang seeks to minimize the distinction between Rev 4 and what precedes it, discussing "the great disjunction which is not" ("The Interpretation of Ezekiel in the Apocalypse" [Ph.D. diss., Harvard University, 1985], 263–65).

70. See Ferdinand Hahn, "Die Sendschreiben der Johannesapokalypse: Ein Beitrag zur Bestimmung prophetischer Redeform," in *Tradition und Glaube: Das frühe Christentum in seiner Umwelt* (ed. Gert Jeremias, Heinz-Wolfgang Kuhn, and Hartmut Stegemann; Göttingen: Vandenhoeck & Ruprecht, 1971), 357–94; Aune, *Prophecy in Early Christianity*, 275–79; idem, "Form and Function of the Proclamations," 184.

71. Barr deals with these features in "Apocalypse of John as Oral Enactment," 244–47.

formality, fixity and repetition that were described above as strategies characteristic of the process of ritualization.

Aune takes note of the numerous unusual grammatical and stylistic features concentrated in Rev 2:1–3:22.[72] To some extent, several of these features represent a ritual formalizing strategy. Clearest among these is the *tade legei* formula, an intentional archaism which can aptly be rendered in English as "thus saith." According to Aune, ancient readers might have recognized the phrase as the LXX rendering of the OT prophetic messenger formula and/or as the sort of proclamation formula that was often found in royal and imperial edicts.[73] The formal quality of this expression is compounded by its repetition in all seven messages.

It is the *narrations* (2:2–4, 6; 2:9; 2:13–15; 2:19–20; 3:1b, 4; 3:8; 3:15), introduced by the stereotyped "I know" clause, and in the *dispositiones* (2:5–6; 2:10; 2:16; 2:22–25; 3:2–4; 3:9–11; 3:16–20) that the messages become specific in order to offer a divine assessment of each church's situation (the *narratio*) and an appropriate course of remedial action (the *dispositio*).[74]

The prophetic salvation-judgment oracular mode of the central sections of the messages confers on them the traditional authority of their biblical background, combined with an authority based on control over the production of these texts-within-the-text, texts which John sets in writing in obedience to a divine command.[75] As oracular diagnoses, these proclamations prompt reflexivity. In the betwixt-and-between of ritual time, they challenge the *churches* to consider those features of their situations which are singled out for attention, with some behaviors singled out for reinforcement and others for reform.[76]

The messages to the seven churches are specific but not private: the message addressed to each church is available to all of the others. As a sort of sanctioned eavesdropping, a device which promotes reflexive engagement with the text, such reading of other people's mail establishes the kind of distance from each church's particular situation that makes reflexive objectification possible. The proclamation formula serves as an invitation to reflexivity and the use of the plural, "let the one who has ears listen to what the Spirit is saying to the churches," urges listeners to eavesdrop on all seven messages.[77] This exhortation effectively extends to readers and hearers beyond the circle of the seven churches.

---

72. "Form and Functions of the Proclamations," 184.
73. Ibid., 187.
74. Ibid., 190–93.
75. See Aune, *Prophecy in Early Christianity*, 274–79; idem, "The Form and Function of the Proclamations," 182–204.
76. See John T. Kirby, "The Rhetorical Situations of Revelation 1–3," *NTS* 34 (1988): 197–207. Aune writes, "Just as the announcement of salvation was a prophetic speech form in ancient Israel that was apparently more characteristic of the cult and court prophets than of the free prophets, so the salvation-judgment oracles of Rev. 2–3, which have a cultic setting in early Christianity also have a basic salvific orientation" (*Prophecy in Early Christianity*, 277).
77. On the proclamation formula as "hermeneutical imperative," see Jean-Pierre Ruiz, *Ezekiel in the Apocalypse: The Transformation of Prophetic Language in Revelation 16, 17–19, 10* (European

The concepts of liminality and reflexivity help to make sense of a particularly difficult and disturbing feature of the Apocalypse. Specifically, the Apocalypse takes full advantage of the opportunities which ritual liminality provides for identifying and dealing with opponents by direct insults, name calling and derogatory allusions. Adela Yarbro Collins has already addressed this from the standpoint of conflict theory, suggesting that vilification in the Apocalypse is a strategy for group formation and maintenance. Outsiders are labeled in a derogatory manner so as to define the boundaries within which insiders stand.[78] Another approach, based on the sociology of deviance, suggests that "Negative labeling serves as a social distancing device, underscoring differences and thus dividing social categories into polarities such as the good and the wicked," and that it "serves to underscore societal values by setting apart those who lack or flaunt them."[79]

In the Apocalypse, this boundary setting by name calling is a ritual activity. That is, the betwixt and between condition of the assembly for worship on the Lord's Day makes it possible to identify those who are to be considered opponents by the churches, and makes it possible for the addressees to keep their distance from these enemies.[80]

Name calling in the Apocalypse is articulated along lines that correspond to the two levels on which ritual facilitates reflexivity. Name calling on the first level of reflexivity occupies 2:1–3:22, while name calling on the second level takes place from Rev 4:1 on.[81]

On the first level of reflexivity, which involves attending to proximate experience, the messages to the seven churches focus mainly (though not exclusively) on the author's Jewish and Christian opponents. Jewish opponents are vilified in 2:9,

---

University Studies, ser. 23; Theology 376; Frankfurt: Lang, 1989), 196–99. Schüssler Fiorenza notes that "Revelation's roots in the early Christian eschatological tradition come especially to the fore" in the *Weckruf* (*Revelation*, 47).

78. "Vilification and Self-Definition in the Book of Revelation," *HTR* 79 (1986): 308–20. Also see Yarbro Collins, "Insiders and Outsiders in the Book of Revelation," in *"To See Ourselves as Others See Us": Christians, Jews, "Others" in Late Antiquity* (ed. Jacob Neusner and Ernest S. Frerichs; Chico, Calif.: Scholars Press, 1985), 187–218; and idem, "Women's History and the Book of Revelation," *SBL Seminar Papers, 1987* (SBLSP 26; Atlanta: Scholars Press, 1987), 80–91; as well as Schüssler Fiorenza, *Revelation*, 132–36. On the rhetoric of vituperation in Greco-Roman antiquity, see Séan Freyne, "Vilifying the Other and Defining the Self: Matthew's and John's Anti-Jewish Polemic in Focus," in Neusner and Frerichs, *"To See Ourselves as Others See Us,"* 118–19.

79. Bruce J. Malina and Jerome H. Neyrey, *Calling Jesus Names: The Social Value of Labels in Matthew* (Sonoma, Calif.: Polebridge, 1988), 37–38, and 35–42 on labeling theory.

80. The expression of unity or its establishment through the language of worship (Thompson, *Apocalypse and Empire*, 53–73, esp. 69–71) is therefore a matter of boundary-setting that enforces the borders around insiders by labeling outsiders negatively.

81. This is not only a matter of negative labeling, but also of the positive affirmation that is its opposite. On such "status elevation rituals," see Malina and Neyrey, *Calling Jesus Names*, 103–5. The doxologies of the Apocalypse can be said to function in this way as acclamations of God and of Christ. From the standpoint of ritual reflexivity, vilification and doxology are two sides of the same coin, identifying villains and heroes.

"I know the slander on the part of those who say they are Jews but are not, but are a synagogue of Satan," and in similar terms in 3:9.[82] Christian opponents are labeled in 2:2 as "those who claim to be apostles but are not" and in 2:6 and 2:15 as Nicolaitans.[83] In 2:14 and 2:21, different Christian opponents are accused of "teaching and beguiling my servants to practice fornication and to eat food sacrificed to idols,"[84] and they are labeled as "Balaam" and as "that woman Jezebel, who calls herself a prophet."[85] In 2:24, the church at Thyatira is warned against learning "the deep things of Satan." Revelation 2:13 describes Pergamum as "where Satan's throne is" and "where Satan dwells."[86]

Moving from a level of reflexivity that identifies local opponents in the particular churches to a second level of reflexivity that encompasses a broader horizon, the Apocalypse depicts political opponents on a global scale as grotesque beasts (Rev 13 and 17) and reappropriates pornographic metaphors from Israel's prophetic literature to depict Rome as "the harlot Babylon" in chapters 17–18.[87]

The shift to a second level of reflexivity begins with the heavenly ascent in 4:1. John narrates the invitation he receives, "Come up hither, and I will show you what must take place after this." Having crossed the temporal threshold into ritual time in 1:10, the visionary narrates the invitation he accepts to ascend through the door across the spatial threshold into heaven. This visionary ascent grants him a higher and broader perspective from which to see and to encode in writing "what must take place after this." The spatial transition accompanies an analogous movement from the particular situations of the churches on the ground to a more comprehensive outlook. This facilitates the sort of reflexivity that involves reflection "on other contexts of meaning . . . in the social and cultural world out of which ritual emerges."[88]

Just as the messages to the seven churches facilitate reflexivity by proffering intratextual intertexts, the second level of reflexivity is also prompted by the introduction

---

82. See Yarbro Collins, "Vilification and Self-Definition," 310–14; idem "Insiders and Outsiders," 204–10. See also chapters 6 and 7 in this volume.

83. See Colin J. Hemer, *The Letters to the Seven Churches of Asia in Their Local Setting* (JSNTSup 11; Sheffield: JSOT Press, 1986), 87–94; Yarbro Collins, "Vilification and Self-Definition," 316–18.

84. Yarbro Collins demonstrates that this charge indicates the Apocalypse's attitude toward polytheists ("Insiders and Outsiders," 210–15).

85. See Hemer, *Letters to the Seven Churches*, 117–23; Yarbro Collins, "Women's History and the Book of Revelation," 80–84.

86. Revelation 2:13 may constitute the only clear reference to the emperor cult in the messages to the seven churches. See Hemer, *Letters to the Seven Churches*, 82–87; Yarbro Collins, "Insiders and Outsiders," 215–16. On Pergamum as the site of the first provincial imperial cult in Asia, see Steven Friesen, "Ephesus, Twice Neokoros" (Ph.D. diss., Harvard University, 1990), 1–14, published as *Twice Neokoros: Ephesus, Asia, and the Cult of the Flavian Emperors* (Religions of the Greco-Roman World; Leiden: Brill, 1993).

87. See Yarbro Collins, "Vilification and Self-Definition," 314–16, on Rev 13; idem, "Oppression from Without: The Symbolisation of Rome as Evil in Early Christianity," in *Truth and Its Victims* (ed. Willem Beuken, Séan Freyne, and Anton Weller; Edinburgh: T&T Clark, 1988), 66–74; and Ruiz, *Ezekiel in the Apocalypse*, 292–378, on Rev 17–18.

88. Kapferer, "Ritual Process and the Problem of Reflexivity," 181.

of a text: the seven-sealed scroll introduced in 5:1. As a distinct organizational unit within the Apocalypse, the Scroll of the Letters is followed by the Scroll of the Liturgy and the Scroll of the Heavenly Signs.[89] The gradual unsealing of the scroll introduced in Rev 5 presents a progressively broadening perspective, which moves listeners from the particular focuses of the messages to the seven churches to the cosmic vision of the new Jerusalem.

In *The Combat Myth in the Book of Revelation*, Adela Yarbro Collins closes her discussion of the structure of the Apocalypse by suggesting that "The phenomenon of recapitulation, the repetition of the same basic pattern in a variety of specific formulations ... seems to be an essential characteristic of mythic language."[90] Following Lévi-Strauss, Yarbro Collins suggests that repetition in myth and other types of oral literature functions to bring the structure of the myth to the surface.[91] In the light of the present discussion, it is tempting to suggest that the literary phenomenon of recapitulation might also be understood in terms of the repetitiveness which often characterizes strategies of ritualization.

Conclusion

With the ambitious aim of exploring the intersection of literary critical and social scientific approaches to the Apocalypse, we now step back to sum up the modest, yet measurable results of this study. We do so under two interrelated headings: (1) writing rite; (2) rite makes might.[92]

Writing Rite

The messages to the seven churches, usually neglected in studies of the Apocalypse's ritual features, furnish a number of key insights when examined in specifically ritual theoretical terms. First, on the literary level, the concept of reflexivity helps to clarify how the ritual setting of the Apocalypse affects the organization of the book. On this literary level, Kapferer's delineation of two ways in which ritual can provoke reflexivity clarifies the relationship between the scroll of the letters and the rest of the book. Second, also on the literary level, the recognition of formality, fixity and repetition as strategies which characterize the process of ritualization helps us to recognize the Apocalypse as a text which stands betwixt and between orality and textuality.

On the social scientific level, the concept of liminality opens up a new approach to the disturbing phenomenon of name calling in the Apocalypse. Separated from

---

89. Barr, "Apocalypse of John as Oral Enactment," 247–48. Also, Edith M. Humphrey, "The Sweet and the Sour: Epics of Wrath and Return in the Apocalypse," *SBL Seminar Papers, 1991* (SBLSP 30; Atlanta: Scholars Press, 1991), 453–60.

90. (HDR 9; Missoula, Mont.: Scholars Press, 1976), 44. For the discussion of the recapitulation theory and its revival by Günther Bornkamm, see 8–13, 32–44.

91. Ibid., 44.

92. The latter is borrowed from Kertzer, *Ritual, Politics, and Power*, 102–24: "Rite Makes Might: Struggling for Power through Ritual."

ordinary life within the boundaries of ritual time and space in their assembly for worship on the Lord's Day, the churches were urged to safeguard their identity by keeping their distance from those identified in the text as their enemies. It must be underlined that while this helps to explain the negative and positive name calling of the Apocalypse in terms of the dualistic enforcement of social boundaries, it offers neither any justification nor any excuse for this deeply disquieting canonization of hatred.

RITE MAKES MIGHT

As a prophetic letter, the Apocalypse represents a reconfiguration of congregational prophecy in early Christianity in the direction of textualization. In the text of the Apocalypse, congregational prophecy came to be an explicitly literary activity. The authority of the sender over the text's addressees was established mainly as a matter of control over the production of a text for recitation in a ritual setting: the voice of the prophet was heard across the distance which the text simultaneously created and mediated.

Schüssler Fiorenza's political analysis of the rhetorical function of ritual symbolism in the Apocalypse underlines the importance of the connection between ritual and power, and prevents us from considering the ritual features of the Apocalypse in isolation. Because John's voice was but one among the many which competed for the attention of Christians in first century western Anatolia, rite made might by claiming the superiority of this text's authority over against the manifest sociopolitical, economic and ideological expressions of Roman imperial authority.[93] By reappropriating biblical language and by subverting imperial ideology and ceremonial, the Apocalypse stubbornly claimed its own ground.[94]

---

93. On the Apocalypse's voice as that of a cognitive minority, see Thompson, *Apocalypse and Empire*, 191–97. Also see Dieter Georgi, "Who Is the True Prophet?" *HTR* 79 (1986): 100–126. On the cognitive majority, see S. R. F. Price, *Rituals and Power: The Roman Imperial Cult in Asia Minor* (Cambridge: Cambridge University Press, 1984); David Cannadine and Simon Price, eds., *Rituals of Royalty: Power and Ceremonial in Traditional Societies* (Cambridge: Cambridge University Press, 1987).

94. Aune remarks that "one of the more fascinating and problematic features of the Apocalypse is the extent to which the author *consciously* juxtaposed and blended traditions to diverse origin" ("Apocalypse of John and Graeco-Roman Revelatory Magic," 418). It might be suggested that such manipulation of diverse material itself represents an expression of authority through control over texts and traditions.

Babylon the Great: A Rhetorical-Political Reading of Revelation 17–18

Elisabeth Schüssler Fiorenza

The seminar "Reading the Apocalypse: The Intersection of Literary and Social Methods" under the leadership of David Barr has worked toward a paradigm shift in Apocalypse studies.[1] This is a shift from the hegemony of literalist-positivist historical and literary (i.e., source criticism) "scientific" methods and essentialist, universalist, or salvation-historical approaches to a rhetorical paradigm of interpretation. Such a rhetorical paradigm thrives on multiple methods and multi-hued critical hermeneutical and theological[2] perspectives. To elucidate the shift from a "scientific-positivist"[3]

This essay was prepared for the Reading the Apocalypse Seminar and has appeared in my book *The Book of Revelation: Justice and Judgment* (Minneapolis: Fortress, 1998), 205–37. The notes have been slightly updated for this publication.

1. See David Barr, ed., *Reading the Book of Revelation: A Resource for Students* (Atlanta: Society of Biblical Literature, 2003), 6.

2. See Elisabeth Schüssler Fiorenza, "The Words of Prophecy: Reading the Apocalypse Theologically," in *Studies in the Book of Revelation* (ed. Steve Moyise; Edinburgh: T&T Clark, 2001), 1–20.

3. Bruce Malina, *On the Genre and Message of Revelation: Star Visions and Sky Journeys* (Peabody, Mass.: Hendrickson, 1995), insists however on such a "how it actually was" historical reading of Revelation. While I agree that it is important to reconstruct the historical situation of the book, I would argue that we "reconstruct" the mind-set of the author or the beliefs of the ancients only in and through our contemporary linguistic and theoretical assumptions. Hence, Malina is not critically aware that his reconstruction of the Mediterranean first-century universe often reads like a counter-caricature to what he believes to be the modern American understanding of the world. See also his very instructive essay "Rhetorical Criticism and Social-Scientific Criticism: Why Won't Romanticism Leave Us Alone?" in *Rhetoric, Scripture, and Theology: Essays from the 1994 Pretoria Conference* (ed. Stanley E. Porter and Thomas H. Olbricht; Sheffield: Sheffield Academic Press, 1996), 72–101, where he identifies himself as "a member of that small, literary challenged, band of socio-rational empiricists." He defines socio-rational empiricists as "those who are socialized to believe that lightning, by whatever signifier one might signify it, will have an effect on us if it directly strikes us" (72 n. 1). While I agree with Malina that a reality is signified by the signifier "struck by lightning," I disagree with him that we have direct access to this reality. His polemics against "feminism, deconstructionism, fundamentalism and hermeneutics" (in that order!) as Gnosticism and Romanticism indicates the authoritarian character of his own position. "What all of these have in common," in his view, "is that they all dismiss the concrete, physical, situation—conditioned, culturally based orientation of the first telling of the Christian story,

to a rhetorical-political paradigm[4] I will center on a feminist hermeneutical debate in the study of Revelation which is of methodological significance to Christian Testament[5] studies in general and to Apocalypse studies in particular. By focusing on a particular text such as Rev 17–18,[6] I sought to make a contribution to the discussions of the Seminar on how to read the Apocalypse. The disagreements between different readings of Revelation's polysemic language, I argued, can be adjudicated only in a rhetorical-political paradigm of inquiry and not in a "literalist" or positivist scientific one.

In a first step I will therefore sketch the basic tenets of a critical rhetorical-political paradigm of interpretation.[7] With this theoretical frame in place, I will in a second step return to the feminist controversy concerning how to read the gendered polysemic language of Revelation and explore the ramifications of a rhetorics and ethics of inquiry with regard to a particular text. The feminist debate[8] over the misogynism of Revelation, and the theoretical issues and assumptions undergirding this debate,

---

much like Gnosticism in antiquity." Yet this advocacy of literalist empiricism overlooks that a sociohistorical feminist analysis, for instance, questions the culturally-conditioned rhetorical constructions of texts and interpretations because it is very much concerned with the concrete, physical presence of wo/men in history.

4. For a fuller development of the argument for a rhetorical approach, see my book *Revelation: Vision of a Just World* (Minneapolis: Fortress, 1991).

5. I use this expression in conjunction with Hebrew Bible in order to overcome the supersessionism implied by the nomenclature "Old and New Testaments."

6. For a comprehensive discussion of this text, see the work of my student Barbara Rossing, *The Choice between Two Cities: Whore, Bride, and Empire in the Apocalypse* (Harrisburg, Pa.: Trinity Press International, 1999); see also her book *The Rapture Exposed: The Message of Hope in the Book of Revelation* (Boulder, Colo.: Westview, 2004).

7. For the elaboration of this approach, see now my book *Rhetoric and Ethic: The Politics of Biblical Studies* (Minneapolis: Fortress, 1999). I proposed a political reading of Revelation for the first time in my article "Religion und Politik in der Offenbarung des Johannes," in *Biblische Randbemerkungen: Schülerfestschrift für Rudolf Schnackenburg zum 60. Geburtstag* (ed Helmut Merklein and Joachim Lange; Würzburg: Echter, 1974), 261–72. See also my feminist work, e.g., *In Memory of Her: A Feminist Reconstruction of Early Christian History* (New York: Crossroad, 1983); *Bread Not Stone: The Challenge of Feminist Biblical Interpretation* (Boston: Beacon, 1984); *But She Said: Feminist Practices of Biblical Interpretation* (Boston: Beacon, 1992); *Sharing Her Word: Feminist Biblical Interpretation in Context* (Boston: Beacon, 1998); *Jesus and the Politics of Interpretation* (New York: Continuum, 2000); *WisdomWays: Introducing Feminist Biblical Interpretation* (Maryknoll, N.Y.: Orbis, 2001). For paradigm research in biblical studies, see also Fernando F. Segovia, "'And They Began to Speak in Other Tongues': Competing Methods of Contemporary Biblical Criticism," in *Reading from This Place*, vol. 1: *Social Location and Biblical Interpretation in Global Perspectives* (ed. Fernando F. Segovia and Mary Ann Tolbert; Minneapolis: Fortress, 1995), 1–32, and idem, "Introduction: Pedagogical Discourses and Practices in Contemporary Biblical Criticism," in *Teaching the Bible: The Discourses and Politics of Biblical Pedagogy* (ed. Fernando F. Segovia and Mary Ann Tolbert; Maryknoll, N.Y.: Orbis, 1998), 1–28.

8. For a short review of this debate, see Alison Jack, "Out of the Wilderness: Feminist Perspectives on the Book of Revelation," in *Studies in the Book of Revelation* (ed. Steve Moyise; Edinburgh: T&T Clark, 2001), 149–62.

can serve to look at the methodological issues that surface in a rhetorical paradigm of interpretation.[9]

1. The Rhetoricality[10] of Revelation

1. Toward a Political-Rhetorical Paradigm of Interpretation[11]

As historical-critical studies form and redaction criticism[12] already implicitly use a literary-rhetorical analysis insofar as they look for the forms and arguments of a writing as well as for the "Sitz im Leben," that is, the generative rhetorical situation of literary forms and texts. However, since they are critical studies indebted to the Enlightenment they also share in the Enlightenment's "scientific" ethos, which negates rhetorical argument and obscures the power relations that constitute it.[13] In contrast, in a rhetorical paradigm of interpretation, one does not need to claim that only one interpretation is correct and all the others are wrong. While having to decide for one definite overall reading in order to be able to make sense out of the book, one nevertheless can appreciate the rich multiplicity of interpretations all of which shed new light on Revelation's different aspects. A rhetorical approach understands these differences as discursively constructed and seeks to adjudicate them both in terms of the overall rhetorics of the book and the interpretive lenses used.

Already in 1973 I had argued that the polemics against the Nicolaitans, the followers of "Jezebel" and of "Baalam" must be understood as integral to the overall polemics

---

9. For a postcolonial discussion of Rev 18, see Allen Dwight Callahan, "Revelation 18: Notes on Effective History and the State of Colombia," in *Walk in the Ways of Wisdom: Essays in Honor of Elisabeth Schüssler Fiorenza* (ed. Shelly Matthews, Cynthia Briggs Kittredge, and Melanie Johnson-DeBaufre; Harrisburg, Pa.: Trinity Press International, 2003), 269–85.

10. I have taken over this expression from John Bender and David E. Wellbery, eds., *The Ends of Rhetoric: History, Theory, Practice* (Stanford, Calif.: Stanford University Press, 1990), 25: "[R]hetoric today is neither a unified doctrine nor a coherent set of discursive practices. Rather it is a transdisciplinary field of practice and intellectual concern, a field that draws on conceptual resources of a radical heterogeneous nature and does not assume the stable shape of a system or method of education.... The classical rhetorical tradition rarefied speech and fixed it within a gridwork of limitations: it was a rule-governed domain whose procedures themselves were delimited by the institutions that organized interaction and domination in traditional European society. Rhetoricality, by contrast is bound to no specific set of institutions.... [I]t allows for no explanatory metadiscourse that is not already itself rhetorical. Rhetoric is no longer the title of a doctrine and practice, nor a form of cultural memory; it becomes instead something like the condition of our existence."

11. See Elisabeth Schüssler Fiorenza, "Challenging the Rhetorical Half-Turn: Feminist and Rhetorical Biblical Criticism," and Dirk J. Smit, "Theology as Rhetoric ? Or Guess Who's Coming to Dinner," in Porter and Olbricht, *Rhetoric, Scripture, and Theology*, 28–54, 393–423.

12. See my dissertation, *Priester für Gott: Studien zum Herrschafts- und Priestermotiv in der Apokalypse* (Münster: Aschendorff, 1972), which has been much utilized but has never been translated into English.

13. For the advocacy of a postmodern rhetorical approach in biblical studies in terms of the New Rhetorics, see The Bible and Culture Collective, *The Postmodern Bible* (New Haven: Yale University Press, 1995), 149–77. This volume is dedicated to Wilhelm Wuellner, who has pioneered the New Rhetoric in Christian Testament Studies.

of the book.[14] But whereas I have maintained that this intramural polemics is based on a different attitude toward accommodation with Roman imperial power, more recently scholars have utilized this argument in order to bolster the "perceived crisis"[15] or "no crisis at all"[16] reading of the rhetorical-historical situation which Revelation addresses. In a recent article Harry O. Maier, for instance, elaborates this intramural argument in sectarian[17] terms:

> Consequently chapter 17 recasts in the role of the harlot the rhetorically named Jezebel of Rev 2:20, whose colorful Hebrew Bible career includes the charge of harlotry. . . . In this parodic, fantastic cast of characters, the alleged idolaters of Rev 2:14–15, 20–22 thus unsuspectingly encounter themselves not only sharing the character of the one drunk on the blood of its model citizens,—namely, the Christian community to whom they would appeal by their alleged false prophecy—but also excluded from the heavenly city. The similarity of depiction functions rhetorically to persuade John's wavering audience to resist his opponents teaching.[18]

While I have read John's polemics against his prophetic rivals as attempting to persuade the audience to follow John's politics of consistent resistance and thus as crucial for the persuasive power of Revelation's argument against the Roman empire, other scholars have tended to make this intramural, sectarian argument the primary rationale for Johns polemics against his internal opponents. Rather than speaking to a situation of oppression, powerlessness, and destruction, John's sole concern allegedly is to prove that he and not the prophet called "Jezebel" is the true prophet and

---

14. See also *Vision of a Just World*, 130–39.

15. Adela Yarbro Collins, *Crisis and Catharsis: The Power of the Apocalypse* (Philadelphia: Westminster, 1984).

16. Leonard Thompson, *The Book of Revelation: Apocalypse and Empire* (Oxford: Oxford University Press, 1990), 185–95, argues that John's dualistic rhetoric is not primarily directed against Rome but seeks to establish "binary opposition and boundary formation—to distinguish insiders from outsiders." His work is part of a depoliticizing trend in Revelation research that has gained widespread acceptance. In a similar fashion, Stephen L. Cook, *Prophecy and Apocalypticism: The Postexilic Social Setting* (Minneapolis: Fortress, 1995), challenges the conventional "conventicle" approach pioneered by Otto Plöger and Paul Hanson, which assumes that apocalyptic writings stem from the losers in political power struggles and argues that apocalyptic texts "are *not* products of groups that are alienated, marginalized, or even relatively deprived" (2). This depoliticizing trend in apocalyptic research needs to be problematized and discussed critically in light of the conservative political use of Revelation in particular and of apocalyptic symbolism in general.

17. For the understanding of Revelation as sectarian, see David A. deSilva, "The Revelation to John: A Case Study in Apocalyptic Propaganda and the Maintenance of Sectarian Identity," *Sociological Analysis* 53 (1992): 375–95; see also idem, "The Social Setting of the Revelation to John: Conflicts within, Fears Without," *WTJ* 54 (1992): 273–302.

18. Harry O. Maier, "Staging the Gaze: Early Christian Apocalypses and Narrative Self-Representation," *HTR* 90 (1997): 149–50.

leader of the community.[19] At stake is here a political reading which such a politics of interpretation displaces with a sectarian parochial one.[20]

Feminist scholars of Revelation also have taken up my argument but have made John's polemics against "Jezebel" the predominant hermeneutical key for the whole book. They have argued that Revelation is a misogynist tract, which advocates the dehumanization of wo/men[21] and eradicates them from its community because the only actual historical wo/man mentioned is vilified. Tina Pippin's work,[22] which is an original and creative attempt to reread the book of Revelation in and through the unmasking of its gender codes, has greatly contributed to such a reading of Revelation. Hence, the growing consensus among feminist scholars that seems to be emerging regarding the feminine figures of Revelation is best summarized in Pippin's own words:

> Females in the Apocalypse are few but noticeable, and their future is prophesied. The prophetess Jezebel and her unrepentant followers will be thrown upon a bed and will die (2:22–23). The Whore of Babylon is dethroned and made desolate and totally destroyed, as the ceremonial lines proclaim: "Fallen, fallen is Babylon, the great" (18:2). Even the Woman Clothed with the Sun is "banished" for protection and safekeeping to the wilderness. . . . The female becomes the absent cause—the cause of both evil and good—but nonetheless is erased from the text. The bride image (the New Jerusalem) alone is left standing, but only briefly; she is replaced by the imagery of the city. . . . I want to show that all females in the Apocalypse are victims; they are objects of desire and violence because they are all stereotyped archetypal images of the female. . . .[23]

At another place she sums up her reading of Rev 17–18: "Having studied the

---

19. See Paul B. Duff, "Whoever Is Not with Me Is against Me: Witchcraft Accusation and the Revelation of John," paper presented in the SBL Reading the Apocalypse Seminar, New Orleans, 1996.

20. It is curious that in his new fascinating narrative commentary, *Tales of the End* (Santa Rosa, Calif.: Polebridge, 1998), David Barr distances himself from my argument that Revelation has adopted a "perspective from below," the perspective of those who were poor, powerless and in constant fear of denunciation, but then goes on to state that "it is worth remembering that the writing is addressed to the urban poor" (165). Although Barr uses a narrative rather than a rhetorical analysis is reference to the correspondence of Trajan for illuminating the rhetorical situation of the book, his characterization of its aim as "consistent resistance" and his integration of the sectarian argument into an overall political one, adopts similar interpretive strategies to those which I have elaborated in my work.

21. In order to reflect the ambiguity and inclusivity of the term, I write the word wo/men in this broken form. See Denise Riley, *Am I That Name? Feminism and the Category of "Women" in History* (Minneapolis: University of Minnesota Press, 1988).

22. See especially Tina Pippin, *Death and Desire: The Rhetoric of Gender in the Apocalypse of John*. Literary Currents in Biblical Interpretation (Louisville: Westminster John Knox, 1992).

23. Tina Pippin, "The Heroine and the Whore: Fantasy and the Female in the Apocalypse of John," *Semeia* 60 (1992): 69

evils of Roman imperial policy in the colonies, I found the violent destruction of Rome very cathartic. But when I looked in the face of Rome, I saw a *woman*."[24]

Contrary to such a naturalized readings of the text simply in terms of gender, I have argued that the androcentric/kyriocentric language of Revelation is conventional. Without question the rhetoric of Revelation is determined by its androcentric language. The question is whether such gendered language functions as exclusive of wo/men or as inclusive generic language. If one reads the androcentric language of Revelation as exclusive one comes for instance to the conclusion that there are no wo/men sharing in the New Jerusalem.[25] If one reads the language of Revelation as conventional, generic language in an inclusive way, one can comprehend the rhetoric of the book as shaping the desire of both wo/men and men but *not of all* wo/men and men.

In other words, any gender analysis that does not reflect on the constructedness and inflection of gender in and through relations of domination is in danger of becoming apolitical. Like any other text Revelation needs to be analyzed critically as to its rhetorical strategies and the power relations it inscribes. Rather than, for instance, evaluating Revelation's symbolic depiction of Babylon and its destruction simply in terms of gender, one must explore what kind of different effects identification with the image of Babylon, the Great City, would have had if the hearer or reader were, for example, a Roman slave or a Jewish freeborn wo/man in the first century.

If one reads Revelation as an argument that depends on its rhetorical-historical situation one can investigate and critically assess its power of persuasion. Rather than focus on "woman" in Revelation, one must explore its politics of meaning in order to adjudicate whether or not the discourses of Revelation are misogynist. In order to do so one needs to investigate whether and how much the rhetoric of Revelation shares in the hegemonic discourses of domination and dehumanization. If one situates the adjudication of the meaning of Revelation not on the level of text but on the level of interpretation, one can perceive the differences in the interpretation of Revelation as epistemological differences. An ethics of interpretation accordingly has the task of critically reflecting on the theoretical frameworks or "lenses" and their implications for the understanding of Revelation's rhetoric. Hence, before I take up the feminist hermeneutical debate in more detail, I need first to clarify what I mean by a rhetorics and ethics of inquiry.

2. Toward a Rhetorics and Ethics of Inquiry

By asserting that a given interpretation of the text represents an objective, value-free, disinterested "scientific" reading, "scientific" exegesis supposedly is able to be

---

24. Tina Pippin, "The Revelation to John," in *Searching the Scriptures: A Feminist Introduction* (ed. Elisabeth Schüssler Fiorenza; New York: Crossroad, 1993), 2:119.

25. For this thesis see Pippin, "Reading for Gender in the Apocalypse of John," 195: "The new Jerusalem is a woman, but women are not included in the utopian city. God's future world excludes women but not before marginalizing them first."

able to comprehend the definitive meaning intended by the author and to overcome its own perspectival understandings. Admittedly, exegetical commentary is not free from rhetorical argument but such argument must be restricted to showing how competing interpretations have misread the text as well as to establish a single and true meaning. Yet, "scientific" exegesis allegedly produces a correct understanding of Revelation and its historical contexts insofar as it curbs the text's multivalent meanings. It does not acknowledge and reflect upon the fact that it interacts with the text from a particular socio-political and religious-theological location. Consequently, it remains oblivious to the fact that it engages not just in hermeneutical but also in rhetorical practices.

In contrast to "scientific" exegesis a rhetorics of inquiry asserts that in the act of interpretation one does not just understand and comprehend texts and symbols (hermeneutics) but also produces new meanings by interacting with them and the audience which one seeks to persuade. As Lorraine Code puts it, rhetorical "discourse becomes a *poiesis*, a way of representing experience and reality, that remakes and alters it in the process.[26] Biblical scholarship as a rhetorical or communicative practice shows how biblical texts and their contemporary interpretations are political and religious discursive practices. Authorial aims, point of view, narrative strategies, persuasive means, and authorial closure, as well as audience perceptions and constructions are rhetorical practices that have determined not only the production of Revelation but also its subsequent interpretations.[27]

The understanding of rhetoric/rhetorical as a persuasive, communicative practice of interpretation that involves interests, values, and visions, must carefully be distinguished from its popular use. Popular parlance often labels those statements as "rhetoric/rhetorical" which it believes to be "mere talk," stylistic figure, or deceptive propaganda, as a clever form of speech that is not true and honest but rather lacks any substance. Rhetoric is often misunderstood as "mere" rhetoric, as stylistic ornament, technical device or linguistic manipulation, as discourse utilizing irrational, emotional devices that are contrary to critical thinking and reasoning. When I use these terms rhetoric/rhetoricity/rhetorical, I do not use them in this colloquial sense.

I also do not conceive of rhetorical analysis as just one more mode of literary or structural analysis. Rather I understand it as a means for analyzing how Revelation and its interpretations participate in creating or sustaining oppressive or liberating theo-ethical values and socio-political practices. In distinction to formalist, structuralist, or aesthetic literary approaches, a critical rhetorics insists that context is as important as text. What we see, depends on where we stand. One's social location or rhetorical context is decisive for how one sees the world, constructs reality, or inter-

---

26. Lorraine Code, *Rhetorical Spaces: Essays on Gendered Locations* (New York: Routledge, 1995), x.

27. Cheryl Glenn, *Rhetoric Retold: Regendering the Tradition from Antiquity through the Renaissance* (Carbondale: Southern Illinois University Press, 1997), 1: "Rhetoric always inscribes the relation of language and power at a particular moment."

prets biblical texts. Biblical scholarship that continues to subscribe to a value-neutral epistemology covertly advocates an apolitical reading of canonical texts and does not take responsibility for its political assumptions and interests.

Once biblical scholarship begins to acknowledge its own social locations and interests, whether of race, gender, nation or class, scholars will be held accountable as to why they privilege one particular interpretation over other possible readings. Competing interpretations of Revelation are not simply either right or wrong, rather, they constitute different ways of reading and constructing socio-historical and theo-ethical meanings. Not detached value-neutrality but an explicit articulation of one's rhetorical strategies, interested perspectives, ethical criteria, theoretical frameworks, religious presuppositions and socio-political locations for critical public discussion are appropriate in a rhetorical paradigm of biblical scholarship.

Hence, a rhetorics[28] of inquiry cannot limit itself to analyzing the text of Revelation but must attend to the argumentative discourses of contemporary scholarship and their theoretical presuppositions, social locations, investigative methods, and socio-political functions. In distinction to aesthetic, structuralist, and psychological literary criticism, which works with a "deeper " archetypal meaning of gender and conceptualizes interpretation in universalizing terms, rhetorical criticism stresses the importance of the particular speech context and socio-historical matrix for understanding the persuasive force of the various arguments of scholars.

> Treating each other's claims as arguments rather than findings, scholars no longer need implausible doctrines of objectivism to defend their contributions to knowledge. At a practical level, to stress rhetoric is to discount claims to neutrality. . . . Detailed attention to rhetoric can reveal underlying issues and better ways to consider them responsibly. It also fosters more effective thinking, speaking and acting by . . . students and by audiences outside the academy.[29]

Feminist epistemological studies have greatly contributed to the revival of such a cross-disciplinary rhetorics of inquiry.[30] Nevertheless, their pioneering contributions are almost never recognized. For instance, in a discussion in *SBL Seminar Papers, 1997,* "The Rhetorics of Revelation," Robert Royalty does not mention once for instance that for a long time my work has advocated and developed such a rhetorical approach to Revelation.[31] This neglect of feminist epistemological work becomes un-

---

28. In speaking of a rhetorics of inquiry, I adopt W. Wuellner's suggestion to distinguish between rhetorics as theory and rhetoric as practice, although such a differentiation is in danger of reinscribing the dualism between theory and practice.

29. John S. Nelson, Alan Megill, and Donald N. McCloskey, "Rhetoric of Inquiry," in *The Rhetoric of the Human Sciences: Language and Argument in Scholarship and Public Affairs* (ed. Alan McGill and Donald McCloskey; Madison: University of Wisconsin Press, 1987), 4.

30. See Ricca Edmondson, *Rhetoric in Sociology* (London: MacMillan, 1984).

31. Robert M. Royalty Jr., "The Rhetoric of Revelation," *SBL Seminar Papers, 1997* (SBLSP 39; Atlanta: Scholars Press, 1997), 596–617. Similarly John T. Kirby, "The Rhetorical Situation of Rev 1–3," *NTS* 34 (1988): 197–207.

derstandable when one considers the negative "feminine" gendering of both rhetoric and religion in the anti-rhetorical discourses of philosophy and science.[32]

Like wo/men, religion and rhetoric figure as the excluded or idealized "other" in modern Western discourse. Like wo/men, both religion and rhetoric are reduced to emotion and passion, to style devoid of substance by the modern rationalist tradition. They are identified with custom, fiction, or colorful ornament, likened to opium and pie in the sky, or associated with trickery and treachery[33]. Throughout the centuries, wo/men not only were excluded from public speaking and academic institutions, but "woman" also became a rhetorical figure of exclusion and subordination that has the function of containing not only religious but also rhetorical discourses and their unruly socio-political possibilities.

Yet, not only religion and theology but also rhetoric has been coded as "feminine other" in contrast to the masculine "hard" sciences. Coded as feminine, theology and rhetoric have been banished by the Enlightenment university to the margins of intellectual activity and public discourses. This marginalization and suppression of rhetoric has been achieved in part through its feminization. According to a well known maxim, "facts are masculine, and words are feminine." Like wo/men, rhetoric is said to be about ornamentation and seduction. Rhetoric has been called "the harlot of the arts" which needs to be kept in place and under surveillance so that it will not corrupt the chaste mind of masculine science and inflict upon its adherents relativistic opinion in place of the certainty of scientific or religious truth.

Like the proverbial "bad girl," rhetoric is said to play loose with scientific truth and objective fact, and like the virtuous wife, "good rhetoric" has been confined to departments of preaching in theological schools.[34] Thus, metaphor, trope, and manner of speaking have been gendered in the anti-rhetorical Western tradition and likened to the treacherousness of wo/men. False eloquence reminds one of the garrulousness and endless gossiping of wo/men, whereas decorum demands that an orator does not speak with the small and shrill voice of a woman.[35] However, it must not be overlooked that this gendered discourse on rhetorics and religion does not speak about actual wo/men but about feminine metaphorization.

Biblical criticism, as I have argued elsewhere,[36] has also remained in the captivity of empiricist-positivist science for far too long insofar as it has until now spent much of its energy applying to and reinscribing into Christian Testament texts ancient rhetorical categories, disciplinary technologies, esthetic stylistics and the scattered

---

32. Susan Shapiro, "Rhetoric as Ideology Critique: The Gadamer-Habermas Debate Reinvented," *JAAR* 62 (1994): 123–50.

33. Susan Jarrattt, "The First Sophists and Feminism: Discourse of the 'Other,'" *Hypatia* 5 (1990): 29.

34. For this characterization, see M. Calvin McGee and J. R. Lyne, "What Are Nice Fellows Like You Doing in a Place Like This?" in Nelson, Megill, and McCloskey, *Rhetoric of Human Sciences*, 381–83.

35. Patricia Parker, *Literary Fat Ladies: Rhetoric, Gender, Property* (London: Methuen, 1987), 109.

36. Schüssler Fiorenza, "Challenging the Rhetorical Half-Turn," 28–53.

prescriptions of oratorical handbooks in antiquity.[37] Hence one could ask the following rhetorical question also of biblical studies in general and those on Revelation in particular.

When respectable academics come to rhetoric's abode, have they really abandoned their old faith in the mythical value-freedom of academic discourse? Or do they entertain a hope of transforming rhetoric into a practice that pious ex-positivists can embrace in good conscience, while they continue to devalue the passions and logic of the political (and religious) economy?[38]

The resistance of biblical studies to a rhetorics of inquiry becomes even more intelligible when one considers that beginning with Plato and Aristotle not only logic but also rhetoric had strong links with political conservatism and has legitimated relations of domination.[39] Even though Aristotle developed an elaborate theory of rhetoric,[40] he kept it in place as an imperfect system, subordinate to science and reason in which freeborn wo/men had only a partial and slave wo/men had no share at all.

Although they differ in their politics of inquiry, most of the recent studies of Revelation recognize the symbolic-rhetorical character of Revelation's language and imagery.[41] Nevertheless, they do not always affirm the paradigm shift from a "scientific," descriptive, reflective, representational, and propositional understanding of Revelation's language to a constructive, evocative and rhetorical one as most appropriate for understanding the book's symbolic universe. To reduce a critical rhetorical-political approach to "social functionalism," as Leonard Thompson does,[42] is a gross misreading of this paradigm shift. In a rhetorical understanding, language is not a straitjacket into which our thoughts must be forced nor is it a naturalized, closed, gendered linguistic system. Rather, it is a medium that is shaped by its socio-political contexts and that changes in different socio-political locations.[43]

Rhetorical criticism recognizes that grammatically androcentric language can function either as "natural," as gender specific or as generic inclusive language. I have

---

37. See especially the introduction and conclusion of Nancy Sorkin Rabinowitz and Amy Richlin, eds., *Feminist Theory and the Classics* (New York: Routledge, 1993), for the institutionalization of classics as modern "gentlemen" disciplines dedicated to the study of philology, text, and history—pure and simple.

38. McGee and Lyne, "What Are Nice Fellows Like You Doing in a Place Like This?" 382.

39. Jarratt, "First Sophists and Feminism," 28.

40. See A. H. M. Jones, *Athenian Democracy* (Baltimore: John Hopkins University Press, 1957); Susan Moller Okin, *Women in Western Political Thought* (Princeton: Princeton University Press, 1979), 73–98; Page duBois, *Centaurs and Amazons: Women and the Prehistory of the Great Chain of Being* (Ann Arbor: University of Michigan Press, 1982).

41. For a short discussion of the variegated readings of Revelation, see Loren L. Johns, *The Lamb Christology of the Apocalypse of John* (WUNT 167; Tübingen: Mohr Siebeck, 2003), 1–21.

42. Thompson, *Book of Revelation*, 206. Yet the analysis of the rhetorical situation does not "mirror its originating situation" but rather makes it more complex.

43. Jan Feckes III, *Isaiah and Prophetic Traditions in the Book of Revelation* (Sheffield: Sheffield University Press, 1994), completely misunderstands my proposal that John uses in a rhetorical and not exegetical fashion the Hebrew Bible and apocalyptic traditions as "language" to express his own vision.

proposed the following four socio-linguistic assumptions as crucially important for a rhetorical-political understanding of the rhetoricity of Revelation.[44]

1. Language and knowledge of the world are rhetorical. That is, they are articulated in specific situations, by particular people, for a certain audience and with certain interests in mind. This is the reason, why a critical rhetorics and ethics of inquiry must pursue a hermeneutics of suspicion with regard to biblical texts understood as rhetorical texts, their persuasive narrative worlds and their ideological functions for inculcating the Western kyriarchal, that is, lord/master/father/husband, that is, elite male-centered order. Such a hermeneutics of suspicion is an interpretive activity through which thinking "escapes the power of the linguistic even while it is itself linguistically constituted."[45]

2. Grammatically, androcentric/kyriocentric language is not simply reflective or descriptive of reality but, as an ideological production, it is also regulative. A hermeneutics of suspicion insists that practices of understanding the "world," such as speaking, writing, reading, or reasoning, are never outside of language or outside of time and history; that is, they are never transcendentally located outside of the "world." Hence, a rhetorics of inquiry focuses on the ambiguity and instability of grammatically gendered language and text and works with a theory of language that does not assume linguistic determinism. It understands language as a convention or tool that enables writers and readers to negotiate linguistic tensions and inscribed ambiguities and thereby to create meaning in specific contexts and socio-political locations.

3. Language is not just polysemic, performative and constructive-poetic[46]: it is also political. Language shapes and is shaped by preconstructed notions of kyriarchal reality or of how the world "really" is. For that reason, a critical intratextual analysis of the language and rhetoric of texts does not suffice. It must be complemented by a critical systemic analysis of socio-political and religious structures of domination and exclusion. Consequently, a hermeneutics of suspicion is called for that interrogates not only how the text but also how the reader is linguistically constituted. It does not

---

44. On the question of language, see Mary Vetterling-Braggin, ed., *Sexist Language: A Modern Philosophical Analysis* (Totowa, N.J.: Littlefield, Adams, 1981); on the problem of "natural" versus "grammatical" gender, see Dennis Baron, *Grammar and Gender* (New Haven: Yale University Press, 1986). Similar observations can be made for race classifications. See Gloria A. Marshall, "Racial Classifications: Popular and Scientific," in *The "Racial" Economy of Science: Toward a Democratic Future* (ed. Sandra Harding; Bloomington: Indiana University Press, 1993), 116–27; Christina Hendricks and Kelly Oliver, *Language and Liberation: Feminism, Philosophy, and Language* (Albany: State University of New York Press, 1999).

45. Brice R. Wachterhauser, ed., *Hermeneutics and Modern Philosophy* (Albany: State University of New York Press, 1986), 30.

46. See Ian Paul, "The Book of Revelation: Image, Symbol, and Metaphor," in Moyise, *Studies in the Book of Revelation*, 131–47.

reduce text or reader to an a-historical core, to the "truth" or to "human nature," but seeks to understand them as produced in or against the interest of kyriarchal relations of domination; that is it understands them sociopolitically.

4. Taking up my rhetorical and political emphasis as crucial for understanding Revelation's grammatically incorrect, bizarre and extraordinary anti-language,[47] Allen Dwight Callahan has called for a "nonrepresentational criticism" in Apocalypse studies that is indebted to postcolonial theories and practices.[48] Utilizing postcolonial criticism he has elaborated, that the language of the oppressor can be subversively used by those disenfranchised to construct an alternate symbolic universe and understanding of the world. For instance, for the Rastafarians, a prophetic messianic sect of Jamaica, biblical language functions, as Theophus Smith has pointed out, "iconically to configure and reconfigure Jamaican history and ongoing experience."[49] According to Callahan, the Rastafarians do not use the language of the King James Bible typologically or allegorically but as a "nonrepresentational glossary of reality" and "counter-hegemonic lexicon."[50]

In short, a rhetorics of inquiry understands the persuasive power of Revelation's anti-imperial discourse in terms of rhetorical convention, compositional arrangement, social location, and the speaker-audience relationship. It analyzes Revelation as a moment of rhetorical exchange and cultural-religious argumentation between John and his audience, a moment that is determined by their common socio-political and cultural-religious situation. Thus it pays special attention to the constraints placed on Revelation's rhetorical discourse by its socio-cultural-religious location and rhetorical situation.

Consequently, a rhetorics and ethics of inquiry must first of all critically analyze

---

47. Following A. K. Halliday, *Language as Social Semiotics* (Baltimore: University Park Press, 1978), John E. Hurtgen, *Anti-language in the Apocalypse of John* (Lewiston, N.Y.: Mellen, 1994), 50–51, defines anti-language as follows: "Anti-language is the language of social resistance. It is a language like any other language, that it functions to express and maintain the social structure. . . . For groups who perceive themselves as relegated to the outer margins of society (the Apocalypse of John fits here), anti-language offers one form of protest against the standard society to which it stands opposed." According to Halliday (165–66), anti-language is determined by *relexicalization* that is new words for old, and *overlexicalization* that is, multiple words for the same concept, both of which are characteristic for the language of Revelation.

48. Allen Dwight Callahan, "The Language of Apocalypse," *HTR* 88 (1995): 453–70.

49. Theophus Smith, *Conjuring Culture: Biblical Formations of Black Culture* (New York: Oxford University Press, 1994), 133.

50. Callahan, "Language of Apocalypse," 464; see also Pablo Richard, *Apocalypse: A People's Commentary on the Book of Revelation* (Maryknoll, N.Y.: Orbis, 1995), 175: "Finally Revelation is having a decisive Influence especially in the so-called Third World (the poor countries and the poor within those countries) in the reconstruction of liberation theologies. . . . The Book of Revelation is helping to create a new historical and liberating language. . . . Revelation is coming to be the preferred book of the Base Christian Communities and of all the ecclesial movements that hope to transform the present situation and reform the church, movements that are born among the poor, the oppressed and the excluded (both women and men)."

whether proposed interpretations do justice to the text's rhetoric. It must critically ask, for instance, whether interpretations of Revelation re-inscribe the kyriarchal sex/gender system or whether they interrupt it's ideological strategies. Such a rhetorics of inquiry concurs with postmodern discourse analysis in that all texts, interpretations, and historical reconstructions are relative and perspectival. If what one sees, depends on where one stands, social-ideological location and rhetorical context is as decisive as text for how one re-constructs historical reality, or interprets biblical texts. The sociopolitical locations and interests of interpreters[51] determine all knowledge production on Revelation.

By understanding different interpretations as discursive arguments that construct reality and are shaped by it, one can place into the center of attention their politics of interpretation and develop an ethics of reading. In the following I will return to the feminist debate on how to read the androcentric/kyriocentric gendered language of Revelation and engage the rhetorics of inquiry for exploring its implications for research on Revelation. However, it must not be overlooked that the debate on how to read the gendered language of Revelation is part of a broader feminist discussion on the basic categories of analysis. Whereas white western feminist scholars have stressed gender as a basic category of analysis, feminist subaltern and postcolonial studies have argued that gender is one of various multiplicative, interactive ideological categories of oppression that determine wo/men's identity. In other words what "wo/man" or "gender" means is differently constructed depending on one's positioning within kyriarchal power relations.[52]

2. Reading the Rhetorical Politics: Revelation 17–18

I return to the feminist discussion of and disagreement about the misogynism of Revelation in order to stage a rhetorical debate on the politics of interpretation and the theoretical frames of meaning[53] produced by different reading paradigms, In so doing I do not seek to prove that my own interpretation is the superior one. Rather I want to elucidate that all interpretations are perspectival and determined by their socio-historical location. Although it is not usually admitted to because of the scientistic ethos of the academy, one always must choose a perspective and standpoint from where to read, if one wants to make sense out of the polyvalence of a text and it becomes thus important to critically reflect and assess the hermeneutical ramifications of such a choice.

---

51. Exemplary here is Brian K. Blount, *Can I Get a Witness? Reading Revelation through African American Culture* (Louisville: Westminster John Knox, 2005).

52. For the exploration and literature on this epistemological debate, see my books *But She Said* (Boston: Beacon, 1992); *Jesus, Miriam's Child and Sophia's Prophet* (New York: Crossroad, 1994), and *Sharing Her Word* (Boston: Beacon, 1998).

53. For the theoretical elaboration of this expression, see Rosemary Hennessy, *Materialist Feminism and the Politics of Discourse* (New York: Routledge, 1993), and my book *Jesus, Miriam's Child and Sophia's Prophet*.

Moreover I want to explore and investigate this rhetorical debate not just on exegetical or feminist grounds but also in terms of the methodological issues raised by a rhetorics of inquiry. I am not interested here in an apologetic defense of Revelation which denies the powerful negative impact of the book's androcentric, or better, kyriocentric,[54] that is, lord/master/father/husband, that is, elite male-centered, language and symbolic universe.[55] Rather, I want to point out that the interpretation of Revelation depends on the theoretical lenses and methodological approaches employed.

In short, I elaborate on the feminist debate of Revelation kyriarchal language and imagery in order to argue that the book of Revelation can not be adequately understood through an analysis simply in terms of gender because gender is always already constructed and inflected by other relations of domination. This does not mean that it is not important to study the "conventional" gendered metaphors and language of the book. I do not want to argue that they have not and do not produce misogynist readings because they have done so and continue to do so. Instead I want to stress that one must avoid absolutizing and universalizing gender as basic category of analysis. Hence on must look carefully at both Revelation's and one's own frames of meaning and their understanding of language "as a reality- generating system."[56]

1. Reading Gender in Revelation

In her contribution to the *Wo/men's Bible,* Susan Garrett has elaborated the significance of reading Revelation in terms of gender:

> Each of these symbols reflects the male- centered view of the first century: women are caricatured as virgins, whores or mothers. . . . The stereotyped feminine images in the book do not represent the full spectrum of authentic womanhood, either in John's day or in our own . . . Exploring the cultural roots of John's metaphoric language about women will enable us to understand what he was trying to say at those points, but the dehumanizing way in which he phrased his message will remain deeply troubling.[57]

This statement clearly indicates that Garrett does not differentiate between actual wo/men and the feminine as trope or metaphor.[58] She equates wo/men as persons with the stereotypical feminine images of Revelation. Tina Pippin also seems to remain within the boundaries of the naturalizing sex/gender system when she

---

54. For the definition and elaboration of this neologism, see *But She Said* and *Sharing Her Word*

55. For a deconstructive reading of Revelation androcentric G*d language, see Stephen D. Moore, "The Beatific Vision as a Posing Exhibition: Revelation's Hypermasculine Deity," *JSNT* 60 (1995): 27–55

56. M. A. K. Halliday, "Anti-languages," *American Anthropologist* 78 (1976): 570–584.

57. Susan R. Garrett, "Revelation," in *The Women's Bible Commentary* (ed. Carol Newsom and Sharon Ringe; Westminster John Knox, 1992), 377.

58. Cf. Suzanne Dixon, *Reading Roman Women: Sources, Genres, and Real Life (*London: Duckworth 2001); Léonie J. Archer, Susan Fischler, and Maria Wyke, eds., *Women in Ancient Societies: An Illusion of the Night* (New York: Routledge, 1995).

identifies Revelation's female-feminine symbols and images—such as mother, whore, and bride—with "real women." She repeatedly states that she wants to focus on "real women," in order to uncover the misogyny of the text. However, she then goes on to read the female images of the Apocalypse as feminine archetypes[59]:

> I want to focus on the clearly identified women in the text who are destroyed and on the general "apocalypse of women" brought about in the utopian vision of the New Jerusalem. By the "apocalypse of women" I mean the misogyny and disenfranchisement that are at the root of gender relations, accompanied by (hetero)sexism and racism along with violence, poverty, disempowerment and fear.... The text of the Apocalypse, with its female archetypes of good and evil, virgin and whore is an account of a political and religious and also gender crisis of the end of the first century CE.[60]

My objection to such an approach is not directed against a deconstructive reading that brings to the fore the gender inscriptions of the text. Rather, my objection is and has been that such a deconstructive reading does not go far enough since it employs an archetypal approach that re-inscribes and naturalizes the andro/kyriocentric feminine representations of the text as a self-evident and self-contained totality. By establishing a one to one relationship between female/feminine language and symbol on the one hand and actual wo/men on the other, a gender reading does not destabilize but rather literalizes the gender inscriptions of Revelation.

Although, for instance, Garrett recognizes the "mixed" character of the image of Babylon that refers to a city, she nevertheless insists that it is the image of a wo/man rather than the feminine image of the empire. Similarly, Tina Pippin goes on to read Rev 17–18 in a universalizing fashion as referring to a wo/man, although she recognizes the class markers of the feminine figure of Babylon.[61] Such a literalization and naturalization of the book's gendered language and symbolism can not comprehend the vacillation and ambiguity of a text that slips and slides between feminine and urban characterization, between masculine and beastly symbolization, between images of war and justice, violence and salvation, defeat and hope, ethical struggle and divine predestination. It is this ambiguity and slippage inscribed in the text, I would suggest, that "reveals" an unresolved political, religious crisis at the end of the first century.

To reify such textual ambiguities into a closed system of antagonistic dualisms reinscribes linguistic-religious gender determinism. It does not allow for ambiguity and change in meaning but only for an "either or" dualistic alternative. By naturalizing and reifying the text it ends up in the same place as a literalist religious, historical or linguistic positivism does. By over-interpreting the text in gender terms it negates

---

59. For a trenchant feminist critique of Carl Gustav Jung's theory of archetypes, see Naomi Goldenberg, *Important Directions for a Feminist Critique of Religion in the Works of Sigmund Freud and Carl Jung* (Ann Arbor, Mich.: University Microfilms International, 1977).
60. Pippin, *Death and Desire*, 47.
61. Pippin, "Reading for Gender in the Apocalypse of John," 195.

the possibility of readers' ethical decision and resistance insofar as it does not leave a rhetorical space for wo/men who desire to read Revelation "otherwise." Although a gender reading of Revelation seeks to interrupt the gender ideologies inscribed in the book, it is in danger of naturalizing and reinscribing them in feminist terms. Although this interpretive approach delights in the post-modern language of multiplicity, surplus of meaning, and play of desire, it does not allow for a *different feminist* reading of Revelation's symbolic world.

By contrast, a critical rhetorical multi-systemic interpretation of the gendered language of Revelation in terms of socio-political and cultural-linguistic systems of domination, that is, in terms of Roman imperialism, I argue, is able to avoid an archetypal gender reading that reinscribes the dualistic sex/gender system. Such an approach insists that the "female" personifications of mother, virgin or whore in Revelation must be problematized not only in terms of gender but also in terms of the systemic structures of race, class, and imperialist oppression.

A systemic analysis of domination can show that the Western gender discourse does not produce and negotiate just *androcentric* but *kyriocentric*, that is, master/lord/father/husband—*elite male-centered* relations of domination, not only between wo/men and men but also between wo/men and wo/men. For instance, the image of the Whore in Rev 17–18 does not speak about a female person or refer to actual historical wo/men. Rather, Revelation deploys it as figure of speech in order to characterize the idolatrous[62] imperial power of Rome. Such a reading, I submit, is able to destabilize the Western construction of gender by pointing out that it functions as a politics of meaning that does not speak about actual wo/men but inculcates the kyriarchal gender ideology of femininity i.e. that of the "white lady."

In difference to a complex systemic feminist analysis, reading *as a woman* or reading simply in terms of gender reinscribes cultural femininity by naturalizing Rev's symbolic figurative language. It perpetuates the western sex/gender system according to which wo/men and men are essentially different and in which masculine and feminine represent antagonistic or complementary archetypes of being human. In so doing, its reading of Revelation reifies and stabilizes socio-cultural gender constructs as natural, essential, or "universal." At the same time *reading as a woman* unifies and naturalizes gender identity by obfuscating or denying that the subjectivity of wo/men readers is traversed by multiple structures of oppression. Yet, for Tina Pippin's reading of Revelation, gender remains the overarching lens of interpretation.

> The ideology of gender in the text is a neglected area in studies on the Apocalypse, so a focus on gender and misogyny is partially justified by the history of the neglect of these topics. But in this reading for gender I am promoting a western, white

---

62. For the feminine coding of idolatry in later theological work, see Susan Shapiro, "The Feminization of Idolatry: Reading Jewish Philosopher Moses Maimonides for his Views on Rhetoric, Gender, and Idolatry," *Harvard Divinity Bulletin* 27 (1998): 27–28; see also idem, "A Matter of Discipline: Reading for Gender in Jewish Philosophy," in *Judaism since Gender* (ed. Miriam Peskowitz and Laura Levitt; New York: Routledge, 1997), 158–73.

feminist reading and hermeneutic. Gender oppression has to be linked with other forms of oppression that women experience. Since I am not third world or living in poverty or in the midst of war, my voice is limited. In my gender analysis of the Apocalypse I cannot claim to speak for any women readers of this text except myself. The majority of women suffer multiple oppressions—sexism, racism, ableism, classism, ageism, heterosexism, colonialism. I am not listing these oppressions just to be "politically correct." Rather, I am called by women of color to face my own role in their multiple oppressions and our mutual enslavement.[63]

This "confessional" statement at once assumes and elides responsibility for its construction of white elite wo/men's agency and identity as universal. It unwittingly re-inscribes the privileged position of the white educated elite woman by privatizing and individualizing its own theoretical "reading *as a woman*." Thereby it mystifies the fact that it produces its reading of Revelation from the cultural position of "the white Lady" and that it does so for readers who are differently positioned in the kyriarchal systems of oppression. Without question, every feminist voice is limited and cannot speak *for* wo/men, but insofar as we "speak" we always speak *to* and seek to communicate *with* others.

2. A Critical-Systemic Political Analysis of Revelation 17–18

I have problematized and critically explored here the hermeneutical underpinnings of the re-inscription of the sex/gender system which is at stake in a one-dimensional gender reading *as a woman* in order to point to a different reading of Revelation in general and Rev 17–18 in particular. A rhetorical political feminist reading utilizing the lens of the multiplicative structures of domination engendered by Roman imperialism[64] points to four areas of ideological struggle over the meaning of gender in Revelation:

1. Although Babylon is figured as an elite woman, the rhetorical-symbolic discourse of Revelation clearly understands it as an imperial city and not as an actual woman. Just as the figure of "beast" does not connote "animal" or that of the "ten horns" an animal's "bony outgrowth," neither does "harlot" in the rhetorics of Revelation connote "wo/man". The rhetorical markers in the text again and again refer the reader to a certain "city" and not to an actual wo/man.

---

63. Pippin, *Death and Desire*, 55.
64. For a political reading of Rev 17–18, see Klaus Wengst, "Babylon the Great and the New Jerusalem: The Visionary View of Political Reality in the Revelation of John," in *Politics and Theopolitics in the Bible and Postbiblical Literature* (ed. Henning Graf Reventlow, Yair Hoffman, and Benjamin Uffenheimer; Sheffield: Sheffield University Press, 1994), 189–202; see also Wes Howard-Brook and Anthony Gwyther, *Unveiling Empire: Reading Revelation Then and Now* (Maryknoll, N.Y.: Orbis, 1999); Richard Bauckham, ed., *The Bible in Politics: How to Read the Bible Politically* (Louisville: Westminster John Knox, 1989), ch. 6.

Whereas, in chapter 17,[65] Babylon is seen primarily as a feminine figure (17:1–7, 9, 15–16) and secondarily as a city (17:5, 18), in chapter 18 Babylon is primarily characterized as a city (18:2, 4, 10, 16, 18–19, 21) and only three times as a "woman" (18:3, 7, 16). This reversal in emphasis indicates that the rhetorical argument shifts from feminine figuration to that of city. The author's explanatory identification of "the woman" vision as that of the "great city which has dominion over the kings of the earth" in 17:18 serves as a rhetorical directive telling the audience that they should understand this image in terms of imperial Rome.[66] In any case, at no time does Rev 17–18 refer to an individual wo/man but only to a feminine figuration.[67]

The narrative sequence concerning Babylon in 17:1–19:10 may be compared to a triptych with three panels. After a general introductory headline in 17:1–2, the first panel (17:3–18) describes and interprets the world capital, Babylon. The second panel (18:1–24)[68] differs stylistically insofar as the destruction of the great city is not described but only reflected in the dirges of the kings, merchants, and ship-owners. The legal claim of the persecuted victims against Babylon is now granted. The powerful capital of the world is destroyed not just because it has persecuted Christians but also because it has unlawfully killed many other people. Rev 18:24 must therefore be understood as the hermeneutical key to the whole Babylon series of judgments. That the question of justice is at the heart of Rev's politics of meaning is also underscored by the third panel (19:9–10) which presents a heavenly liturgy praising the justice of G*d's[69] judgments and announcing the marriage feast of the Lamb.[70]

This whole narrative rhetoric ratifies Rev 14:8, the announcement of imperial Babylon/Rome's judgment, which the second angel proclaims in traditional prophetic language (cf. Isa 24:19; Jer 51:7–8; Dan 4:27). The expression "Babylon the great" recurs in Rev 16:19; 17:5; and 18:2, 10, 21. Most exegetes hold that in the context of Revelation Babylon is a prophetic name for Rome, since Rome was understood in Jewish (2 Esd 3:1–2, 28–31; *Apoc. Bar.* 10:1–3; 11:1; 67:7; *Sib. Or.* 5:143.159) and

---

65. Ian Boxall, "The Many Faces of Babylon the Great: *Wirkungsgeschichte* and the Interpretation of Rev 17," in Moyise, *Studies in the Book of Revelation*, 51–68.

66. For the imperial context of Revelation, see also D. Aune, "The Form and Function of the Proclamations to the Seven Churches (Rev 2–3)," *NTS* 36 (1990): 182–204; idem, "The Influence of Roman Imperial Court Ceremonial on the Apocalypse of John," *BR* 28 (1983): 5–26; the discussion by Heinz Giesen, "Das Römische Reich im Spiegel der Johannes-Apokalypse," *ANRW* 26:2501–614; H. J. Klauck, "Das Sendschreiben nach Pergamon und der Kaiserkult in der Johannesoffenbarung," *Biblica* 73 (1992): 153–82.

67. The study of gender has amply documented that gender images do not need to refer to actual wo/men or men.

68. Susan M. Elliott, "Who Is Addressed in Revelation 18:6–7?" *BR* 40 (1995): 98–113.

69. In order to mark the inadequacy of our language to speak about the divine, I write G*d in such a broken form. For a discussion of the term G*d, see Francis Schüssler Fiorenza and Gordon Kaufman, "God," in *Critical Terms for Religious Studies* (ed. Mark C. Taylor; Chicago: University of Chicago Press, 1998), 136–59.

70. When read literally we have here a marriage between an animal and a wo/man. However, scholars do not read "lamb" as "animal" but see it as a figuration of Christ.

early Christian literature of the time as "Babylon." Both Babylon and Rome shared in the dubious distinction of having destroyed Jerusalem and the temple. However, Babylon must not be reduced to a simple code or steno-symbol for Rome since John uses the name Babylon in order to evoke a whole range of scriptural-theological-political meanings.[71]

For its image of the imperial city as "whore," Revelation not only utilizes the conventional metaphor of woman for a city or country—which is still in vogue today—but also relies on the prophetic language of the Hebrew Bible that indicts Jerusalem and the people of Israel for idolatry, metaphorically likened to "prostitution,"[72] a figure of speech which was by then conventional language and would have been understood by the hearers/readers of Revelation as such. Just as, for example, the image of the Lamb refers to an actual historical person, Jesus, and not to an actual sheep-animal, so the label of prostitute refers to an actual imperial city and not to a sexually lewd female. In short, the vision of Babylon the great does not tell us anything about the author's understanding of actual wo/men.

2. Whereas a feminist analysis solely in terms of gender identifies Rev's references to *porneia/porneuein* as expressions of sexual desire, a complex-rhetorical-political analysis argues that the sexual metaphor of "whoring" or "practicing immorality" is a *conventional metaphor* connoting idolatry. Rev's gendered language of economic-political realities, I have argued, needs to be scrutinized both for its ideological–misogynist evocation and its religious exclusivist bias. Since the "harlot" trope is taken over from the classical prophets who also spoke of nations and cities as prostitutes and harlots. (Nah 3:4: Nineveh; Isa 23: Tyre and Sidon; Isa 1:21, Hos 1–4, Jer 3:6–10, Ezek 16, 25:5–21: Jerusalem and Israel), this trope must be problematized as engendering an ideological tradition that has been and is activated against wo/men in the interest of a misogynist politics.

The controverted question remains as to whether Revelation wants to activate this tradition for misogynist ends or whether it intends it as an argument against idolatry. For, the language of prostitution and immorality signifies in the classical prophets unfaithfulness to Israel's G*d which was enacted in foreign alliances and the worship of other Gods. It is not femininity and sexual morality, I contend, but the politics of power that is central for the argument of Revelation. As Adela Yarbro Collins has pointed out:

> Like Nineveh, Rome has seduced many nations into alliance because of its overwhelming and attractive power. Like those of Tyre, its commercial enterprises are widespread, enriching some and making the poverty of others harder to bear. Idola-

---

71. Jean Pierre Ruiz, *Ezekiel in the Apocalypse: The Transformation of Prophetic Language in Revelation 16:17–19:10* (New York: Lang, 1989).

72. For a feminist discussion of this language tradition of idolatry as prostitution and the rhetoric of Israel as harlot, see Renita Weems, *Battered Love: Marriage, Sex, and Violence in the Hebrew Prophets* (Minneapolis: Fortress, 1995).

try is a factor here as well, although the image has shifted. Rather than depicting the people of G*d as a prostitute who has lusted after male gods . . . instead of remaining faithful to Yahweh, Revelation presents the foreign god as female, as a prostitute who seduces the inhabitants of the earth.[73]

Rather than exploring the politics of meaning coming to the fore in this specific rhetorical accentuation of Revelation, Yarbro Collins's interpretation, however, resorts to the archetypal theory of Carl Gustav Jung and Erich Neumann. While she finds no evidence of sexual desire in the depiction of Babylon/Rome, she sees in it the depiction of the "Terrible Mother."

> Her character as a prostitute symbolizes the seductive and charming power of the Great Mother's lure toward self-dissolution in the unconscious sea of participation, of non-individuation. . . . The beast upon which she rides is her phallic consort, showing her power over the animal world of fertility. . . . The Terrible Mother must be appeased by blood and needs to be soaked with and nourished by blood in order to be fruitful.[74]

Such an archetypal gender reading depoliticizes Revelation's imperial language and imagery in order to make sense out of the feminine figuration of Rome as prostitute. This Jungian perspective finds in the depiction of Rome as the Great Mother "a struggle of Christian faith as a religion of individuation to free itself from Greco-Roman 'participation mystique.'"

However, if one reads the sexually charged language of Revelation not in psychological but in political terms one can understand it as conventionally coded feminine language for a city. Hence, one is able to explore its significance for Revelation's political critique of imperialism. "The wine of its fornication" from which the "dwellers of the earth have become drunk" stems from the intercourse of Babylon with the "kings of the earth" by which "the wealth of its wantonness" has enriched the merchants of the earth.[75] Not sex but power, wealth, and murder are the ingredients of Babylon/Rome's "fornication." The conventional use of "practicing immorality" as signifying idolatry is here redefined as political "intercourse" that negotiates wealth, power and violent death.

Whereas the merchants ship owners, kings and all the nations of the earth were "drunk" with Babylon's wantonness, that is, their sharing in its power and wealth, Babylon is drunk with "the blood of the witnesses of Jesus," (17:6) and that of "prophets, and of saints, and of all who have been slain on earth." (18:24). If one reads the problematic statement "these who have not defiled themselves with wo/men" (Rev

---

73. Adela Yarbro Collins, "Feminine Symbolism in the Book of Revelation," *BibInt* 1 (1993): 27.
74. Ibid., 30
75. See J. Nelson Kraybill, *Imperial Cult and Commerce in John's Apocalypse* (Sheffield: Sheffield Academic Press, 1996), 102–43; see also Robert M. Royalty Jr., *The Streets of Heaven: The Ideology of Wealth in the Apocalypse* (Macon, Ga.: Mercer University Press, 1998).

14:4)[76] in light of the rhetorics of Rev 17–18, then it becomes clear that Revelation's use of conventional Hebrew Bible language[77] does not refer to sexual intercourse with actual wo/men.

3. If one reconstructs the rhetorical situation of Revelation as one of debate and struggle over right action, one can recognize John's voice as one voice but not as the only or the most authoritative one in this debate. Revelation 2:20 refers to a wo/man prophet whom John calls Jezebel after the Phoenician queen Jezebel, for teaching Christ's servants to "practice immorality and to eat food sacrificed to idols." Read against the grain Revelation tells us that one of the renowned leaders of the churches in Asia Minor was a wo/man who could claim the official title "prophet." Such a reading is possible because in difference to Rev 17–18 the text refers here to an actual wo/man.

Since John further claims that like Jezebel the Balaamites and Nicolaitans, whom he also vilifies with Hebrew Bible invectives—are teaching the "sons of Israel" that they might eat food sacrificed to idols and practice immorality" (2:14–15), it is obvious that Revelation's "othering" and vilifying invectives are hurled against *both* wo/men and men.[78] Insofar as John uses the same expressions "practicing immorality or fornication" to refer to the followers of "Jezebel" and to those of "Balaam," he does not vilify her alone. He does not accuse her of moral depravity because she is a "woman" but because he disagrees with her theological stance. John does not argue against the wo/man prophet "Jezebel" because she usurped prophetic office and leadership *as a woman*, but because he did not agree with her teachings. It seems that their difference is not just doctrinal but political-cultural. It is rooted in a quite different experience and evaluation of Roman power and influence in Asia Minor.

This is the only time when Revelation refers to an actual wo/man in sexually coded language. To read this reference in an essentialist manner as directed against wo/men qua women is to seriously misread it. Instead, a rhetorical-political reading can understand this sexually coded reference to a wo/man prophet as the "tip of the iceberg" or as a "symptom" for what has been submerged of wo/men's historical reality through Rev's grammatically masculine language and vituperative polemics. Red against the grain this reference to "Jezebel" indicates that wo/men were not only

---

76. Richard, *Apocalypse*, 120, suggests the following translation of 14:4a: "these are those who did not contaminate themselves with idolatry, for they are clean of heart." However, as I have pointed out above "idolatry" must not be misread in purely religious modern sense but must be understood as economic, political and religious perfidy.

77. See Judith Plaskow, *Standing Again at Sinai* (San Francisco: Harper &Row, 1990), who has problematized Exod 19:15: "Be ready on the third day; do not go near a woman." According to her, for a feminist this is one of the most disturbing verses in the Bible because wo/men are rendered invisible at the central moment in Jewish history.

78. For the polemics against his Jewish compatriots, see Peder Borgen, "Polemic in the Book of Revelation," in *Anti-Semitism and Early Christianity* (ed. C. Evans and D. Hagner; Minneapolis: Fortress, 1993), 199–211; Luke T. Johnson, "The New Testament Anti-Jewish Slander and the Conventions of Ancient Polemic," *JBL* 108 (1989): 419–41.

members of the communities of Asia Minor but had also leadership in them. Their presence in the audience of Revelation could be one of the reasons why the book uses female figures as central images in its politics of meaning.

Against such a political-rhetorical interpretation that I have proposed here, a reading just in terms of gender would insist that grammatically masculine language must be read as gender specific having a one to one relation of meaning and hence the audience of Revelation must be seen as male. However, this argument does not interrupt but reinscribes the kyriocentric androcentrism produced by grammatically masculine language that marginalizes and eliminates historical wo/men from our cultural and religious records.

4. Finally, a dualistic reading of Revelation just in terms of gender is in danger of reinscribing the widespread cultural-religious dichotomy between the "good" and the "bad woman." Barbara Rossing's dissertation has convincingly shown that the author of Revelation was familiar with the feminine coding of the dualistic cultural pattern of ethical choice found in Greco-Roman and in Jewish Wisdom literature.[79] However, it must not be overlooked that this ethical dualism symbolized by two feminine figures is embedded in a tripartite symbolism. A binary reading of Rev's female representations as "good and bad woman" does not appreciate that the author introduces and relates to each other three, and not just two, powerful feminine figures—Babylon, the Whore, and New Jerusalem, the Bride. Revelation does not work with a simple either-or dualism but dialectically[80] mediates this ethical dualism by inserting as a third figure the birthing Wo/man (not the Mother) of chapter 12.[81] They symbolize in a dialectical fashion the Powerful Queen of Heaven, the Powerful Queen of Earth and the Powerful Queen of the New Heaven and New Earth. Such a three-part structure also can be observed in Rev 17–18 and in that of chapter 12, as well as in that of the New Jerusalem segment.[82]

---

79. Barbara Rossing, *The Choice between Two Cities: Whore, Bride, and Empire in the Apocalypse* (Harrisburg, Pa.: Trinity Press International, 1999). For a deconstructive reading of the Wisdom language in Revelation, see Tina Pippin, "Wisdom and Apocalyptic in the Apocalypse of John: Desiring Sophia," in *In Search of Wisdom* (ed. Leo Purdue; Louisville: Westminster John Knox, 1993), 285–95.

80. Roger Fowler, *Linguistic Criticism* (Oxford: Oxford University Press, 1986), 146, points to "the dialectical semantics" of anti-language at work.

81. See Edith McEwan Humphrey, *The Ladies and the Cities: Transformation and Apocalyptic Identity in Joseph and Aseneth, 4 Ezra, the Apocalypse, and The Shepherd of Hermas* (Sheffield: Sheffield Academic Press, 1995), 103–11, who argues against Yarbro Collins's disassociation of the woman of chapters 12 and 21 (*Combat Myth in the Book of Revelation* [Missoula, Mont.: Scholars Press, 1976], 233–35) that the two figures "have a close relationship, but not an exact identity" (110). However, she does not explore the links between the three "queen" figures in Revelation. This seems to be remedied in her article "A Tale of Two Cities and (at Least) Three Women: Transformation, Continuity, and Contrast in the Apocalypse," in Barr, *Reading the Book of Revelation*, 81–96, in which she follows my lead in drawing out the three "Queen" figures of Revelation.

82. However, it must not be overlooked that the feminine metaphor of the bride, which serves to allude to synoptic messianic banquet traditions, is quickly replaced by that of the city, the New Jerusa-

Chapter 12 takes the form of an inclusion. Between the great portent of the glorious wo/man and the powerful dragon (12:1–6), on the one hand, and the vision of the dragon's persecution of the wo/man (12:13–17) on the other, John inserts the vision about war in heaven waged by the dragon (12:7–12). He first draws the audience's attention to the glorious sign in heaven, but at the end of each section he shifts the focus again toward the earth. The whole vision appears to be a mythological elaboration of the *eschatological war* motif already sounded in 11:7.

The myth of the Queen of Heaven with the divine child was—as Adela Yarbro Collins has shown[83]—internationally known at the time of John. Variations appear in Babylonia, Egypt, Greece, Asia Minor, and especially in the texts about astral religion. Elements of this myth are the Goddess and the divine child, the great red dragon and his enmity to mother and child, and the motif of the protection of mother and child. Revelation 12 also incorporates these elements. As in other versions of the myth, the dragon seeks the child not yet born in order to devour and kill it. The dragon therefore pursues the pregnant wo/man for the child she carries. In other forms of the myth the wo/man is either carried away to give birth in a protected place, or she gives birth in a miraculous way and escapes the onslaught of the dragon together with the newborn. In Rev 12, the child is exalted to heaven while the wo/man is carried to the desert for the sake of her own protection.[84]

Some features of this international myth appear also in the Roman imperial cult. A coin of Pergamum, for example, shows the goddess Roma with the divine emperor. In the cities of Asia Minor, Roma, the Queen of Heaven, was worshiped as the Mother of the Gods.[85] Her oldest temple stood in Smyrna. Her imperial child was celebrated as the "world's savior," incarnation of the Sun-God Apollo. John probably intends such an allusion to the imperial cult[86] and the Goddess Roma insofar as he pictures the wo/man clothed with the sun as the anti-image of Babylon, the symbol of the world-power of his day and its allies (chs. 17–18).

Revelation reinterprets this international ancient myth in terms of Jewish expec-

---

lem. Contra Jan Fekkes III, "Revelation 19–21 and Isaian Nuptial Imagery," *JBL* 10 (1990): 283, who argues that Rev 21:18–21 is a continuation of the bride scheme.

83. See Yarbro Collins, *Combat Myth*.

84. In her "Response to Tina Pippin, 'Eros and the End,'" in *Ideological Criticism of Biblical Texts* (Semeia; Atlanta: Scholars Press, 1992), 220, Jane Schaberg comments: "[H]elped by the wings of the great eagle (12:14) and by the earth (v. 16), she almost seems like a character from the Native American traditions. She represents a third option: she does not follow the beast, nor is she a martyr/companion/bride of the Lamb. Refusing this either/or she flees. She has become interesting in a new way." However, Schaberg overlooks this positive understanding of the "earth" in Revelation (see also the hymn [11:18], where judgment is announced as "destroying the destroyers of the earth") when she claims that reverence for the earth is missing from Revelation (223).

85. See Ronald Mellor, *Thea Roma: The Worship of the Goddess Roma in the Greek World* (Göttingen: Vandenhoeck & Ruprecht, 1975). See also idem, "The Goddess Roma," *ANRW* 17.2:950–1030.

86. S. R. F. Price, *Rituals and Power: The Roman Imperial Cult in Asia Minor* (Cambridge: Cambridge University Press, 1984); see also Steven J. Friesen, *Twice Neokoros: Ephesus, Asia, and the Cult of the Flavian Emperors* (Leiden: Brill, 1993).

tations. Its emphasis on the travail of the wo/man does not derive from the ancient pagan myth but takes inspiration from the Hebrew Bible's image of Israel-Zion in messianic times. The vision of the wo/man in labor pains alludes to Israel-Zion seen as a pregnant wo/man awaiting the delivery of the messianic age in Isa 26:16–27; 54:1; 66:7–9 (cf. also Mic 4:9–10).[87] With the symbolic language of Isaiah and this ancient pagan myth, Revelation invokes the image of the messianic child being born accompanied by the birth-pangs of the messianic woes.

While the "wo/man clothed with the sun" is clearly a female figure, as Rossing has elaborated, the New Jerusalem, like Babylon is strongly characterized as a cosmic city. If a dualistic contrast is intended it is the *political contrast* between the capital of the world of oppression and the capital of the world of G*d in which tears, hunger, and death — the characteristics of the world of injustice— have passed away. It is not a contrast between two types of wo/men.

The "first" heaven and earth now belong to the past. The antagonistic dualism between the reign of G*d and Christ in heaven and that of Babylon, the Dragon and his allies on earth and in the underworld no longer exists. The "new heaven and earth" stands in continuity with the former heaven and earth but they form a qualitatively new and unified world. This new reality is characterized by G*d's presence among the peoples of G*d. The vision of the New Jerusalem, arrayed like a bride in the splendor of the "righteous deeds of the saints,"[88] makes symbolically present G*d's eschatological salvation and reign which entails that heaven will move down to earth.[89]

The last series of visions in 21:9–22:9 magnificently elaborate in visionary symbolization the eschatological salvation announced in 21:1–8. This series is structurally designed to form the third panel in the triptych 17:1–22:9, insofar as like the Babylon visions, it is introduced by one of the seven bowl angels (21:9; cf. 17:1) and concludes with a dialogue between the angel and the seer (22:6–9; cf. 19:9–10). In contrast to 17:1 where John is carried into the wilderness, in 21:10 he is carried to a great mountain where one of the bowl angels shows him the "bride, the wife of the lamb"[90] (21:9) as contrast image to the "great harlot," Babylon/Rome (17:1). Just as Babylon is arrayed in scarlet and purple, adorned with gold, jewels and pearls (17:4, 16–17), so the New Jerusalem sparkles with precious jewels and pearls (21:18–21). It radiates from the glory of G*d like a most rare precious gem like jasper, clear as crystal (21:11). Nothing "unclean" and no abomination scars the beauty of the New Jerusa-

---

87. See Claudia Suter Rehmann, *Geh frage die Gebärerin: Feministisch-befreiungstheologische Untersuchungen zum Gebärmotiv in der Apokalyptik* (Gütersloh: Gütersloher Verlagshaus, 1995).

88. Pippin stresses that the New Jerusalem is a controlled and subdued female figure ("Reading for Gender in the Apocalypse of John," 195). However, there is no evidence for this in the text which does not stress wifely subordination but splendor, bliss, and well-being.

89. Richard, *Apocalypse*, 172: This "is not the end of history, but rather a new creation within history. It is a transcendent world, not because it is beyond history, but rather a new creation within history. This new creation is the final achievement of our history."

90. Note that here the masculine-feminine dualism is interrupted through the figuration of Christ as an animal.

lem (21:27; 22:3a) in contrast to the gaudy appearance of Babylon who is called "the mother of abominations (17:5). Just as Babylon has a "name on its forehead" (17:5) so the citizens of the New Jerusalem have "G*d's name on their foreheads" (22:4). Their names are written in the "Lamb's book of life" (21:27) in contrast to Babylon's followers whose names are "not written in the book of life (17:8).

The "kings of the earth" who are not only vassals of Babylon/Rome but also destroy it (17:15–18), bring their glory to the New Jerusalem (21:24). Thus Revelation depicts the eternal glory of the New Jerusalem as the dwelling place of G*d (21:10–22:5) by contrasting it with Babylon's doom as the dwelling place of demons (18:1–3, 9–19). Through these rhetorical parallels John draws the picture of the New Jerusalem as the alternative image of the Great City Babylon/Rome. He contrasts the splendor and power of the Roman empire with that of the empire of G*d and Christ in order to encourage readers to resist the murderous power of Rome. Read in rhetorical-political terms Revelation speaks not primarily of gender and sex but of power used either for destruction or for well-being.

Conclusion

In the beginning of this essay I stressed that a rhetorics of inquiry does not have just the task of adjudicating, on exegetical-textual grounds, which interpretations are right or plausible and which are not. Rather, its task is to assess ethically and politically what kind of reality and vision texts and interpretations generate. Moreover, it must clarify the underlying methodological assumptions and interpretative lenses used in certain readings and assess their implications for shaping the symbolic/moral universe of texts and interpreters. A rhetoric of Revelation calls for an ethics of interpretation.[91]

I have tried to show, here, that a reading of Revelation in terms of a dualistic gender framework inscribes or re-inscribes the Western sex/gender system[92], whereas a rhetorical-political reading is able to underscore the socio-political-religious power of Roman imperialism that affects wo/men differently. I have argued further that a rhetorical-political analysis which reads Revelation in terms of the structures of oppression inscribed in the text, is more appropriate for a historical-postcolonial reading, whereas a gender reading is more apt to underscore the Western sex-gender frame and misogynist assumptions of biblical texts and their readings.

As I pointed out almost twenty years ago,[93] when reading Revelation, contemporary "audiences," always interpret the text in terms of the sex-gender system, and they are bound to activate unconsciously the most prominent reading paradigm in

---

91. See also David Barr, "Doing Violence: Moral Issues in Reading John's Apocalypse," in Barr, *Reading the Book of Revelation*, 97–108.
92. For this expression see my book *Jesus: Miriam's Child, Sophia's Prophet*.
93. Elisabeth Schüssler Fiorenza, "The Followers of the Lamb: Visionary Rhetoric and Social-Political Situation," in *Discipleship in the New Testament* (ed. F. Segovia; Philadelphia: Fortress, 1985), reprinted as chapter 7 in Schüssler Fiorenza, *Book of Revelation*.

Western culture. Hence, the work of feminists who uncover and demystify the gender code of Revelation is crucially important as long as it does not "naturalize" this dualistic code. As I have argued throughout this essay, a reading approach that single-mindedly focuses on gender and identifies gender constructs with actual women is in danger to revalorize the symbolic sex-gender system of the text in modern Western terms although it seeks to deconstruct it. Hence, a reading in terms of gender must remain embedded in a socio-political-religious rhetorics and ethics of inquiry that can adjudicate which texts and interpretations use androcentric language as conventional generic language but reinscribe misogynism and the language of hate if they are not read against the grain.

A reading of Revelation in terms of the multiplicative structures of oppression, I have argued here, can correct a dualistic-androcentric feminist lens and help Western readers to read "against the grain" of their own cultural religious assumptions or prejudices as well as against those of the grammatically and symbolically kyriocentric text. A feminist rhetorical-political reading of Revelation utilizes gender as one but not as the sole lens. It does not naturalize and reify the text in terms of the dualistic kyriocentric Western sex-gender system. Instead it points out that gender is an ideological construct that is produced by and in turn legitimates and "naturalizes" relations of domination. Hence the constructedness of gender in texts and interpretations can come only to the fore when the structures of domination become the focus of feminist readings.

Julia Esquivel's poem "Thanksgiving Day" expresses poetically the politics of interpretation that animates a reading strategy that is critical of all forms of domination. Unlike Tina Pippin, when Julia Esquivel, a Guatemalan refugee, looks into the eye of Babylon/Rome, she does not see a wo/man. Rather she sees U.S. imperial power that has been and still is so destructive of all native peoples.

> In the third year of the massacres
> by Lucas and the other coyotes
> against the poor of Guatemala
> I was led by the Spirit into the desert
> And on the eve
> of Thanksgiving Day
> I had a vision of Babylon:
> the city sprang forth arrogantly . . .
> Each day false prophets
> invited the inhabitants
> of the Unchaste City
> to kneel before the idols of gluttony
> money
> and death:
> Idolaters of all nations
> were being converted to the American way of life . . .
> The Spirit told me

>in the River of death
>flows the blood of many peoples . . .
>the blood of the Indian's ancestors
>who lived on those lands, of those who
>even now are kept hostage in the Great Mountain
>and on the Black Hills of Dakota
>by the guardians of the beast. . . .[94]

This poetic interpretation of Revelation's Babylon vision does not use gender but a postcolonial analysis of imperialism as its analytic lens. It foregrounds the experience of colonial oppression and death-dealing political-religious power. Although Esquivel does not engage in a critical exegetical reading but in an imaginative-poetic one, the theoretical issues undergirding such a reading of Revelation in terms of imperialism can be brought into conversation with a feminist gender reading

In sum, I have juxtaposed two different feminist strategies of reading Rev 17–18 in particular and the female images of the book in general. One reading practice subscribes to an ideological-archetypal gender politics, the other reads gender in contextual-rhetorical-political terms. A rhetorics and ethics of inquiry can alert us to the fact that the disagreement between these reading practices is not exegetical-textual but rather rhetorical-hermeneutical. Whereas a scientific-positivist paradigm would argue for one interpretation over the other as the only correct one, a rhetorical paradigm seeks to understand why and on what grounds different interpretations privilege different rhetorical markers in the text. The determination of which interpretation is most appropriate, however, cannot be settled on purely exegetical grounds but only in terms of a rhetorics and ethics of inquiry. Both feminist reading strategies highlight important aspects of the rhetorical discourse of Revelation.

While a feminist reading of Revelation solely in terms of gender underscores the ways the discursive sex/gender system determines the rhetoric of Revelation and our own readings of it, an interpretation of it in terms of the "imperial" code insists that gender is not a discrete category but that it is inflected by other relations of domination such as race, status, religion, and colonial imperialism. It points out that western middle class wo/men readers will activate the sex/gender system but not that of class, race or ethnicity. They privilege gender markers when reading Revelation whereas oppressed and marginalized readers stress the political language and rhetoric of the book. Both readings must remain dialectically related to each other if they should fruitfully correct each other. Such a correction and fine-tuning of the feminist lens and interpretive focus is especially necessary for those who read from the social location of Western elite male status and privilege. A rhetorics of inquiry must therefore be accompanied by an ethics of inquiry that is able to critically assess the scholarly frameworks and interpretive patterns that determine all interpretation of Revelation in light of its utopian vision of justice and well-being for all.

---

94. Julia Esquivel, *Threatened with Resurrection: Prayers and Poems from an Exiled Guatemalan* (Elgin, Ill.: Brethren Press, 1982), 79–91.

Select Bibliography

Aune, David E. *Revelation*. WBC 52A–C. 3 vols. Nashville: Nelson, 1997–1998.
———. "The Apocalypse of John and the Problem of Genre." *Semeia* 36 (1986): 65–96.
———. *The Cultic Setting of Realized Eschatology in Early Christianity*. NovTSup 28. Leiden: Brill, 1972.
———. "The Influence of Roman Imperial Court Ceremonial on the Apocalypse of John." *BR* 28 (1983): 5–26.
———. *Prophecy in Early Christianity and the Ancient Mediterranean World*. Grand Rapids: Eerdmans, 1983.
Barr, David L. "The Apocalypse as a Symbolic Transformation of the World: A Literary Analysis." *Int* 38 (1984): 39–50.
———. *Tales of the End: A Narrative Commentary on the Book of Revelation*. The Storytellers Bible 1. Santa Rosa, Calif.: Polebridge, 1998.
———, ed. *Reading the Book of Revelation: A Resource for Students*. SBLRBS 44. Atlanta: Society of Biblical Literature, 2003.
Bauckham, Richard J. *The Climax of Prophecy: Studies on the Book of Revelation*. Edinburgh: T&T Clark, 1993.
———. *The Theology of the Book of Revelation*. Cambridge: Cambridge University Press, 1993.
Beale, Gregory K. *The Book of Revelation: A Commentary on the Greek Text*. Grand Rapids: Eerdmans, 1999.
Beasley-Murray, G. R. *The Book of Revelation*. Edited by Matthew Black. Rev. ed. NCB. London: Oliphants, 1978.
Berrigan, Daniel. *The Nightmare of God*. Portland, Oreg.: Sunburst, 1983.
Bloomquist, L. Gregory., and Greg Carey, eds. *Vision and Persuasion Rhetorical Dimensions of Apocalyptic Discourse*. St. Louis, Mo.: Chalice, 1999.
Blount, Brian K. *Can I Get a Witness? Reading Revelation through African American Culture*. Louisville: Westminster John Knox, 2005.
———. "Reading Revelation Today: Witness as Active Resistance." *Int* 54 (2000): 398–412.
Borgen, Peder. "Polemic in the Book of Revelation." Pages 199–211 in *Anti-Semitism and Early Christianity*. Edited by Craig A. Evans. Minneapolis: Fortress, 1993.
Boring, M. Eugene. "The Apocalypse as Christian Prophecy: A Discussion of the Issues Raised by the Book of Revelation for the Study of Early Christian Prophecy." Pages 2:43–62 in

Society of Biblical Literature 1974 Seminar Papers. Edited by G. W. MacRae. SBLSP 36. Missoula, Mont.: Society of Biblical Literature, 1974.

———. *Revelation*. IBC. Atlanta: John Knox, 1989.

Bousset, Wilhelm. *Die Offenbarung Johannis*. 6th ed. Göttingen: Vandenhoeck & Ruprecht, 1906.

Caird, G. B. *A Commentary on the Revelation of St. John the Divine*. HNTC. New York: Harper & Row, 1966.

Carey, Greg. *Elusive Apocalypse: Reading Authority in the Revelation to John*. Macon, Ga.: Mercer University Press, 1999.

Charles, R. H. *A Critical and Exegetical Commentary on the Revelation of St. John*. ICC. Edinburgh: T&T Clark, 1920.

Clifford, Richard J. "The Roots of Apocalypticism in Near Eastern Myth." Pages 3–38 in *The Origins of Apocalypticism in Judaism and Christianity*. Edited by John J. Collins. New York: Continuum, 2000.

Collins, Adela Yarbro. *The Combat Myth in the Book of Revelation*. HDR 9. Chico, Calif.: Scholars Press, 1976.

———. *Crisis and Catharsis: The Power of the Apocalypse*. Philadelphia: Westminster, 1984.

———. "Vilification and Self-Definition in the Book of Revelation." *HTR* 79 (1986): 308–20.

———, ed. *Early Christian Apocalypticism: Genre and Social Setting*. Semeia 36 (1986).

Collins, John J. *The Apocalyptic Imagination: An Introduction to the Jewish Matrix of Christianity*. 2d ed. Los Angeles: Crossroad, 1984. Repr., Grand Rapids: Eerdmans, 1998.

———. "From Prophecy to Apocalypticism: The Expectation of the End." Pages 129–61 in *The Origins of Apocalypticism in Judaism and Christianity*. Edited by John J. Collins. New York: Continuum, 2000.

———, ed. *Apocalypse: The Morphology of a Genre*. Semeia 14 (1979).

———, ed. *The Origins of Apocalypticism in Judaism and Christianity*. Vol. 1 of *The Encyclopedia of Apocalypticism*. Edited by Bernard McGinn, John J. Collins, and Stephen J. Stein. New York: Continuum, 2000.

Collins, John J., and James H. Charlesworth, eds. *Mysteries and Revelations: Apocalyptic Studies since the Uppsala Colloquium*. JSPSup 9. Sheffield: Sheffield Academic Press, 1991.

Derrida, Jacques. "The Law of Genre." *Critical Inquiry* 7 (1980): 55–91.

Duff, Paul Brooks. *Who Rides the Beast? Prophetic Rivalry and the Rhetoric of Crisis in the Churches of the Apocalypse*. Oxford: Oxford University Press, 2001.

Eco, Umberto. "The Poetics of the Open Work." Pages 1–23 in *The Role of the Reader: Explorations in the Semiotics of Texts*. Edited by Thomas A. Sebeok. Bloomington: Indiana University Press, 1979.

Farmer, Ron. *Beyond the Impasse: The Promise of a Process Hermeneutic*. Macon, Ga.: Mercer University Press, 1997.

Farrer, Austin. *A Rebirth of Images: The Making of St. John's Apocalypse*. 1949. Repr., Gloucester: Mass.: Smith, 1970.

Flaceliere, Robert. *Greek Oracles*. London: Elek, 1965.

Frankfurter, David. "Early Christian Apocalypticism: Literature and Social World." Pages 415–53 in *The Origins of Apocalypticism in Judaism and Christianity*. Edited by John J. Collins. New York: Continuum, 2000.

———. "Jews or Not? Reconstructing the 'Other' in Rev 2:9 and 3:9." *HTR* 94 (2001): 403–25.
Friesen, Steven J. *Imperial Cults and the Apocalypse of John: Reading Revelation in the Ruins.* Oxford: Oxford Press University, 2001.
———. "Revelation, Realia, and Religion: Archaeology in the Interpretation of the Apocalypse." *HTR* 88 (1995): 291–314.
———. *Twice Neokoros: Ephesus, Asia and the Cult of the Flavian Emperors.* Religions of the Greco-Roman World. Leiden: Brill, 1993.
Frilingos, Christopher A. *Spectacles of Empire Monsters, Martyrs, and the Book of Revelation.* Divinations. Philadelphia: University of Pennsylvania Press, 2004.
Gager, John G. *Kingdom and Community: The Social World of Early Christianity.* Edited by John Reeder. Prentice-Hall Studies in Religion Series. Englewood Cliffs, N.J.: Prentice-Hall., 1975.
Genette, Gerard. *Palimpsestes: La Littérature Au Second Degré.* Paris: Éditions du Seuil, 1982.
Gibson, Leigh, and Shelly Matthews, eds. *Violence in the New Testament.* New York: T&T Clark, 2005.
Hanson, Paul D. *The Dawn of Apocalyptic: The Historical and Sociological Roots of Jewish Apocalyptic Eschatology.* Rev. ed. Philadelphia: Fortress, 1979.
Harris, Michael A. "The Literary Function of the Hymns in the Apocalypse." Ph.D. diss. Southern Baptist Theological Seminary, 1989.
Hellholm, David. *Apocalypticism in the Mediterranean World and Near East: Proceedings of the International Colloquium on Apocalypticism, Uppsala, August 12–17, 1979.* 2d ed. 1983. Repr., Tübingen: Mohr Siebeck, 1989.
Howard-Brook, Wes, and Anthony Gwyther. *Unveiling Empire: Reading Revelation Then and Now.* Maryknoll, N.Y.: Orbis, 2001.
Humphrey, Edith M. *The Ladies and the Cities: Transformation and Apocalyptic Identity in Joseph and Aseneth, 4 Ezra, The Apocalypse, and the Shepherd of Hermas.* JSPSup 17. Sheffield: Sheffield Academic Press, 1995.
Iser, Wolfgang. *The Act of Reading: A Theory of Aesthetic Response.* Baltimore: Johns Hopkins University Press, 1978.
Johns, Loren L. *The Lamb Christology of the Apocalypse of John: An Investigation into Its Origins and Rhetorical Force.* WUNT 2/167. Tübingen: Mohr Siebeck, 2003.
Koester, Craig R. "The Message to Laodicea and the Problem of Its Local Context: A Study of the Imagery in Rev 3.14–22." *NTS* 49 (2003): 407–24.
Kraybill, J. Nelson. *Imperial Cult and Commerce in John's Apocalypse.* JSNTSup 132. Sheffield: Sheffield Academic Press, 1996.
Lambrecht, Jan. *L'Apocalypse Johannique Et L'Apocalyptique Dans Le Nouveau Testament.* BETL 53. Louvain: Louvain Univesity Press, 1980.
Mack, Burton L., and Vernon K. Robbins. *Patterns of Persuasion in the Gospels.* Sonoma, Calif: Polebridge, 1990.
Maier, Harry O. *Apocalypse Recalled: The Book of Revelation after Christendom.* Minneapolis: Fortress, 2002.
Marshall, John W. *Parables of War: Reading John's Jewish Apocalypse.* Waterloo, Ont.: Published for the Canadian Corporation for Studies in Religion = Corporation canadienne des sciences religieuses by Wilfrid Laurier University Press, 2001.

Mathewson, David. *A New Heaven and a New Earth: The Meaning and Function of the Old Testament in Revelation 21:1–22:5*. JSNTSup 238. London: Sheffield Academic Press, 2003.
Miller, Patricia Cox. *Dreams in Late Antiquity: Studies in the Imagination of a Culture*. Princeton: Princeton University Press, 1998.
Moore, Stephen D. "Revolting Revelations." Pages 183–200 in *The Personal Voice in Biblical Interpretation*. Edited by Ingrid Rosa. London: Routledge, 1999.
Mounce, Robert H. *The Book of Revelation*. NICNT. Grand Rapids: Eerdmans, 1977.
Moyise, Steve, ed. *Studies in the Book of Revelation*. Edinburgh: T&T Clark, 2001.
Osiek, Carolyn. *Shepherd of Hermas: A Commentary*. Minneapolis: Fortress, 1999.
Pattemore, Stephen. *The People of God in the Apocalypse: Discourse, Structure, and Exegesis*. Cambridge: Cambridge University Press, 2004.
Pippin, Tina. *Apocalyptic Bodies: The Biblical End of the World in Text and Image*. London: Routledge, 1999.
———. *Death and Desire: The Rhetoric of Gender in the Apocalypse of John*. Louisville: Westminster John Knox, 1992.
Price, S. R. F. *Rituals and Power: The Roman Imperial Cult in Asia Minor*. Cambridge: Cambridge University Press, 1984.
Prigent, Pierre. *Comentary on the Apocalypse of St. John*. Translated by Wendy Pradels. Tübingen: Mohr Siebeck, 2001.
Reddish, Mitchell. *Revelation*. Smyth & Helwys Bible Commentary. Macon, Ga.: Smyth & Helwys, 2001.
Richard, Pablo. "Plagues in the Bible: Exodus and Apocalypse." Pages 45–54 in *The Return of the Plague*. Edited by José Oscar Beozzo and Virgil Elizondo. London: SCM, 1997.
Roloff, Jürgen. *The Revelation of John: A Continental Commentary*. Translated by John E. Alsup. Minneapolis: Fortress, 1993.
Rossing, Barbara R. *The Choice between Two Cities: A Wisdom Topos in the Apocalypse*. Harrisburg, Pa.: Trinity Press International, 1999.
———. *The Rapture Exposed: The Message of Hope in the Book of Revelation*. Boulder, Colo.: Westview, 2004.
Rowland, Christopher. "The Apocalypse: Hope, Resistance, and the Revelation of Reality." *ExAud* 6 (1990): 129–44.
———. *The Open Heaven: A Study of Apocalyptic in Judaism and Early Christianity*. New York: Crossroad, 1982.
Royalty, Robert M., Jr. *The Streets of Heaven: The Ideology of Wealth in the Apocalypse of John*. Macon, Ga.: Mercer University Press, 1998.
Ruiz, Jean-Pierre. *Ezekiel in the Apocalypse: The Transformation of Prophetic Language in Revelation 16:17–19:10*. European University Studies, ser. 23; Theology 376. New York: Lang, 1989.
Russell, D. S. *The Method and Message of Jewish Apocalyptic: 200 B.C.–100 A.D.* OTL. Philadelphia: Westminster, 1964.
Schüssler Fiorenza, Elisabeth. *Aspects of Religious Propaganda in Judaism and Early Christianity*. Notre Dame, Ind.: University of Notre Dame Press, 1976.
———. *The Book of Revelation: Justice and Judgment*. 2d ed. Minneapolis: Fortress, 1998.
———. "Challenging the Rhetorical Half-Turn: Feminist and Rhetorical Biblical Criticism."

Pages 28–53 in *Rhetoric, Scripture and Theology: Essays from the 1994 Pretoria Conference*. Edited by Stanley E. Porter and Thomas H. Olbricht. JSNTSup 131. Sheffield: Sheffield Academic Press, 1996.

———. "The Ethics of Interpretation: De-centering Biblical Scholarship." *JBL* 107 (1988): 3–17.

———. "The Followers of the Lamb: Visionary Rhetoric and Socio-Political Situation." *Semeia* 36 (1986): 123–46.

———. *Revelation: Vision of a Just World*. Minneapolis: Fortress, 1991.

Sweet, J. P. M. *Revelation*. Westminster Pelican Commentaries. Philadelphia: Westminster, 1979. Repr., Philadelphia: Trinity Press International, 1990.

Swete, Henry B. *The Apocalypse of St. John*. 3d ed. London: Macmillan, 1909.

Thompson, Leonard L. *The Book of Revelation: Apocalypse and Empire*. Oxford: Oxford University Press, 1990.

Turner, Victor W. *The Ritual Process: Structure and Anti-structure*. Ithaca, N.Y.: Cornell University Press, 1969.

Vanni, Ugo. "The Ecclesial Assembly: 'Interpreting Subject' of the Apocalypse." *Religious Studies Bulletin* 4/2 (1984): 79–85.

———. "Liturgical Dialogue as a Literary Form in the Book of Revelation." *NTS* 37 (1991): 348–72.

Vorster, W.S. "'Genre' and the Revelation of John: A Study in Text, Context and Intertext." *Neot* 22 (1988): 103–23.

Wainwright, Arthur. *Mysterious Apocalypse: Interpreting the Book of Revelation*. Nashville: Abingdon, 1993.

Watson, Duane Frederick, ed. *Persuasive Artistry: Studies in New Testament Rhetoric in Honor of George A. Kennedy*. JSNTSup 50. Sheffield: Sheffield Academic Press, 1991.

Wilson, Robert R. "From Prophecy to Apocalyptic: Reflections on the Shape of Israelite Religion." *Semeia* 21 (1982): 79–95.

Zanker, Paul. *The Power of Images in the Age of Augustus*. Ann Arbor: University of Michigan Press, 1990.

Contributors

David E. Aune
Professor of New Testament and Christian Origins, University of Notre Dame

David L. Barr
Professor of Religion, Brage Golding Distinguished Professor, Wright State University

Greg Carey
Associate Professor of New Testament, Lancaster Theological Seminary

Paul Duff
Professor of Religion and Associate Dean for Undergraduate Studies, George Washington University

Steven J. Friesen
Louise Farmer Boyer Chair in Biblical Studies, University of Austin

Jan Willem van Henten
Professor of Bible, University of Amsterdam, Head of the Department of Art, Religion and Culture

Edith M. Humphrey
William F. Orr Professor of New Testament, Pittsburgh Theological Seminary

Gregory L. Linton
Vice President for Academic Affairs and Professor of New Testament, Great Lakes Christian College

Jean-Pierre Ruiz
Associate Professor, Department of Theology and Religious Studies, St. John's University

Elisabeth Schüssler Fiorenza
Krister Stendahl Professor, Harvard Divinity School

Index of Ancient Writings

Hebrew Scriptures

Genesis
3 — 189

Exodus
19:4 — 187
20:3 — 183
23:24 — 183
34:14 — 183
34:27–28 — 50

Numbers
22:1–25:3 — 134

Deuteronomy
4:2 — 69
6:13 — 183
34:19 — 50

Judges
4–5 — 230
5:4–5 — 66

1 Kings
16:31 — 134
18:12 — 61
22:11 — 62
22:19–22 — 52

2 Kings
2:16 — 61
9:37 — 134
13:14–19 — 62
22:19–20 — 52

Job
1:6–12 — 52
1:6–12 — 52
2:1–6 — 52
31:10–13 — 190

Psalm
2:9 — 64
18:7–15 — 66
29 — 98
46 — 65
48 — 65
56:8 — 66
68:7–8 — 66
76 — 65
78:43–51 — 54
87:4 — 189
98 — 120
105:27–36 — 54

Proverbs
3:11 — 158
3:11–12 — 158
8:27 — 158

Isaiah
1:21 — 261
06 — 30, 50
6:1–13 — 52
7:10–12 — 62
17 — 65
17:4–5 — 60
19:25 — 28
22 — 140
22:15–25 — 139

(Isaiah) 22:20–22	139	16	261
22:22	161	25:5–21	261
23	261	26:15–18	62
24:19	260	27:1–8, 26–36	62
26:16–27	266	28:1–10	202
27:3	54	28:2	202
29	65	28:6–10	203
30:18	28	29:3–5	189
30:8	50	38–39	65
45:1–02	140	40–48	67
45:14	140	48:30–35	144
49:23	140		
51:9–10	189	DANIEL	
54:1	266	3	198
56:2	28	3:12, 18	198
58:1	54	3:2, 4	198
60:14	140	3:7: 10, 14–15, 18	198
63:1–6	60	4:27	260
65:6	66	7	29
66:7–9	266	7: 8	189
		7:9–14	50
JEREMIAH		7:10	66
1	30, 50	7:13	49
1:1–2	47	7:13–14	52
017:7	28	7:9–12	52
3:6–10	261	7–8	190
4:4–5	62	8:10–12	190
4:6:1	62	8:26	68, 92
22:30	66	10:5–9	50
42:1–6	93	11:36	202
48:6–8	62	11:44	187
50:8–10	62	12:4	99
51:7	260	12:4, 9	68
51:33	60		
51:34	189	HOSEA	
51:6–8, 45–48	62	1–4	261
EZEKIEL		JOEL	
1:4–28	52	2:2–3	54
1:4–3:11	52	2:4	65
1:1–3	47	3:13	60
1–3	30, 50		
2:8–3:11	95	AMOS	
2:8–3:3	55, 91, 103	1:1	47
3:14	61	1–2	66
9	143	3:7	95

3:7–8	99, 109	19:43–44	65
4::6–11	54	21:20	65

MICAH

		JOHN	
1:3–4	66	1:1–2	64
4:13	60	9:22	151, 161
4:9–10	266	21:25	91

NAHUM

		ACTS	
3:4	261	1:24–26	78
		2:15	83

ZEPHANIAH

		7:48–50	67
1:15–16	54	11:26	142
		12:22–23	203

ZECHARIAH

		14:27	140, 161
4:1–14	56	17:24	67
9:14	54	26:28	142
12	29	27:14	191
12, 14	65		
12:10b	49	**ROMANS**	
		2:28–29	135

MALACHI

		2:5	96
3:16	66	8:19	96
		11:36	49

Christian Testament

		13	181
		14:1–15:4	176

MATTHEW

		1 CORINTHIANS	
3:12	60	1:7	96
9:15b	63	8:4–6	181, 183
9:37–38	60	8–10	176
19:28–30	52	10:23–30	135
24:31	54	10:26	176
25:31–46	52	14	27
		14:6, 26	96

MARK

		15	102
2:20	63	15:26	219
4:29	60	15:52	54
4:34	91	16:22	68
14:58	67	16:9	140, 161

LUKE

		2 CORINTHIANS	
5:35	63	2:12	140, 161
10:17–24	114, 115, 118	10	95
10:18	116	10:10	106
13:39	187	11:2	63
14:15	63		

(2 Corinthians)	12	101	
12:1–10		104, 109	
12:1–13		96	
12:4		91	
12:1, 7		92	
12:4		91, 94, 101, 106	

GALATIANS
1:1–5	49
1:12	27, 96
1:1–5	29

EPHESIANS
5:25–32	63

COLOSSIANS
4:3	140
4:3	161
1–02	102
2:2	96
6:7–9	60

1 THESSALONIANS
4:16	54

2 THESSALONIANS
2:3–12	59
2:4	199, 202

1 TIMOTHY
1:17	49
2:1–6	181

TITUS
3:1–8	181

HEBREWS
9:11	67
10:34	150
12:22–24	52, 53

1 PETER
2:1–17	181
4:11	49
4:16	142

1 JOHN
1:1	64

REVELATION
1:1	36, 143
1:1–3:22	175
1:1–20	26–32
1:1–3	47
1:3	33, 217, 231, 233
1:4–5a	48
1:5	64
1:5–6	143
1:5b–6	49
1:6	179
1:7–8	49
1:9	50
1:9–20	50, 232
1:10	51, 231
1:11	95
1:4	143
1–3	2, 70
2:1–3:22	50
2:2	134
2:4–6	51
2:8–11	137
2:9	136, 150, 157, 207
2:10	154
2:12, 16	64
2:13	150, 239
2:14	133
2:14, 20	147
2:14–15	246, 263
2:14–16	51
2:20	143, 246, 263
2:20–22	51
2:21	179
2:21–23	155
2:22–23	247
2:23	133, 143, 158
2:24	134
2:26	64
2–3 3 1:	51, 130, 133, 141, 217, 232, 234, 237
3:4	174
3:7–10	160
3:7–13	138, 141, 143
3:9	136, 139
3:12–13	139
3:14	64
3:14–19	51
3:16–17	133

3:17	207	11:3–13	55, 56
3:21	52, 207	11:3–19	94
4:1	51, 235, 239	11:7	179, 213, 265
4:1–6	52	11:7–10	107
4:1–6:17	51, 52	11:8	162
4:5	98	11:15–18	52, 57
4:7	52	11:18	143
4:17	52	11:19	98
5	95	11:19–12:17	58
5:1	240	11:7	183
5:2–6	219	12	87, 122, 143, 162, 182, 185, 186, 264
5:3, 13	52	12:1–12	118
5:8	143	12:1–17	115, 118
5:9	137	12:1–3	188
5:10	179	12:3	197
5:12	209	12:5	64
5:6	202	12:7–12	265
05–1–14	52	12:7–8	209
6:1–17	52	12:9, 14–15	183
6:10	174, 211, 219	12:1	188
6:11	212	12:10–12	120
6:16	207	12:11	209, 219
6:16–17	215	12:14	187
7:1–17	53, 215	12:18	189
7:2–8	143	12:9	136
7:3	143	12–13	183, 201
7:9–17	53, 143	13	87, 178, 189, 190, 197, 239
7:10	53	13:1	197
7:17	207	13:1–18	58, 220
8:1	51, 53	13:4	179
8:2	53	13:6–7	184
8:2–9:21	54	13:7	179
8:3–4	143	13:8, 12, 14	174
8:5	98	13:10	143
9:7	98	13:11–17	205
9:12–21	94	13:14–15	198
9:20–21	174	13:15	182, 198, 207
9:21	211	13:7	198
10	95, 97	14:1, 10	207
10:1–11:14	54	14:1–20	59
10:1–11:2	55	14:1–5	52, 53, 98
10:1–7	53	14:6–02	53
10:2, 8–10	95	14:8	260
10:4	91, 92, 98, 99, 100, 101, 102, 103, 104, 232	14:13	50, 232
		14:20	207, 213
10:8+11	233	14:9–11	208
10:10	103	14:9–12	183
11	121, 162	15:1	53

(Revelation) 15:1–16:21	60	19:15	207
15:2	217	19:17	211
15:2	183	19:17–18	53
16:1–21	54	19:17–21	213
16:6	212	19:18–21	174
16:9, 11	211	19:19–21	183
16:9–11	174	19:20	155, 198, 218
16:13	189	19:21	207, 210
16:18	98	20:1–10	65
16:19	260	20:1–3	53
16:2, 10–15	183	20:1–4, 7–10	183
17	246	20:2	184
17:1	266	20:4	198
17:1–18	36, 47, 60	20:4–6	52
17:2	174	20:6	179
17:3	198	20:6, 14	218
17:3–18	260	20:10	189, 218
17:5	260	20:10–21	68
17:6	219, 262	20:11–15	52
17:14	64	20:14	207
17:15–18	267	20:14–15	218
17:16	210	20:15	210
17:17–18	214	21:1–22:9	66
17–18	178, 239, 244, 247, 255, 259	21:1–8	266
18:1–19:10	62	21:5	50, 232
18:1–24	260	21:8	155
18:1–3	53	21:9–14	36
18:1–3, 21–24	36	21:9–22:11	47
18:1–3, 9–19	267	21:9–22:5	144
18:2	213, 247	21:9–22:9	266
18:2, 10, 21	260	21:10	61
18:8	213	21:12	140
18:21	213	21:13	187
18:24	262	21:19	179
19	87	21:21	179
19:1–10	62	22:6	36
19:1–8	52	22:6–20	2, 70
19:3	213	22:7, 10, 18	47
19:8	179	22:7, 10, 18, 19	33
19:9	36, 50, 232	22:8–9	140
19:9–10	260	22:10	92, 99
19:10	33, 140	22:14	140
19:11	215	22:14–21	175
19:11–21:8	64	22:16	55, 143
19:12	197	22:18–19	233

| 22:21 | 48 | 13.5–50 | 53 |
| | | 14 | 50 |

Other Ancient Sources

4 Maccabees
| 18.24 | 49 |

1 Clement
20.12	49
32.4	49
38.4	49

Acts of Philip
| 135 | 63 |

Ad Herenium
| IV.55.68 | 114 |

1 Enoch
1.1	47
10.4–14	65
14.8–16.2	52
39.6–40.10	53
45.3	52
47.3–4	52
56.5–8	65
62	158
62.1–6	52
90.28–29	67
93.1–3	47

Aelius Aristides
Orationes
| 26.32 | 201 |
| 48.2 | 50 |

Aeneid
| 2.604–631 | 80 |

Aeschylus, Prometheus Bound
| 362 | 195 |

2 Apocalypse of Baruch
| 31.5–32.4 | 67 |

Anthrologia Paletina
| 3.6 | 191 |

2 Clement
| 20.5 | 49 |

Antoninus Liberalis
| 28.2–4 | 195 |

3 Apocalypse of Baruch
| praef 1–2 | 47 |

Apocalypse of Abraham
| 21.7–29.21 | 61 |
| 30.3–8 | 54 |

3 Enoch
| 1:6–12 | 52 |

Apocalypse of Baruch
10.1–3	260
11.1	260
67.7	260

3 Maccabees
| 7.23 | 49 |

Apocalypse of Elijah
| 4.7–17 | 56 |

4 Ezra
2.42–45	53
2.42–48	52
3.1–2, 28–31	260
6.23	54
7.83–87	158
13.5–11, 33–38	65

Apocalypse of Moses
| 22.1–29.6 | 52 |
| 22.3 | 54 |

Apocalypse of Zephaniah
09–12	54
12.1	54

Apollodorus
Bibliotheca
1.6.3	187, 190

Apuleius
The Golden Ass
11.23	93

Aristides
Apologia
12	187

Aristotle
Rhetoric
3.2.2	177
3.2.4	178
3.7.1–2	177

Poetics
5.7	177
17.1	177
21.4	178

Arratus
92	194

Ascension of Isaiah
9.22	66
10.1–16	52

Callimachus
Aetia
1.1.21–22	50

Cassius Dio
45.1	192
62.20.5	192

Cicero
Academica priora
2.16.51	50

De officiis
1.118	196

De Oratore
100	177
3.202	114

Cyprian
Ad Quirinum   57

Dead Sea Scrolls
1QH
3.32–66	66
1QpHab	83
7.1	83

Didache
10.6	68
11.3–6	133
16.6	54

Dio Cassius
59.28	199
62.11.3	196
62.11.3–12	196
63.20.5	192
67.5.7	199
73.23.2	50

Dio Chrysostom
Orationes
1	193
1.58–84	196
40.12, 45.1, 50.8	196

Diodorus Siculus
Bibiotheca
1.21–22	187, 189

Epiphanius
Panarion
1.1.1	47

Eusebius
Praeparatio evangelica
9.27.1–37	54

Historia ecclesiastica
7.15.2	197

Index of Ancient Writings

Ezekiel the Tragedian
Exagoge
68–82 ... 52

Gospel of Thomas
104 ... 63
73 ... 60

Greek Apocalypse of Ezra
4.36 ... 54

Hermas
Similitude
6, 9 ... 61
Vision
1.1.3 ... 61
2.1.1 ... 61
3 ... 61

Herodotus
Historiae
2.144 ... 187, 189
2.59, 152, 155 ... 188

Hesiod, Theogonia
183–68, 306 ... 195

Hipparch
1.2.5 ... 194

Homeric Hymn to Apollo
305–55 ... 195

Hyginus
Fabulae
140 ... 185, 187
196 ... 195

Hymn of Amen-Mose ... 187

Ignatius
Philadelphia
6.1 ... 148
Magnesians
10.3 ... 142, 148

Irenaeus
Against Hereses
2.30.7 ... 101

Josephus
Antiquities
15.339 ... 199
18.261–309 ... 199
Jewish War
1.414 ... 199
2.184–203 ... 199

Jubilees
5.1–7 ... 50
30.22, 36.10 ... 66

Judith
3.8 ... 203

Lactantius *Divine Instutes*
7.17 ... 56, 59
7.26.5–7 ... 57

Longinus
On the Sublime
15.1 ... 177
15.8–9 ... 177

Lucan
De *Bello Civili* 5.79–81 ... 185
Dialogi Marini 9 ... 185, 187

Martyrdom of Pion
8, 18 ... 197

Martyrdom of Polycarp
8–10 ... 197

Melito of Sardis
Peri Pascha ... 163

Mishna Abot
5.8 ... 54

Nonnus of Panopolis Dionysiaca
1.165–218 ... 191

Odes of Solomon
36   52, 53

Origen
Contra Celsum
6.6   91
In Ioannis Evangelium
13.5   91

Ovid
Metamorphoses
5.321–33   187

Paralipomena Jeremiae
3.2   54
4.1   54

Pausanias
1.21.2   50

Philo Legum
Allegoriae
184–388   199
95–96   199
On the Special Laws
1.66–67   67

Plato
Phaedo
4.60e–61b   50
Timaeus
13 41c   203

Pliny
Natural History
2.23.91   191

Pliny the Younger
Letters
3.5.4   50
10.96   *197*
10.96, 10.97   150

Plutarch
De Iside et Osiride
12–13   189
18, 38   188
21.38, 61   188
Moralia
355E, 356AB, 371AB   189
359D, 365F, 376A   188

Propertius
3.3   50

Psalms of Solomon
2.25–29   202
2.26–27   203

Pseudo-Demetrius
On Style
2.120   177
2.36   177
2.75   177
3.128   178
3.150   178

Pseudo-Seneca
Octavia
237–41   195
288–34   194
33, 87, 110, 620, 899, 959   194

Quintilian
Institutio Oratoria
7.10   115
9.2.40   114
10.2.1   177
10.2.22   177

Sepher ha-Razim
7   52

Shepherd of Hermas   27

Sibylline Oracles
3.657–58   65
4.174f   54
5.143, 159   260
5.28–34   182
5.34   203
5.34   202

3.388–392	82	15.23	195
3.762–766	82	15.45	196
5.34, 138–40	203		

SIRACH

		TESTAMENT OF BENJAMIN	
16.18–19	66	7.1–4	54
18.13	158		

SOPHOCLES
Oedipus the King

TESTAMENT OF DAN
5.8 — 54

897–910 — 80

TOBIT
12.20 — 50
14.15 — 49

SUETONIUS
Augustus
94 — 192

VIRGIL
Fourth Eclogue
6–10 — 192

Caligula
22 — 199

Domitian
13 — 199

WISDOM OF SOLOMON
3.5 — 158
5.1 — 158
11.1–14 — 158
11.1–19.9 — 54

Nero
32 — 196

TACITUS
Annals
14.22, 15.22 — 194
14.47 — 195

XENOPHON
Memorabilia
2.1.21–34 — 196

Index of Modern Authors

Altenmüller, B., 193
Amidon, Philip R., 47
Anderson, Janice Capel, 207, 212
Anthony, Dick, 164
Archer, Léonie J., 256
Ashcroft, Bill, 176, 179
Aune, David, 29, 30, 31, 32, 35, 39, 40, 45, 47, 51, 55, 67, 84, 85, 119, 121, 123, 134, 147, 149, 150, 152, 153, 154, 156, 160, 181, 184, 187, 202, 215, 224, 225, 235, 236, 237, 241, 260

Babcock, Barbara, 234
Baldic, Chris, 130
Ballaira, G., 194
Barbe, Kathrina, 129, 131, 132
Barnett, P., 202
Baron, Dennis, 253
Barr, David L, 1, 28, 31, 38, 85, 147, 183, 206, 208, 209, 211, 212, 213, 219, 221, 224, 227, 231, 236, 240, 243, 247, 264, 267
Barrett, C. K., 102, 106, 147, 151
Barta, Levi W., 193
Barthes, Roland, 11, 24, 25
Bartlett, David L., 224
Barton, John, 10, 15
Bartsch, Shadia, 61
Bauckham, Richard, 30, 35, 40, 98, 103, 107, 108, 202, 259
Beagley, Alan James, 118
Beale, G. K., 30, 149, 161, 189, 190
Beasley-Murray, G. R., 14, 37, 39, 99, 202
Beaujeu, J., 193
Beauvery, R., 61
Beckwith, I. T., 100

Bell, Catherine, 222, 229, 230, 232
Berg, Temma F., 24
Berger, Klaus, 31
Berger, Peter L., 206
Bergmeier, R., 103, 184, 188
Berrigan, Daniel, 77
Bertram, Georg, 158
Betz, H. D., 101, 102, 104, 110
Bhaba, Homi K., 175
Biguzzi, G., 186
Bird, Frederick B., 165
Black II, C. Clifton, 113
Blevins, James L., 30, 31, 39
Bloomquist, Gregory, 114
Blount, Brian K., 172, 255
Bøe, Sverre, 65
Boesak, Allen A., 172
Boll. F., 188, 191
Borgen, Peder, 127, 134, 136, 263
Bornkamm, Günther, 240
Bousset, W., 99, 100, 103, 184, 198
Bowker, J. W., 92, 93
Bowman, John Wick, 31, 39, 227
Boxall, Ian, 260
Boyle, Robert, 113
Braden, G., 191
Braggin, Mary Vetterling, 253
Brinkmann, B., 222
Broadbent, Donald, 23
Brooks, Cleanth, 20
Brown, Mary, 130
Bultmann, Rudolf, 96, 115

Cabaniss, Allen, 222
Caird, G. B., 28, 149, 150, 160, 235
Calder, William M., 228

Callahan, Allen Dwight, 172, 176, 245, 254
Cannadine, David, 241
Carey, Greg, 114, 208, 210, 218
Carnegie, David R., 223
Carson, D. A., 30, 33, 39
Castagnoli, F., 61
Cawelti, John G., 17
Charles, R. H., 38, 99, 100, 103, 140, 149, 156, 198
Charlesworth, James H., 63, 183
Chatman, Seymour, 216
Clifford, Richard J., 84
Code, Lorraine, 249
Cohen, Ralph, 10, 11
Cohen, Shaye J. D., 137, 142, 151, 152
Colie, Rosalie, 19
Collings, Virginia B., 23
Collins, Adela Yarbro, 27, 28, 30, 35, 37, 40, 58, 85, 86, 118, 127, 134, 136, 141, 143, 147, 149, 150, 151, 160, 161, 162, 163, 181, 184, 185, 186, 187, 188, 190, 206, 216, 217, 227, 238, 239, 240, 246, 261, 262, 264, 265
Collins, John J., 2, 34, 36, 38, 40, 76, 82, 84, 85, 100, 114, 183, 190, 203
Cook, Stephen L., 246
Cornford, Francis Macdonald, 228
Corti, Maria, 9, 15, 19
Coser, Lewis, 164
Cothenet, Edouard, 222
Court, John M, 38
Crafton, J. A., 96
Croce, Bernedetto, 20, 21
Csikszentmihalyi, Mihaly, 234
Cuddon, J. A., 131
Culler, Jonathan, 11, 12, 13, 15, 16, 231
Cuss, D., 181, 192, 198, 199, 202

Davis, E. F., 92
Davis, Ellen F., 233
Davis, Robert Con, 21, 22
Deflem, Mathieu, 226
Dégh, Linda, 47
Deininger, J., 198
Deissmann, A., 181, 202

Delling, Gerhard, 222
Derrida, Jacques, 10, 16
Desideri, P., 196
deSilva, David A., 246
Dewey, Joanna, 212
Dieterich, A., 184
Dixon, Suzanne, 256
Dochhorn, J., 189
Draper, J. A., 222
Dreyden, John, 80
duBois, Page, 252
Dubrow, Heather, 12, 15, 19, 20, 34
Duff, Paul, 134, 149, 154, 156, 157, 161, 165, 206, 247
Dunand, F., 187

Eberwein, Robert T., 25, 26
Eco, Umberto, 24, 25
Edmondson, Ricca, 250
Ehrman, Bart D., 45
Eitzen, Kim Haines, 44
Eliade's, Mircea, 223
Elliott, Susan M., 260
Esler, Philip F., 174
Esquivel, Julia, 269

Farmer, Ron, 208, 218
Fauth, W., 191
Fears, J. R., 181, 200
Fekkes, Jan, 189, 252, 264
Feuillet, Andre, 92, 103
Fischer, Walter R., 114, 116, 123
Fischler, Susan, 256
Fishwick, D., 197
Flaceliere, Robert, 78
Flusser, David, 57
Fontenrose, Joseph, 184, 185, 186, 187, 188, 190, 228
Ford, J. Massyngberde, 209
Fowler, Alastair, 10, 11, 12, 13, 19, 22
Fowler, Roger, 130, 131, 264
Fox, Robin Lane, 149
Frankfurter, David, 85, 135, 136, 153, 154, 159, 165, 168, 175, 193
Frazer, James B., 227
Freyne, Séan, 238

Friesen, Steven J., 72, 144, 149, 153, 181, 182, 197, 198, 200, 201, 217, 239, 265
Frilingos, Chris, 207
Frye, Northrop, 131
Furnish, Victor Paul, 96, 97, 105, 106, 109

Gager, John G., 31, 86, 118, 151, 223, 224, 225, 233
Garrett, Susan R., 256
Gaster, Theodor H., 228
Gaston, Lloyd, 147, 151, 153
Geertz, Clifford, 229
Geisau, H. von, 194
Genette, Gérard, 9, 15
Georgi, Dieter, 192, 241
Giblin, Charles Homer, 67, 94, 100, 103
Giesen, Heinz, 260
Giet, S., 198
Gitay, Yehoshua, 115
Glenn, Cheryl, 249
Gloer, W. Hulitt, 31
Glucksberg, Sam, 130
Golden, Leon, 85
Goldenberg, Naomi, 257
Gollinger, H., 184, 186, 189
Goody, Jack, 226
Gregory, Richard L., 23
Griffiths, Gareth, 176, 179
Griffiths, J.G., 187
Grimes, Ronald, 222, 226, 227, 228, 229, 230
Guenther, Heinz O., 116
Guery, D. E., 189
Gundry, Robert H., 63, 67
Gunkel, H., 184
Gwyther, Anthony, 172, 259

Hadorn, W., 188
Hahn, Ferdinand, 236
Haiman, John, 129, 131, 132
Hall, Stuart, 174
Halliday, M. A. K., 254, 256
Halver, Rudolf, 227
Hänlein-Schäfer, H., 198
Hanson, J. S., 92
Hanson, Paul D., 33, 38, 84, 118, 246

Hardin, Richard F., 228, 230
Harlow, Barbara, 175
Harris, Michael Anthony, 29, 35, 217, 222, 231
Harrison, Jane Ellen, 227
Hartman, Lars, 65
Hawkes, Terence, 13
Hawthorn, Jeremy, 14
Heckel, Ulrich, 96, 97, 106
Hellholm, David, 27, 28, 35, 37, 51, 76, 224, 232
Hemer, Colin, 72, 149, 239
Hendricks, Christina, 253
Hennecke, Edgar, 74
Hennessy, Rosemary, 255
Hernadi, Paul, 34
Hill, David, 39, 40
Himmelfarb, Martha, 93, 101
Hirsch Jr, E. D., 11, 12, 13, 14, 15, 16, 26
Hochberg, Julian, 23
Höistad, R., 196
Hooke, S. H., 228
Hopfner, T., 193
Howard-Brook, Wes, 172, 259
Hull, Michael F., 92
Humphrey, Edith M., 114, 118, 183, 240, 264
Hurtgen, John E., 254
Hutcheon, Linda, 131

Iser, Wolfgang, 213

Jack, Alison, 244
Jameson, Fredric, 9
Janzen, Waldemar, 93, 110
Jarrattt, Susan, 251, 252
Jauss, Hans Robert, 10, 12, 19, 20, 21
Jenkins, Jerry B., 73
Jenks, G. C., 183
Jenny, Laurent, 9
Jeremias, Jörg, 65
Johns, Loren L., 252
Johnson, Luke T., 263
Johnson, S. E., 152
Jones, A. H. M., 252
Jones, Bruce W., 40

Jones, D. L., 181, 197, 198
Jones. C. P., 193, 196
Jörns, Klaus Peter, 120, 223
Judge, E. A., 104

Kallas James, 40
Kalms, J., 189
Kapferer, Bruce, 236, 239, 240
Karrer, Martin, 30, 48, 232
Katz, Albert N., 130
Katz, David S., 73
Kaufman, Gordon, 260
Kavanaugh, M. A., 68
Kennedy, George A., 113
Kent, Thomas L., 12, 13, 14, 15, 18, 19, 20, 22, 24, 26
Keresztes, P., 197, 198
Kerkeslager, A., 185, 199
Kermode, Frank, 24
Kertzer, David I., 226, 240
Kim, Jean K., 172
Kirby, John T., 237, 250
Klauck, H. J., 92, 93, 101, 190, 200, 260
Koch, Klaus, 33, 34, 84
Koenen, L., 193, 196
Koester, Craig R., 72, 149
Koester, Helmut, 35, 151
Kraabel, A. T., 163
Kraft, H., 188, 189, 198
Kraft, Heinrich, 135, 153
Kraybill, J. Nelson, 262
Kreitzer, L., 183
Kristeva, Julia, 24
Kumon-Nakamura, Sachi, 130
Kyle, Richard G., 73

Labrecque, Y., 187
Lacocque, A., 100
Ladd, George Eldon, 40
LaHaye, Tim, 73
Lambrecht, Jan, 94, 98
Lambrechts, P., 192
Lämmer, M., 200
Läuchli, Samuel, 222
Lawrence, D. H., 210
Laws, Sophie, 178

Lebram, J. C. H., 51
Lee, J. A. L., 51
Leitch, Vincent B., 21
Levi, Annalina, 193
Lévi-Strauss, Claude, 223
Lewalski, Barbara, 19
Liew, Tat-Siong Benny, 173
Lincoln, A. T., 93, 97, 102
Lindsey, Hal, 73
Lineck, Kara M., 130
Lloyd, A.B., 188
Lohmeyer, E., 94, 98, 103
Longman III, Tremper, 12, 13, 15, 16, 32
Loyen, A., 196
Lücke, Friedrich, 33, 74
Luckmann, Thomas, 206
Lyne, J. R., 251, 252

MacAloon, John J., 222, 234
MacCormack, Sabine, 121
Mack, Burton, 123
Mack, Burton L., 113, 116
Maier, Harry O., 122, 128, 130, 131, 246
Malina, Bruce, 224, 226, 238, 243
Marino, Adrian, 20
Marshall, Gloria A., 253
Marshall, John W., 135, 136, 142, 148, 151, 153, 162, 165, 175
Martin, Ralph P., 96, 97, 101, 102
Mathewson, Dave, 36, 37
Mazzaferri, Frederick David, 27, 30, 35, 36, 40, 84
McBurney, Donald H., 23
McCant, J. W., 96, 105
McCloskey, Donald, 250
McDonald, M. F., 56
McDonald, P. M., 209
McGee, M. Calvin, 251, 252
Mead, George Herbert, 234
Meeks, Wayne, 224
Megill, Alan, 250
Mellor, Ronald, 200, 265
Michie, Donald, 212
Míguez, Nestor, 172
Millar, F., 197
Miller, Patricia Cox, 79

Moo, Douglas J., 30, 33, 39
Moore, Stephen D., 207, 210, 212, 218, 220, 256
Moray, Neville, 23
Morris, Leon, 27, 30, 33, 39
Mounce, Robert H., 27, 37, 38, 40, 140
Mowry, Lucetta, 222
Moyise, Steve, 23, 172, 189, 207, 208, 218, 243, 244, 253, 260
Murphy, Frederick J., 147
Murray, Gilbert, 227
Mussies, G., 46, 56, 197
Myerhoff, Barbara, 234

Nanos, Mark D., 160
Nelson, John S., 250
Newman, Jr, Barclay M., 151
Neyrey, Jerome H., 238
Nitzsch, K. I., 33
Nock, A. D., 199

O'Donnell, Patrick, 21, 22
O'Collins, G. G., 106
Ogilvie, R. M., 57
Okin, Susan Moller, 252
Oliver, J. H., 201
Oliver, Kelly, 253
Onasch, C, 193
O'Rourke, John J., 120, 223
Ortega y Gasset, José, 10
Otting, M. Dean, 92

Pagels, Elaine, 201
Palmer, Susan J., 164, 165
Parke, H. W., 81
Parker David C., 44
Parker, Patricia, 251
Pattemore, Stephen, 213, 216, 217
Patterson, Mark, 73
Patterson, S. J., 188
Paul, Ian, 253
Paulien, Jon, 189
Peirce, Charles S., 212
Pérez Firmat, Gustavo, 17, 21, 32, 34
Perrin, Norman, 38
Pescheck, Josef, 222

Pexman, Penny M., 130
Phillips, Oliver, 228
Piper, Otto, 31, 222
Pippin, Tina, 78, 214, 215, 218, 247, 248, 257, 258, 259, 264, 265, 266, 268
Plaskow, Judith, 263
Poggioli, Renato, 14
Popkin, Richard Henry, 73
Potter. David S., 78, 81, 87
Powell, Mark Allan, 212
Price, Robert, 104
Price, S. R. F., 149, 181, 197, 198, 199, 241, 265
Priest, John, 63, 85
Prigent, P., 97, 107, 181, 197, 199, 222, 235
Prümm, K., 106

Rabinowitz, Nancy Sorkin, 252
Ramsay, William M., 72, 148
Rappaport, Roy A., 226, 234
Rehmann, Claudia Suter, 266
Reicke, B., 198
Resseguie, James L., 214
Rhoads, David M., 212
Richard, Pablo, 172, 211, 212, 254, 263, 266
Richards, I. A., 24
Richlin, Amy, 252
Ricoeur, Paul, 15
Riddell, Joseph N., 21
Riley, Denise, 247
Robbins, Thomas, 164, 165
Robbins, Vernon K., 113, 116
Robinson, John A. T., 149
Roloff, Jürgen, 30, 39, 92, 99, 138, 140
Rosmarin, Adena, 11, 17, 18, 20
Rossing, Barbara, 244, 264
Rowland, Christopher, 38, 76, 97, 101
Rowley, H. H., 34
Royalty, Robert M., 165, 172, 179, 250, 262
Ruby, Jay, 234
Rudd, Niall, 131
Ruiz, Jean-Pierre, 28, 107, 189, 237, 239, 261

Ruprecht, Hans-George, 11
Russell, D. A., 178
Russell, D. S., 34, 74
Ryan, Marie-Laure, 13, 14, 15

Sacks, Sheldon, 11
Saffrey, H. D., 184
Sanders, E. P., 37, 76
Schaberg, Jane, 265
Schafer, P., 92, 93
Schechner, Richard, 228
Scherrer, S. J., 198, 199, 225
Schmid, Josef, 46
Schmidt, J., 185, 187, 191
Schmithals, Walter, 34
Schoedel, William R., 152
Scholem, G., 93, 105
Scholes, Robert, 10
Schowalter, D. N., 199
Schüssler Fiorenza, Elisabeth, 27, 28, 30, 31, 32, 33, 35, 36, 37, 38, 39, 40, 84, 114, 118, 136, 147, 149, 151, 153, 154, 172, 178, 181, 206, 221, 224, 225, 227, 237, 238, 241, 243, 245, 251, 267
Schüssler Fiorenza, Francis, 260
Schweizer. E., 107
Scott, James C., 175, 179, 180
Segal, Alan F., 93
Segovia, Fernando F., 244
Seippel, G., 185
Shapiro, Susan, 251, 258
Shepherd, Massey H., 31, 152, 222
Simmel, G., 164
Slugoski, Ben R., 129, 132
Smit, Dirk J., 245
Smith, Jonathan Z., 224
Smith, Morton, 27, 152
Smith, Theophus, 254
Sordi, Marta, 150
Spittler, R. P., 101
Stauffer, E., 181
Sternberg, Meir, 231
Stone, M. E., 101
Stringfellow, Jr, Frank, 131, 132
Sweet, J. P. M., 72, 103, 149, 150, 160, 161, 235
Swete, H. B., 98, 99, 103, 149, 151, 198

Tabor, J. D., 92, 93, 97, 101, 102
Te Velde, H., 185, 188
Terdiman, Richard, 179
Thompson, Leonard L., 33, 119, 120, 124, 136, 147, 149, 150, 160, 163, 165, 196, 206, 217, 224, 225, 238, 241, 246, 252
Tiffin, Helen, 176, 179
Todorov, Tzvetan, 9, 15, 19, 20, 23
Tolbert, Mary Ann, 244
Toplak. Maggie, 130
Tran Tam Tinh, V., 187
Türk, G., 185, 191
Turnbull, William, 129, 132
Turner, Max, 116
Turner, Victor W., 86, 225, 226, 228, 229, 230, 234

Ulfgard, Håkan, 222

van Gennep, Arnold, 86, 233
van Henten, Jan Willem, 183, 185, 187, 189, 190, 193, 196, 206
van Unnik, W. C., 30
Vanni, Ugo, 48, 68, 94, 95, 98, 99, 100, 221, 231, 232, 236
Vázsony, Andrew, 47
Versnel, H. S., 186, 192, 198, 201
Versnel, Henk, 181
Vielhauer, Philipp, 27, 36, 40, 74
Vivas, Eliseo, 17, 21
Vogelgesang, Jeffrey, 236
Vögtle, A., 184
Vollenweider, Samuel, 116
Vorster, Willem S., 30, 39, 40

Wachterhauser, Brice, 253
Wainwright, Arthur, 71, 74
Walker, Andrew, 73
Wallis, Roy, 164
Watson, Duane F., 114
Weber, Max, 164
Weems, Renita, 261
Wellbery, David E., 245
Wengst, Klaus, 259
Whitman, L. Y., 194, 196
Williams, Sam K., 158
Wills, Lawrence, 113

Wilson, Brian R., 174
Wilson, Robert R., 84
Wilson, Stephen G., 135, 137, 147, 151, 152, 154, 175
Wimbush, Vincent, 172
Wimsatt Jr, William K., 20
Winterbottom, M., 178
Wuellner, W., 113, 245, 250
Wyke, Maria, 256

Young, B. H., 93

Zabkar, V, 193
Zanker, P., 192
Zeller, D., 181
Zielinski, T., 187
Zmijewski, J., 97, 106

Subject Index

1 Enoch, 28, 33
144,000, 53, 143
    on Mount Zion, 59, 88
2 Baruch, 33
4 Ezra, 33

Adventus, 121, 122, 123
Aeneas, 79, 88
Alpha and the Omega, 29
Ancient of Days, 50
angels
    epiphany, 53, 55
    as interpreter, 28, 36, 61, 64
    as interpreter in Apocalypse of John, 47
    speech, 53
    worship of, 63, 108
anti-language, 254
Antiochus IV, 59
Antipas, 161
anti-Semitism
    in New Testament studies, 128, 142
Aphrodite, 187
Apocalypse. *See also* Apocalypses
    genre definition, 34, 76
    meaning of, 78
    as unveiling, 80
Apocalypse of Elijah, 85
Apocalypse of John. *See also individual entries*
    angel interpreter, 47
    as anti-imperial, 201
    as Apocalypse, 26
    astral imagery, 188
    authority struggles, 107
    authority defended, 107

    autobiographical style, 50
    cherubim compared with Ezekiel, 52
    "Christian" not appropriate term, 142
    churches split, 165
    coercion and, 207
    commissioning scenes, 94
    compared with other Apocalypses, 50, 51, 52
    contradictions in, 208
    cosmology of, 51
    differences from prophecy, 74
    as drama, 227
    dual attitudes toward, 169
    ending as liturgical dialogue, 68
    ethics of, 211
    feminist debate, 244, 255–67
    feminist interpretations, 267
    four living creatures, 52
    gender language, 248
    genre, 9, 74
    genre anomalies, 35
    genre as synthesis of prophetic and apocalyptic elements, 48
    genre traits, 74
    genre, significance of, 36
    Greek of, 176
    as hybrid genre, 21–25, 39
    hymns, 224
    Greco-Roman traditions and, 202
    as identity politics, 174
    ideology of domination, 128, 208
    images for church, 143
    importance of genre for interpretation, 37, 38
    internal divisions, 174
    interpretations of, 246

(Apocalypse of John)
   2, 9, 10, 40
   irony in, 128, 138
   Isaiah usage, 141
   Jesus as conqueror, 207
   Jesus as lamb, 209
   Jesus as warrior, 64
   Jesus' character, 213, 214
   Jesus' death, 214
   Jesus in, 51, 88, 179, 205
   Jews in, 128, 136, 140, 141, 158, 160
   Lamb in, 52, 179
   language as postcolonial, 177
   language as symbolic, 252
   as letter, 29, 232
   letter elements, 48
   letter ending, 69
   letter frame, 36
   letters as edicts, 31, 235
   Lion Lamb figure, 124
   Little Scroll in, 103, 118
   liturgical dialogue and, 48, 68
   liturgical language, 225
   liturgy and, 28, 31
   misogyny of, 247, 248, 255, 261
   mixed genre, 39–41
   moral ambiguities, 169
   morality, 210–12
   moral logic, 212
   myth and, 30, 223
   narratees, 216
   narrative, 212–20
   narrative levels, 216
   not sealed, 68
   Old Testament allusions, 45
   as oral performance, 28, 222
   paraenesis in, 51
   as parody, 178
   persecution and, 150
   political reading of, 244
   precursors, 45–47
   prophetic traits, 51
   prose style of, 62
   pseudonymity and, 35
   pseudonymity lacking, 50
   psychoanalysis and, 223
   purpose of, 206, 217
   intertextuality of, readers reconstructed, 44
   rhetoric of, 114, 127, 175
   rhetorics of inquiry, 254
   as resistance literature, 178
   ritual setting, 221
   rituals in, 121
   sarcasm in, 127
   scroll eating, 104
   scrolls in, 95
   seals in, 99
   second coming and, 87, 205
   second coming omitted and, 215
   as sectarian, 173, 174
   Seven Thunders, 93, 111
   social function, 85
   as story of Jesus, 87
   stylistic features, 51
   symbolic inversions, 210
   symbolic reading of, 218
   symbolism, 206–10
   Thunders, 98
   title, 47
   twenty-four elders, 52
   Two Witnesses, 107
   unlike other Apocalypses, 36
   use of definite article, 46
   verbal strategies of, 132
   vilification in, 127
   violence in, 169, 174, 208, 209, 210, 214, 215, 216, 218
   as vision, 232
   voice of God in, 66
   wealth in, 179

Apocalypse of Paul, 101
Apocalypse of Peter, 85
Apocalypses
   common schema, 84
   features of, 36, 51
   functions of, 76, 85
   future and, 86
   illocutionary function, 114
   not about future, 76
   other types of revelation and, 84
   as prophecy, 32
   pseudonymous, 35, 50
   ritual and, 86
   textual history of, 44

themes of, 85
apocalypticism
    differentiated from prophecy, 70
    transformed by John, 70
Apollo, 265
    Apollyon and, 178
    Augustus and, 191
    birth of, 185
    emperor and, 199
    Nero and, 192
    Pythios, 186
Apuleius, 83
aretalogy, 104
archetypes
    Jung's theory, 257
Aristophanes, 178
Aristotle, 85, 252
Artemis, 188, 200
Ascension of Isaiah, 85
ascent to heaven, 51
Asclepius
    dream divination, 81
astrology, 83
Atargatis, 188
Atia, 192
Azazel, 65

Babylon
    contrasted with Jerusalem, 266
    fall of, 62
    gender and, 248
    as Rome, 261
    as U.S. imperialism, 268
    as woman and city, 259
Balaam, 133
beasts, 58, 189
    of Revelation, 178
Behemoth, 59
Bildungsroman, 12
Book of Life
    traditional image, 66
Bradley, Ed, 171
brain theory, 23
bride of Christ, 63

call narratives, 30
Carmen Saeculare, 192

catharsis
    in Apocalypses, 85
charismatic leadership
    problems, 164
cherubim, 52
chreia, 116, 117, 123
Christian
    as term, 148
    use of term, 142
church
    images for in Apocalypse, 143
    synagogue and, 128, 135, 143, 151, 161
    as true Israel, 136, 137, 138, 141, 144
Cicero, 78
Cloisters manuscript of the Apocalypse, 75
combat myth, 58, 184
    Apocalypse and, 195
    astrology and, 194
    inverted in Apocalypse, 202
    John's plot and, 213
    pattern, 184
    political use of, 191–97
    Seth-Typhon elements, 190
    two types, 185
    two variants, 59
commissioning scene, 94
conflict
    purposes of, 164
Cynic, 116
Cyrus, 140

Daniel, 28, 33
Dead Sea Scrolls, 67, 82, 136
Delphi
    Apollo's shrine, 81
Dialogue with Trypho
    date, 160
Diefenbaker, John, 116
Dio Chrysostom, 196
Domitian, 148, 149, 178
    Horus and, 193
    rites at Ephesus, 200
    as tyrant, 196
    as Zeus, 199
doxologies
    purpose of, 49

Draco (constellation), 194
Dragon
    Apollo myth differences, 187
    combat myth, 183
    as emperor, 72
    in imperial ideology, 181
    Isis and Seth-Typhon and, 188
    Lamb and, 209
    as opponent, 119
    Python and, 185
    Python and Apollo, 185
    queen of heaven myth, 265
    red, 190
drawing lots, 78
dreams
    as revelations, 81

ekphrasis
    in other Apocalypses, 61
    in Revelation, 61
Elijah, 61
emperor. *See also* imperial cult
    divine titles, 198
empyromancy, 83
enthronment scenes, 52
Ephesus, 133, 200
    Temple of Artemis, 186
    theater, 31
Esquivel, Julia, 268
ethics
    of John, 211
ethics of inquiry, 248
Eusebius, 71
ex eventu prophecy, 36
eyes, 52
Ezekiel, 61, 91
    call of, 55

feminism
    scholarship neglected, 250
final judgment
    in Apocalypse, 65
fiscus Ioudaicus, 149
food of idols, 173
Four Horsemen, 52

Gaius, 199

Garden of Eden
    as heavenly place, 68
genre, 9
    anomalies, 35
    audience perspective, 77
    as boundary setting, 16
    definition, 10, 14
    definition of apocalypse, 34
    as expectation, 12, 15
    fool's speech, 95
    as heuristic devices, 17
    hybrid, 10, 18–21, 39
    hybrid and interpretation, 21–25
    hybrid and perception, 23
    interpretation, 12–14
    literary conventions, 14–16
    metaphors for, 16
    naive readers, 14
    need for, 10–12, 16
    role of the reader, 36
    as supertext, 17
    synchronic and diachronic views, 34
Gog and Magog, 65
Gospel of Peter, 142
Gospel of Thomas, 142
Great Bear, 188
Great Red Dragon, 72

Hadrian, 193
    as Zeus Olympios, 200
Hebrews
    relation of Revelation, 150
Hekate, 30
Hellenistic cosmology, 51
Heracles, 196
Herod Agrippa II, 142
Herod the Great, 199
history of religions method, 182
holy war. *See* combat myth
Homer, 79
Horace, 131
Horus, 191
hybridization of discourse, 176
hymns
    rhetoric of, 120

Ignatius of Antioch, 141, 152, 153

Subject Index

Iliad, 79
imperial cult
    ceremony undermined, 122
    in eastern Mediterranean, 198
    goddess traditions and, 265
    ideology, 181
    mythology of, 197–201
    obligations to, 197
imperial decrees, 51
imperial ideology
    claims of, 182
    inverted in Apocalypse, 201
imperial imagery
    reversed, 178, 183
imperialism
    resistance to, 171
integrity formula, 69
intercalations, 94
internal divisions
    related to imperial pressure, 175
interpretation
    distortion of, 73
    ethics of, 248
    factors in, 219
    feminist, 247
    genre determination, 13
    hermeneutics of suspicion, 253
    multiple, 24
    political and social, 255–67
    psychological, 262
    rhetorical political paradigm, 244
    sectarian versus political, 246
    tests of, 255
    three worlds of a text, 71
intertextuality, 9, 21
    definition, 43, 129
    irony, 128, 129
    as method, 43
    motives for, 129
    structural, 130
Isaiah, 139
Isis, 78, 187, 188, 191
    hymns to, 193
    representations, 187

Jeremiah
    influence on John, 62

Jerusalem, 139, 162
    attack on, 65
    heavenly, 67
Jesus. *See also* Apocalypse of John, Jesus in
    Ancient of Days, 50
    as character in Apocalypse, 205
    coming of, 49, 87, 89, 205
    contrasted with emperor, 206
    as Divine Warrior, 207
    John's characterization, 208
    Luke's characterization, 116
Jewish War, 136
Jews
    attraction of, 166
    John's view of, 148, 160
    purpose of hostility toward, 163
    theory of persecution by, 149
Jezebel, 134, 154, 158, 175, 206, 217, 239, 245, 247, 263
    fate of, 155
    status of, 165
John
    authority of, 176, 232, 241
    conflict with other leaders, 163
    opponents, 238
    as prophet, 55
    roles of, 108
Judaism. *See also* church and synagogue
    continuity with, 53, 162
    distinguishing from Christianity, 141
    in interpretation of Apocalypse, 142
judgment scenes, 52, 64
Jung, Carl Gustav, 262
Juvenal, 131

key of David, 139, 161
King Lear, 19
King, Martin Luther, 116

Lactantius
    relation to Revelation, 57
lake of fire, 218
Lamb. *See also* Apocalypse of John, Jesus as Lamb
    Dragon and, 209
    Lion and, 209, 216
    main character in Apocalypse, 214

(Lamb) marriage of, 63
    violence of, 208
lament
    in Revelation 18, 62
language
    gender of, 256
    ideological production, 253
    political, 253
Laodicea, 133
    hot and cold, 72
Lawrence, D. H., 210
Left Behind novels, 73
Leto, 185, 188
Leto-Apollo-Python myth, 58
letters, 50. *See* Seven Letters
Leviathan, 59, 189
liminality, 233
Lion Lamb figure, 52
liturgical dialogue, 48
liturgical language, 48, 49, 68, 69
liturgy
    Apocalypse and, 221
Lucian, 81
Luther, Martin
    attitude toward Apocalypse, 169

magical papyri, 29
Martyrdom of Pionius, 149
Martyrdom of Polycarp, 149, 150
Melville, Herman, 19
Merkavah mysticism, 52
messianic banquet, 63
    Great Supper of God and, 64
Michael
    war with Satan, 58
Moby-Dick, 13, 19, 22
morality
    delayed response, 211
    use of power, 211

narratees
    of John's story, 216
narrative analysis, 212
Necker cube, 23
Nero, 183
    Tryphon and, 195
    connection with Apollo, 192

divine honors, 192
as head of Beast, 194
New Jerusalem, 143
    no temple in, 67
    Qumran text, 67
Nicolaitans, 147, 152, 155, 159, 239, 245
Niebuhr, Reinhold, 88

Odes of Solomon, 224
open door
    meaning of, 139
    purpose of, 167
optical illusion, 23
oracles, 80
    of Hystaspes, 57
    questions asked, 81
    yypes of responses, 81
Origen, 91

Papias, 71
Paradise Lost, 19
parody, 178
parousia, 205, 215
Paul
    fool's speech, 96
    revelation of, 104
    on the end, 219
    thorn in the flesh, 105
Peirce, C. S.
    on John's Apocalypse, 212
Pergamum, 239, 265
persecution, local, 150
Pesher, 82
Philadelphia, 134, 136, 138, 154, 157, 159
Philo, 136
plagues
    of Egypt, 54
    literary motif, 54
Plato, 252
Plutarch, 191
porneia
    as idolatry, 261
    meaning of, 173
Poseidon, 187
postcolonial criticism, 172, 254. *See also*
    resistance criticism
prefaces, role of, 47

prophecy
    differentiated from apocalyptic, 70
    not about the future, 87
prophets
    authority of, 93, 109
    conflicts, 107
    final prophet, 56
Psalms
    genres, 13
pseudonymity, 35
Pythian Games, 192
Python, 188
    compared to Seth-Typhon, 186, 188

queen of heaven, 265
Quintilian, 115
Qumran
    John's community and, 163
    New Jerusalem, 67

Rahab, 189
rapture
    origins in nineteenth century, 73
Rastafarians, 254
realized eschatology, 224
reflexivity
    in apocalypse, 238
    apocalypse structure and, 236
    meaning of, 234
resistance
    rhetoric of, 172, 176
    in ritual, 234
    symptoms of, 173
resistance criticism, 172
    as discourse, 173
resistance discourse
    reinscribing oppression, 179
resistance rhetoric
    purpose of, 178
Revelation. *See* Apocalypse of John
revelations
    astrology, 83
    by dreams, 81
    empyromancy, 83
    intuitive, 80
    kinds of, 78
    modern analogies, 87

oracle collections, 82
oracles, 80
revenge
    as motive, 53
    desire for, 171
rhetoric
    classical versus Hebrew, 113
    concept of propriety, 177
    as hermeneutical model, 243
    of hymns, 120
    Jewish and Greco-Roman, 115
    meaning of, 249
    as politics, 178
    of resistance, 171, 176
    of visions, 114
rhetoricality, 245
rhetorics of inquiry, 248
    defined, 250
    tasks of, 267
rider on white horse, 64
rites of passage, 233
ritual
    analyzed, 225–27
    in texts, 232
    various definitions, 226
ritual process, 86
rituals
    kinds of, 86
Roma, 200
    queen of heaven, 265
Roman art, 62

Salvador Dali, 23
sarcasm, 129, 131
Sardis, 133
Satan
    defeat of, 64, 219
    fall of, 115, 124, 190
satire, 129
    defined, 130
    purposes of, 131
    Roman, 131
SBL Genres Project, 34, 75
scroll
    compared to Paul's thorn, 102
    eating of, 91, 104, 108, 124, 233
    meanings of, 103

(scroll) opening as judgment, 52
    theme in Apocalypse, 95
selective attention, 22
September 11, 2001, 169
Seth
    animals, 193
Seth-Typhon, 188, 191
Seth-Typhon myth, 187
Seven Letters, 214. *See also* under Apocalypse of John
    as edicts, 235
    genre of, 31
    issues in, 175
    structure of, 154
Seven Thunders, 94
Seven Trumpets, 54
Shepherd of Hermas, 28
Sibylline Oracles, 82
Smyrna, 134, 136, 137, 154, 159, 265
Son of Man, 30
    in Daniel, 50
sonnet, 13
suffering
    manliness and, 207
synagogue
    expulsion, 161
synagogue of Satan, 134, 138, 175
    fate of, 157
    as member of the church, 151
    various views, 147

Tabitha, 56
tense shifting, 56
theophany
    final judgment, 65
throne visions, 52, 53, 57, 59
    functions of, 52

Thueris, 187
Thyatira, 134, 155
    as central letter, 155
torture, 211
Trajan, 200
Trallians
    letter to, 152
Tristram Shandy, 19
Troy
    destroyed by gods, 80
trumpets
    in apocalyptic literature, 54
Two Witnesses, 55, 56, 107, 162, 213
    role of, 57
Typhon, 191
    attack of Zeus, 190
    birth, 195

Venus, 79
Victorinus of Pettau, 103
vilification, 127
violence
    kinds of, 208, 218
visions
    rhetoric of, 114

whore of Babylon
    destruction of, 214
    as Roman economic power, 178
    as Roman imperial power, 258
woman
    Dragon and, 58
    giving birth, 264
    goddess traditions and, 188, 265
women
    contrasting images, 196
Wright, Richard, 180

www.ingramcontent.com/pod-product-compliance
Lightning Source LLC
Chambersburg PA
CBHW031706230426
43668CB00006B/130